INSIGHT GUIDE

BARBADOS

About This Book

Editorial
Project Editor
Caroline Radula-Scott
Managing Editor
Lesley Gordon
Editorial Director
Brian Bell

Distribution
UK & Ireland
GeoCenter International Ltd
The Viables Centre , Harrow Way
Basingstoke, Hants RG22 4BJ
Fax: (44) 1256-817988

United States
Langenscheidt Publishers, Inc.
46–35 54th Road, Maspeth, NY 11378
Fax: (718) 784-0640

Canada
Prologue Inc.
1650 Lionel Bertrand Blvd., Boisbriand
Québec, Canada J7H 1N7
Tel: (450) 434-0306. Fax: (450) 434-2627

Australia & New Zealand
Hema Maps Pty. Ltd.
24 Allgas Street, Slacks Creek 4127
Brisbane, Australia
Tel: (61) 7 3290 0322. Fax: (61) 7 3290 0478

Worldwide
Apa Publications GmbH & Co. Verlag KG (Singapore branch)
38 Joo Koon Road, Singapore 628990
Tel: (65) 865-1600. Fax: (65) 861-6438

Printing
Insight Print Services (Pte) Ltd
38 Joo Koon Road, Singapore 628990
Tel: (65) 865-1600. Fax: (65) 861-6438

First Edition 1986
Fourth Edition 1999

CONTACTING THE EDITORS
Although every effort is made to provide accurate information, we live in a fast-changing world and would appreciate it if readers would call our attention to any errors or outdated information that may occur by writing to us:
Insight Guides, P.O. Box 7910, London SE1 1WE, England. Fax: (44 171) 403-0290. insight@apaguide.demon.co.uk

This guidebook combines the interests and enthusiasms of two of the world's best known information providers: Insight Guides, whose titles have set the standard for visual travel guides since 1970, and Discovery Channel, the world's premier source of nonfiction television programming.

The editors of Insight Guides provide both practical advice and general understanding about a destination's history, culture, institutions and people. Discovery Channel and its Web site, www.discovery.com, help millions of viewers explore their world from the comfort of their own home and also encourage them to explore it first hand.

This fully updated edition of *Insight Guide: Barbados* is carefully structured to convey an understanding of the island and its culture as well as to guide readers through its sights and activities:

◆ The **Features** section, indicated by a yellow bar at the top of each page, covers the history and culture of the country in a series of informative essays.

◆ The main **Places** section, with a blue bar, is a complete guide to all the sights and areas worth visiting. Places of special interest are coordinated by number with the maps.

◆ The **Travel Tips** listings,

with an orange bar, provides a reference for information on travel, hotels, shops, restaurants and more.

The contributors

This new edition of *Insight Guide: Barbados* was edited by **Caroline Radula-Scott**, who also edited *Insight Guide: Caribbean.* Several people proved invaluable to the update project. Barbadian **Alison Pile** was for months at the end of a computer link in Barbados, researching and updating the bulk of the Places section and Travel Tips listings. Barbadian writer **Tracy Johnson** reworked the two Bridgetown chapters and wrote the picture story on Rum. Photojournalist **Mike Toy** not only contributed new photographs, but also updated the South and West Coast chapters and provided text on Architecture and Watersports.

Award-winning writer **Nailah Folami Imojah**, cultural officer for the Literary Arts at the National Cultural Foundation, helped coordinate updaters for the Features section and updated A Storytelling Tradition, originally by the late Barbadian poet and playwright **Timothy Callender**, and **Annette Trotman**'s Street Beats, Stage Treats. **Therese Hadchity**, an art critic who lives in Barbados, wrote a new chapter on art, and songwriter **Eric Lewis** wrote Ridin' de Riddim, The Young Brigade and the piece on Street Festivals.

The Land of Flying Fish and Cou-Cou was rewritten by **Sally Miller**, co-publisher of *Ins and Outs of Barbados* and *Barbados in a Nutshell*, and her colleague **Christine Wilkie** wrote Island Hopping. **James Ferguson**, author of *A Traveller's History of the Caribbean*, wrote A Singular Island, Barbados National Trust and updated All 'o We is Bajan by Barbadian historian **Trevor Marshall** who added to his own history chapters. Journalist **Peter "Adonijah" Alleyne**, updated photographer **Tony Arruza**'s piece on fishing, **Addinton Forde**'s A Religious Mosaic and **Tony Cozier**'s cricket feature, and **Dr Elizabeth Best** wrote an essay on Bajan dialect.

Contributors also include **Peggy McGeary, Myra Murby, Christine Barrow, Mark DaCosta Alleyne, Angela Carter** and **John Wickham**. **Lesley Player** provided new photographs. Thanks go to **Paul Foster**, former president of the Barbados National Trust, to **Jane Ladle** for editing Travel Tips, to **Bryony Coleman** for proofreading and to Liz Cook for the index.

Map Legend

— · ·	International Boundary
– – – –	Parish Boundary
— • —	National Park/Reserve
✈ ✈	Airport: International/ Regional
🚌	Bus Station
P	Parking
i	Tourist Information
✉	Post Office
† ☦	Church / Ruins
†	Monastery
☪	Mosque
✡	Synagogue
♜	Castle / Ruins
∴	Archaeological Site
∩	Cave
ⵊ	Statue/Monument
★	Place of Interest

The main places of interest in the Places section are coordinated by number with a full-colour map (e.g. ❶), and a symbol at the top of every right-hand page tells you where to find the map.

INSIGHT GUIDE
BARBADOS

CONTENTS

Maps

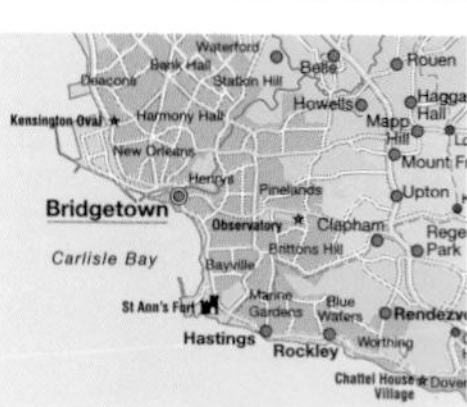

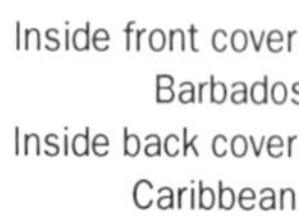

Introduction

History

Features

Fishing on the beach

Insight on ...

Information panels

Travel Tips

◆ Full Travel Tips index is on page 329

Places

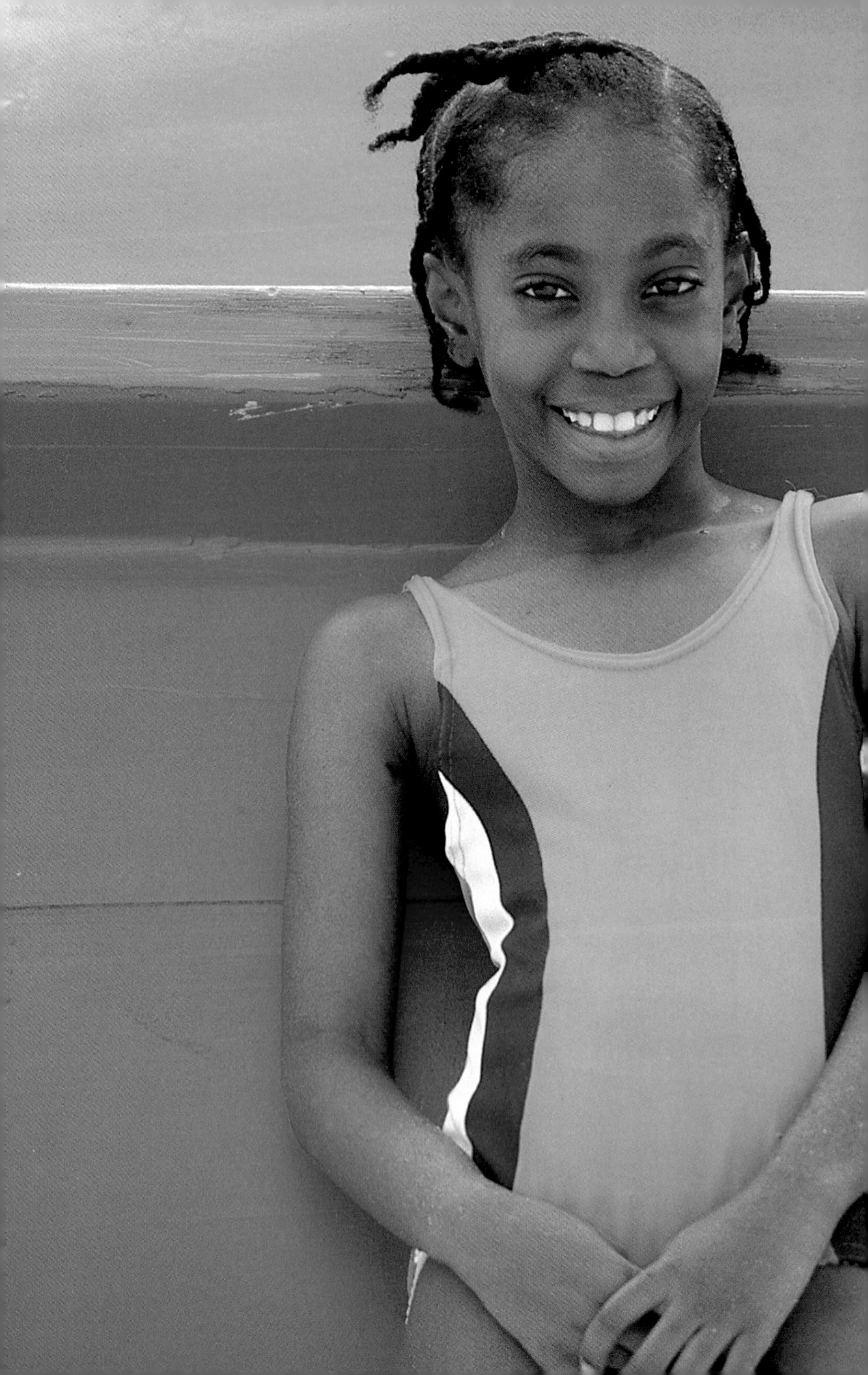

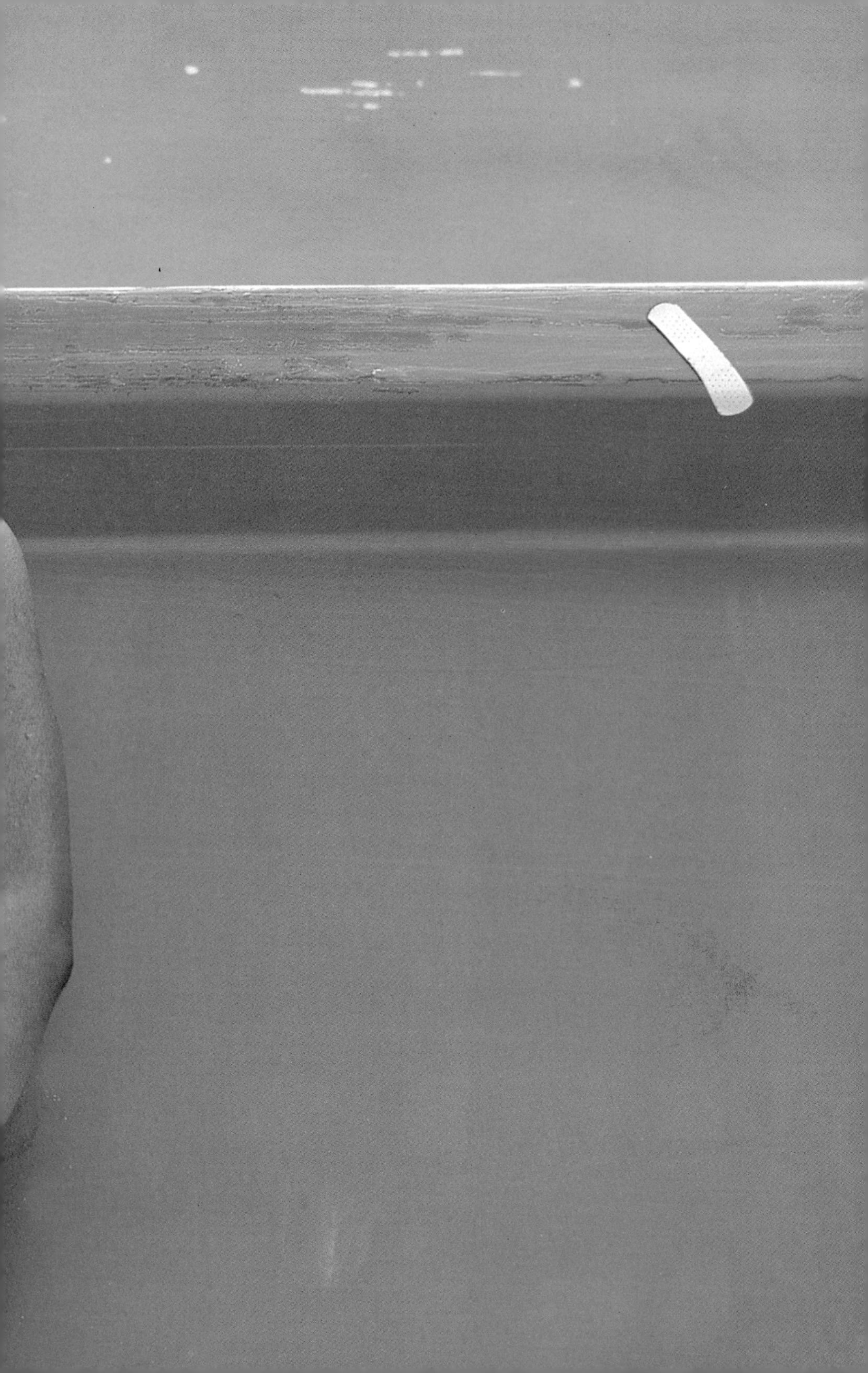

A Singular Island

Scratch the surface of this sunny island and you'll find a wealth of history, a rich culture and a bottomless pot of friendliness

Sir Henry Colt, one of the first English visitors to Barbados, arriving in 1631, remarked: "To confess truly, of all the islands that I have seen unto this day, not any pleaseth me so well." For well over three centuries, visitors to its glittering shores have been impressed by this "gem of the Caribbean Sea". Barbados "has an air of neatness, politeness and opulence which one does not find in other islands", wrote a French missionary back in 1700, and it is still true today. Barbados is the only place outside the United States that George Washington ever visited: in 1751, he was "perfectly ravished by the beautiful prospects on every side" of the island.

Barbados confirms the theory that the character of a people is shaped by the landscape they inhabit. Ever since the English landed on its shores in the 1600s, the entire island has been intensely cultivated, even to the tops of its modest hills. The patchwork of flat, tidy fields which stretches to the sea has produced a hardy, down-to-earth people with a reputation for seriousness, self-assurance and frugality. In the small, crowded space of the Barbadian environment, order and discipline have always been essential. Perhaps that's why Barbados has supplied so many teachers, preachers and policemen to neighbouring islands. Barbadians, or Bajans, are not slow to trumpet their own virtues. They firmly believe, as a piece of doggerel from more than 50 years ago says, that "when the great trump shall blow, all other nations will please stan' back and Buhbadians march up first."

Even more so today as, proud of their unique cultural heritage – which has encouraged the exploration and celebration of some of the African-inspired aspects of the island's music, art and literature – and confident in the high standards of living reached at the turn of the millennium, they can look forward to a future of prosperity as one of the world's top developing countries, highly respected by the international business fraternity.

Often called a singular island, Barbados lives up to this analogy as Barbadians know and visitors quickly discover. It may have glorious sunny days, a glistening azure sea and spectacular scenery, but it is a fascinating cultural vantage point too – an example in miniature of the way history and geography shape both a people and a place. ❑

Preceding Pages: waterskiing into the sunset on the West Coast; having a laugh at the market; a self-conscious smile; tuning up for the big parade.
Left: dressed up smart for town.

Why Bajans Are Different

Set apart from the rest of the Caribbean islands, this pear-shaped coral island has a distinct identity of its own

Barbados is different, distinctive, an island apart. In a part of the world where every territory is dissimilar, where diversity is almost commonplace, Barbados still stands out with its own specific identity. Partly a question of geography, partly a result of history, this sense of separateness is not so much a matter of pride, more a fact of life.

Not, of course, that Barbados stands alone. First and foremost, it is unmistakably Caribbean, as much a part of the region as, say, Jamaica or Trinidad. A shared history and common culture bind the island to its neighbours. Sugar, slavery, migration: all the scourges and challenges of Caribbean history have affected it as much as any other island. And Barbados thrives on many of the same forms of self-expression and enjoyment as the rest of the region. Music, sport, religion are all as central to Barbadian life as elsewhere.

But even so, there is something special about Barbados, a feeling unique to an island that seems very much bigger than its 166 sq. miles (430 sq. km). Everyone in the Caribbean knows that Bajans are different, a special case.

Gentle landscape

Standing some 100 miles (160 km) to the east of St Vincent, pear-shaped Barbados somehow keeps its distance from the archipelago of small islands that stretch down towards the coast of South America and make up the Lesser Antilles. Topographically, that distance is far greater. Barbados is a mostly low-lying coral island surrounded by reefs – the chalky secretions of countless colonies of tiny living creatures – while its nearest neighbours are volcanic and often mountainous.

Its rolling hills, pastures and extensively cultivated plains stand in stark contrast to the rugged and inhospitable terrain of the central arc of islands. There is little of the savage grandeur of a place like Dominica, where nature can seem overwhelming, but more a gentle, if still tropical, landscape dominated by agriculture and human settlement.

Much of the island is topped by a covering of coral limestone, which geologists think may be up to 600,000 years old. Rain percolates through the limestone, forming underground lakes, such as at Harrison's Cave, where subterranean streams have carved out dramatic caverns. Underneath the limestone is older, softer rock, and in certain areas, such as the hilly northeast Scotland District, erosion has exposed this substratum of chalk and clay. The relentless battering of the Atlantic Ocean against the northeastern coastline has also revealed sedimentary rocks that may be 70 million years old. The result is a spectacularly tortured panorama of giant rocks, jagged inlets and cliffs assaulted by "white horses" or breakers.

Nothing could be further from the placid beaches of the South and West coasts (in fact,

LEFT: the deep pinks of bougainvillea create bright splashes of colour all over the island.
RIGHT: small roads wind through acres of cane fields.

only 20 miles/32 km away), where the Caribbean Sea laps at long palm-lined stretches of white sand. Here, protected from the ravages of the Atlantic, a series of reefs shelter powdery beaches from strong currents and waves.

Coral reefs

These reefs have been a matter of concern for the islanders, however, as more and more visitors discovered their holiday paradise in Barbados and coastal development had to increase at a rapid rate to keep up. By the 1980s, pollution was having an adverse effect on the reefs, reducing their ability to protect the shoreline from the might of the sea and causing the erosion of several South Coast beaches.

In the mid 1980s, the Government took stock and set up a coastal conservation programme and since then new sewage plants have been built on the South and West Coasts to relieve the stressed reefs and, to revive the beaches, submerged breakwaters have been made out of limestone boulders that have already attracted new coral growth and fish.

Two separate worlds

The contrast between wild Atlantic windward coasts and calmer leeward Caribbean shorelines occurs in all the islands of the Lesser Antilles, but in Barbados it is particularly dramatic, creating two separate worlds. The more remote, sometimes desolate, East Coast is reminiscent of a Cornish or Scottish seascape, as waves crash over the cliffs amidst the roar of ebb and flow. To the west and south, the beaches are those captured a million times in tourist brochures, bordered by a sea whose colour changes constantly as the day progresses.

Mountainous it is not, but Barbados is not entirely flat. The view from the island's highest point, Mount Hillaby (1,115 ft/340 metres), reveals an expanse of steep hillsides and modest peaks, dotted with palm trees and villages and hillsides swathed in bananas and sugar cane. Further south, the hills become gentler, sloping down towards the sea, until they level out into the fertile sugar-growing plains of the island's southern parishes.

Balmy temperatures

The gentleness of the landscape is reflected in a mostly benevolent climate. The weather is mild all year round, with an average balmy temperature of 80°F (27°C). It's usually cooler in February and hottest in August. Trade winds deliver welcome breezes from the northeast, while rain tends to pass quickly in brief squalls, except during the June to November hurricane season when downpours can be more intense. Still, even here Barbados is relatively blessed compared to its neighbours, since hurricanes generally spare the island, passing harmlessly by to the north.

Flora and fauna

Since the earliest English settlement, Barbados has been intensively cultivated. It is also one of the most densely populated places on the planet, with an average of 1,500 people packed into each square mile concentrated mostly around the capital, Bridgetown, and its surrounding areas, but even so there are few real wildernesses left. As a result, what remains of the island's tropical flora and fauna is protected with unusual zeal – the assortment of trees, including mahogany, in Turners Hall Wood gives an idea of what the island was like before its forests were chopped down to make way for sugar plantations,

The Barbados National Trust manages a number of beautiful nature sites, including the Andromeda Botanic Gardens, which contains exceptional collections of tropical flowers and trees, including a huge bearded fig tree, supposed to be the inspiration behind the naming of Barbados.

The green monkey still runs riot in the pockets of woodland. They arrived as stowaways on the slave ships more than 350 years ago and became such a menace to farmers that the Government offered rewards for their tails. The mongoose was introduced in the 19th century to help keep the rat population down, but it turned out they only operated by day whereas rats are nocturnal. There are no poisonous snakes or spiders. At Graeme Hall Bird Sanctuary, the mangrove swamps are being revived and attracting birds such as the large white cattle egrets, green herons, yellow warblers as well as around 150 migratory birds. A small number of Amazon parrots have also made their home on the island.

EVENING SONG

As soon as dusk falls, the most enchanting orchestra of sound strikes up in the bushes. This is the song of countless tiny whistling frogs, not much bigger than a thumb nail.

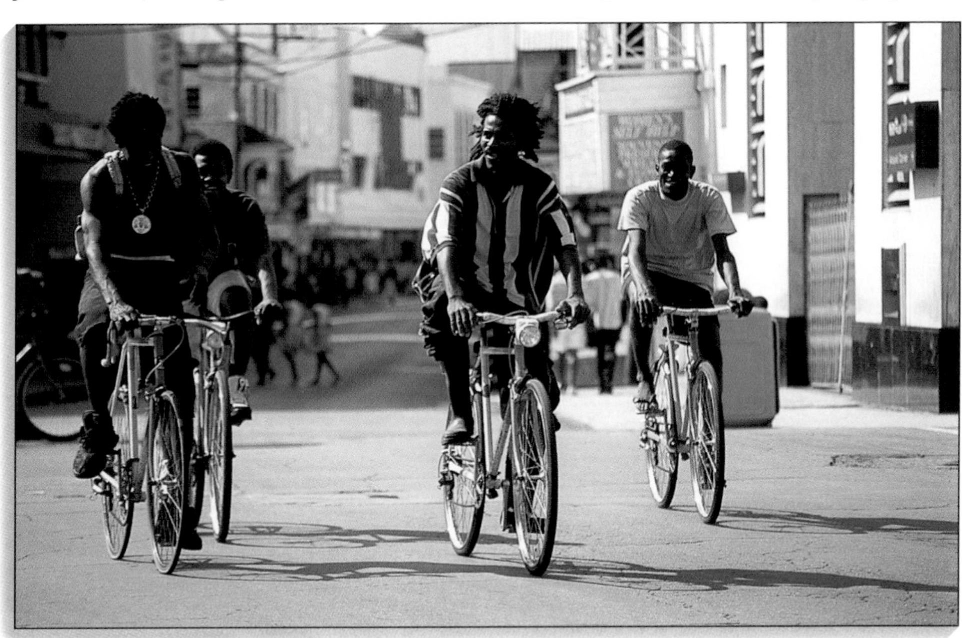

LEFT: horseback riding near Ragged Point.
ABOVE: a useful form of transport.

New horizons

Verdant expanses of sugar cane still cover large areas of Barbados, and when the delicate, wispy flowers appear on top of the 12-ft (3.5-metre) high canes it makes an impressive sight. But diversification has had to be the watchword throughout the Caribbean since sugar (and, more recently, banana) plantations began to face bankruptcy in the early 1990s.

However, Barbados has been ahead of many of its neighbours in actually restructuring its economy to take account of new markets and opportunities. Small-scale manufacturing plants have sprouted around Bridgetown, making garments and electrical components for North American companies. Information technology has brought employment, as Barbadian workers process large amounts of electronic information – airline reservations, credit card bills – online. And a programme to make Barbados a digitally literate society by 2005 is well underway in schools and colleges.

The glitzy new office blocks outside Bridgetown testify to the presence of a burgeoning offshore financial sector, dealing in banking, insurance and other international money flows.

The holiday idyll

The biggest money spinner of all is tourism. As early as 1887 the Crane Beach Hotel on the island's southeast coast opened its doors to winter-weary American visitors. "Winter in the West Indies" became a chic concept among well-heeled British tourists from the 1920s, and gradually an embryonic tourist industry began to take shape. But it was only with the advent of regular and affordable long-haul flights from Europe and the US that tourism really came into its own. Since the 1960s, Barbados has been at the forefront of what has developed into a highly competitive industry and has proved popular enough with the wealthy to merit Concorde flying out weekly during the winter.

About one in five Bajans work in tourism-related jobs, while foreign visitors bring in more than 10 times more money than the ailing sugar business. You only have to drive along the South Coast road from Hastings to Oistins to appreciate how tourism has utterly changed

BUSINESS IS BOOMING

At the turn of the new millennium there were more than 6,000 international financial service businesses in Barbados. This has been due to a strategy of tax incentives since 1969 to encourage offshore business to the island.

After a slow start, when the emphasis was on training Barbadians in all aspects of the financial services, Barbados now prides itself on being able to support a global business centre with a highly skilled workforce.

With plenty of scope for corporate entertainment on the doorstep and a quality of life claimed to be the best in the developing world, the benefits of international business are being felt across the board.

the island's landscape. A congested strip of hotels, condominiums, restaurants and shopping centres absorbs more than half a million tourists a year (another half million make fleeting excursions from cruise ships). The overall effect sometimes lacks charm, for taste has occasionally been on the altar of quick construction and profitability.

> **CONCORDE**
>
> During the winter, Concorde flies from London to Barbados once a week and takes just four hours, making a long weekend in the Caribbean a viable proposition…

But not all the aesthetic or environmental impact of tourism is negative. The luxurious establishments that line the so-called Platinum West Coast are often tastefully remodelled and landscaped versions of plantation properties. Some fine old-fashioned hotels still stand on the less crowded parts of the coastline, including the Crane Beach and the legendary Atlantis Hotel at Bathsheba.

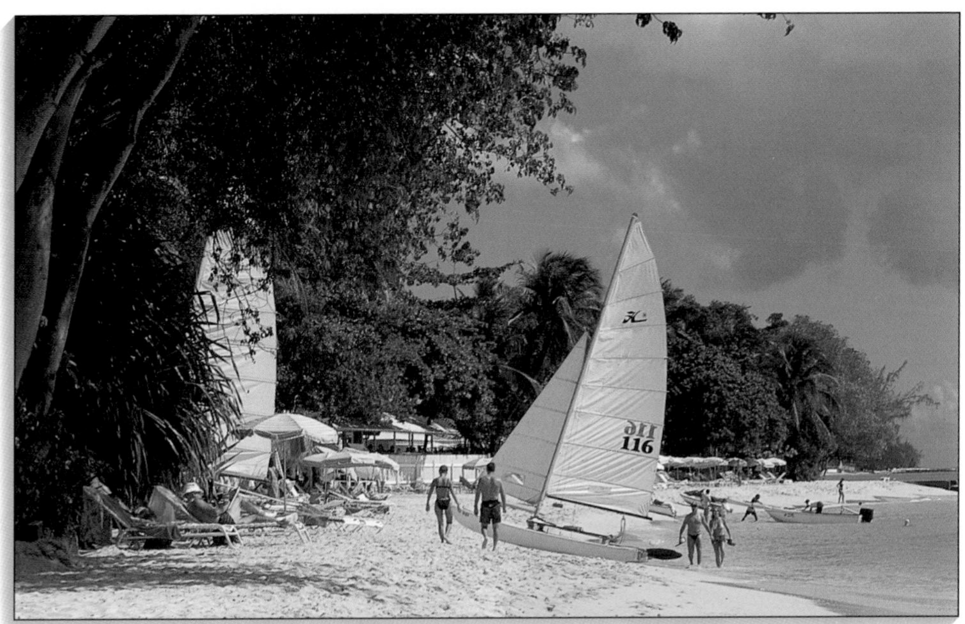

Most important, however, is the way that tourist dollars filter into environmental and architectural conservation, funding the invaluable work of the Barbados National Trust in preserving historic sites and nature reserves.

With its excellent infrastructure and relatively short distances (even if getting from A to B isn't quite as simple as it looks on the map), Barbados offers the visitor an impressive range of excursions. Tourism is, of course, a mixed blessing. But Barbados has shown that when it is carefully managed and largely kept in local hands, it can be a force for good as well as a vital economic lifeline.

Politically stable

Since independence in 1966, Barbados has been pretty much a model of political and social stability. Apart from a few Black Power-related disturbances in the 1970s, the island has experienced little of the inter-party violence or ethnic tension that have plagued Jamaica and Trinidad. What political conflict does occur takes place through the formal channels of the "Westminster-style" parliamentary democracy or, more entertainingly, through a lively local press and radio. Some of the best political commentary is to be found in the calypsoes which accompany the annual Crop Over Festival in late July and early August. This, understandably, is not an event that erring politicians relish.

The rewards of such political maturity have been steady economic growth (apart from a brief recession in the early 1990s) and an envi-

LEFT: sunset at Warrens International Business Centre.
ABOVE: visitors flock to the West Coast.

able level of social development. In terms of health and education, Bajans enjoy a First World lifestyle. Per capita income is on a par with Portugal. Illiteracy is almost unknown, life expectancy is on a par with Europe and North America, the mass poverty and epidemics of the 1930s have been all but eradicated.

Not everything is perfect. A wealthy minority, some descended from the white British "plantocracy", continue to wield disproportionate power. Unemployment runs at just over 12 percent and pockets of deprivation, both rural and urban, remain, but for the great majority of Barbadians, the prospect of old age and illness is no longer grounds for despair. To this extent, modern-day Barbados is a singular success story, especially in a region where poverty is all too common.

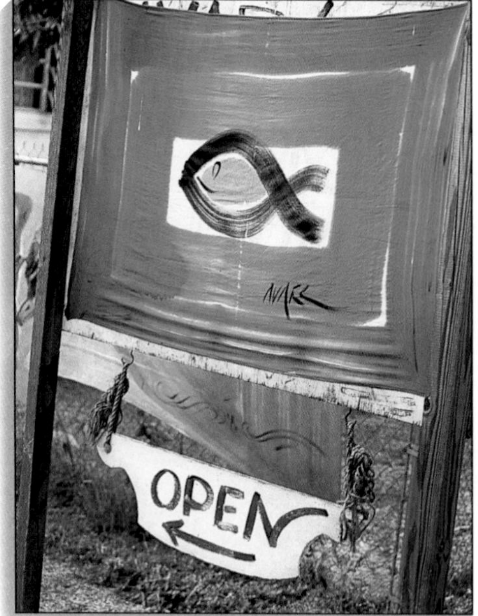

TREAD LIGHTLY ON THIS ISLAND...

...and help preserve it for future generations:

- choose a locally owned and run hotel, preferably with Green Globe accreditation.
- be mindful of your use of energy and water.
- leave coral for the fish, don't stand on it and never drop anchor on a reef.
- ask people for their permission before taking a photograph of them.
- enjoy watersports that don't need a motor.
- the landscape is fragile so keep four wheels on the roads, not on the hillsides.
- video or report any pollution you may see.

A new identity

The prevailing northeasterly trade winds meant that, in the past, Barbados was difficult to reach, let alone attack, from other islands. And while these regularly changed hands between French, Dutch and Spaniards, Barbados remained resolutely British. From this continuity sprang the idea of "Little England", the belief that Barbados was – and still is – the most British of Caribbean islands.

Sometimes the illusion is still there. A grey stone Anglican church reminds you of a Cotswold village, old signposts direct you to Worthing and Hastings. But illusion it is. The days of blind loyalty to Britain, mocked in George Lamming's anti-colonial masterpiece *In The Castle of My Skin* are long gone.

Most young Barbadians aspire more to Miami or New York than London; satellite dishes beam in not the BBC, but CNN and a solid diet of US chat shows and soaps. Proximity to North America has eroded the island's Englishness. And there are even plans afoot to make the island a republic and replace the Queen as head of state with a president.

But Barbados has not simply replaced one imported cultural model with another. Instead, by reassessing its past, by fusing British influences with those from Africa, from other Caribbean islands and from North America, it has produced a cultural blend that is distinctively Bajan. Writers like Lamming and Kamau Brathwaite have won international acclaim by exploring authentically local themes of village life, migration and exile.

In re-evaluating and celebrating the island's African heritage, in making links with a neglected past, new writers and artists of all sorts are busy creating a vibrant and evolving culture that encompasses calypso, poetry, theatre, the visual arts and, of course, cricket.

Neither Little England, nor Little Miami, Barbados is happy with its own identity. A singular island it may be, but it is also a place of multiple attractions and infinite charm. ❑

LEFT: West Coast attractions.
RIGHT: an enterprising craftsman.

A PROSPECT OF BRIDGE TOWN

BARBADOS . 1695 By Samuel Cop

Decisive Dates

1600–2000 BC Amerindian fishers and foragers arrive from the lowlands of South America in dug-out canoes and settle on Barbados. Others follow, including the Saladoid ceramic-using Indians who come from Venezuela in around 200 BC and form the origin of the people generally referred to as Arawaks or Tainos.
23 December AD 1511 First known mention of Barbados in an official document. Issued by King Ferdinand of Spain, it authorised the capture of Amerindians on the island and their removal to Hispaniola (now Haiti and Dominican Republic) for slave labour.

Establishment of a British Colony 1627–44

English, Irish and Scottish immigrants start new lives in Barbados either as plantation owners and managers or indentured servants.
1625 Captain John Powell, employed by London merchant Sir William Courteen, claims a deserted Barbados for James 1, King of England.
February 1627 Captained by John Powell's brother Henry and financed by Courteen, the *William and John*, carrying around 80 British settlers, arrives at Holetown.
1628 Bridgetown is founded when Charles Wolverston, sent by the island's new owner, the first Earl of Carlisle, lands there with more settlers.
1630–44 Around 30,000 white settlers, including convicts committed to forced labour on the plantations, indentured servants and a stream of African slaves, arrive in Barbados.
1637 Sugar cane from Brazil is introduced to the island by Dutchman Pieter Blower for making rum.
1639 The House of Assembly is set up creating the third oldest Parliament in the world.

The Sugar Boom Years 1640–1700

As sugar grew rapidly in importance, the African slave trade came into its own providing vast numbers of slaves to work on the plantations.
1640 The manufacture of sugar begins in earnest supplanting cotton and tobacco, creating wealthy planters and establishing a "plantocracy".
1647 An epidemic of yellow fever kills 6,000 people.
1649 After the execution of Charles I at the end of the English Civil War, Royalist Barbados refuses to recognise Oliver Cromwell's leadership.
1652 Barbados capitulates to Cromwell's troops but is given a degree of autonomy in the signing of what becomes known as the Charter of Barbados.
1663 A conspiracy by a group of white servants to revolt due to their inhumane living conditions is cruelly crushed and 18 are executed. England levies a 4½ percent tax on all exports out of Barbados.
1670s Poorer white planters and farmers leave for other parts of the Caribbean and the Carolinas in America as a handful of wealthy planters monopolise the sugar industry.
1675 A highly organised black slave rebellion is foiled and the ringleaders are executed. More uprisings are put down in 1683, 1686, 1692 and 1702.
1679 Black slaves outnumber whites nearly two to one (total population: 57,000).
1685 After the failure of the Monmouth Rebellion, at the Bloody Assizes Judge Jeffreys sentences 100 of the rebels to transportation to Barbados.

Reform and Rebellion 1700–1840

During the 18th century, world opinion moved towards abolishing slavery while the Caribbean rocked with European warfare.
1700 The world market value of Barbados's sugar drops due to competition from other Caribbean islands.
1713 Britain wins more sugar trading concessions from Spain as a result of the Spanish War of Succession.
1748 Codrington College is established as the first educational institution in the Caribbean.
1766 Bridgetown is mostly destroyed by fire.
1780 A hurricane causes massive destruction to the island and its crops and claims 3,000 lives.
1805 Lord Nelson docks in Bridgetown with his fleet, a few months before his final heroic victory at Trafalgar.

1807 Britain officially abolishes the slave trade.
1816 Rebellion of 5,000 slaves, led by Bussa, who thought a new slave registration law was to free them.
1831 Free coloured people are granted legal equality with whites. The "Great Hurricane" hits Barbados.
1834 With the Emancipation Act, slavery is abolished and an "apprenticeship" system is introduced.
1838 Slaves wake up as free men on 1 August, but still nothing changes as plantation owners seek ways to prevent their labour force from moving on.

EMANCIPATION AND INDEPENDENCE 1840–1966

Although officially free, repression of the former slaves continued and many left Barbados to work elsewhere. Great political strides were made for true freedom.
1843 Samuel Jackman Prescod becomes Barbados' first non-white member of Parliament.
1861 Fresh water pipes are laid in Bridgetown.
1876 Plans for Barbados to join the other Windward Islands in a confederation lead to bloody riots.
1884 Franchise Act gives vote to smaller landowners.
1886 Mulatto politician William Conrad Reeves becomes the British Empire's first black Chief Justice.
1887 The Crane Beach Hotel opens.
1902 An outbreak of smallpox isolates the island, followed by yellow fever in 1908.
1904–1914 Around 20,000 Barbadians leave for Panama to help build the canal. Cheap sugar from European beet forces sugar prices down.
1937 Trinidadian-born trade unionist Clement Payne is deported, triggering bloody riots over inequality and harsh economic conditions.
1938 Barbados Labour Party (BLP) is founded under the leadership of Grantley Adams, followed by the formation of the Barbados Workers Union in 1941.
1951 After universal suffrage is granted, the BLP wins the first free elections. A break-away group forms the Democratic Labour Party (DLP).
1954 Grantley Adams becomes the island's first premier as major constitutional changes get under way.
1958 Grantley Adams leads a short-lived federation of the British West Indies which dissolves in 1962.
1961 The DLP win the elections led by Errol Barrow.
30 November 1966 Barbados granted independence from Britain but remains within the Commonwealth.

AN INDEPENDENT NATION, 1966 – TODAY

The second half of the 20th century saw Barbados decline as the sugar industry dwindled; later it was revitalised by tourism and international business.
1973 CARICOM (Caribbean Community) is set up to provide the framework for a single Caribbean market.
1974 Crop Over Festival is revived.
1976 The BLP wins back the Government with Tom Adams as Prime Minister.
1979 A new enlarged airport is opened with a runway long enough for Concorde.
1983 Barbados assists America in the invasion of Grenada with a Defence Force founded in 1978 with US financial assistance.
1986 The DLP are voted back in power.
1992 Economic crisis pushes Barbados to the brink of bankruptcy.

LEFT: mulattoes enjoying a dance. **RIGHT:** Owen Arthur, Prime Minister of Barbados, whose BLP party won a sweeping victory in the 1999 elections.

1994 General election is brought forward and Owen Arthur heads a new BLP administration.
1997 Edutec 2000 Project is set up in schools to create a new computer literate generation by 2005. President Bill Clinton attends a Caribbean/ USA summit at the new Sherbourne Conference Centre in May. International business is attracted to Barbados as a result of its offshore tax advantages.
1998 10 National Heroes are announced on 28 April and the day, Sir Grantley Adams' 100th anniversary, is made a public holiday. Sandy Lane Hotel closes for major rebuilding work.
1999 Owen Arthur celebrates a landslide election victory and presses on with plans for a republic; Trafalgar Square is renamed National Heroes Square. ❑

THE FIRST BAJANS

Home to Amerindians since prehistoric times, Barbados was bypassed by the Spanish and settled by the British, who hung on to "the Rock" for more than 300 years

Although Columbus missed it completely on all of his trips to the West Indies, Amerindians, Africans and Europeans have all left their mark on this tiny island.

The story began 5,000 years ago, when Amerindians were "island hopping" in the Caribbean, and probably visited Barbados. This early history has become much more clear recently as, in the late 1990s, major archaeological discoveries were made at Heywoods, the site of the new Port St Charles development on the West Coast, north of Speightstown, which has literally rewritten the history books.

The finds have pushed back the date of the first settlement on the island by nearly 2,000 years, as radiocarbon dating of Amerindian shell tools unearthed here have revealed a date of 1630 BC, which means that Heywoods has been a site of continued human occupation for almost 4,000 years.

These first settlers were Pre-Ceramic fisher/foragers who are believed to have come from around the Orinoco delta, in what is now Venezuela in South America, and used tools fashioned from conch shells. Much later, between 200 and 400 BC, a group of ceramic-using people arrived from the Venezuelan coast, crossing the sea in canoes up to 90 ft (27 metres) long, carrying women, children, animals, water, plants, religious objects, navigational devices and weapons.

Farmers and fishermen

Originally referred to as Arawaks, these Amerindians are now known by historians as Tainos, and the pottery they used is classified by archaeologists as Saladoid. They farmed and fished and brought with them a calendar system and a unique tradition of pottery-making. Pot-lined wells, which would have been a major source of fresh water, and remains of their round houses have been found at Heywoods, Silver Sands and other sites around the island. People of the same origin then remained living in Barbados until they disappeared in the early 16th century when it is believed they were taken as slaves to Hispaniola by the Spanish. The first known mention of Barbados in an official document is that of the Spanish king, Ferdinand, dated 23 December 1511, authorising slaves to be taken from "Los Barbudos".

A differing theory is that they were wiped out by another race from South America known as the Caribs or Kalinagos, a somewhat less sophisticated tribe of hunters and fishermen, who settled the other islands of the Lesser Antilles. But there is little or no evidence to show that they inhabited Barbados, only visited it in their canoes from St Vincent, just 100 miles (160 km) away and St Lucia, 128 miles (205 km) away. These visits continued even after the English had arrived, as they were documented by contemporary observers.

Many Europeans who visited the West Indies in the 16th and 17th centuries told tales of Carib

LEFT: portrayal of an Amerindian family.
RIGHT: sacred object to the deity "Giver of Cassava".

cannibalism. But anthropologists now say that these were probably stories put around by the Spanish so they could justify enslaving them.

First English settlers

So when the English arrived in 1627, all they found was a flourishing population of wild hogs, left by Portuguese explorers who had anchored briefly there in 1536. They soon set about clearing the densely forested land that they found and persuaded some Amerindians from Guyana to come and teach them how to grow their crops.

The voyage from Europe to Barbados is made easy by the currents and trade winds. Even today, it is possible to float on a raft from the Canary Islands to Barbados. Still, the fortune-hunting Spanish explorers bypassed Barbados, as there was no promise of gold.

Barbados' name is Portuguese. At some point during the Caribbean exploration, the Portuguese referred to the island as Los Barbudos, meaning "the bearded ones". It's generally acknowledged that the reference is to Barbados' bearded fig trees, but other theories are that bearded men – some say Africans – were among the island's pre-European "citizens".

It fell to English explorers, led by Captain John Powell, in 1625 to land near today's Holetown and claim Barbados in the name of James I, King of England, who unbeknown to them had died while they were at sea.

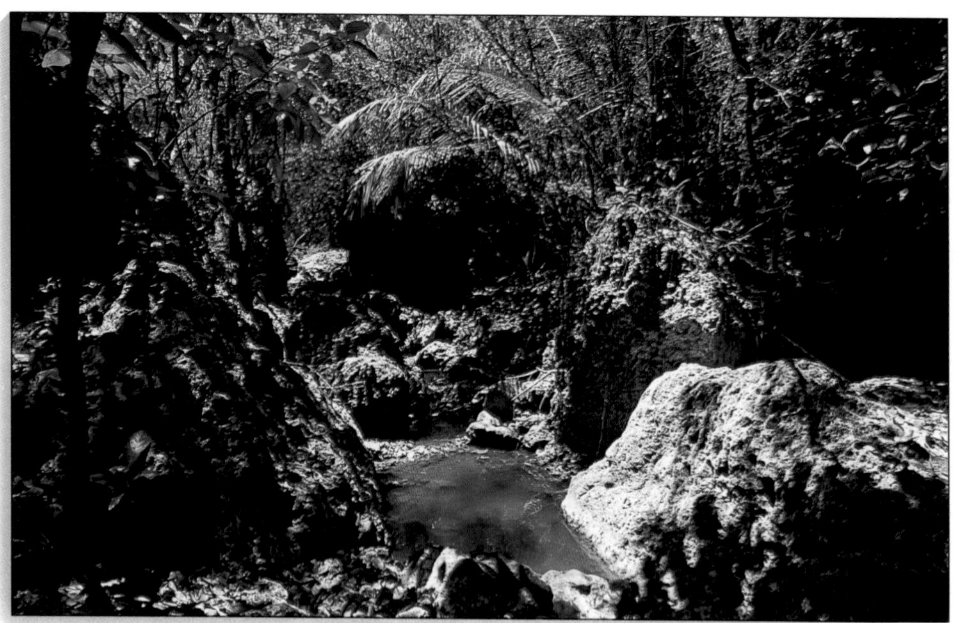

The first European settlement began in earnest on 17 February 1627, when 80 English settlers and 10 black slaves (captured from a Spanish vessel) landed on the West Coast funded to the tune of £10,000 by Sir William Courteen, a London merchant.

A difficult start

These first settlers and those that followed were intrepid, willing to risk their lives for the promise of wealth and power. Many of them

Amerindian Language

We still utter the sounds of the ancient Amerindian language when we use these familiar words: hurricane – *huracan*; maize or corn – *maiz*; canoe – *canaua*; tobacco – *tobaco*; hammock – *hamaca*; savannah – *sabana*; guava – *guayaba*.

Other Caribbean Indian terms, literally translated, are jewels of creativity: father of the fingers – thumb; soul of the hand – pulse; my heart – wife; he who makes me little children – son-in-law; God's plume of feathers – rainbow; the pot is boiling – earthquake.

A European was called a "misshapen enemy" because of his clothing and armour.

were second or younger sons of well-placed Englishmen who would receive none of the inheritance earmarked for first-born sons. During the first 50 years, nearly all the new arrivals were men causing a severe imbalance of the sexes. Life on the island took on an anything-goes quality described as being "beyond the line", outside territorial limits of European treaties.

BEYOND THE LINE

Out of reach of European treaties, Barbados became a stage for gamblers, fighters, fortune hunters, political refugees, outcasts and kidnappers.

The first settlers did not own land or stock, but acted as freeholders or tenants, often keeping a small plot and two or three indentured

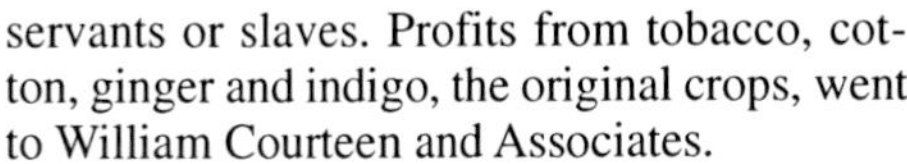

servants or slaves. Profits from tobacco, cotton, ginger and indigo, the original crops, went to William Courteen and Associates.

During the first 10 years, white indentured servants from Europe did most of the servile and agricultural work. They were lower-class labourers without money to buy land, who agreed to serve as indentured servants on the island for two to 10 years, for a small parcel of land or start-up sum at the end. Unfortunately, few employers kept their promises and many left for the British colonies of North America or other Caribbean islands.

Slaves were a minority. According to historian Hilary Beckles, the number of blacks on Barbados didn't exceed 800 throughout the 1630s. Even in 1643, the population numbered roughly 37,000 whites to nearly 6,000 blacks.

If the island was "owned" by one man, at least Courteen was a sympathetic and able administrator. His successor, the Earl of Carlisle (a Scot and a favourite of the English crown) was less of a

humanitarian. He convinced Charles I to grant him rights to Barbados and, although in direct conflict with Sir William Courteen's deed, he sent his own band of settlers to a southwestern bay, which became Bridgetown.

Great Barbados Robbery

Dumbfounded by the turn of events, Courteen enlisted the help of the Earl of Pembroke in restoring his rights to the island. Charles I acquiesced. In a turnabout, however, the King then re-granted ownership rights to Carlisle, whose will prevailed. The dispute, and especially its outcome, was later dubbed the "Great Barbados Robbery".

LEFT: Joe's River – how the island looked in 1627.
ABOVE: the first Englishman to land in Barbados.
ABOVE RIGHT: jewellery found in slaves' graves.

Political duelling between Carlisle and Courteen factions sapped the island's economic momentum. Infighting was compounded by drought and a drop in food production that shook optimism. Carlisle made sure his personal profit margin from Barbados exports also increased substantially. Islanders called the mid 1630s "the starving time".

Carlisle appointed as governor Henry Hawley, who, says one account, was "a restless and a scheming soul". However, to appease powerful planter opposition to his appointment, in 1639 he set up a House of Assembly, a "representative" body of citizens added to the island's system of government. Many of the first representatives of the Assembly – all white male landowners – became big planters and heads of influential families. In the 1630s, a Captain Futter commented to the island's Judge Read about the character of Barbados's appointed officials, "If all whore-masters were taken off the Bench," he inquired, "what would the Governor do for a council?"

When Royalist Richard Ligon arrived in 1647, an epidemic of yellow fever was sweeping the island. Planters who had begun "sugar workes" were "laid in their dust, and their estates left to strangers", he wrote from a

HOW SLAVES LIVED

During the sugar boom of the 17th century, slaves were housed in floorless huts, sustained on meagre food supplies, and worked six days a week, 12 hours a day. "The day began at half-past five, when the plantation bell summoned them to the main estate yard to receive instructions," writes historian Karl Watson. "After an issue of hot ginger tea, they were divided into three groups. The able men and women were sent out to dig cane holes, to manure, or to cut and crop mature cane. Less able adults, children and nursing mothers performed less arduous tasks.

"Slaves were given food weekly. A typical weekly ration consisted of 28 lb (13 kg) of yams or potatoes, 10 pints (5 litres) of corn, 8 oz (225 g) of fish, and 1½ pints (900 ml) of molasses. The yearly ration of men's clothing might be a flannel jacket, a shirt, a pair of trousers and a cap. Women might get a flannel jacket, a gown, petticoat and a cap."

Slaves in skilled positions fared better and domestic slaves were more trusted, and better treated, than field workers. A visitor to one household wrote: "It surprised me... to observe the unchecked and even disputatious familiarity of the house Negroes and servants; and at dinners... I have frequently observed them wholly occupied in listening to any good stories and laughing at them much louder than any of the Company."

debtors' prison after he'd returned to England three years later.

Reaping the sweets

By the 1650s, the sugar plantation system was established (*see page 37*). The tropical forests had all been chopped down, and the landscape transformed into a patchwork of cane fields. This was the start of the sugar boom years and, for the white upper class, a period of unparalleled prosperity when Barbados became known as "the brightest jewel in the English crown".

Without slaves, plantations could not have existed. The white indentured servants were not used to toiling all day under a tropical sun and were ill nourished – they were often treated worse than the slaves by the planters, as they were not their property and so of no value.

The slave trade

Slaves were brought from West Africa to the West Indies by the Portuguese and Dutch, from areas which are now Sierra Leone, Guinea, Ghana, the Ivory Coast, Nigeria and the Cameroons. They came from the Fanti-Ashanti peoples of the Gold Coast, from the Dahomey and the Yoruba and Bini peoples of areas in western Nigeria.

From different ethnic groups and places, and speaking different languages, the Africans brought to Barbados were extremely diverse. However, they also shared a number of expectations, attitudes and everyday practices. From these they were able to communicate and secretly recreate their own folk traditions.

During the sugar boom, the number of slaves increased from 5,680 in 1645 to 60,000 in 1684. Slaves outnumbered whites by three to one – a threat to their masters which resulted in severe measures of control. They were purposely kept in awe and not discouraged from believing, for instance, that Anglican church services were sessions of witchcraft that were directed against them.

LEFT: colonial good life portrayed in the 18th century.
ABOVE: an artist's view of a working plantation.

Police action, usually brutal, was a major tactic against uprisings. Slave laws, reports historian Karl Watson, "tried to limit mobility. A pass system was devised to prevent slaves from moving about freely. Rigid laws were enacted for the capture and punishment of runaway slaves… Efforts also were made to reduce the risk of rebellion by the prohibition of drumming, blowing of horns… assemblies." In the 18th century these laws were relaxed.

Barbadian slaves were the property of their

owners – a kind of property seen partially as chattel and partially as real estate. Slaves could be sold, or traded against debts. The rare planter freed his slaves, sometimes upon his own death, according to his will, or out of compassion, after the slaves had reached a certain age. Economics as well as compassion were at work – aging slaves were plantation liabilities.

Ultimate penalty

During the English Civil War, as a joke, if anyone called a person a Cavalier or Roundhead the offender had to invite that person and all who had heard to dinner.

During Barbados' growing years, inter-marriages were few, according to church records, or perhaps just kept secret. However, inter-racial liaisons were many, especially between white planters and black slaves. A mulatto population grew up, creating a new class of "coloureds" generally treated better than blacks. It was not uncommon for a planter who had fathered a mulatto child to baptise it and free it from slavery.

Roundheads and Cavaliers

Throughout the English Civil War in the 1640s, Barbados had tried to remain neutral and became a refuge for those looking for "a quiet life". But after Charles I's execution in 1649, the Royalists, or Cavaliers, who were in the majority, could not contain themselves and open hostilities began. This finally resulted in the expulsion of the Roundheads to England who reported the island's strong Royalist faction and that they were trading with the Dutch who were Commonwealth enemies. In 1651, Oliver Cromwell sent a fleet carrying 4,000 men to invade Barbados, which they finally managed after strong resistance from the island's Governor, Lord Willoughby, and his troops at Oistins.

Eventually, a peaceful settlement was reached with the 1652 Charter of Barbados, in which the islanders had to pledge obedience to the Commonwealth, but were still allowed self-government and to continue their policy of free trade. The latter did not last though, as Cromwell reinforced a previous Act banning trade between other nations, which had a detrimental effect on the sugar industry. After years of protest from the Barbadians, a compromise was reached in 1663 allowing them some free trade but the sting in the tale was a 4½ percent duty on all exports, lasting until 1837.

Slave revolts

Meanwhile, Royalist prisoners were being sent out to Barbados to be sold as slaves. Unable to tolerate the dismal living conditions, a group of white servants plotted a revolt. The conspiracy was crushed and 18 servants executed. But such open resistance to the planters was a harbinger of changes to come. The British Parliament had granted planters in the West Indies the right to "fight, kill, slay, repress and subdue all such as shall in a hostile or mutinous manner… disturb the peace." A trained militia in Barbados was the chief weapon against slave rebellion.

Scares and plots occurred in 1675, 1683, 1686, 1692 and 1702. But, unlike Jamaica, Barbados, small and highly cultivated, was too open for successful hiding. And the irony was that most of the revolts were thwarted by the slaves themselves reporting the conspiracies to their masters.

Bussa's Rebellion

In 1807, the slave trade was officially abolished by the British Parliament, but humanitarians in England feared it was still going on. So in 1815, to hedge against this possibility and to discover the extent to which it existed, the British passed a bill which declared that all slaves in the West Indian colonies had to be registered. This caused a furore among planters, who saw it as a threat to their right of self-government.

The slaves got wind of the controversy, too, but misunderstood it. They thought that the bill everyone was talking about was to free them not register them and resentment grew as they wondered, "Why Bacchra (white man) no do that the King bid him?"

The ensuing revolt, nicknamed "Bussa's Rebellion", as one of the leaders was a slave called Bussa (*see page 201*), took place on the night of 14 April 1816 and was eventually suppressed by the British militia only after a fifth of the sugar crop had been destroyed.

LEFT: an emancipation society's view of slavery. **ABOVE:** a register listing slaves by age and race. ("Coloured" means mulatto or mixed race).

Emanicipation

The rebellion triggered reforms and was another step on the road to Emancipation. The humanitarian and abolitionist movements were now irrevocably underway. But it would not be until 1834 that slavery was abolished, transforming the 84,000 slaves into apprentices.

British humanitarians had campaigned zealously for 40 years to bring about the official abolition of slavery against the planters' wishes. As a compromise, the slaves became "apprentices". This meant that they continued to work for their particular plantation, with food, clothing and shelter provided in return for 45 hours of work a week. In exchange, the apprentices could remain in their meagre huts, eating with what utensils they had and sleeping on boards of dried foliage covering themselves with crocus bag blankets. They were worse off than before.

The planters' worries that their labourers would emigrate, and the sugar industry would collapse were unfounded. Finally, some came to believe that they could cultivate their land more cheaply with a freed labour force than with apprenticed help for whom they had to provide. Thus, on 1 August 1838, the former slaves were freed from their apprenticeships. They could now hope that "licks" (whippings) and "lock-up" (jailings) were "done wid" and that "Jin-Jin" (the young Queen Victoria) had come to the rescue. Unfortunately, the descendants of these people would not see true, harmonious emancipation for more than a century.

CARING GOVERNOR

John Pope Hennessy, Governor of Barbados (1875–76) gave money to the poor and declared that children under eight should not be jailed for stealing sugar cane.

Legal shackles

To prevent the new labour force from "shopping around" for the highest wages, a law was made binding labourers firmly to the plantations as tenants. Here, they could live on tiny "house-spots" at the discretion and whims of the master – and for a weekly rent – in return for work, stripping the labourers of most of their rights. Consequently, there was no "fall of the planter class" as had occurred in other colonies and Barbados recorded steady economic growth between 1838 and the 1870s.

The people's tribune

One man who would not allow this virtual return to slavery to destroy the hope of true emancipation was Samuel Jackman Prescod, the son of a slave mother and white father. He became a powerful speaker and writer, championing the cause of justice, freedom and equality. In 1843, he became the island's first non-white member of Parliament in 204 years.

In the House of Assembly, Prescod provided a strong voice for the plight of the masses, and helped found the Liberal Party, whose adherents included small landowners, businessmen, and mulatto and black clerks. His death in 1871 removed a stalwart "tribune of the people".

Five years later, the island was in the middle of yet another governmental shake-up, one that pitted whites against blacks, poor against rich.

The confederacy question

In 1876, the British government proposed linking Barbados with the Windward Islands in a loose association of British colonies. The Governor, John Pope Hennessy, tried to persuade the Barbadians to accept this scheme, but the island's decision-makers didn't want to become a Crown Colony; after all, they reasoned, Barbados had enjoyed self-rule for more than 230 years. The planters also feared they would lose control over cheap labour, as it would provide the masses with an outlet to seek fair wages and gainful employment in other, less densely populated colonies. For the same reason, blacks were in favour of the move.

This conflict was not to be resolved without bloodshed and riots erupted in April 1876 as the blacks reacted violently to the stubbornness of the plantocracy.

Pope Hennessy was blamed for inciting the riots and was transferred to Hong Kong. The confederacy plan was shelved but the problems continued to rage, and by the end of the century the plantation system with its dependence on cheap labour still dominated the social and economic life of the island. ❑

King Sugar

The 1640s were a pivotal decade for Barbados. These were the years in which the colonists "retooled" to produce sugar, making Barbados the first country in the Western world to plant sugar and export it on a large scale.

The first man to bring sugar cane to the island was a Dutch Jew, Pieter Blower, in 1637; he had learned how to grow and process it in Brazil. At first, canes were used to produce rum, but by 1642 sugar was producing sweet profits. "There is a greater change on this island of late, from worse to better, praise be God," wrote one Barbadian in 1646. That change was the crystallised and refined juice of the sugar cane.

Everything grew – canes, population and land values. In 1646, one plantation was sold for £16,000 – which, according to historian Dunn, was more than the Earl of Carlisle had been offered for the proprietary rights to the whole of the island a few years before.

Barbados' success story was partially underwritten by the Dutch. In the late 1600s, the Dutch dominated European and Caribbean trade. They brought slaves from Africa, and offered high prices for Barbados sugar, cash on the barrelhead. Producing sugar was costly too, and they came forward with financial backing and sugar-making expertise – a double enticement.

Of course, England frowned upon its colony's close ties with Amsterdam. Once Britain's own house was in order, following the Civil War which resulted in the formation of the British Commonwealth, Parliament passed several Navigation Acts to limit foreign imports to English-owned colonies. In Barbados, the Dutch had been enjoying brisk business selling food, provisions and luxury items to rich planters – a seller's market of which Britain was jealous. In fact, producing sugar on Barbados was so profitable that planters were reluctant to "waste" land to grow food. As one observer wrote in the 1640s, Barbadians were "so intent upon planting sugar that they had rather buy foods at very dear rates than produce it by labour, so infinite is the profit of sugar workes after once accomplished." In Barbados, the Dutch and English had a captive market with money burning in their pockets.

Along with sudden wealth, sugar-making dictated two other sweeping social changes on the island. The more far-reaching was the large numbers of slaves brought in to work the sugar fields, mills, boiling houses and distilleries. The other change was that it favoured the big planters with access to capital, over small planters without any, squeezing them out, as sugar-producing required a large outlay.

During the 18th and 19th centuries the sugar economy ebbed and flowed, until cheap sugar beet in Europe priced Barbados sugar out of the market. Production also fell as planters turned to other means of making a living. In 1994, the European Union (EU) came to the rescue by agreeing to buy a fixed quota of sugar at preferential prices every year. In order to meet this 54,000-ton quota, Barbados has to export its entire crop and import sugar from Central America for its own use.

Today, although still a principal export, with electrical components, chemicals and rum, sugar as an industry has been superseded by tourism and offshore business. ❑

LEFT: champion for justice and equality.
RIGHT: cutting cane.

The Advocate

REDIFFUSION
PROUDLY SERVING
A
PROUD
NEW NATION

BARBADOS, WEST INDIES — WEDNESDAY, NOVEMBER 30, 1966 — 12 CENTS

Midnight: Darkness encompasses Savannah...then the Barbados flag emerges

● Duke gives P.M. Barrow constitutional instruments.

BARBADOS IS INDEPENDENT

By Tony Vanterpool

AT one minute after midnight today, Barbados threw off the shackles of colonialism, when during a tense and historic moment at the traditional Garrison Savannah the British Union Flag was lowered and the 166 square mile nation's ultra-marine blue and gold flag with broken trident was hoisted.

A deafening applause came from the thousands and thousands who came from every nook and cranny of the sugar coated territory, braving the threats of inclement weather, to witness the most significant achievement since the freedom of the island's slaves 132 years ago.

And so ended 339 years of association with Britain as a colonial territory and so began the membership of Barbados to the British Commonwealth of Nations as its 26th member.

After receiving the Constitutional Instruments from the Duke of Kent, who presided at the ceremony as the Queen's Special Representative, Barbados' Prime Minister, Mr. Errol Walton Barrow, 46, said: "This is a very proud moment in the history of the people of Barbados."

In an address obviously packed with emotion, the Prime Minister added: "I am glad, and I am sure the members of my Government are equally glad, that we were born at a time when we could see this eventful day."

In his moment of glory the Prime Minister continued: "On behalf of the people of Barbados, on behalf of the Government, on behalf of the young people, I should like you to convey to Her Majesty the Queen the heartfelt thanks of us all that she was on this eventful day the Head of the Commonwealth and that she elected to send you, her trusted cousin, to see us through the dawn of independence."

There was a mad rush for the Garrison Savannah by Barbadians who wanted to get proper vantage points. And from as early as 7 p.m. traffic policemen were battling with numerous road blocks along Bay Street.

At the Garrison some people gathered on roof tops and in trees. Virtually one half of the savannah was filled and people even filled some of the grand stands which were not very close to the ceremonial square.

Children and adults alike were crushed through pressure of numbers and first-aid had to be admitted at regular intervals.

Prime Minister Barrow and Mrs. Barrow arrived at 10.40 after attending the state banquet at the Barbados Hilton Hotel. By the time they took their seats in the Royal Box, the stand for invited guests was practically filled.

But due to congestion, less than 10 minutes before the actual flag-raising, invited guests were still arriving.

The Royal party arrived at 10.55 which was already 15 minutes behind schedule and after a shortened version of the displays, which excluded the motor-cycling Rockets due to the wet condition of the ground, four religious leaders representing the Barbados Christian Social Council mounted the dais and read the prayers.

Then came the real prelude to the great moment as the Governor-General-designate, Sir John Stow, and the Prime Minister, left the Royal Box and took up positions facing the flagstaff.

At 11.58 the guards of honour saluted the Union Flag and the first verse of the British National Anthem was played.

Then at midnight the guards of honour saluted the Flag of Barbados and the first verse and chorus of the Barbados National Anthem were played.

Suddenly darkness — the Union Flag was lowered and the Barbados Flag hoisted. And when the lights went on again the ultra-marine blue and gold coloured Barbados Flag with broken trident was fluttering in the wind.

A REMINDER

● Be sure you are GIVEN your 96-page Independence supplement when you buy this issue of The Advocate!

● Up goes the Barbados flag of ultra-marine blue and gold with broken trident (left), and down comes the British Union Flag. Within seconds of the completion of this operation, Barbados became an independent State within the British Commonwealth of Nations.

● Barbados' Governor-General-designate, Sir John Stow, raises Prime Minister Errol Barrow's right hand as a sign of victory seconds after Barbados became independent today.

Russia recognises Bimshire

THE Soviet Union has declared its recognition of Barbados as an independent and sovereign state. In a message yesterday to Prime Minister Errol Barrow, the Chairman of the Council of Ministers of the USSR, Mr. Alexi Kosygin, expressed the Soviet Union's readiness to establish diplomatic relations with Barbados.

Mr. Kosygin, in a congratulatory telegram, said: "On the occasion of the declaration of the independence of Barbados, please accept, Mr. Prime Minister, sincere felicitations and best wishes of well-being and progress for the people of Barbados on the road of independent development."

From Chou En-Lai, Premier of State Council of the People's Republic of China, came the telegram: "On occasion of proclamation of independence of Barbados I extend sincere congratulations to Government and people of Barbados on behalf of Government and people of People's Republic of China. May people of Barbados achieve new successes in cause of combating imperialism, colonialism and neo-colonialism, safeguarding national independence and building their own country."

West Germany also recognised Barbados as an independent State and declared its readiness to open diplomatic ties.

IMPROMPTU ROAD MARCH

A GROUP of Trinidadians who are in Barbados for the island's independence celebrations were the centre of attraction in Bridgetown yesterday when they staged an impromptu road march through Broad Street and Swan Street.

With their improvised steelband, the group marched up and down in true festive spirit and had soon attracted a large crowd of Barbadians to do likewise.

Meanwhile, the official road march in Barbados was staged early this morning when thousands of Barbadians and visitors marched and jumped to the rhythm of steelbands from the Garrison Savannah following the Flag-Raising Ceremony, down Bay Street to Pelican Village.

MISS BARBADOS ARRIVES

MISS JUDY ROSITA WALKER, 18, Miss Barbados (United Kingdom), arrived in Barbados last night from London to take part in Barbados' Independence celebrations.

Miss Walker, who was crowned at the Lyceum Ballroom, Strand, London, on Saturday night, won from six lovely Barbadian belles now living in Britain.

Second in the competition was Miss Marguerite Rocheford. Miss June Gill placed third.

Victor's hand is raised

Barbados' Governor-General-designate, Sir John Stow, typical of a referee in a boxing match, held Prime Minister Errol Barrow's right hand in the air to denote victory during the Flag-Raising Ceremony at the Garrison Savannah last night.

And, as if to be outdone by Sir John, Guyana's Prime Minister Forbes Burnham also raised the hand of his contemporary.

POPE'S CONGRATS

VATICAN CITY, Tuesday —Pope Paul today cabled his congratulations, best wishes and blessing to the island of Barbados, which becomes independent tomorrow.

He said he was confident that the Catholic members of the population would contribute generously to, and work effectively for, the good of their new country.

The Queen's thoughts are with us

QUEEN ELIZABETH II has assured Barbadians that her thoughts are with them as they step into independence.

The Queen's message on the occasion of the flag-raising ceremony, which was read at the Garrison Savannah last night by her cousin, the Duke of Kent, was as follows:

"I have asked my cousin, The Duke of Kent, to represent me at the independence celebrations of Barbados and it is with real pleasure that I send you this message at such an important and happy moment in your history.

"My husband and I are very glad to have been able to visit your beautiful island earlier this year and to meet its people. With that enjoyable memory still fresh in my mind, I join with you in celebrating your country's independence and in welcoming you as a member of the Commonwealth.

"My thoughts go with you as you step into independence. In sending you my good wishes, I pray that God may bless and guide you throughout the coming years.

MUD AND WATER ON THE GROUNDS

MUD and three inches of water in some parts failed to spoil an excellent show by the Royal Barbados Police Force, the Police Band, the Barbados Regiment and the Cadet Corps at the Garrison last night.

The display put on by these units drew applause from the Royal Box and from the thousands of spectators who had converged on the Garrison for this history-making occasion.

The Regiment marched past and the display began. This was followed by the marching on of the guards

TODAY'S WEATHER

TODAY'S FORECAST: Generally fair apart from a few early morning showers.

[illegible]

TV BINGO

Numbers called in the 1.am TV bingo last night

SPECIAL ISSUE

The Advocate's special Independence supplement (96 pages) is being circulated today along with your regular copy of The Advocate.

This historic document carries stories of all aspects of Barbadian life and Barbadian personalities.

On Page five in today's issue is a pen picture of the major contributors to this special publication.

Traffic jams as thousands flock city

HUNDREDS of Barbadians, young and old, flocked the city last night to window shop and see the buildings and stores which were brilliantly illuminated and gaily bedecked with flags and bunting in Barbados' national colours of ultra-marine and gold.

The City Council's building cut a colourful show. City stores were also points of attractions and so, too, were the Public Buildings and the Barbados Workers' Union building on Fairchild Street which has been illuminated since the start of the silver jubilee celebrations last week.

Other focal points were the arch south of the Chamberlain Bridge.

Hours before the flag-raising ceremony, pedestrians, cyclists and motorists were seen wending their way to the Garrison to secure early vantage points.

All roads leading to the Garrison from the city had traffic jams and many people who left home by car did not get to the Garrison for the ceremony.

One of the busiest streets was Bay Street, the main road to the Garrison. With the seemingly never ending line of traffic, policemen at point duty were kept busy.

Vice-president of Lions here

Mr. David Evans, vice-president of Lions International, arrived in Barbados last night to attend the island's Independence celebrations.

Mr. Evans, who lives in Texas, United States, leaves Barbados tomorrow for visits to Trinidad, Surinam, Curacao, Panama, Costa Rica, and Mexico City before returning home.

China rejected

UNITED NATIONS, New York, Tuesday — The General Assembly today administered a crushing defeat to advocates of Peking's admission to the United Nations, rejecting their resolution to seat the Communists by 57 votes to 46 with 17 abstentions, one member (Laos) being absent.

748 die in U.S.

CHICAGO, Tuesday — More people died on American roads during the four-day Thanksgiving weekend than in any previous holiday period, it was announced today.

NEXT ISSUE

The next publication of The Advocate will be on Saturday, December 3, 1966.

AN INDEPENDENT ISLAND

The 20th century saw great social reforms and the end of colonialism, coinciding with the demise of sugar, the rise of tourism and a future full of promise

At the turn of the 20th century, the sugar industry was in trouble and was having an adverse effect on the island's economy. Hurt by stiff competition from sugar beet in Europe and by disease, planters had to lay off workers to cut costs. But as they still owned 90 percent of the land the only course open to many blacks was to emigrate.

Between 1904 and 1914, 20,000 labourers left for Panama to help build the canal. Others went to Brazil, British Guiana, Trinidad and Curacao – anywhere that promised employment and relief from the lowest rung of the socio-economic ladder.

Panama money

The men toiled industriously to build the canal and sent home money to their families. Most of them returned wearing flashy clothes, their pockets stuffed with US currency. But there were a few who talked big and then returned to Barbados with nothing – much to the chagrin of their girlfriends or families. One such case was related in the folk song *Panama Man*:

Oh de Panama man 'ent got no money
Still de Panama man want love...
But 'e cahn get me wid-out de money
To buy me a taffeta dress!
If de Panama man gwine court wid me,
He gwine treat me like a queen...

The money brought home was used to educate their children, raise their standard of living and, above all, to buy land on which they could provide for their own livelihood.

Planters in debt

For the first time, labourers were able to buy land from planters, who were sorely in debt. Between 1900 and 1920, the number of estates fell from 437 to 305, and the major portions of more than 60 estates were converted into free villages. While labourers' families battled against starvation with remittances from Barbadians abroad, the planters scrambled to modernise their troubled industry. The keys to the salvation of the sugar industry and economy were the development of fertilisers, the introduction of a new kind of sugar cane and the discovery of new markets.

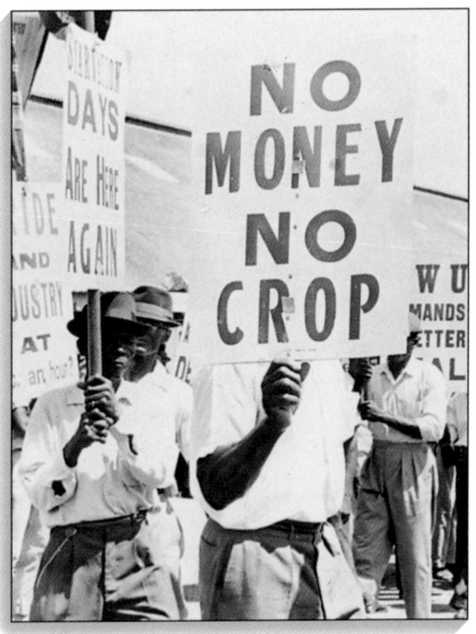

In 1859, J.R. Bovell, a botanist, and J.B. Harrison, a chemist, had experimented with sugar cane germination techniques, dabbled with new cane varieties and studied the incidence of cane diseases in Barbados – with profitable results.

Royal Commission

Growers had begun using manures as fertilisers, producing record crops in the 1890s and offsetting the low price of sugar. By 1900, the old "Bourbon" type cane had been successfully replaced by the "white transparent" variety. And the problem of finding a ready market was eased a little by trade with the US.

Meanwhile, the British Government had

PRECEDING PAGES: carrying sugar cane fibre for fuel.
LEFT: front page story.
RIGHT: farm workers on strike in the 1940s.

recognised the possibility of an economic collapse in her West Indian islands and, in 1897, set up a Royal Commission under Sir Henry Norman to look into the problems of the Caribbean sugar industry. Upon the recommendations of the Commission, Britain invested large sums of money in the sugar industry. With its £80,000 share, granted in 1903, Barbados set up the Sugar Industry Agricultural Bank, to grant loans to individual planters and finance new sugar factories.

Another £50,000 was given for plantation repairs after the 1898 hurricane, and the then Secretary of State for the Colonies, Joseph Chamberlain (1863–1937) succeeded in having the bounties on sugar beet removed. Barbados began to benefit from easy access to the British market.

Cruel forces of nature

Although the island's economy was in better standing, the Barbadian masses were still in trouble, plagued by the cruel forces of nature. The hurricane of 1898 killed 80 people, blew down 18,000 ramshackle houses and increased the incidence of dysentery and typhoid already common among the poor. In 1902, an epidemic of smallpox struck, followed by yellow fever in 1908. Yet the Barbados Government did not improve health or sanitation or pay workers enough to help them improve their standard of living. There were not even the meanest social welfare programmes for the majority of Barbadians. Children went to "ragged" schools until they were old enough to work. Meanwhile, higher-class children attended such exclusive schools as Harrison College, Queen's College and Codrington High.

INSIDE A SUGAR FACTORY

To make sugar, the cane is ground mechanically under a steady flow of water and the resulting juice is clarified to remove impurities. It is then channelled to a series of evaporators, which remove the water from the solution leaving a thick, brown syrup which goes into a vacuum pan to form crystals. The sugar boiler, one of the most important workers, regulates the amount of syrup in the pan to ensure large crystals. He also decides when to let the thick, syrupy mixture of crystals and molasses pass on to the centrifugals – a metal basket that spins at very high speeds, throwing the molasses through holes in its sides. The sugar falls out at the bottom into bins.

Workers' rights

In 1914, the construction of the Panama Canal was finished, shutting off a dependable outlet for industrious workers. And by the 1930s, workers could only go to Trinidad, British Guiana, Brazil, Cuba or Costa Rica in small numbers. Those that remained mostly lived in tenantries that were part of the plantations where they worked. And when the depression shook the American, Canadian and British economies in the 1930s, these workers were hit hardest.

> **WAGE FREEZE**
>
> In 1937, plantation workers were still earning the same as they had been almost 100 years earlier – one shilling (five pence) a day.

New political movements developed in response to these harsh social and economic realities. Charles Duncan O'Neal (1879–1936), a doctor, rose to the cause and devoted his life to fighting for the improvement of the masses in the same way that Prescod had done 60 years earlier. In 1924, O'Neal founded the Democratic League, the first mass-based, radical, political force to be launched on the island in the 20th century.

The league attracted many non-white, middle-class professionals and sent several candidates to the House of Assembly. O'Neal won a seat in 1932, and though his health was failing, he left behind the twin legacy of the early trade union, the Workingmen's Association (founded in 1925), and the League. Both organisations influenced the formation of the Barbados Labour Party in 1938 and the Barbados Workers Union in 1941, which fought for workers' rights.

Equally significant to the cause was the emergence of the Garveyite movement in the 1920s and 1930s. Marcus Garvey was a black Jamaican who fought the oppression of blacks and wanted to see an exodus from the Americas back to Africa, toward the creation of a black nationality.

Garvey spoke to the increasingly dissatisfied Bajans. Emancipation had occurred 100 years earlier, but equality had not followed. Barbadians took their frustration to the streets in the riots of 1937. In fear of famine and disease, with little hope for education or land to cultivate, and an ever-increasing population threatening to compete for jobs and resources, their anger exploded.

LEFT: sugar cane ready for the harvest.
ABOVE: half a million tourists fly in every year.

Riots in the streets

Clement Payne (1904–41) was the spark that ignited the social disturbances. Payne was Trinidadian by birth, but both his parents and his brothers and sisters were born in Barbados. He began advocating the formation of trade unions at public meetings in Bridgetown and incited such a fever among the people that on the night of 26 July 1937, the authorities deported him.

Crowds gathered to protest his deportation. And, as the number of people grew, so did the sense of outrage, which suddenly exploded. The rioting lasted three days and spread quickly to the isolated rural areas. Windows were smashed, cars were broken into, shops were looted and fields were raided. These responses were prompted less by the deportation of Payne than

DEEP WATER HARBOUR

Before Deep Water Harbour was built in 1961, all sugar and molasses for export had to be rowed out in heavy barges to ships anchored in Carlisle Bay.

by hunger and the genuine fear of starvation.

The fervour of these days produced the kind of myths and folksongs that sprang forth out of the excitement of emancipation. One such song is *The Riot Song*, a personal and tangible look at the events of this time:

Listen friends to what was composed
De twenty-seventh of July I couldn't
show much nose.
Civilian wid rocks, policemen wid guns
Doan doubt me friends it wasn't no fun
For everything dat yuh hear a sound
Somebody dead and somebody wound.

The most colourful account of the riot is found in W.A. Beckles' *The Barbados Disturbances*, a report summarising the findings of a commission appointed to pinpoint the causes of the 1937 riot. Beckles likens the violent riots to a volcanic eruption: "While the rumblings revealed the presence of a 'volcano', it gave no indication whatever of the gigantic crash that was to take place shortly after... In two days the hot lava that belched forth from the crater had spread its ravages to practically all parishes of the Island... Reviewing the situation dispassionately... it is manifest that circumstances, and not the qualities of a leader, made Payne, a slim, slight unimpressive stranger, a Moses in our midst."

For the first time, Bajan masses had come to the centre of the political stage. Unlike in 1816 and 1876, they challenged the fact that 70 percent of the population was still unable to vote on an island that called itself a democracy and touted its "long and proud tradition of Parliamentary government".

Democratic vistas

The riots had not been in vain and had led to change with Grantley Adams as the primary catalyst. Between 1938 and 1945, Adams became the acknowledged leader of an emerging mass movement that coalesced around a political party and a labour union. He firmly believed in the British monarchy and the sanctity of the British parliamentary institutions, but he was determined to modernise the Barbadian political system by narrowing the traditional boundaries between the planters and labourers.

In 1938, Adams, along with C.A. Brathwaite and several others, formed the Barbados Progressive League, also known as the Barbados Labour Party. Adams headed this coalition and vowed to work for greater equality until the island's wealth and resources would be controlled by the Government on behalf of the people. Adams demanded fair labour laws, and formation of tribunes to monitor wage fairness and factory conditions. He also advocated a slum clearance and housing plan.

The party gained its first political victory in 1940 when it won five seats in the House of Assembly and Adams set about modernising the political system. He met with strong opposition: a bill to provide for adult franchise was consistently voted down.

In 1942, however, the members of the Assembly recognised the mood of the times and agreed to a compromise. The bill passed reduced the income qualification of voters to £20 and permitted women to vote and to be eligible for membership to the Assembly on the same terms as men. At the instigation of the Governor, a constitutional change was made and Adams was elected leader of the new executive committee.

Working out the kinks

These changes – though conceptually sound and well-intentioned – did not make any significant impact because the Legislature was still

LEFT: cruise ships visit regularly.
ABOVE: communing with nature.

FREEDOM FIGHTER

The peaceful transformation of Barbados from a feudal plantocracy to a modern democracy was largely due to Grantley Adams (1898–1971). The son of a Barbadian headteacher, he studied law at Oxford, returning to Barbados in 1925. He was elected to the House of Assembly at 36, where he began his fight for social justice in Barbados using his tact, careful timing and mastery of debate as his "weapons".

A revered leader, his legacies to the nation are still evident today: free elections, new homes, union representation at work, a minimum wage and improved health facilities. He was knighted by the Queen in 1957.

controlled by white planters. When reforms such as the nationalisation of public utilities, paid holidays for workers and adult franchise came up, the two bodies inevitably clashed.

By 1949, however, this kink was worked out by limiting the powers of the Legislature to the functions of revision and delay, thereby leaving the ultimate say in the enactment of legislature to the House.

A new federation

With Adams' strong leadership, Barbados was able to modernise its system of government in only two decades. The island was clearly heading towards independence. At the same time leaders of various British West Indian islands began discussing – once again – the merits of federation.

With Adams representing Barbados, the Federation of British West Indies was, in fact, inaugurated in 1958. Unfortunately, it never achieved the kind of momentum needed to grab international attention because each island seemed to have different goals for the union. Also, the Queen maintained legislative authority in matters of defence, external affairs and finance of the Federation, and the Governor had the power to veto any laws passed. These

NATIONAL HEROES OF BARBADOS

On 28 April 1998, the 100th anniversary of the birth of Barbados' greatest social reformer Sir Grantley Adams, 10 National Heroes of Barbados were announced:

- **Sir Grantley Adams** (1898–1971) – a social reformer and leader (*see page 45*).
- **Bussa** – the slave leader of the 1816 Easter Rebellion (*see page 201*).
- **Sarah Ann Gill** (1795–1866) – the only female hero, she risked her life to save the Methodist Church before and after Emancipation (*see page 83*).
- **Samuel Jackman Prescod** (1806–71) – writer and parliamentarian who championed the cause of the suppressed masses after Emancipation (*see page 36*).
- **Charles Duncan O'Neal** (1879–1936) – organiser of the first trade union and mass political party (*see page 178*).
- **Clement Payne** (1904–41) – the catalyst for the 1937 riots which triggered social reforms.
- **Sir Hugh Springer** (1913–94) – pioneer of trade union movement, educator and governor-general (1984–90).
- **Sir Frank Walcott** (1916–99) – progressive trade unionist.
- **Errol Barrow** (1920–87) – father of Independence and founder of the Democratic Party (*see page 48*).
- **Sir Garfield Sobers** (1937–) – the "greatest cricketer on Earth or on Mars" (*see pages 90–91*).

problems led to the dissolution of the Federation on 31 May 1962, after only four years.

The rise of Barrow

When Adams returned from his dealings with the Federation, much had changed in the political and social life of Barbados. And his nemesis, Errol Walton Barrow, had succeeded him. In 1961, Barrow, with his liberal Democratic Labour Party (DLP), held the reins of power in the Government.

> **THE RIGHT TO VOTE**
>
> At the 1951 general election for the first time every adult was allowed to vote – and the Barbados Labour Party (BLP) was the clear winner.

Barrow, the nephew of reformer Charles Duncan O'Neal, immediately instituted reforms that were severely lacking during the years of constitutional rearrangement. He carried out a programme of public works to provide relief for the unemployed.

Independence...

Although he, like all preceding reformers, had his share of problems and opposition, Barrow was able to put the finishing touches on an island prepared for imminent independence. And Barbados was ready at a time when Britain was clearly liquidating its empire.

Although the decision to proceed to independence was one of the most significant in Barbados's history, it was accepted with little opposition or fanfare. After having fought so many battles for the cause of justice and equality, Barbados began a new life as a free nation, within the British Commonwealth, on 30 November 1966.

The actual transition from colony to sovereign state involved only a change of titles and functions. The DLP had been re-elected, and Errol Barrow changed from Premier to Prime Minister. Four weeks later, amid pomp and solemnity, the new flag was unfurled.

As the new nation's first leader, the charismatic Barrow served for over 10 years. By 1976, Barbadians were ready for a change, and Barrow's party lost to the BLP. Five years later, the BLP, led by Tom Michael Geoffrey Manningham Adams, won again. He took Barbados confidently into the 1980s. The son of Sir Grantley Adams, he entered 1985 without a political care, but on 11 March, he died of a heart attack at the age of 53, leaving his party and the country bereft of his guidance.

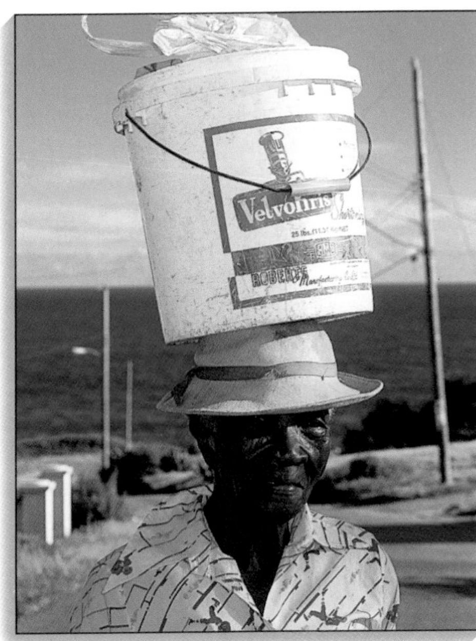

LEFT: surfing by the Arawak Cement Plant.
ABOVE: taking the day's catch to market.
ABOVE RIGHT: North American influences.

Full circle

Adams' successor, the energetic Bernard St John (now Sir Harold), moved swiftly to allay fears of a disintegration of the ruling BLP, continuing the policies of his predecessor with the same dedication. Errol Barrow, then 65 and with 33 years' experience in Parliament (a Caribbean record) seized the opportunity. His party hammered away incessantly at the St John administration as Barbados experienced an economic slowdown.

St John decided to hold the election in May 1986 – in order, some say, to avoid the harsh criticism in song that would come from the

calypsonians during the Crop Over Festival. Despite a huge advertising blitz by the BLP, the Barbadians voted back Barrow by the largest landslide in Barbados' history.

Tragically, Barrow, now a National Hero (*see page 46*), died in 1987 while still in office, following a heart attack. The smooth transfer of leadership to Erskine Sandiford, of the DLP, testified to the political stability of Barbados.

Meteoric rise

Nevertheless, in the early 1990s, the economy took a dive again and came close to bankruptcy. This was mainly due to the recession in the United States, the island's biggest investor, which had a detrimental effect on the tourist trade and exports. In return for help from the IMF, Sandiford cut salaries and laid off hundreds of public servants, making the Government very unpopular.

In 1994, the BLP returned to power and Owen Arthur, with the same political roots as Grantley and Tom Adams, became the island's fifth Prime Minister. Diminutive, cheeky-looking and, unlike Sandiford, a warm, approachable Prime Minister, Arthur had transformed himself into an Errol Barrow-style character. An economic expert born in 1949, he picked a woman, lawyer Billie Miller, as the island's first Deputy Prime Minister.

His policies renewed the confidence of investors in the island, reduced unemployment to manageable levels and made bold initiatives with the private sector that sent the economy soaring to new heights. When Arthur called elections in January 1999, the day before Errol Barrow's Day, Barbadians responded by giving his BLP a 26–2 control over Parliament.

Battle of Trafalgar Square

At the turn of the millennium, Arthur had the power to make sweeping constitutional changes. One of them was to create a Ministry of Social Transformation, a social welfare move that was even congratulated by the Pope, and plans are afoot to renovate the centre of Bridgetown. However, his most controversial decisions have involved bringing Barbadians face to face with their history and have brought to the fore deep feelings among white and black over the heritage of slavery and Barbadian "petty apartheid".

In 1998, the Government established a pantheon of 10 National Heroes (*see page 46*), but no white Barbadians were included in the list. This has been seen by some as a rejection of the contribution made by Anglo-Barbadians to the nation since 1627. However, the list has not been closed at 10 and more heroes are expected to be chosen. Another storm arose in April 1999 over the hasty vote of Parliament to rename Trafalgar Square as National Heroes Square and to find a new site for the statue of Lord Nelson, who has been officially deemed "a British not a Barbadian hero".

Some say that it is healthy that white and black Barbadians are now talking about subjects that were once taboo, but others wonder about the necessity or wisdom of removing a historical landmark which symbolised the British connection.

A new culture

Although Barbados was ready for independence way back in 1966, it took years before its indigenous culture could flourish, steeped as it was in its Britishness.

In the early 1970s, inspired by the Black Power and Rastafari movements from the US and Jamaica, Barbadian youths began forging a

CARIBBEAN COMMUNITY

Barbados and the other Caribbean islands of the Commonwealth got together in 1973 to form CARICOM – an area of free trade with a pool of resources.

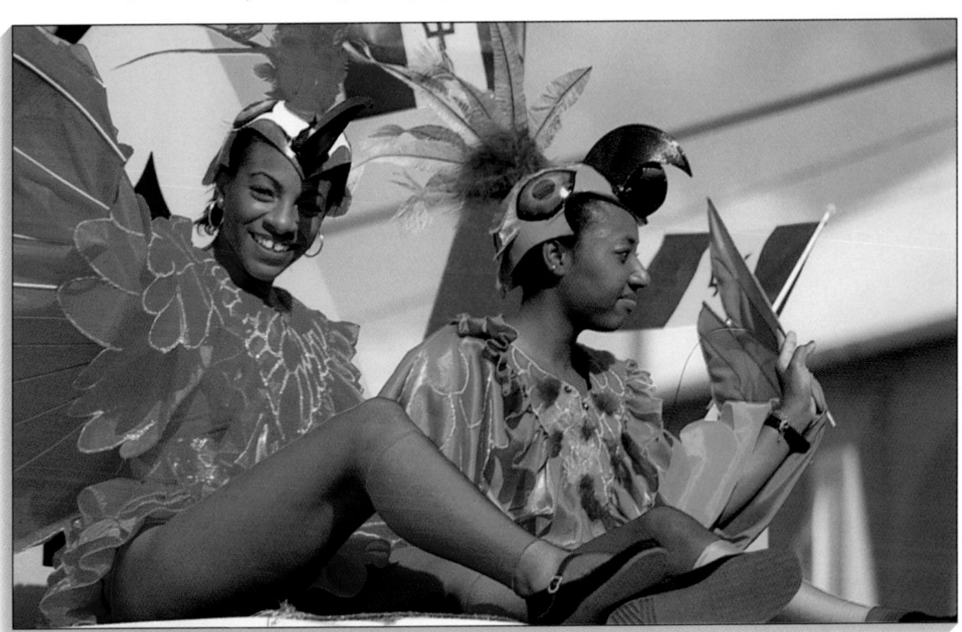

new identity. But the most powerful influence came from American television.

Today, Barbadians are appreciative of things Bajan and more interested in preserving their own culture in the face of foreign influences. Bajan dialect has been elevated to the status of Nation Language and is often the main tool in the new literary and performance arts movement that has bloomed in the 1990s.

The enthusiasm that the Crop Over Festival generates is a sign of cultural pride. Crop Over originated in the days of plantation society. Revived in the 1970s and managed by the National Cultural Foundation (NCF) since 1982, it has played a major part in promoting cultural awareness, and is responsible for reviving the calypso tradition, which in turn has spawned numerous hybrid offspring making Barbados a musical focal point of the Caribbean. The wildly popular calypsonians are now a major force speaking for the people, providing social commentary, protest and a constant source of indigenous entertainment.

In the top 10

Barbadians are quietly up-beat about their economy, their standard of living and their ability to face the challenges of the 21st century and many are set to throw off the mantle of the Commonwealth to forge ahead as a republic. New houses, new cars, opportunities for jobs, travel and trade are theirs for the taking. There is a new emphasis on telecommunications and the wonders of cyberspace are now considered a Barbadian's birthright.

At the end of the 20th century, the UN ranked Barbados as the most prosperous small state in the Caribbean and one of the top 10 developing countries in the world. ❑

LEFT: Sir Garfield "Gary" Sobers in his heyday.
ABOVE: colourful Independence Day celebrations.

ALL O' WE IS BAJAN

The peaceful determination, quick sense of fun and united friendliness of Barbadians have earned them a quality of life to be proud of

Pride and Industry is the motto of Barbados and local poet Bruce St John reveals in this extract from *Bumbatuk I* that whatever the shade of a person's skin or wherever he originates from, there is a deep-seated national pride that unites them all:

All o' we is Bajan!
Bajan to de back-bone...
Bajan black, Bajan white,
Bajan hair curly, Bajan hair straight,
Yo' brother red, yo sister brown,
Yo' mother light-skin, yo father cob skin...

There are Afro-Bajans, Anglo-Bajans, Euro-Bajans, Bajan Jews and Bajan Hindus and Muslims. Smaller groups include an American community, a Canadian element, some South American expatriates and an influential group of Arab-Bajans from Syria and Lebanon.

Over 70 percent of today's Barbadians are directly descended from Africans who were part of the greatest involuntary migration in world history. Another 20 percent are of mixed black and white blood – described as "brown-skin", "light-skin", "fair-skin", "high brown", "red" and "mulatto". Another 7 percent of the population is white, either "overseas" white (of traditional Caucasian features and skin tone) or "Bajan" white (containing "a tip of the tar-brush" or a small amount of black ancestry). The remaining 3 percent is drawn from immigrant groups.

Quick sense of fun

Despite this diversity, a national character, or sense of identity, has emerged. Bajans, on the whole, are pragmatic people with a native capacity for quick wit and irony. They do not take offence easily, and they have a quick sense of fun, often quite subtle, that is capable of being effectively directed, in true British fashion, against any form of pretentiousness.

They have a refreshing realism in their outlook and a sturdy resistance to change for the sake of it – a characteristic that stands out in sharp relief against the apparent excitability and enthusiasm of some of the other Caribbean peoples.

Some have interpreted this Barbadian trait as smart-aleck cynicism, and it is not all that unusual to hear other Caribbean people use terms such as "smug", "smart Bajan" and "know-alls" to refer to Barbadians they've met.

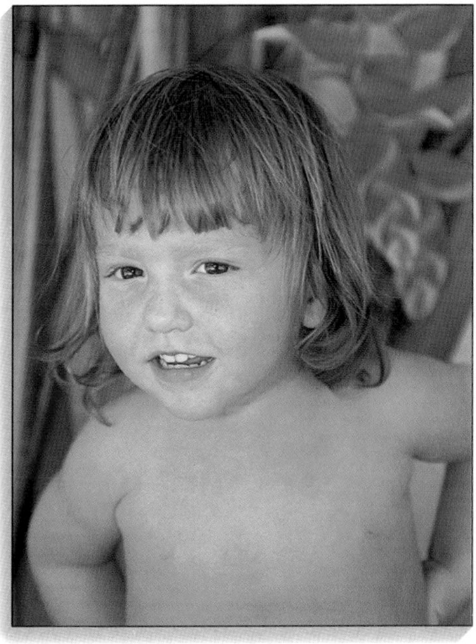

At least in one regard, however, Barbados and Bajans conform to the Caribbean norm: their slowness of tempo to which visitors must try to adjust if they want to avoid frustration. This is balanced by a readiness to oblige, exhibited with such unforced courtesy that the recipient of favours feel no sense of obligation.

Haves and have-nots

That today's Bajans are the result of three-and-a-half centuries of settlement, slavery and migration makes this relaxed social atmosphere all the more miraculous. Most, of course, can

PRECEDING PAGES: all o' we is Bajan.
LEFT: roasting flying fish on the beach.
RIGHT: a sun-kissed smile.

trace their ancestry back to the horrors of slavery, but the significant minority of whites are descended from two distinct social backgrounds – the wealthy "haves" who owned the plantations, and the hard-up "have-nots" who came to the island as indentured labourers and political convicts.

These were unwilling Scottish, Irish and Welsh men of various classes. They had been on the losing side in the English Civil War and were exiled, or "Barbadosed". They became bonded servants, and they stayed at the bottom of the social and economic pile until the 20th century. They married their brothers and sisters in defiance of the injunctions of the English *Book of Common Prayer*, thus keeping their bloodlines pure. The fact that they passed on debilitating diseases to their descendants was a price to be paid for their lily-whiteness.

Red Legs

Over the centuries, the Afro-Bajans have ribbed their fellow Bajans about these practices and lampooned them with such nicknames as "Red Shanks" and "Red Legs" because the kilts their ancestors wore exposed their legs to the sun, "Ecky-bekky", "white niggas" and "Poor Backra-johnnies" – "Backra" comes from the West African word *bakara*, meaning white man.

The sun-intolerance of Celtic skin aside, poor whites did benefit from the generosity of planters. Schools, jobs and even clubs were provided for them to help them pull themselves up by their boot straps.

Today there are only a few small groups left as, for the most part, they have integrated into Barbadian society.

The island's elite

And what became of Barbados' original English settlers? Roughly 20 families dominated the island's history and economic development during the early period of colonisation. Even

THE STANDPIPE

Today, almost all island homes have running water. But modern plumbing is a relative Johnny-come-lately: a generation ago most Bajans trekked to the village standpipe to fill their buckets with water. The standpipe became a community centre of sorts – the place where people gathered to gossip and exchange news, where young men and women flirted, and where children played games. It was practically impossible for people "who didn't nuse to 'gree" to avoid one another at the standpipe which was the venue for a fair few fights. Today, the standpipes are still there and you can stop for a drink of the pure, fresh water that flows from any of them.

now many of these families still rank among the island's elite, known as "high whites".

Today, the great wealth of Barbados' first planter families has been dispersed, but the descendants of these families still remain, along with some of their beautiful and well-preserved plantation houses. But gone is the era of exclusivity which saw the coining of the phrase, "The Sealys talk only to the Piles, and the Piles talk only to God."

LOYAL TO THE CROWN

Until Independence in 1966, it was usual for white Bajans to openly support visiting English cricket teams over local West Indian sides.

The island's high whites still speak the purest Bajan dialect, with a rich West Country brogue. He is a cricket fanatic, a horse-racing addict, and a sturdy believer in the pursuits of polo, tennis, rugby and soccer, a love of which he has passed on to black Bajans. He named his houses and plantations after the Royal family and British districts and towns, even though he might never have been to England. In fact, until independence in 1966, it was usual for white Bajans to openly support visiting English cricket teams over local West Indian sides.

In control

High whites continue to control much of the commercial and economic life of the island, just as they have since the 17th century. And many are actively involved in all the things that make Barbados a nation, from cricket to calypso-singing, from loyally drinking Cockspur rum to unswervingly defending the island's institutions against any reproach or criticism that may come from outsiders.

In the past, they have heavily influenced the island's cultural life as well. It was the privileged class which launched the tourism industry and founded the now defunct monthly magazine called *The Bajan*.

The coming together of blacks and whites in Barbados began during the slave period, when blacks and poor whites lived "cheek by jowl" on the plantation tenantries and in free villages. Afro-Bajan men had children with poor white women, and vice versa, despite the latter's determination to keep themselves to themselves. Co-mingling was trickier with the high whites, however. They didn't mind having a black "outside woman", because, as a rhyme says, "de blacker de woman, de sweeter de tail", but accepting blacks or mulattos socially was something else altogether.

Changing attitudes

Open race discrimination used to be practised in commerce, the civil service and, until the 1930s, within the Anglican Church where whites sat at the front and blacks had to stay at the back. In sports, there were racially exclusive clubs until as late as 1970 when St Winifred's became the last school to desegregate.

While today there is an easy tolerance between the black majority and whites in Barbados, there still remain areas of prejudice. The many interracial couples that are seen are almost all foreigners: the number of marriages between black and white Bajans can be counted on the fingers of two hands. The best-known black politician of this century, the late Sir Grantley Adams, squeezed under the barrier by marrying into a white planter-class family in the late 1920s. Sir Grantley was, of course, a "man of the future" at the time: he was a Barbados Scholar, a lawyer, a better-than-average-

FAR LEFT: a happy Bajan.
LEFT: there are still standpipes all over the island.
RIGHT: keeping an eye on things.

cricketer and an agitator for political reform. Today, Bajans of all groups will tell you that "it doesn't bother anybody". Others will reveal the not-very-secret secret that "black and white Bajans ent gwine marry one anodder, but nuff 'living-wid' does go on dat a lotta people don't know 'bout!" Attitudes are changing, if slowly.

African descendants

The Bajan black is a descendant of West Africans brought to the island between 1627 and 1807 as slaves. They mostly came from the Gold Coast (modern-day Ghana) or the area that is now Nigeria. Unlike Jamaica, Guyana or Trinidad, Barbados was the destination of few African-born slaves after 1800. Thus African blacks became "Bajanized" relatively early on in the island's history. This tended to make them less resistant to local culture, with its anglicised language, religion and customs.

The slaves attempted open revolts four times and after each showdown, the whites gained further ascendency. With their dreams of freedom thwarted, slaves sometimes resorted to many forms of passive aggression and to indirect trickery, deceit and quiet defiance. Nevertheless, they had the reputation of being the most obedient slaves in the region.

Experience and education eventually proved to be two great levellers, however. Hundreds of black Bajans served in the two World Wars and suddenly saw life in a radically different way. They saw whites doing menial jobs and even being ordered around by non-whites. Since then the agitation of Clement Payne and Marcus Garvey, the performances of Jack Johnson, Joe Lewis and Muhammed Ali in boxing, of Jesse Owens in athletics, Pele in soccer and Gary Sobers, Wes Hall and Frank Worrell in cricket all prompted new pride.

When black Bajans went overseas, they often became eager to defend the rights of the labouring classes of all races. In Panama, the United States, Canada and Trinidad, Bajan blacks helped organise workers and unions long before such action could be taken on "the Rock".

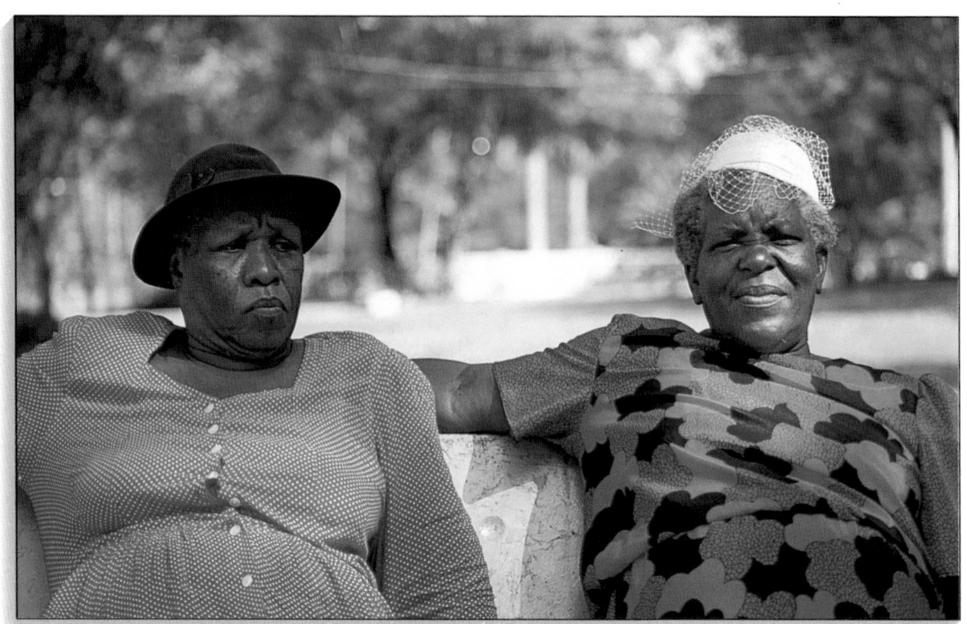

Racial pride

In the 1960s, many of the black politicians who worked towards independence had spent time abroad in their early childhood, and were proud to be black and Bajan. Among these men were former Prime Minister Errol Barrow, who had been a World War II airman and was trained in London as a lawyer and economist, and Sir Grantley Adams, who was trained in London as a lawyer after attending Oxford University.

By contrast, the leader of the island's blanket

trade union, the Barbados Workers Union, Frank Walcott, came by his racial pride by remaining on the island and fighting discrimination. These men led Barbados into the 1970s and gave the following generation a new understanding of what it could mean to be a Barbadian.

During this period of ferment, a process of cultural revaluation took place. Blacks began to challenge the notion that to be a respectable citizen required rejecting African traditions. African folklore and practices were resurrected; schoolchildren read the African-inspired poetry of Kamau Brathwaite and the writings of George Lamming, Bruce St John, Timothy Callender, Austin "Tom" Clarke and Jeanette Layne-Clarke – all literary explorations of what it means to be Bajan.

A Union Man

National Hero, Sir Frank Walcott (1916–99) was an active trade unionist for more than 50 years, describing himself as "Frank by name, frank by nature".

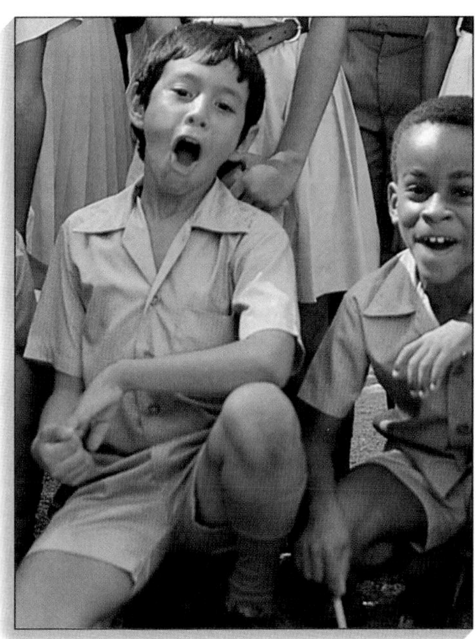

My mother who fathered me

Life has rarely been easy for many black Bajan women, as they have often been left behind by migrating menfolk to raise large families on their own. They have had double workloads – earning a living and bringing up children – and this has meant that the extended family has often been a life-saving support system. But don't imagine that Bajan women are downtrodden in any way. Long renowned for their resilience in the face of hard work and hard knocks, they are benefiting from changes in Barbadian society. There are already more women than men students at the Barbados campus of the University of the West Indies (UWI), and more women are joining the hitherto male professions of the law and business every year.

Not every girl's dream is marriage. A pattern not uncommon for some women is that of delaying marriage and entering into a number of different unions, serially and with different men. Often couples start out with a "visiting union" in which the man visits his girlfriend at her house. Children may be born, and the couple may either move in together and eventually marry, or they may remain casual for a while before ending the relationship. It is not uncommon for a woman to have given birth to children from more than one man.

While it is accepted that a woman will enter

LEFT: taking it easy.
ABOVE: a photograph for the family album.
ABOVE RIGHT: a happy mix.

into unions with more than one man during her lifetime, to do so simultaneously and to "have children all about" (from a number of men) is cause for considerable scorn. There is a Bajan proverb that goes "When yuh pick corn 'pon more than one row, yuh don't know where yuh get yuh bag full up." It means that a woman involved with too many men won't know which one has made her pregnant.

Fame and shame

For a man, however, the situation is different. It is often said in Barbados, "What is fame for the man is shame for the woman." Even when a man is married or involved with one woman, he often continues to maintain a relationship with another woman and produce "outside" children. This is often accepted by wives until money they feel is theirs goes to support the other family.

Though many women work, and have done so since the days of slavery, home and children are their main concerns. Children are so important to womanhood that it is a great insult to be called a "mule" or, worse still, a "graveyard" (a term for a woman who has had an abortion). But while one or two children are proof of womanhood, males are esteemed for their success with several women and their fathering of

A Ship on Land

Founded in the 1860s by a retired black seaman, the Barbados "Landship" began as a collaboration of ex-sailors wanting to strengthen the camaraderie of their time at sea. Seeking to bring discipline and a sense of worth into their "evening years", they styled a naval-theme self-help organisation – a land-based "brotherhood of the sea".

Today, the Landship has evolved into a "club" of talented performers. It is also a savings and loan society with a "Meetings Turn" – a community pool which is funded through regular dues payments by members, to aid individuals in time of fire, flooding and unemployment.

The Landship is divided into local chapters called "ships", each with a complement of "officers", "mates", "engineers" and "doctors". The "crew" dresses in white bell-bottoms and shirts, British Navy style, complete with epaulettes and ratings. And – call it progressive or just a sailor's answered prayers – women were allowed to come aboard as "nurses" in the early 1920s.

The most visible aspect of Landship has always been its hilarious public performances, spoofs of real-life situations. With all the starch and shoeshine afforded to a serious review of arms, the sailors demonstrate their formation marching in time to the African rhythm of a tuk band that would leave Lord Nelson spinning in his briny grave.

many children. Women are expected to be the carriers of respectability in the community. As the saying goes: "Women in de church; men in de rum shop."

Respectability for a woman has its roots in the family and the church and is symbolised primarily by marriage.

A WOMAN'S PLACE

Women are expected to be the carriers of respectability in the community. As the saying goes: "Women in de church; men in de rum shop."

Separate lives

Family is "woman's business", and the mother-centred family is another feature of life in Barbados. Ties between the couple are weak and they generally lead fairly separate lives. They usually engage in different leisure activities. Money and property matters are rarely entered into jointly, and separations are common.

The relationship between a mother and her children is close and often lasts to the end of her days. Mothers assume responsibility for their children and take their duties very seriously, always making sure their children are well-groomed and neatly dressed. The sight of scrubbed young girls on their way to Sunday school, all dressed up in pink frills with matching bows in their tightly braided hair, is a delight to visitors and locals alike.

Discipline is strict with "plenty licks and lashes" (slaps) – licks for being late for school and for arriving home late, licks for forgetting to say "good morning" or "good evening" or "yes, please" to their elders.

The exchanges between female relatives go beyond that of occasional babysitting and borrowing of money, food and other goods. If a woman has a large number of children who prove to be a handful, one or even two may be "adopted" and sent to live with an aunt, sister, sister-in-law, or even a neighbour or friend. This is not legal adoption, though the woman assumes full maternal responsibility and may be addressed as "Ma" or "Mum". Tightly-knit villages and extended families make this kind of cooperation possible.

In Barbados, a family can extend beyond the confines of mother, father and children. Supportive networks between female relatives – sisters, mothers and daughters – are especially strong, and sometimes include men as well – uncles, brothers, cousins and grandfathers.

Households may contain a mixture of relatives

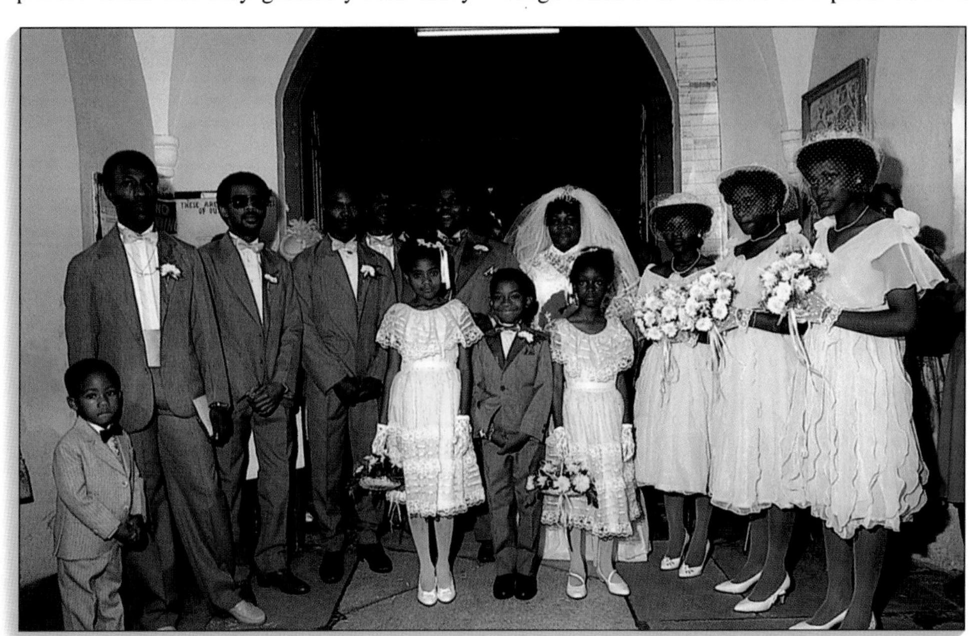

LEFT: Landship ceremonials.
ABOVE: an elaborate wedding.

and friends, often on a permanent basis. Friends may call each other "Sis" or "Brother". A friend is often said to be "like family to me" or sometimes even "better than family to me". Indeed, it is difficult for a stranger to tell who is "family" and who is not.

No place like home

Three-generation households are common, particularly those containing grandmother, mother and children. The question of "What to do with mother?" asked by many adults in Europe and America is less of a problem in Barbados, where grandmothers lead functional lives for much of their old age. The family home continues to play an important part in the lives of many Bajans; it is a haven to which they can return at any stage.

Family ties also stretch internationally, and although some links with migrants may weaken, they are likely to be reactivated in later years and many are coming back to the Rock for good. Links with migrant family members are maintained by letters, remittances and visits, often for funerals and weddings. Starting in early December plane loads of Bajans laden with gifts arrive "home" for Christmas and more arrive for Crop Over in the summer.

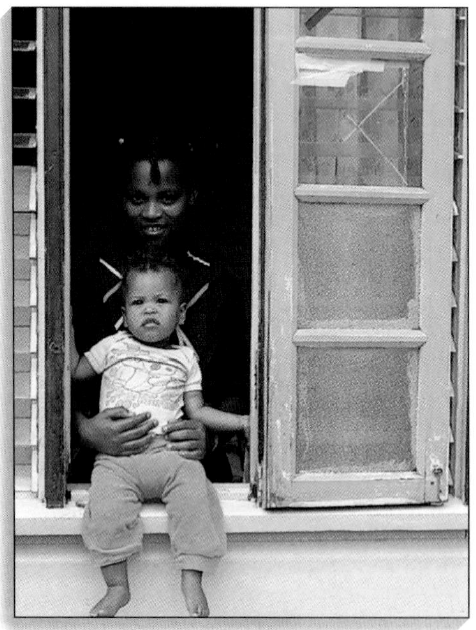

COMING HOME

Due to the booming economy during the late 20th century many Barbadians who went abroad to work returned to their homeland to share their new skills.

Return tickets

For most of the 20th century, Barbados has been a place that its people left, pushed out by unemployment and land shortages to seek greener pastures elsewhere. Finding more lucrative jobs, they have sent back monthly cheques to the family left behind. The Panama Canal and the sugar plantations of Cuba acted like magnets to hungry workers in the early 20th century, and later Bajan men sought jobs in Trinidad's oilfields or in a gloomy 1950s London, where work was plentiful after World War II.

But the island's economic success story in the 1990s has reversed the trend, and nowadays many Bajans are choosing to return home, either to retire with what they saved during a lifetime overseas or to take advantage of new jobs or investment opportunities. From the US, Canada and Britain, Bajans are coming back with high-tech expertise to work in the burgeoning financial sector or in tourism. Salaries may not quite equal those in North America or Europe, but many returnees feel that Barbados has much more to offer besides money alone. After many generations of brain drain, it is a positive reflection on modern-day Barbados that arrivals are beginning to overtake departures among younger educated Bajans.

The "new" Bajans

The "new" Bajans who have moved to Barbados present a slightly different scenario. These groups include Indians and Pakistanis, Lebanese and expatriates from America, Canada, England, Germany, China and South America. According to Kamau Brathwaite's poem *Negus* it is not enough for these "arrivants" to enjoy the "sweets" of Barbados without first becoming part of the culture and supporting the strides the country has made in race relations. To be a Barbadian you have to respect the rights of the people, and this is non-negotiable.

Modern Bajans, in other words, hope outsiders won't jeopardise a hard-won culture, and come "mashing our corns". They "ent mekking no sport" about their national pride and can share in the refrain, "All o' we is Bajan". ❑

LEFT: hanging out in St Joseph.
RIGHT: on duty.

A LETTER FROM THE ROCK

Most families have relatives living abroad and here a mother writes to her daughter in England portraying village life on "The Rock", as Barbados is fondly called

Dear Grace, I got yuh last letter and I glad to hear yuh keepin' well – yuh old mother her alright too. I hope yuh tekin' care o'yuhself and de cold weather in England 'en killin' yuh. Yuh mus' remember to use de mixture – dat candle grease and coconut oil and camphor – which I send for yuh to rub yuh feet 'gainst de cold. Doan' mind de smell – it good.

Yuh ask muh so many questions 'bout so many people here in Maynard's village in yuh las' letter dat it goin' tek a long time fuh muh to write 'bout all o' dem. And muh eyes 'ent so good now. Las' time I went to de doctor he tell muh to wear de glasses all de time but yuh know how it is – Mum 'ent get 'custom to dem yet. Dis old grey head o' mine can't deal with dis new-fangle ting. And besides de glasses mussee mek for white people nose 'cause dey keep slippin' down on my wun.

Yuh father still here de same way. Yuh would t'ink now he gettin' old – he did 65 las' birthday – yuh would t'ink dat he would change. He still chasin' de women – dey goin' kill he! But I lef' he to de Lord. I know yuh doan like muh to bad talk yuh father and he 'ent all bad – I should know after 50 years!

He still usin' de money dat yuh send good – fixing up de place. We change de winders in de front from de old-time jalousies to glass ones. Dat wasn't so much problem. But dis changin' from de wood to de wall is a real headache. De dust from de cement and de cleanin' up every day after de workmen gone. So far de back part finish – paint up and everyt'ing. It 'ent so much to be done now – Praise de Lord! And I hope he goin' let muh live to see it done.

Yuh know dat yuh sister Shirley daughter stayin' wid me now. We does call she "Tammy" for short. But she's a sweet girl doh! And helpful too – washin' wares and tidyin' de house and so every mornin'. I gotta admire she 'cause she doan get on like dese young vagabonds o' today. Yuh can't speak to non o' dem 'cause dey 'ent got no respect and no shame neidder. When you did commin' up any big person could correc' yuh and yuh would have to hear. But today yuh know dem too hard-ears.

But I was tellin' yuh 'bout Tammy. She bright too yuh know. She jus' pass de exam and she reach der de top. And its does mek muh old heart feel so good to see she steppin' out 'pon a mornin' in she school uniform.

But child I gotta tell yuh dis – yuh remember Bertha daughter dat name Mavis – de foolishy, foolishy one – dat used to play dat she more Christian dan anybody else? And de only place dat she used to go to is church. Well, nobody 'ent see she for a few months very well. And yuh know what – jus' yesterday I did commin' from in town and I butt up 'pon lickmout' Doreen. She tell muh dat Mavis got a baby boy – six weeks now. And nobody 'ent see it yet. To t'ink dat Bertha is muh friend and she 'ent tell muh – not a word! But Doreen now – she does

PRECEDING PAGES: rocky reverie on South Coast.
LEFT: a loving son's kiss before dinner.
RIGHT: watching the world go by in St Philip.

know everyt'ing 'bout everybody – she say dat de child ugly, ugly like de Pastor. De Lord sure does move in mysterious ways nowadays!

I going stop writin' for now I goin' to look for something to put in de pot. I still can't do like de young people and cook Sunday for Monday. I goin' cook some stewfood wid sweet potato, a piece o' pumpkin, some breadfruit and a piece o' pigtail and some light dumplin' – 'cause yuh known yuh father like dat. Doan' mind de women – he still doan' eat out. He mussee frighten for what dey might put in the food to mek he bewitch. Doan' mind me – I know he does like muh cookin'.

I doan' know ef I remember to tell yuh but I did get a invitation to Tiny weddin'. At de St Michael Cathedral – ef yuh please!

And de talk, girl – everybody wonderin' who de groom is. He name write 'pon de invitation – Sylvester MacDonald Dacosta Broome! Some say dat he livin' in America, some say England. One body say he white, but yuh Aunt Cintie say doan' mind de name – is de skinny little boy dey used to call "Bones" – dat used to run 'bout here barefoot. But she vex 'cause she didn't get no invitation.

For an occasion like dat dis old girl had to look real smart – everyt'ing new from head to toe – hat, dress, shoes, bag and gloves 'cause gloves in fashion now. I didn't bother you 'bout sending de outfit 'cause my meeting turn was commin' up and dat money was sufficient.

De big day come. Riding in de taxi wid yuh father mek muh remember de day we get married. Yuh father lookin' something like he did den, t'ree piece suit and all. I did feel too sweet.

Tiny did look real good but she mother – I ent know what it is dat she had on! De hat did like a upsided-down lampshade. She face didn't make-up bad but de eye shadder did too blue and too tick and when she start to cry all o' it run down she face. Lord what a mess!

De bridegroom look dapper. He is a Bajan – but he been 'way for donkey years. She mussee find he when she went to England – only 17 days and she come back talking like she swallow a dictionary.

But I did tellin' yuh 'bout de changes in de village. Mos' people try to improve de house, doh I still keep muh oil lamp – one in each room jus' in case – 'cause yuh doan 'get no warnin' when de light goin' off. Nowadays everybody got dey video.

Mos' people got in runnin' water now but de standpipe still dere. Sometimes we old folk still find weself by de standpipe talkin' like de old days. Look how t'ings change nuh! Yuh remember how you and Shirley get dere 'bout five o'clock 'pon a mornin' to avoid de cussin' and quarrellin' and pushin' in de line?

Mr Pilgrim rum shop still dere and yuh father still tekin' one dere in between. But dat is one place I would like to see move from 'bout here. De young boys tek over from where de old men lef' off. Yuh see dem 'pon a Friday or Saturday – as dey get pay. De money dat shoulda gone to feed dem family gone in Pilgrim pocket. Dis is de second house he buildin' now.

Edna doing well too. She 'ent got no more shop – is a Mini Mart now – ef yuh plese! And move out to de front road – sellin' all kind o' fancy t'ings. And she doan' trust no more – no credit for we poor people again.

Dis mussee de longest letter I ever write in muh life but I goin' stop now. Give muh love to muh grands – How dey doin'? I hope dey behavin' duhself. And muh best to yuh husband.

May de Lord bless yuh, real good.

Your lovin' Mum. ❑

Left: playing with Santa.

Right: a farmer on his patch of land in Martins Bay.

A DAY IN THE LIFE OF A FISHERMAN

Despite the island's fishing industry being increasingly controlled by big business, there will always be room for fishermen like Philip and David

Above, the clouds whisk by at a steady clip, their shapes altering every minute. The mind's imagination conjures heads of lions, shapely mermaids and gliding flying fish. Below, the white-cap sea pulsates with the forces of wind and gravity. Between these two natural elements is the fisherman.

In Barbados, a fisherman's day begins before dawn. At 4am Speightstown residents Philip and David are pushing their small rowing boat down to the water's edge. Sensing a lull in the sets of rolling breakers, they quickly hop aboard the dinghy and row under the stars to their fishing vessel, some 200 yards (180 metres) offshore. This pre-dawn ritual is a daily one during autumn and winter. They start early so they can bring in a big catch of flying fish – one of the island's staple foods and the visitors' favourite treat.

Setting off

Loading their supplies on to the single engine fishing boat and untying the anchor line, Philip and David get ready to set out on a course 12 miles (19 km) due west. It's a long, slow, bouncy journey. Near the coast, the island's land mass blocks the strong southeast trade winds, keeping the water smooth as glass. But a mile or so offshore the wind is strong, bucking the swells and current, creating a frothy, turbulent sea.

By the time these two brave fishermen reach their destination, shut off the diesel engine and set adrift, light is just beginning to break over the distant silhouette of Barbados' West Coast. David begins his chores: inspecting the engines, sharpening hooks, preparing the nets and palm fronds. Philip turns on the radio to channel 16 and gives fellow fishermen their location and a weather report. He then washes some pots and cups and prepares the day's meal: a stew of macaroni, pork and fish and hot tea. The two men have some tea, along with cold fried fish and home-baked bread, for breakfast.

Now there's light to work by: they dip one net about 60 yards (55 metres) long with palm fronds attached to each end, in the water. The palm fronds create a shadow: flying fish gather under it to hide from the sun, and become trapped. This

PRECEDING PAGES: casting the net for bait.
LEFT: working on board.
RIGHT: a reef fisherman with his catch.

FISHING FACTS

There are around 2,000 regular fishermen in Barbados and about 6,000 people are employed in the industry. These include people who clean and bone fish as well as small-scale processors, who store the catch. There are just over 400 active registered fishing boats.

With technological advancements, long line fishing is now seen as the major area of investment. This, however, necessitates some retraining since different skills are needed. The Government's Fisheries Management Plan calls for setting up a boat builders' guild, training in boat design and construction as well as improvement of fishers' and owners' business skills.

net will stay out until the end of the day, when Philip, a strong, husky man, will haul it in.

Working the nets and lines

The men drop a shorter net about 30 yards (27 metres) long right next to the boat. A chum bucket filled with cut fish and oil dangles from the side of the boat and attracts the fish to the net. David and Philip work this net every hour or so; pulling it in, cleaning it of its catch – usually about 500 fish – and setting it out again.

In between, they spend the time fishing with handlines: one, a thick monofilament with a large hook and live flying fish for bait, is set a fair distance behind the boat in the hope of hooking a blue marlin or any of the other large fish that feed on flying fish. They also use smaller handlines, with tiny hooks and cut bait, to catch the fish that are swarming around the chum.

All the while the seas ceaselessly roll and tumble the boat in every way. After years of this, the two are oblivious to the 7-ft (2-metre) swells. David stares out at the horizon as if in a trance and Philip loudly sings his favourite calypso. In the background, the non-stop chattering of other fishermen comes over the radio – seamen sharing information on their luck.

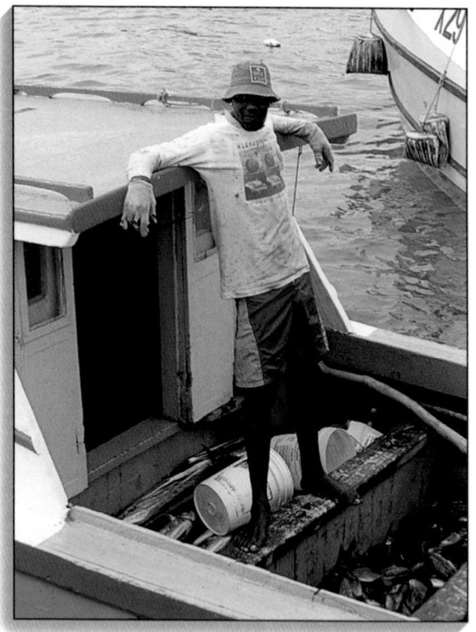

Brightly coloured boats

In the back of each fisherman's mind is the thought that one day his engine may fail to start after a day of drifting. If that happens, he must simply roll with the tides and waves and hope that eventually he will be found by a passing freighter or run aground on the island of St Vincent or St Lucia. That's why fishing boats are painted such bright colours: they're easier to spot if lost at sea. This fateful uncertainty has led to the daily sermon and prayer that comes over the boat radio at 9.30 every morning, given at sea by a fishing minister.

The work is hard, the hours long, the danger imminent and the rewards fair but not great. It is a life that calls to hardy and adventurous souls. Philip and David are two such characters. On their way back they bag their catch, wash the boat and themselves down, and change their clothes. All that is left to do is to hand over the fish to the market vendors. ❑

LEFT: homeward bound. **RIGHT:**; vantage point.

THE FUTURE OF FISHING

The fishing industry in Barbados is a perfect example of the position in which the country finds itself at the dawn of the new millennium. Traditionally carried out by fishermen in small boats, with an occasional bigger vessel, called an ice boat, the industry's future is now firmly in the hands of more organised operators, with the lure of foreign investment ever increasing.

For several years, Barbados has been experiencing some difficulty in thrashing out acceptable fishing agreements with neighbouring countries. With a monotonous regularity Bajan fishermen are found in waters in which they are not legally entitled to fish. This can have some dramatic results, as occurred in 1998 when a local fisherman was shot when his boat was discovered in waters off Guyana. Bajan fisheries officials are now calling for an organisation which will oversee fishing in the region, as well as help to share resources. The officials also believe that the country needs to enter the global fishing arena, becoming signatory to international agreements. Improvements are underway in fish landing sites and fish markets islandwide, and Philip and David may have to get some training in the near future, but they can rest assured that fishing in Barbados will always have room for their way of life.

A Religious Mosaic

More than 140 religious denominations and sects practise their beliefs side by side in peaceful harmony on this tiny island

Religion is not far from hand at any turn in Barbados. The island is reputed to have the highest concentration of churches per square mile in the world. Whether in the staid stone Anglican churches, testimony to the colonial past, or in the often simple wooden buildings whose rafters are rocked with Pentecostal passion, the Barbadian people are, on the whole, believers and practitioners.

Almost all schools begin the day with prayer, and a significant amount of radio time is devoted to religious programming.

Each Sunday afternoon, the Caribbean Broadcasting Corporation's television station (CBC TV) hosts a half-hour of religious choral singing. Island choirs join a year-long waiting list to appear on the popular "Time to Sing" which was first broadcast in 1976.

At last count, there were over 140 different religious denominations and sects practising on the island: among these are Protestants, Catholics, Rastafari, Jews, Mormons, Bahais, Muslims and Hindus.

Royalist settlers

The earliest settlers were British Royalists and Anglicans who, in 1627, claimed Barbados "at one and the same time for the King of England and the King of Kings." Later, at the time of England's Civil War, others fled to Barbados because of their conflict with Oliver Cromwell's Parliament. But when a Cromwellian invasion party gained a footing on the island in 1651, the two opposing factions quickly reached a compromise which proclaimed "liberty of conscience in matters of religion."

Ironically, this pact was ratified by the English Parliament in 1652, at a time when religious freedom in England itself was denied.

The colonists' early religious tolerance was admirable, but it also served a practical end: to ensure the stability and profitability of the plantation system. Indeed, the sugar producers were so eager to avoid the disruptive forces of the English conflict that a local custom insisted "whosoever named the word Roundhead or Cavalier, should give to all that heard him a shoat and turkey to be eaten at his house."

Yet "liberty of conscience" proved to stretch only so far. Irish Catholics exiled to Barbados as indentured servants included teachers and priests, but, upon arrival, they were sold into seven years' labour, and many died as a result. A trickle of Catholic immigrants followed, but it was only after a military garrison requested a Catholic chaplain in 1839, and a mission was established, that this faith gained acceptance.

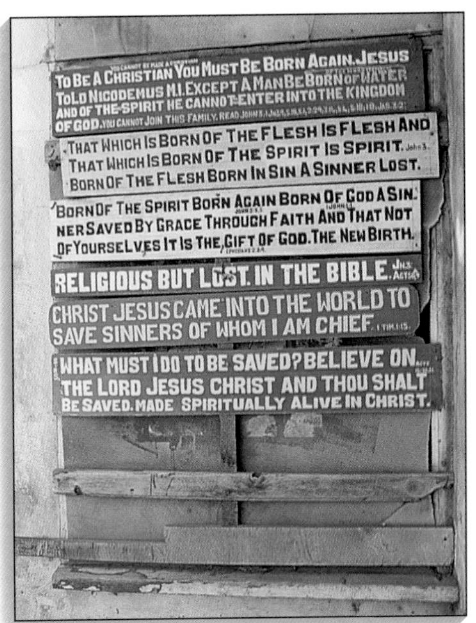

For sake of expedience

By the mid-1600s, sugar was big business in Barbados and traders began importing slaves by the thousands. But the British planters refused to let their slaves become Christians, often against the express wishes of the Anglican

PRECEDING PAGES: Mothering Sunday.
LEFT: an emotional service.
RIGHT: information for the faithful.

authorities in Britain. Their rationale, when offered, was primarily one of expedience. It was commonly believed that one Christian could not enslave another. By excluding them from Christianity, the British ensured that the Africans remained fair game.

When the Church of England attacked this excuse in 1691, by declaring that conversion to Christianity did not make slaves free men, the Barbadian planters retorted, "What? Shall they be like us?"

Planters also developed rigid social divisions between Christians and the Africans to maintain order in circumstances in which they were dangerously outnumbered, sometimes by as many as 13 to 1. They played on the African tradition, that a secret society endowed its members with special knowledge and power, by holding their Christian services in secret, which led slaves to believe that Europeans were witches and sorcerers.

SPIRITS FOR THE SPIRITS

Gifts of liquor are believed to be welcomed by duppies, and it's still a tradition to sprinkle a few drops from a new rum bottle on the ground "for the spirits".

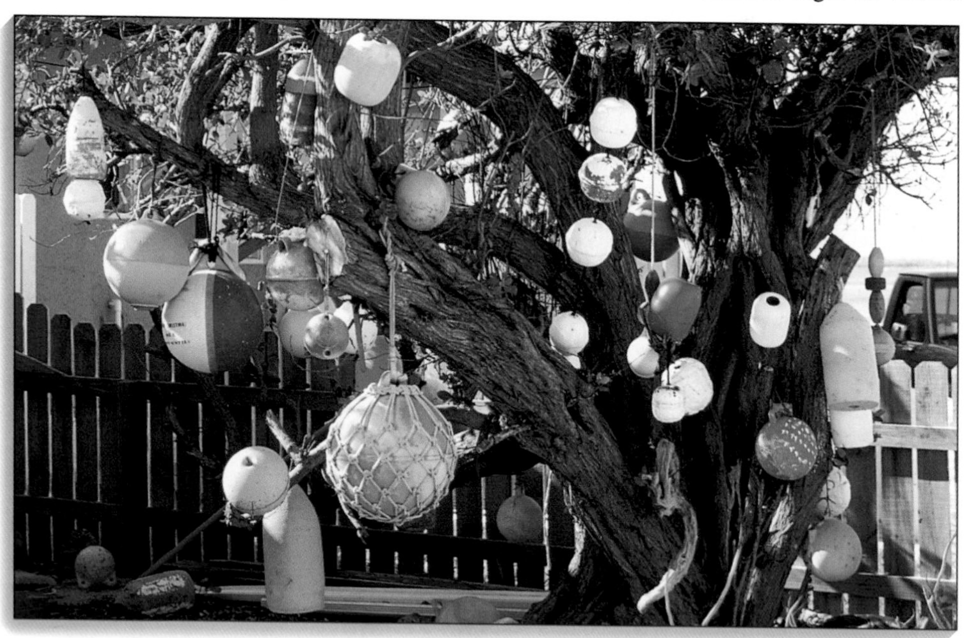

Folk beliefs

While the massive disruption of enslavement and the intermingling of Africans from very different cultures prevented religious systems from remaining wholly intact, the absence of a Christian missionary effort enabled the slaves to retain their African folk beliefs.

Some of these customs persist in diluted form in present-day Barbados. Right up until the 1950s, the placenta and umbilical cord of newborn babies were buried in the ground near the place of birth in order to link the spirit with its homeland. Long and festive funerals were held to ensure that the deceased's spirit would rest in peace.

Some Bajans still speak of duppies, or spirits of the dead, who roam at night in various forms, returning to their favourite "haunts".

Duppies are barred from entering a house by various herbs hung at the windows and doorways, by leaving one's shoes at the door, and scattering sand around the house. (This forces the spirit to stop and count each grain, a task that cannot be completed before daylight.) Older Barbadians still advise against sweeping the house at night, believing that you will sweep out good spirits as well as bad ones, leaving yourself unprotected.

By far the most notorious of these folk beliefs, however, is the system of obeah, a form of witchcraft believed to have come from a West African religion called Obi. The presence of obeah in Barbados today is a matter of opinion. Many hotly claim that it no longer exists, while most will agree that its power is limited to that segment of the population that believes in it. As one Barbadian author writes, "What you believe in, you die in. If you believe that's a duppy 'pon the roof, then one is there."

"Come-to-me sauce"

Obeah "men" can be of either sex, and typically employ a bag of charms which may include rusty nails, feathers, broken glass and pieces of clay, to work their magic for good or evil purposes. Potions are credited with the ability to make one succeed in one's endeavours and give one control over others. Not a few men are alleged to have been tricked into marriage after unwittingly consuming "come-to-me sauce", which makes its victim irresistibly attracted to the woman who slipped it into his food. Wives are also known to have given their husbands "stay-at-home sauce" to curtail extra-marital philandering.

These potent substances are administered in cocoa or in cou-cou (*see page 149*). Legend has it that one potential victim was saved from a tainted dish of cou-cou and flying fish when the cooked fish began to wink at him.

Another apocryphal tale is of the suitor who, suspecting his prospective mother-in-law was "doctoring" his food, threw it out of the window, where it was eaten by a cock. This cock then walked up the church steps every Saturday afternoon, the traditional time for weddings.

Control over others can also take more sinister, and even fatal, forms. "Duppy dust", grave dirt or pulverized human bones, is a particularly dreaded poison, thrown directly on the victim or hidden in his food. Obeah practitioners are supposed to be able to "read up the dead" and direct them to wreak the desired vengeance, sometimes by entering the bodies of their victims.

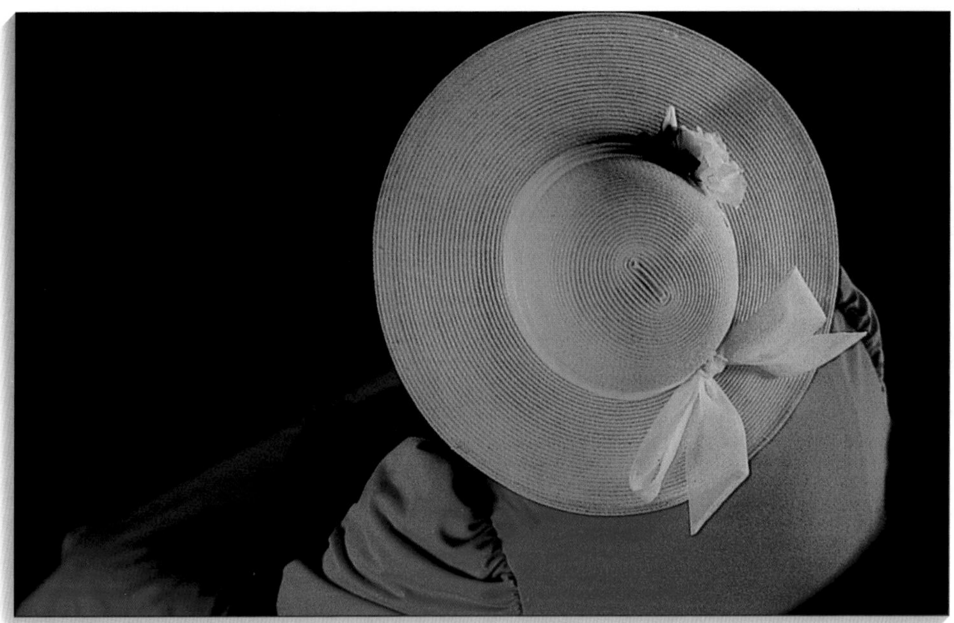

In the early 1960s, one such demon reportedly entered the body of an unfortunate woman. Many people claim to have heard the little fellow, called Conrad, uttering the foulest curses in a high-pitched voice, and making all kinds of demands on his reluctant "hostess". Nobody knows how or why he tormented this particular woman, but it is known that he defied all efforts of an obeah man to exorcise him. Eventually, the wretched woman was admitted to a psychiatric hospital.

LEFT: duppy tree wards off the spirits.
ABOVE: Sunday best.

This is no isolated incident, as indicated by a popular folk song:

De mother-in-law said to de son-in-law
What de hell it could be
Dat every fo-day morning
A man in Della belly.
O Conrad, O Conrad
Conrad come out de woman belly
and he gone to Trinidad
Tra-la-la-la, Tra, la, la, la
Conrad come out de woman belly
and he gone to Trinidad!

As recently as 1998, a family living in the outskirts of the capital Bridgetown experienced mysterious outbreaks of fire in their home, where in one case a bed was consumed by fire and nothing else touched. And a picture of the Last Supper was the only thing burned on a wooden partition. The incidents stopped after a Catholic priest performed exorcism rites.

Though death is sometimes attributed to the force of obeah, induced insanity is the more oft-mentioned result. Certain bush medicines are believed to act upon the nervous system to produce psychotic states, and just the fear of obeah can be enough to drive one mad. In the early 1960s, a man charged with the murder of his wife's lover had his charge reduced to manslaughter on the grounds of temporary insanity due to obeah. The British did their best to crush obeah from the start, forcing the practice underground. Today, obeah remains on the Statute Books of Barbados as a felony.

Conversion efforts

Prior to the emancipation of the slaves in 1838, several religious groups antagonised the planters with their efforts to convert the blacks. The Quakers were the earliest and most influential. They ignored a 1676 Act banning negroes from their meetings and riled the establishment with their controversial stands on such issues as war, and oathtaking in court. Quakers Road in St Michael is believed to be the former centre of the Quaker community. A cemetery west of Government House, and a burial place just north of St Philip Parish Church are all that's left of the Quaker religion in Barbados today.

The Moravians, the oldest Protestant Episcopal Church in the world, arrived in Barbados in 1765 and set to converting the slaves under the leadership of Benjamin Brookshaw. During the slave revolt of 1816, Moravians were granted virtual immunity from the surrounding terror. Today, most of the 1,200 seats in the Moravian Church on Roebuck Street, once the site of a cockfighting pit, are filled with black Bajans on Sundays.

The Methodists met with most opposition and persecution for their efforts to end slavery and bring the blacks into their fold. In 1823, the Methodist minister, William Shrewsbury, had so angered the landed gentry with his "forthright manner" that his church was systematically demolished, its furniture was destroyed, and a proclamation aiming to abolish the faith was posted on the town walls. He and his wife fled to St Vincent, but Sarah Ann Gill, one of the church leaders, defied the authorities and rallied her fellow Methodists into a united front, bravely breaking the law against religious meetings and opening up her home for them. By 1826, the church had been rebuilt on Gill's land in James Street, St Michael, and more than 20 Methodist churches stand on the island today. In 1998, Sarah Ann Gill was named a National Hero *(see page 46)*.

A FITTING TRIBUTE

The gravestone of National Hero, Sarah Ann Gill (1795–1866) reads: "Heroine of Methodism in Barbados, the defender of Methodism when its existence was threatened in 1823–1825; was persecuted and prosecuted."

"Store-front" churches

Neverthess, after Emancipation, the majority of ex-slaves joined the Anglican Church due to the offer of salvation and the desire to be respectable. Yet its complete isolation from traditional African belief, and relative lack of "religious zeal", created a sort of spiritual vacuum eventually filled by the revivalist sects that were sweeping the American South.

Barbados today hosts a staggering number of small sects, often similar in doctrine. As in some African societies, any man who could be a convincing intermediary between his fellows and his Maker was likely to establish a following, and a small wooden "store-front" church would be built for worship, often in impoverished rural areas. The intensely emotional religious experience these Pentecostal churches encouraged and their joyous, hand-clapping gospel music was nearer to black African rhythms than the English hymns of the established churches.

Today, the Pentecostal sects command over 25 percent of the the island's active churchgoers and they are not only confined to the small country churches, now being built in stone. The People's Cathedral and its offshoot Abundant Life Assembly are massive churches. The Reverend Holmes Williams gave up his career in banking to found the People's Cathedral in the 1970s and it now has its own school and television programme. Abundant Life was established in 1980 and has a congregation of about 2,000.

Black pride

By the early 1970s, the Rastafari movement *(see page 84)* was sweeping through the Caribbean from Jamaica in a wave of black pride and was introduced to Barbados in 1975,

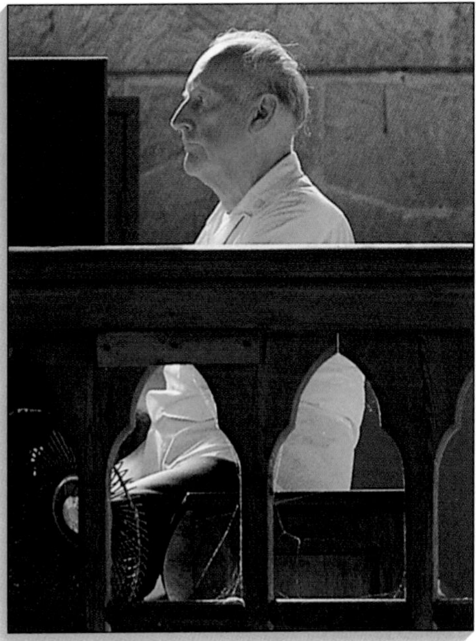

with the visit of a Rastafari elder, Ras Boanerges, and a group of drummers called The Sons of Thunder, where it spread quickly.

However, in addition to the faithful adherents, the movement soon began to attract various undesirables and criminals. Local youths saw it as an extension of their rebellion against school and home, and welcomed the attention their dreadlocks and proud strutting walk – inspired by the image of the lion in Selassie's title – attracted. Rastafari was an excuse, too, to smoke *ganja*, considered to be a sacrament.

Barbadians soon took up arms, sometimes literally, against this wave of "rascals". Whenever a dreadlocked youth fell foul of the law,

LEFT: Seventh Day Adventist baptism in the sea.
RIGHT: organ practice at St Patrick's.

there was always a headline to trumpet the fact: "Rasta fined for possession of drugs"... "Dreadlocked man arrested".

New advances

In 1998, the formation of the Pan African Commission by the Government heralded a change in the relationship between Rastafari and wider society. With Rastafari lecturer at UWI in Barbados, Dr Ikael Tafari, as deputy director, it has meant that some of the Rastafari agenda, such as the need for economic and cultural links with Africa, has been put directly to Government. And Afrika Hall, a non-governmental organisation led by Rastafari activist Bongo Spear, has taken the voice of Rastafari to the halls of the United Nations, where it has been granted observer status.

Despite these advances, however, and Prime Minister Owen Arthur's insistence that groups previously on the fringe of society must be brought within the fold in his "politics of inclusion", there remains significant bias against Rastafari. The Rastaman knows that if he is walking the streets at certain hours he can expect to be stopped and questioned, at least, by the security forces.

Other vibrations

The 2,500-strong Asian population in Barbados is emerging, albeit in small measure, from a self-imposed reclusion. Known previously as itinerant sellers, store-owners and traders, Muslims have recently admitted that they have done themselves no good by not allowing the wider society into their enclaves.

This change of attitude was triggered after a headline-grabbing incident in 1997 when two young Muslim girls ran away from home, protesting at not being allowed to further their education. Drawn into the public eye, the Islamic community undertook some public soul-searching and the Islamic Teaching Centre, set up in 1979 in Hastings, has developed an outreach programme as a means to opening the doors to the Islamic faith.

The Bahais came to Barbados in the 1960s. Membership is close to 1,500, with each of the island's 11 parishes having a local spiritual assembly. Members of these assemblies vote for a nine-member national assembly. Local

RASTAFARI – BACK TO AFRICA

In Jamaica, social inequality and the search for an identity rooted in Africa fostered the Rastafarian movement in the 1930s, making a profound impact throughout the Caribbean. It took a lot of impetus from the teachings and beliefs of the Jamaican, Marcus Garvey, founder of the Universal Negro Improvement Association, who in the 1920s called for self-reliance among Africans "at home and abroad", advocated a "back to Africa" consciousness, and awakened black pride, urging his followers to "look to Africa, when a black king shall be crowned, for the day of deliverance is at hand".

When, in 1930, Ras Tafari was crowned in Ethiopia as Emperor Haile Selassie I (1892–1975), "King of Kings, Lord of Lords, and the Conquering Lion of the Tribe of Judah", to many the prophecy was fulfilled and a way of life was born. His followers stressed black pride, and the need to regain the heritage the black race temporarily lost by straying from holy ways.

Thus, the true Rastafarian lives a peaceful and pious life, desiring nothing beyond material essentials, and engaging in contemplation of the scriptures. At the same time, the Rastafarian rejects the white man's world and its greed, dishonesty, lasciviousness, meat-eating habits, "devil soup" (alcohol) and chemical-oriented technology.

members are mostly those who have rejected other religions, attracted perhaps by the faith's acceptance of all prophets and the absence of teachings which indict other faiths.

The Seventh Day Adventists have 52 congregations in Barbados with a membership of 13,000. A strict Protestant religion believing in Christ's second coming, members have experienced discrimination in the past due to being unable to work on the Sabbath, but nowadays there are rarely problems that can't be sorted with a letter from the church.

TIE-HEAD TRADITIONS

"We can take *Abide with Me* and make you dance to it," says Archbishop Granville Williams proudly. No mean feat, as this Anglican hymn is sung at funerals and is notorious for its dreariness.

Heard God's voice

The only truly indigenous Barbadian religion is the Sons of God Apostolic Spiritual Baptists, or "Tie-head" movement. Archbishop Granville Williams founded the church in 1957 after 16 years in Trinidad, where he had been exposed to the Spiritual Baptists, a West Indian revivalist religion with its roots in Africa.

Maintaining that he had heard God's voice and seen visions, Williams held his first open-air meeting in the fishing village of Oistins, within days of his return to Barbados. There was a terrific response, and soon after, he established the Jerusalem Apostolic Spiritual Baptist Church at Ealing Grove, followed by its Zion sister at Richmond Gap. By 1999, membership had grown to 15,000 and the Jerusalem church has been rebuilt to seat 3,000.

Members wear colourful gowns, each colour symbolic of a particular quality: white stands for purity, cream for spirituality, blue for holiness, gold for royalty, green for strength, brown for happiness, silver-grey for overcoming, and pink for success. Red stands for strength and the blood of Christ. Both men and women wrap their heads in cloth, hence the name "Tie-heads".

As a native faith of Barbados, the church is closely tied to African religious traditions. Its lively music is often accompanied by much hand-clapping, foot-stomping and dancing. About 40 percent of the membership is male, which is quite an achievement, as the innumerable rum shops tend to deprive the traditional churches of men. It's the women who are the backbone of the family and the church, and the primary force behind religion's continuing importance on the island. ❑

LEFT: a welcome for all.
ABOVE: Tie-heads process on Old Year's Night.

ZAMAMA
ASIT ALI
ASIM
KHAN
AZIR

22
C
10
7
LB
7

CRICKET: THE NATIONAL RELIGION

In nearly two centuries, the game of cricket has become almost a way of life, bringing about and reflecting changes in the island's social structure

When Barbados became independent in 1966, it chose to proclaim its political coming of age by challenging the rest of the world to a cricket match.

Barbados lost – an appropriate reward, perhaps, for such arrogance. Yet no one doubted the ability of this country to hold its own against the might of an international all-star team. Barbados may be no more than a pinprick on the world map, but the game of cricket brought it instant and universal recognition. Often called its "national religion", cricket in Barbados is nearly a way of life.

Barbados' only living National Hero, Sir Garfield Sobers (*see page 90*), is a cricketing legend, the greatest the world has seen, as any Bajan will tell you proudly. The pages of *Wisden Cricketers' Almanac*, the Bible-size tome that has chronicled the game for well over a century, are filled with the records of brilliant Barbadians who have fashioned this most intricate sport into an institution.

In Barbados today, cricket is still a source of exuberant pride. After all, even if Barbados did lose that 1966 match against a world team, it has trounced several international touring teams. Since then, it has won the annual regional tournament, more times than not, and, despite the lack of top-class players on its side casting the team into the doldrums during the 1990s, the team won it again in 1999.

A character builder

Cricket was introduced to the colonies almost two centuries ago by the British military. The local white planter and merchant classes soon set up their own clubs, and organised regular competitions. More than any other sport exported throughout the Empire, cricket was seen as a character builder, a reflection of the noble values of British culture.

In the early years, cricket clubs mirrored the clear class and racial structures of Barbadian society. The Wanderers, formed in 1877, drew membership mainly from the white mercantile community. The Pickwick was the club of the plantocracy and, like The Wanderers, strictly white. Spartans' members mainly came from the growing group of black and mixed-race

professionals. When Spartans blackballed Herman Griffith (1893–1980), a public health inspector, because they felt he was socially beneath them, objectors broke away and formed the Empire Club. Griffith went on to become one of the great players of the game, a fast bowler who could sprint 20 powerful strides before hurling the 5½-oz (160-g) leather ball at over 90 miles an hour (145 kph). In 1941, he was the first black captain of a Barbados team and perhaps cemented his place in history by becoming one of the few to bowl the great Australian Don Bradman for a "duck".

These clubs are still active, although the structure of their membership has changed.

PRECEDING PAGES: keeping score at the Oval.
LEFT: congratulations all round.
RIGHT: signed and preserved.

Plantation clubs

All of this early activity was once centred on Bridgetown and confined to a small segment of the population. Yet artisans, labourers and other workers would not be excluded, and soon formed their own clubs. Plantation bosses recognised the game's potential for fostering community spirit and encouraged them to play.

Largely ignored by the official Barbados Cricket Association (BCA), these lesser teams arranged their own competitions. The rivalry was usually intense, particularly on the sugar plantations where outsiders could qualify for membership only by living on or near the plantation or by marrying or courting a girl from the village.

This spirit gave momentum to the formation of the Barbados Cricket League (BCL) at a time of significant social and political upheaval. Ironically, this game that once segregated the classes and colours so neatly, eventually brought disparate groups together in a way not otherwise possible.

Cricketing heroes

In the second half of the 20th century, the best-known players were black, many from humble backgrounds. In the 1950s, the West Indies' scorelines were dominated by three batsmen of grace, style and endurance – Frank Worrell, Clyde Walcott and Everton Weekes, known as the Terrible Three Ws. Worrell, now dead – his ashes are buried under huge concrete cricket stumps at the Cave Hill campus of UWI – was knighted by the Queen in 1964; his image even graces the five-dollar bill. Walcott and Weekes were subsequently knighted.

Garfield Sobers, born into a family of six in the Bridgetown suburb of Bayland, grew up to be the undisputed finest player of all time. In 1958, at the age of 21, he recorded the highest individual score ever made. In an international Test Match for the West Indies against Pakistan

WHAT IS CRICKET, ANYWAY?

Cricket is an intricate game with idiosyncratic rules and traditions, which most non-players find hard to understand. An English cricket club once summed it up: "You have two sides, one out in the field and one in. Each man that's in the side that's in, goes out and when he's out he comes in and the next man goes in until he's out. Then the next man goes in until he's out. When they are all out the side that's out comes in and the side that's been in goes out and tries to get those coming in out. Sometimes you get men still in and not out. When both sides have been in and out including the not-outs, that's the end of the game. Howzat!"

at Kingston's Sabina Park in Jamaica, the lithe left-hander scored an incredible 365 runs.

He was an explosive batsman, a bowler of three distinctive styles, and an incomparable fielder. He played 93 international matches, from 1954 until 1974, when the cartilage in his knees finally gave out. And in 1975, the Queen overturned a tradition and knighted Sobers, not at Buckingham Palace, but in an open-air ceremony on the Garrison Savannah, the site of the earliest recorded matches on the island.

THE GREATEST

"The greatest cricketer on Earth or on Mars" is how Trinidadian Calypso King the Mighty Sparrow described Sir Gary Sobers in a 1965 song.

"make it big". In recent times, however, there has been concern about a decreasing interest in cricket. Young boys that were once inspired by the Three Ws now see Michael Jordan and Grant Hill as their heroes, as satellite technology brings American basketball (NBA) into Barbadian homes.

Still, top cricketers can earn more than US$50,000 a year, a very good living in Barbados. The West Indies team enjoyed a heady run at the top of the international cricketing heap from the late 1970s until the early 1990s. During that

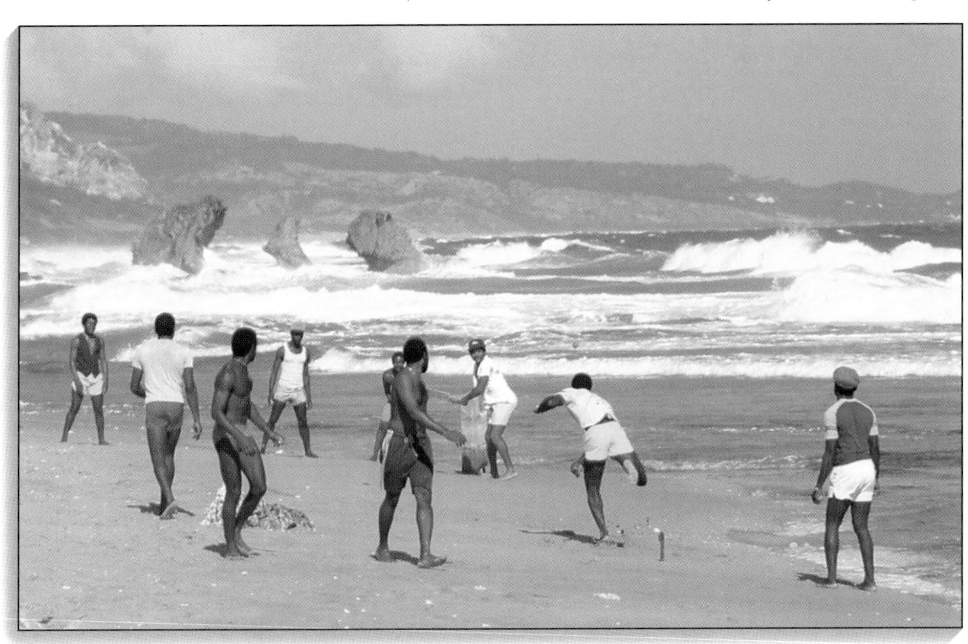

The versatile Sobers has since captained the Barbados golf team and is a sports consultant for the Barbados Tourism Authority as well as being the driving force behind the annual Sir Garfield Sobers International Schools Cricket Tournament.

Making it big

Barbadian cricket has traditionally inspired many personal hopes and dreams as well as national pride. It has been a vehicle for young boys who want to escape from poverty and

LEFT: West Indies v England at Kensington Oval.
ABOVE: beach cricket at Bathsheba.

time captain Clive Lloyd, known as "Super Cat", led a fearsome combination that saw, for the first time, four fast bowlers, all bowling at speeds around 90 miles (145 km) an hour or more, forming the attack. In the mid 1980s, bolstered by batting led by Lloyd, with the dominant Vivian Richards and one of the greatest combinations of opening batsmen in the history of the game, Gordon Greenidge and Desmond Haynes, they were unstoppable.

Batsmen the world over must have had nightmares at the prospect of facing up to speed merchants Andy Roberts, Joel "Big Bird" Garner, Colin Croft, Michael Holding, Malcolm Marshall and Sylvester Clarke in those days.

Hard times

But at the turn of the millennium, after the near simultaneous retirement of the great players, the West Indies team has found itself struggling halfway up the ladder of international cricket, touching the bottom in 1999, when it failed to get through the first round of the World Cup. The saying goes that when Barbados cricket is strong, the West Indies team is strong. In 1966, for example, there were seven Barbadians in a winning team of 11. In 1999 there was only one.

FAITHFUL FOLLOWING

Productivity drops when the West Indies are on tour, as the ball-by-ball commentary is heard on thousands of radios concealed in desk drawers and behind service counters.

Despite 100 association and league matches played every Saturday afternoon from early June until mid September, and a "softball" version using tennis balls played on Sundays, the standard of club cricket has become almost unrecognisably low and the BCA are trying to find ways to stimulate interest among the youth once more and find creative ways to combat the allure of the NBA in the US.

A day at the cricket

Whatever is happening with the West Indies team, nothing will dampen the ardour of a Bajan cricket fan. A day of cricket is a social ritual whether it be at the local village ground kept in trim by sheep, or at the Kensington Oval. An international match runs from 10.30am to 5.30pm each day for up to five straight days, with breaks for lunch and tea. When the action on the pitch is sluggish, and the sun is hot, diversions become mandatory. So fans make a picnic of it, toting their baskets of peas and rice, salted pig trotters, pickled breadfruit and other delights, as well as the island's famous rum.

The Oval is always crammed to its 15,000 capacity on Test Match days against England or Australia, and the atmosphere is electric. It can seem even more crowded at key club matches when as many as 4,000 enthusiastic fans encircle much smaller grounds.

Colourful characters

All the activity surrounding the game has produced some characters whose mission is to entertain the fans when the players are failing to do so. The late "Flannagan" travelled with Barbados teams throughout the 1930s and 1940s, serving as a sort of mascot, heckling and teasing opponents on and off the field with his loud, sharp-witted comments.

"King Dyal" was a regular for more than 30 years until 1995, giving up two years before he died aged 96. He unfailingly supported the other team, particularly if it was the English, and always made a grand entrance to the most conspicuous seat in the most conspicuous stand. At each interval he would reappear in a different, resplendent, three-piece suit in flamboyant scarlet, canary yellow or emerald green.

He has now been replaced by comedian, calypsonian and schoolteacher Mac Fingall who, at every test match, takes up his position in the Kensington Stand with drum, a bugle and a concoction of "duppy dust" he says was passed on to him by his grandmother. He usually goes on to the field and sprinkles some in a corner, and in 1990 when West Indies were failing against England, Fingall went on to the field, sprinkled some of his dust and knelt as if invoking some ancient spirits. Within 15 minutes West Indies star Curtly Ambrose had taken seven wickets and destroyed England! ❑

LEFT: Sir Frank Worrell graces the five-dollar bill.
RIGHT: it's all in the game...

CABLE & WIRELESS

A LIVING ART

A riot of colour, character and contemporary creativity, art in Barbados has undergone a sea change for the new millennium

Art in Barbados developed radically in the last part of the 20th century, with Barbadian artists breaking away from "souvenir" art and finding international acclaim for a variety of work in many types of media – and it is evident in the many new galleries that have sprung up around the island as a result.

However, it can be easily seen from a tour of the galleries that Caribbean art still equals a profusion of colour and echoes of the region's turbulent past – albeit in different forms. Whether it be Ras Ishi's haunting mixed media-constructions or Vanita Comissiong's colourful market-scenes, Annalee Davis' challenging installations or Bill Grace's radiant, stained-glass and clay mandalas, island art is vibrant, direct and more self-confident than ever before.

Before the 1960s, such characteristics did not apply to art in Barbados. Until then, European traditions had been mainly used. Only around independence did art become an outlet for the new national consciousness and the artists' lively impressions of their young nation also happened to fulfill the expectations of art-interested visitors, who were coming to the island in increasing numbers each year. Some artists quickly discovered the potential of this interest and developed what has been termed "souvenir" art which, with such practioners as Jill Walker, whose characterful prints of Barbadian scenes can be found everywhere, is still popular today. However, a breakaway, avant-garde movement emerged soon after.

New trends

During the 1990s, this new avant-garde scene motivated two significant trends: the opening of professional, large-scale galleries and unprecedented attention from the international art world. Travelling exhibitions of contemporary Caribbean art have toured Japan, Europe and the United States. But, in spite of such success abroad, the galleries have still had to capitalise on more popular art to support it.

This has especially been the experience of the Art Foundry, which was established in 1996 as an experimental gallery in a massive, old coral-stone building at Heritage Park in St Philip. For a few years, this unique space was the framework around some of the most interesting and challenging exhibitions ever held in the southern Caribbean.

Facilities of this scale at last allowed a local audience to experience massive installations such as those which Annalee Davis and Joscelyn Gardener, the Art Foundry's former director, had previously exhibited overseas. These young, female artists made a strong and irreversible impact on the traditionally rather conservative Barbadian art scene. Meanwhile, the ungainful nature of such exhibitions eventually necessitated the opening of a second, more commercial gallery at Derricks in St James.

The Art Foundry West maintains a serious

PRECEDING PAGES: Vanita Comissiong's market scene.
LEFT: sculptor Karl Broodhagen, the creator of *Bussa*.
RIGHT: *A Sacred Soliloquy* by Annalee Davis.

profile, but many of the artworks here are simply more marketable, due to their scale. These might include semi-abstract landscapes or fond impressions of the island's beautiful gullies by Alison Chapman-Andrews, Lilian Sten-Nicholson's expressionistic paintings of steel bands, and Nick Whittle's poetic, yet controversial mixed media works, raising questions about gender and identity in today's Caribbean.

Caribbean classics

The Kirby Gallery near the Garrison Savannah in Hastings aims at being the largest regional gallery on the island and offers artworks from the wider, English-speaking Caribbean along with Barbadian best-sellers like Ann Dodson's playfully designed landscapes, Darla Trotman's photo-realistic trees and flowers, or Vanita Comissiong's distinctive, colourful local scenarios. The Kirby Gallery also represents Caribbean "classics" such as those of Trinidadian Boscoe Holder, mostly known for his exotic, creole women, and "naïve" Jamaican painter Seya Parboosingh.

Watercolourist Winston Kellman, whose work is based on faithful observation of how changes in light transform the landscape, is represented by both galleries.

A Round-up of Galleries

More and more galleries are popping up around the island: in restaurants, banks and hotels as well as those with space of their own.

Speightstown Renaissance Gallery features mainly figurative prints and paintings.

Cunard Gallery, Barbados Museum, displays historical prints and another gallery runs temporary exhibitions.

Barbados Gallery of Art, Bush Hill, Garrison, rotates exhibitions from its permanent collection of art from Barbados, the Caribbean, US and South America.

Art Foundry, Rum Factory & Heritage Park, exhibits the avant-garde in large formats by award-winning artists.

Art Foundry West, Derricks, St James, offers more commercially orientated pieces by top Barbadian artists.

Kirby Gallery, Hastings, holds a variety of exhibitions of selected artists' work from Barbados and the Caribbean.

Verandah Art Gallery, Bridgetown, features a wide range of art including the work of young, talented local artists.

Gang of 4 Art Studio, Speightstown, shows paintings and sculpture by renowned local artists.

Pelican Village Gallery, Bridgetown, is run by Barbados Arts Council and hosts temporary exhibitions.

Queens Park Gallery is run by the NCF and used for private exhibitions as well as for general ones.

Gold medal winners

Two of the island's most prominent and top Caribbean artists, Ras Ishi Butcher and Ras Akyem Ramsey are not tied to any gallery, but managed by a private agent. Along with internationally acclaimed Guyanese-born artist Stanley Greaves (who lives in Barbados), Alison Chapman-Andrews, Nick Whittle, Arthur Atkinson and Annalee Davis, these two artists formed the gold-medal winning Barbadian contingent to the Santo Domingo Biennial of Painting from

ARTFUL HOTEL

The Casuarina Beach Club in St Lawrence Gap houses the largest private art collection open to the public on the island including works by Stanley Greaves and Bill Grace.

the Caribbean and Central America in 1996.

Although the careers of Ras Ishi and Ras Akyem have been intertwined, and despite the fact that their work is often indistinguishable to many, their style and message are profoundly different. Both are mostly known for their expressionistic paintings, although Akyem also is a highly admired sculptor and some of Ishi's recent works have been "constructions" in metal and wood, with multiple connotations to slavery, chattel houses and survival. Where Ras Ishi often applies a rural and psychological perspective in his paintings, Ras Akyem uses universal themes, usually in an urban setting and often incorporating graffiti.

LEFT: inside the spacious Art Foundry.
ABOVE: Gordon Webster's *Fruit Bowl* and Ras Bongo Congo's mahogany *One Heart.*

Stanley Greaves has adopted Barbados as his home and some of his surreal, or metaphysical, paintings can be seen at the Casuarina Beach Club in St Lawrence Gap. In fact several hotels have a penchant for art and provide artists with space to exhibit or give them special evenings when they can come and sell their work.

Commercial venues

The Verandah Art Gallery, upstairs at Collins Pharmacy in Broad Street, Bridgetown, frequently offers younger artists an exhibition-debut (prices are often competitive), but is also loyally supported by some well-established artists like watercolourist Neville Legall, who is popular for his paintings of chattel houses and gentle landscapes. Rebuilt in 1999, the Pelican Village Gallery, near Bridgetown Harbour, is operated by the Arts Council and features regular exhibitions. In Bay Street, Perseverance House offers a variety of artworks and crafts.

In Speightstown is a small gallery called the Gang of 4 Art Studio, which displays wooden sculpture by Ras Bongo Congo as well as expressionistic paintings by Sarah Venable, Gordon Webster and Aziza.

National Gallery

While politicians have consented to the establishment of the much desired National Gallery, the only government-operated exhibition space to date is the Queens Park Gallery, which is administered by the National Cultural Foundation (NCF). This gallery occupies the ground level of the old Daphne Joseph-Hackett Theatre in Bridgetown's largest recreational park. When not booked by individual artists, it is used for art shows arranged by the NCF.

Nearby, the Tom Adams Financial Centre (which houses the Central Bank), likewise lends its Grande Salle to changing exhibitions.

Still, the most ambitious non-commercial gallery is the small, privately sponsored Barbados Gallery of Art, at the Garrison Savannah, which mainly aims at public education through follow-up programmes and workshops in connection with the gallery's professionally curated exhibitions selected from a permanent collection of 300 pieces of art.

A Cover Up

The Emancipation Monument, *Bussa*, was planned as a male nude, but such a fuss was made that the artist Karl Broodhagen had to give him some shorts.

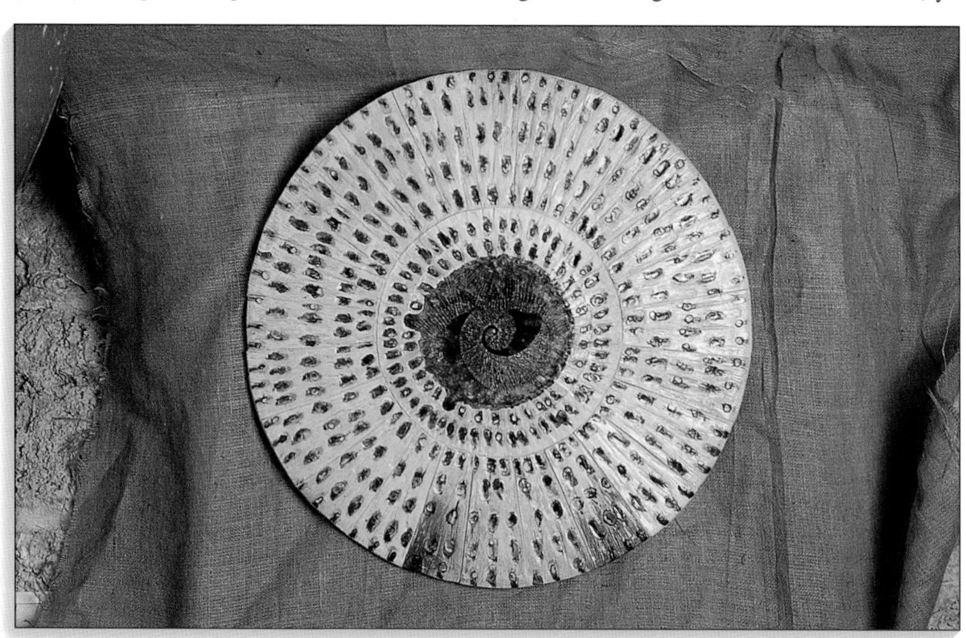

Sculpture – the African touch

Generally, sculpture is not well represented by the commercial galleries – mostly, perhaps, because it does not, like painting, comply with the expectations of "authentic" Caribbean colour, and therefore is harder to sell. Even so, it is only sculpture which can boast a direct lineage to African traditions. This connection is stressed in the work of artists such as Woodpecker, Ras Bongo Congo and Kenneth Blackman. All three draw on the age-old carving traditions of West Africa, yet at the same time giving them contemporary Caribbean relevance.

The most celebrated sculptor of the island is Karl Broodhagen, whose Emancipation Monument, known as *The Freed Slave*, or *Bussa*, was unveiled in 1985 at the St Barnabas roundabout and is now a landmark for all Barbadians. Broodhagen is a well respected master craftsman, painter, thinker and researcher. Born in 1909, he began his career as a tailor and developed into a virtuoso artist. He has sculptured many famous Barbadian busts, including one of the revered politician Sir Grantley Adams which stands in front of Government Headquarters in Bay Street.

Bill Grace – close to the earth

Colour is in fact applied to sculpture in the works produced by the revered ceramist Bill Grace. He combines coral stone, clay and stained glass into startling pieces voicing an environmental concern particularly with reference to Barbados, his homeland. An artist whose work is technically brilliant and commercially successful, his *We Are the Reef* series portrays man as an integral part of nature, and incorporates natural and man-made materials in the work. Many of his sculptures have a turtle theme and are on display in several hotels, banks and galleries, and you can see his deeply coloured stained-glass window in St James Church in Holetown (*see page 220*).

Pottery – an island tradition

The pottery tradition of the island originated at Chalky Mount in St Andrew, an area with rich deposits of clay. Liberated slaves were probably first to settle there in the early 19th century and have handed down their skills for making simple, practical pots. But only a few small potteries are left now, the village's situation on top of a saddleback ridge makes it difficult to get to and the next generation is heading for the town.

This is where the pottery industry thrives, producing items as souvenirs. In St Thomas, Earthworks' pottery is known for its simple designs and bright glazes in the colours of the Caribbean. At Fairfield Pottery, in St Michael, Maggie Bell's characteristic swift brushstroke introduces a "Caribbeanised" version of classical motifs such as hibiscus and flying fish.

These motifs also grace many local crafts sold through Walker's Caribbean World. They are, perhaps, most noted for their prints and souvenirs based on Jill Walker's light and often humorous drawings of local street life. ❑

LEFT: a Bill Grace sculpture.
ABOVE: pots at Chalky Mount.

WEARABLE ART

Sculptural jewellery can be perceived as "wearable art". Fashion designer Nefertari is inspired by nature and her elegant pieces (sold at Earthworks) are created with colourful stones, metalwork and chains, complementing her hand-painted silks that have shells and the movement of water as themes. Ichia draws on West African traditions combining silver with seeds, leather and other natural materials (galleries and Colours of de Caribbean) to create spiral and almost graffiti-like pieces. Andrea Wells' work is simpler; she wraps "gems" of colourful, sea-washed glass with wire to make bracelets and necklaces (Barbados Museum).

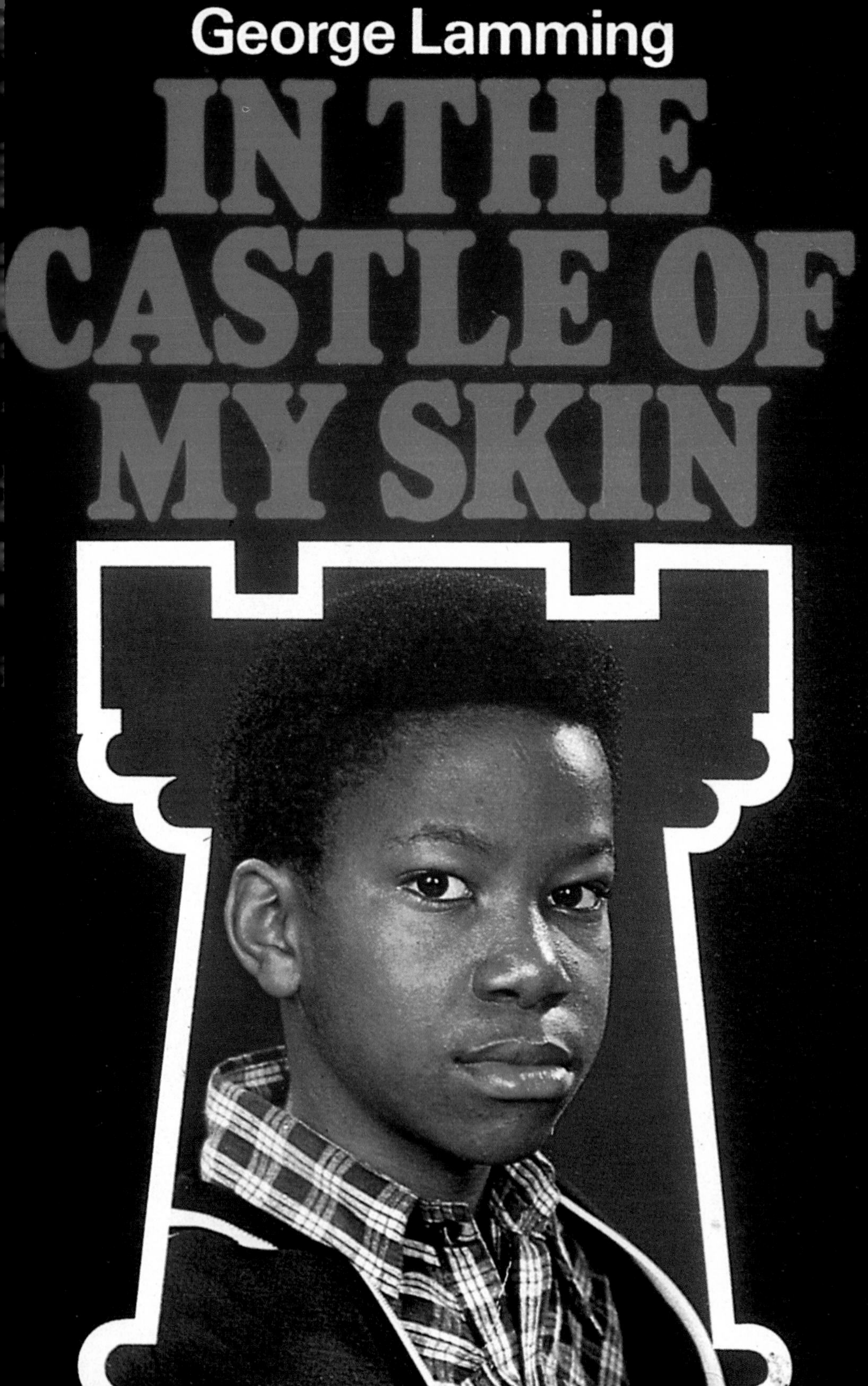
George Lamming
IN THE CASTLE OF MY SKIN

A Story-Telling Tradition

Handed down by word of mouth, Bajan literature has endured across the centuries. Today, the island's contemporary writers are still spreading the word

Once upon a time on a moonswept night in Pie Corner, St Lucy, two men might have entertained one another with stories of ghosts and spirits. And over a family supper in Bridgetown, a grandmother might have admonished children not to "throw stones at a dog or cat when yuh meet them at night – it might not be a cat or dog at all". Of course, that was long before Barbados' shores were inundated with cable TV, but shared myths, legends and musings like these were once part of this island's social currency, as traditional a part of life as flying fish and cou-cou. Today they can be counted part of Barbados' fertile oral tradition.

Barbados also has a rich literary tradition, a number of internationally respected novelists and poets, and one of the world's highest literacy rates: more than 95 percent of the people can read and write and, more importantly, understand what they read and write.

Modern urban myths

These days, folk beliefs are disappearing, replaced by more urban and urbane myths imported from the United States via Hollywood and, more recently, the Internet. The Urban Myth about gang initiation and flashing headlights is a case in point, having arrived in Barbados in the late 1990s in the form of a film entitled *Urban Legends* and via e-mail. As the story goes, a man is driving home one night when he sees a car approaching with no headlights. He flashes his lights as a warning. Immediately, the other car turns around and begins to chase him. The chasing car is full of gang members participating in an initiation ceremony. The initiate that night must kill the Good Samaritan to gain full membership to the gang. The moral? No good deed goes unpunished.

Despite global cultural influences, Barbados' traditional folklore lives on existing alongside the island's literature, each helping to preserve the culture and heritage and to express the society's hopes and fears. Both are an integral part of the many-sided Barbadian character.

Traditional folklore

The traditional folklore side is replete with looming imaginings and supernatural beliefs,

for example, the *duppy* of Bajan folklore is a spirit, a "shadow" of a departed person. The *Conrad* is an avenging ghost that possesses the body, racks it, and shouts nasty things at people.

No less puzzling is the *baccoo* of Barbados, a small man who reportedly lives in bottles. In the baccoo one finds good or evil, prosperity or failure, heroism or villainy, depending on the amount of attention showered on him by his human owner. Local legends also feature entities that throw stones on the houses of the obsessed, and slap the victims of magic with invisible hands. Stories of witchcraft, spells and miracles abound. Ask any Bajan about the Black Rock, St Michael, family whose terrify-

PRECEDING PAGES: chillin' on the beach.
LEFT and **RIGHT:** George Lamming as a boy on the cover of his novel about his childhood and as he is today.

ing experiences of spontaneous combustion and bombardment with stones from unseen sources made front page news – in 1998.

African heritage

The many Bajan tales and beliefs – ancient and modern – are survivors of an oral tradition that harks back to the African heritage of the majority of the island's population. From the villages of West Africa to the village communities and the modern housing developments of Barbados, the oral tradition is used to transmit cultural mores and values.

In Barbados, many folktales and songs are teaching tools; they contain a moral or a lesson. Others are sheer entertainment, vehicles for grassroots creativity. Of all popular Bajan folk tales and practices, however, those that have had the most powerful hold are religious. These are the stories and beliefs directly descended from old-time African lore.

The deities and demons of West African folklore have had an equally strong hold on the Barbadian imagination. Shango, the African deity, once enjoyed a following in Barbados, and myriad are the tales of *obeah* (witchcraft), of duppies and spirits of the dead.

Legends that originate locally tend to be

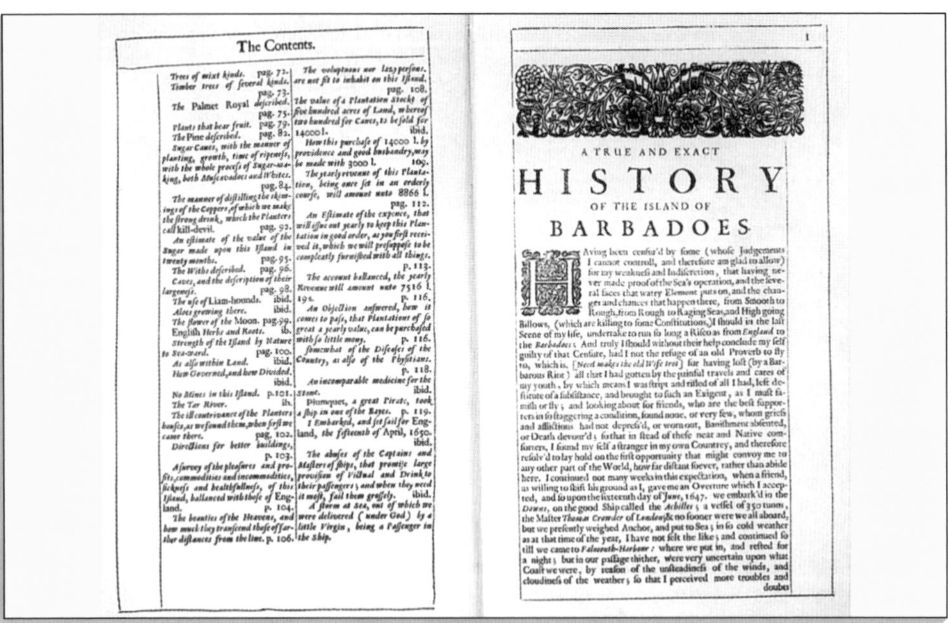

The Contents.

1

A TRUE AND EXACT

HISTORY

OF THE ISLAND OF

BARBADOES

HAving been censur'd by some (whose Judgements I cannot controll, and therefore am glad to allow) for my weakness and Indiscretion, that having never made proof of the Sea's operation, and the several faces that watry Element puts on, and the changes and chances that happen there, from Smooth to Rough, from Rough to Raging Seas, and High going Billows, (which are killing to some Constitutions,) I should in the last Scene of my life, undertake to run so long a Risco as from *England* to the *Barbadoes*: And truly I should without their help conclude my self guilty of that Censure, had I not the refuge of an old Proverb to fly to, which is, [*Need makes the old Wife trot*] for having lost (by a Barbarous Riot) all that I had gotten by the painful travels and cares of my youth, by which means I was stript and rifled of all I had, left destitute of a subsistance, and brought to such an Exigent, as I must famish or fly; and looking about for friends, who are the best supporters in so staggering a condition, found none, or very few, whom griefs and afflictions had not depress'd, or worn out, Banishment absented, or Death devour'd; so that in stead of these near and Native comforters, I found my self a stranger in my own Countrey, and therefore resolv'd to lay hold on the first opportunity that might convoy me to any other part of the World, how far distant soever, rather than abide here. I continued not many weeks in this expectation, when a friend, as willing to shift his ground as I, gave me an Overture which I accepted, and so upon the sixteenth day of *June*, 1647. we embark'd in the *Downs*, on the good Ship called the *Achilles*; a vessel of 350 tunns, the Master *Thomas Crowder* of *London*; & no sooner were we all aboard, but we presently weighed Anchor, and put to Sea; in so cold weather as at that time of the year, I have not felt the like; and continued so till we came to *Falmouth-Harbour*: where we put in, and rested for a night; but in our passage thither, were very uncertain upon what Coast we were, by reason of the unsteadiness of the winds, and cloudiness of the weather; so that I perceived more troubles and doubts

TWO BAJAN FOLKTALES

The Metaphysical Prank A very sick man went to a metaphysician who worked in Bridgetown. The practitioner explained to him what "pain" was all about, saying it only existed in the mind and all he had to do was to affirm and believe that the pain was gone and gradually it would be relieved. With neophyte's zeal, the man successfully made the affirmations. However, when the practitioner asked for his fees, the man said: "Wha' fees? All you have to do is affirm and believe dat you have receive de fees and you have dem."

The Baccoo Mrs Barbara lived in Speightstown. Her daughter was cleaning the house after her mother's death, and in the deceased's bedroom, she attempted to remove a blanket from under the bed. To her surprise, the blanket seemed to resist and pull itself back under the bed. When Mrs Barbara's daughter examined it, she found a baccoo. The tiny man defied all her attempts to root him out. Finally a Roman Catholic priest had to be called to rid the house of this demon. He bagged the baccoo and paid a fisherman $50 to carry it out to sea.

The mysterious small man in the bag proved too much for the curious fisherman. He opened the bag to look, and the baccoo escaped. The story goes that, soon afterwards, the fisherman's house was destroyed by a fire.

vivid and entertaining. Even today there is a persistent folk rumour that certain people can transform themselves into animals and move about inconspicuously.

Stories describing mysteries circulate freely such as the steel donkey who would wreak havoc at night, immortalised by The Merrymen:

The steel donkey coming down...
An' he jumping and prancing 'bout
A long thing like a muffler sticking out
behind him
And 'e tongue sticking out he mout'

In the 1960s and 1970s, there were people who swore they saw this donkey, surrounded by blue light, bawling and galloping along the country roads of Barbados.

History and social events are preserved in folk songs as well. One Bajan folk song documents the activity of a petty thief:

Sly Mongoose, the dog know yuh name.
Sly Mongoose, you ain't got no shame.
You go straight in the lady kitchen
Take up half of she big fat chicken
Hide it down in yuh wes'coat pocket
Sly Mongoose.

And then there's the one about a West African king, captured by the British, and brought to Barbados under a kind of house arrest in the late 1800s. He became something of a folk hero on the island and he fell in love with a local woman, Rebecca, inspiring the ditty, *King Ja-Ja won't leave Becka 'lone.*

The song *Lick and Lock-up Done Wid* commemorates the ending of slavery on the island. and *Panama Man* reminds us of the hundreds of Bajans who went to help in the construction of the Panama Canal, and whose riches, on their returning to Barbados, were legendary. These and other folk songs can be found in *Folk Songs of Barbados*, a collection edited by Trevor Marshall, Peggy McGeary and Grace Thompson, which are still sung in schools and by folk chorales islandwide.

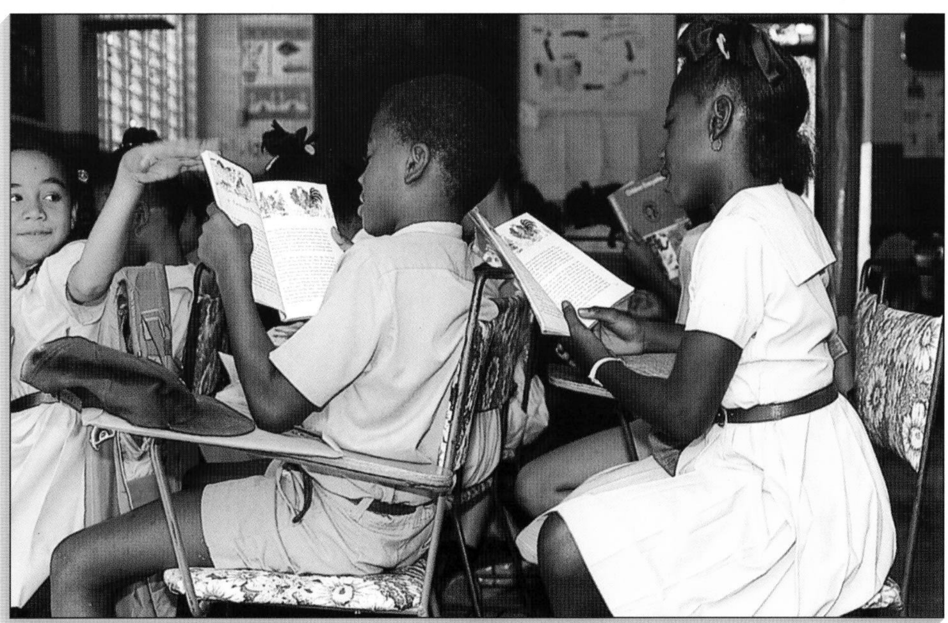

LEFT: Richard Ligon's history of Barbados was published in 1657, with a second edition in 1673.
ABOVE: enthusiastic readers.

True and exact history

For generations, Barbados' folk traditions have been passed on orally, but rarely written or recorded. As is the case with most (former) colonies, the earliest writings were not by Barbadians, but by visitors who reported on the island's history and conditions. The first study was Englishman Richard Ligon's *A True and Exact History of the Island of Barbadoes*, which was first published in 1657. A more definitive work is Robert H. Schomburgk's *The History of Barbados*, published in 1848 and reprinted in 1998. Past editions of two island newspapers, the *Barbados Mercury* and *Bridgetown Gazette*, also contain a wealth of historic information and can be seen in the Barbados Public Library in Coleridge Street, Bridgetown.

COLLY AND *BIM*

Remembered as the Grand Old Man of Barbadian Literature, Frank Collymore helped launch the careers of many leading writers through his magazine *Bim*.

Bim – a literary forum

Indigenous literature, meanwhile, first came to public notice in the 1940s and 1950s through the efforts of a BBC radio programme called *Caribbean Voices*, and through a Barbadian magazine called *Bim*. First published in 1942, *Bim* encouraged local creative writing. Highly acclaimed novels were to flow from the pens of contributors – novels which may not have been written without such a forum or the encouragement of its editor, Frank Collymore (1893–1980). Back volumes of *Bim* are a Who's Who of Caribbean writers, including Kamau (formerly Edward Brathwaite), St Lucian Derek Walcott, Austin Clarke, George Lamming, John Wickham, Oliver Jackman, Geoffrey Drayton, Monica Skeete, Andrew Salkey, Bruce St John and Timothy Callender.

It was to *Bim* that many foreign publishers of Caribbean literature, particularly prose, turned in their search for authors. The English were becoming increasingly interested in West Indian culture, as immigrants poured into Britain. Meanwhile, the spirit of independence was rising among the educated, upwardly mobile blacks. Trade unions, political parties and calls for self-government were the order of the day.

Much of Barbados' best writing grew up in this ferment. Many early indigenous novels, such as George Lamming's *In the Castle of my Skin* and John Wickham's autobiographical stories, deal with childhood, with coming of age, with the search for self, with questions about colour and race, bondage and freedom; that is, a clash of British and African cultures.

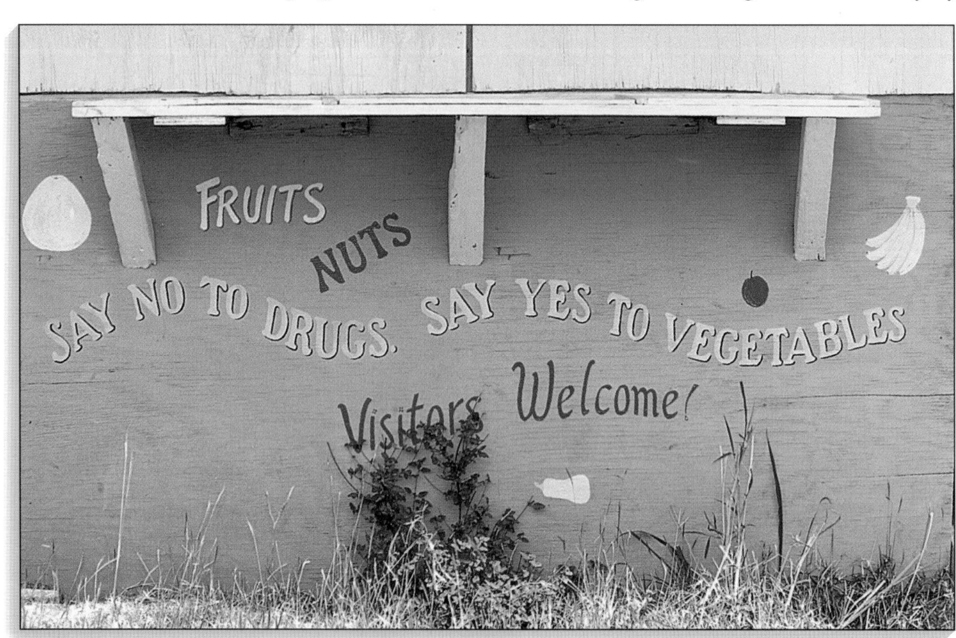

Bubbling with humour

By the 1970s and 1980s, the island's writers were treating the themes of independence and identity with less urgency, an interesting comment on the ongoing and successful synthesis of these two Bajan ways of life. Those novels and writings often bubble with humour, and capture the lives of ordinary people in a positive way. Many Barbadians take special delight in the local radio broadcasts of West Indian stories which often focus on popular culture and village life. Such readings brought to life the stories of Jeanette Layne-Clark, Monica Skeete and Timothy Callender and Barbadians love them. They take pride in hearing about themselves, and Bajan, Barbados' Nation Language, lends itself to public readings. Unfortunately, these stories are broadcast far too seldom these days.

The trends that began in the 1970s and 1980s represented a vigorous, vibrant wellspring of writing in Barbados. The movement has seen efforts to record the oral tradition of the island; to capture its dialect in writing. Bajan authors began to write more honestly and confidently, describing fuller, rounder characters than ever before; writing less for the overseas reader and more for their own people.

That spirit is kindled in the following poem, *Revelation*, by H.A. Vaughn, from his collection *Sandy Lane and Other Poems*, which he wrote in the 1940s and was certainly ahead of its time. The oft-quoted and anthologised poem is the first recorded Barbadian poem that has been dedicated to the black woman:

Turn sideways now and let them see
What loveliness escapes the schools,
Then turn again, and smile, and be
The perfect answer to those fools
Who always prate of Greece and Rome
"The face that launched a thousand ships"
And such like things, but keep tight lips
For burnished beauty nearer home.
Turn in the sun, my love, my love!
What palm-like grace! What poise! I swear
I prize these dusky limbs above
My life. What laughing eyes! What
gleaming hair!

LEFT: getting the message across.
ABOVE LEFT: spreading the word.
ABOVE RIGHT: a relaxing read.

New energy

After a brief lull in the late 1980s and early 1990s, the writing scene at the turn of the millennium is bursting with energy. The recent upsurge in literary creativity is reminiscent, for many of the older writers, to the "*Bim* era" when an air of expectancy prevailed with writers working hard and writing much, developing their craft and hoping for a publishing contract – an affirmation of their talent.

Today, Barbados is home to three literary groups, fostering a wide range of talent, the foremost being VOICES: Barbados Writers Collective, which has been responsible for a marked increase in literary awareness on the island. Established in October 1996 with 12 members to spread the "word", VOICES now has a roll of 160 (including overseas membership) and operates from the Barbados Museum & Historical Society (tel: 427 0201) where open meetings are held every month.

Performance literature

Sponsored by local businesses, each VOICES session comprises an Open Mic Session, when members of the audience share their work, and a performance by a featured writer, such as Kamau, John Wickham, Margaret Gill (winner of the first Frank Collymore Literary Endowment), performance poets Nala (Alan Newton) and Elisheba (Dr Elizabeth Best), as well as science fiction/horror writer James Carmichael.

This inspirational group convenes workshops in poetry and prose writing and facilitates readings at various venues around the island. It has also published (in association with the NCF) a collection of members' work in *VOICES 1 An Anthology of Barbadian Writing* (1998), the first published anthology of contemporary Barbadian writing.

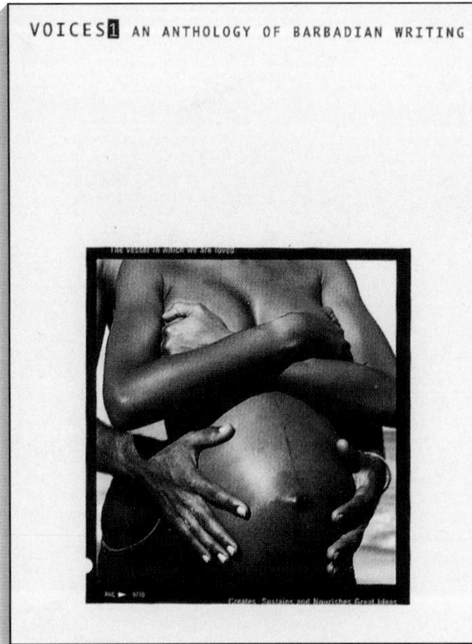

National Cultural Foundation

Set up by the Government in 1983, the National Cultural Foundation (NCF) is responsible for the development of all aspects of Bajan culture, the preservation of the island's cultural heritage, and promotion of local music, visual arts, performing arts and literary arts, and organises writing competitions and workshops. In 1998, it reintroduced the annual Writers' Fest, a three-day writers' conference, and in 1999, launched READ IN!, a series of parish-by-parish readings held the second Sunday of each month, to which the public are welcome. For details of READ IN! programmes and other NCF activities, call 424 0909.

Poetry in motion

Two other organisations also make a contribution to the literary awareness of the island. As well as providing performance opportunities for writers from time to time, Writers' Outreach, headed by poet Norma Meek, put on a literary "concert" in the late 1990s when poets and writers performed their work in front of 300 people. The benefits were donated to the Caribbean Dyslexia Centre.

The Poets' Circle, coordinated by Bajan poet Esther Phillips, comprises seven of the island's top award-winning poets. Several times a year the group puts on an evening of lyrical entertainment (see press for details) in which members weave their poetry, voices and unique performance styles around a theme that often includes music and dance. And poetry merges with jazz, blues and reggae also during the Interludes: Poetry and Jazz season (*see page 131*).

Accolades for writers

Several awards are granted annually to encourage the literary arts in Barbados including The Frank Collymore Literary Endowment ("The Colly") in memory of Frank Collymore. Set up in 1998 and sponsored by the Central Bank of Barbados, a BDS$10,000 prize is awarded for excellent writing each year. The Kamau Brathwaite Award champions poets, but the award is only given if a certain score is reached; and the George Lamming Award, created in 1999, is offered to prose writers.

With community, government and private sector interest, a network of talented, ambitious, dedicated writers has grown, poised to catapult Barbadian literature into the international literary arena of the 21st century. ❑

LEFT: a collection of contemporary Bajan writing.
RIGHT: spreading the word.

Tell Me A Story

THE BOYFRIENDS: A SHORT STORY

Elmina has two boyfriends, but her grandparents want a say in the matter – a delightful short story by Barbadian writer Timothy Callender (1946–89)

Elmina Griffith had two boyfriends. One was short and one was tall. One was ugly and the other was good-looking. One had a lot of money and the other didn't have none. And Elmina did like all two of them.

But from the start she grandmother was giving trouble when it comes to this boy-talk. She start from the time she first see Elmina with James. James was the short one, the one who was ugly and didn't have no money either. One night he come home there and sit down and talk to the grandmother and grandfather good good, and they were all talking to he nice too, trying to find out things 'bout he and where he come from and who he family is, and when James get up and went 'long, seeing that he ain't going get no chance to talk lovey-dovey with Elmina that night, the grandmother ups and says:

"But Elmina, what you getting on with though? This is what I bring you up to do? You mother gone and dead and lef' me with you, and looka how you wanta mek she memory shame after I try so hard with you. What a young little girl like you want with boyfriend already? When I was your age I couldn't even look at a man, and now you got them coming in the house sitting down in all o' we morris chairs like if they own the place. What you want with boyfriend already, Elmina? And he ain't even nice-looking. I wonder where he come from? I aint know he nor none of he family, though he say he born up in St Peter where I used to live meself. And I know everybody that is anybody in them parts. But I ain't know he. And you hear what sorta job he doing?" she say, turning to Grandpa. "Says he does work with Patterson's Garage. What he does do? Motor-mechanic or does drive taxi?"

"Grandma, nothing ain't wrong with them jobs! You got a lot o' old-fashion ideas that collar and tie work is the only work decent men could do. What wrong with honest work? He got to mek money and he doing the job that he like doing best too. He tell me that."

"Elmina would sneak outa the house and go and meet he, and they use to walk to the beach..."

"What you talking 'bout? You wanta tell me you really like he? Why you tekking up for he so strong? You think he like you? How you know he don't go 'round the place chatting down every girl he come across? You know how these men does behave when they reach a certain age. Listen, I want you to get married and thing, but what is you hurry? You still too young to tek on the responsibilities of a wife. You is only twenty-six."

"But grandma, that is old enough."

"Old enough? Girl, when I was thirty my mother beat me because I was walking the road and I speak back to a man that speak to me."

"I like he bad..."

But Elmina only chupse and say, "But Grandma, I like James, though. I can't help it. I like he bad, and he say he like me too."

"Hey, but you ain't got no respect for me and you grandfather? How you can talk that sorta thing in front of we? Look, Zedekiah, you better watch that girl, hear! She feel that she too old to get lashes. You better watch that girl, Zedekiah."

"Listen, however, she mek up she bed she got to lie down 'pon it, yuh know," the grandfather say. "But if I see the young man again, I going ask he a few questions."

So when James pass by another time to see Elmina, the grandfather comes out and sits down in the rocking chair, all dress up in coat and collar and tie like if he feel that this give the atmosphere the sort of seriousness that it demand; like if it is a business conference or something. And he looks at James and say:

"Ahem. Young man, this is the second time I see you and I would like to find out some things 'bout you. You have a family?"

"Well, my father dead, but my mother still living. And I got two sisters that went to school at St Leonard's and St Michael's."

"Them is good schools to go to," the old man say. "So what you sisters doing now?"

"I ain't know. They wasn't home when I left."

He had the old man there. He like he is a fool, yuh, Zedekiah start to think. What sorta idiot this girl encouraging in my house though? Listen, I talking too decent to this idiot. I better talk in language he understand.

"Ahem. Listen, you man, you have money?"

The young man put he hand in he pocket and scratch 'bout.

"Lemme see… 'bout three dollars. How much yuh want?"

The grandfather bend down and hold he head in he hands.

And Elmina, sitting down 'pon the couch beside James, was very embarrass because she did know what the grandfather was getting at; in fact, she did want to find out sheself. So she turn to James and she says:

"All grandfather want to know is what your intentions is."

"Well, right now I intends to ketch the ten o'clock bus," the young man say.

"Don't ever come here again"

"Listen young man. I ain't want you to ever come back inside this house o' mine!" Zedekiah shout out. "Don't ever come here again or I will do as I say as sure as my name is Amos Zedekiah Joshua Zechariah Hedoniah Griffith."

"I believe you, man. You ain't got to tell me you name too," the young man say. "And Elmina, I want you to know that whatever happen I still love you with a eternal love, and I building a house and anytime you ain't feel like standing here no longer, you know what you kin do. I gone for now." And James went 'long.

"You hear what he say?" says the grandmother, coming out from the bedroom where she was listening behind the partition. "But looka this wussless nigger-man though nuh, trying to encourage a nice decent young girl like you to come and live with he. You see what he been intending for you all the time now? You see that we did right?"

So James never went back inside Zedekiah's house again, but every now and then when Elmina coulda think up a excuse she would sneak outa the house and go and meet he, and if it was night, they use to walk to the beach and sit down 'pon the sand and hold one another hand and look out to sea and look at the lights and tell one another how much they like one another and mek plans 'bout getting married and thing, and so on.

Then one day Elmina get a job in a store in town and that is where she meet Bannister. Bannister was the Assistant to the Assistant Manager, so that mean that he had to do all the work. But he still had time to come and chat down Elmina though. And while Elmina ain't like he as much as she like James, she did still like he enough to take on, and she realize too the old people woulda like he better too.

And man, you should see the first evening when Elmina drive up in the car with this good looking young man at the wheel all dress to death in white – white suit, white shirt and collar and tie; and all the neighbors come pepping out through the jalousies and admiring the way he look and the other girls in the village jealous and saying that this time she must be work something 'pon he to get he to like she so. And Bannister gets outa the car and slam the door hard and gone 'round to the other side and open the door for Elmina and Elmina gets out with she head straight in the air and goes inside the house with Bannister. And Zedekiah comes out and starts shaking hands and laughing and talking good good good.

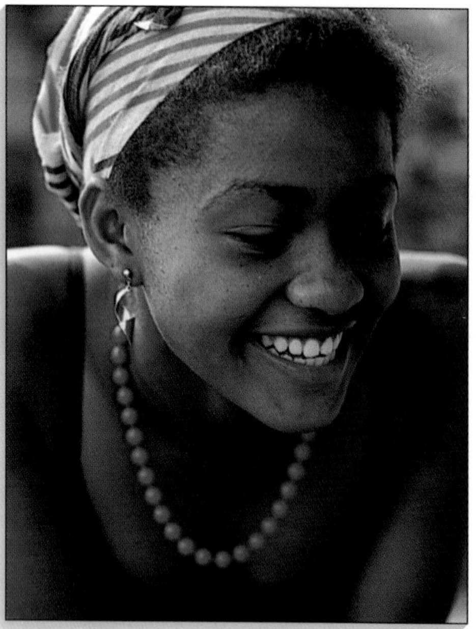

Then out runs the grandmother talking with the best words she could find and says to Bannister that he must excuse the condition that the house in.

So they sit down and talk a lot of small talk and then Bannister ask the grandparents if he could take out Elmina from time to time, and the grandfather say yes, of course, sure, that he know a decent man when he sees one, and that he certainly does admire the way Elmina does pick her friends.

After that Bannister make a date to go to the drive-in theater with Elmina, and then he left. So that is how the two of them start going 'round together. Elmina living it up now, every Saturday night she feting and coming home early in the morning, and she always going this place and that place with this Bannister fellow. And the grandparents watching with interest, wondering when the time going come that Bannister going mek the move to get married to Elmina.

Now Elmina was getting through all right: she

dressing up in a lot of nice clothes and looking real sweet, and though she ain't got time to see James as often as she use to do in the past, sometimes 'pon a night when the old people think that she out with Bannister, she really gone off somewhere to meet James. And is true that she like James more, but she like Bannister too, and it looking like if Bannister is the man most likely to succeed in the long run. James feeling bad 'bout it, and asking she why she don't just stick to he and wait till he get enough money to married she, but she was so excited with the new life she living for the first time that she can't stick to James alone and leave out all o' that fun.

"And is true that she like James more, but she like Bannister too, and it looking like if Bannister is the man most likely to succeed in the long run…"

But some trouble start up that make a big scandal in the village, and all the people say, I tell yuh so, I know it would happen. And the grandparents feeling shame and crying and thing. "Where that man Bannister? What he doing 'bout it?" Zedekiah ups and asks, "Elmina, you know where he live? Looka, come lewwe go up there right now."

"When he coming back?"

So the two of them ketch the bus and gone up by where Bannister live and knock 'pon the door and wait. And then a woman open the door and says she is Mrs Bannister, and that Mr Bannister ain't home. And the old man ask, "Well, when he coming back? I got something important to tell him."

"I ain't certain," the woman say.

"Where he gone?"

"Well, this morning he ketch the plane for South America, where he gone to see after opening a business, and after that he got to go up to Canada to see he uncle, and after that he got to go to Norway and Czechoslovakia and I think he might got to pass through Jerusalem too. So I really can't say when he coming back."

"Well when you see him again, tell him I want to see him," the old man say. That was all he coulda say, too.

So then they gone back home and the old people quarreling and saying that they did know all the time that Bannister wasn't so good but that they was hoping that he woulda behave heself like a gentleman. And they turning on 'pon Elmina and asking she why she couldn't keep sheself to sheself and things like that, and saying that they got five minds to put she outa the house.

So one morning Elmina get up and went straight to where James living and say that she staying there, that she ain't going back home, that she fed up with everything there. And James straightway gone and start taking out marriage license and thing and next thing you know they married and living in the house that James build.

And a lot of people was saying that James is a idiot to act that way after she stop seeing him for such a long time, but they didn't know what was going on for after the baby born and they look at it, it did so ugly, that everybody realize that Elmina had marry the right boyfriend after all. ❑

– from *Bim 52* (1971)

IS TIME
TO EATAH
OOK MEAL
AT Th
VIZZLE

BAJAN DIALECT: A GOOD COOK-UP

Born of a cultural collision between the Africans and English, Bajan dialect is a linguistic "cohobblopot" (spicy stew) cooked into a rich form of expression

There is a Barbadian saying that goes: "When yuh poor, yuh very speech poor" referring to the pervasive effects of poverty. However, those who seek to confer this philosophy on Bajan dialect, the local language of Barbadians, speak an untruth. No language is poor if it constitutes the joys, hopes and pains of a people and descants them in tune to the rhythmic ebb and flow of their fortunes.

Such is the nature of Bajan dialect, born in the 17th century, the offspring of a prodigal union between the English of Great Britain and West African languages of the Niger-Congo family. Far from being poor, Bajan dialect is a veritable linguistic treasure.

In its infancy, Bajan combined features from both languages: English words were pronounced with African intonations; African expressions were translated literally into English. But the African elements of Bajan's formative years have slowly eroded; now the English influence is much stronger. But, of course, English has developed from a vat of languages bequeathed by the invaders of the past so Bajan can be aptly described as a linguistic cohobblopot, a culinary term in dialect for a spicy dish of vegetables and meats.

The Nation Language

It is said that when a hybrid language remains exposed to the influences of one parent, it grows more like that parent and less like the other. When a hybrid and parent language exist side by side, the hybrid is often unfairly seen as inferior, the tongue of the illiterate, a medium for jokes and light matter. The parent is considered the language of the church, the school and the judiciary – the language of the learned, the one more suitable for any and all serious subject matter.

Bajan, like other dialects in the Caribbean, has been treated as a "Cinderella language", restricted to the kitchen and the back yard. But as in the fairytale, helpers appeared as writers, poets and linguists, eager to wipe out the image of Bajan as a "broken" version of English. They showed that, like Cinderella, Bajan had its own beauty, seen in the variations of its stress patterns, pitch levels and internal structures which combine to shape a language that is neither English nor African but is both without being inferior to either. Now instead of being stigmatised as non-standard English, Bajan dialect enjoys the celebrated position of Nation Language, a term favoured by local griot, historian, poet and writer Kamau Brathwaite.

PRECEDING PAGES: "Tekkin' you' time en laziness."
LEFT: Time for a "home-cook" meal at the Swizzle Inn.
RIGHT: "News don' lack a carrier."

Crash course in Bajan

Overall, Bajan dialect is varied and mostly unpredictable in its precarious twists and turns, offering an exhilarating trip across a uniquely delightful speech community. But some have said it is limited and can't be used to express the full range of a person's life experience. In defence, university lecturer and poet, the late Bruce St John, wrote:

We language limit?
Who language en limit?
Evah language
Like a big pot o' Bajan soup:
T'ree dumplin', two eddo,
One beet, two carrot,
Piece o' pig tail, piece o' beef
Pinch o' salt, dus' o' pepper
And don' fuget okra
To add to de flavour.
Boil up, cook up, eat up
An' yuh still wan' rice…

Let's use this poem for a crash course in Bajan dialect and as an insight into its evolution. Line one translates as: Is our language limited? In Bajan, unlike English, one form of a pronoun may be used as subject, object and possessive (e.g. we say; we know; tell we now; it is we book). One African connection can be found in Yoruba where the word *emi* means I or me. Bajan does not invert the subject and the verb when forming this type of question, so by raising the voice at the end indicates that a question is being asked.

Verbs do not have different endings to denote the past even as adjectives (He just finish; I like my meat cook), and there is no auxiliary with verbs (she intelligent; somebody coming). Again this could indicate Yoruban ancestry, as *o lewa* means literally, she beautiful.

In line two "en" means is not and "who" is whose. The numbers "two" and "t'ree" make plurality obvious in lines six and seven, so no final "s" is needed on dumplin' (dumpling) or eddo, although it is used by some.

In line nine "a dust" refers to a small unmeasured portion of any powdered substance. Line 12 gives an insight into the subtle differences between English and Bajan: "boil up" means "bring to the boil". However, you can also hear "boil down" used for boiling away liquid from

African Heritage

African links are ever-present in the Bajan dialect – in the verb structure which reflects patterns of some West African languages; in the Bajan speaker's pronunciation of English words according to an African syllable structure and in derivations of recognisable African words. A stubborn child may be called "hard-ears" or "hard-mout(h)", both direct translations from West African expressions; "cry water" is used for tears; being too "big eye" means greedy, and being "hard-headed" means slow to learn. A Bajan may also speak of getting "jook" (stabbed, poked), using a variant of the term *jukka* in Fulani, spoken in Senegal and Burkina Faso.

sauces and broths to thicken them. "To Cook up" means to mix all of the items together.

I does sing

There is no "th" sound in Bajan so wherever an English word has this sound, the Bajan speaker has either f, v, t, d, z or k, for example breathe becomes "breav"; with becomes "wit", "wid" or "wif"; think is "t'ink" and the is "de".

The verb system of Bajan is different from that of English too. For instance, the present tense is used even when speaking about past action – "He run home last night," instead of "He ran home." Again one African example is enough to make the link here. In Yoruba, *mo o l'ana* translates literally to "I go yesterday".

Present time is also expressed differently in dialect. For example, one may say in English: "The dancer casts strange shadows as she moves to the beat of the drum." But a Bajan would express the immediacy of the action by saying: "De dance' t'rowing strange shadows all de time she movin' to de beat o' de drum."

The expression of habitual action also varies between the two languages. Where the English speaker uses the simple present tense, the Bajan uses the verb "does" to show habit and it does not alter with the subject. So instead of "I sing, he dances and they play the steel pan", you would hear: "I does sing; he does dance and dem does play de steel pan."

ACCENT ON VARIETY

Each of the 11 parishes on this tiny island has its own regional accent, which also varies across the classes. Recently, an American twang has been detected, too.

Even though most Bajan words are English, sometimes their meanings are quite different. For instance, in Bajan, to be "ignorant" is to be mean or very aggressive, not stupid. A woman has "gone cross" or is "pushing bread cart" when she is pregnant.

During your stay, you may be asked whether you've had a "sea-bath" (swim) yet. If you're both going into town, "all two" are going. And if you've gained weight since your last trip, your Bajan friends won't hesitate to tell you that you've "put on some size".

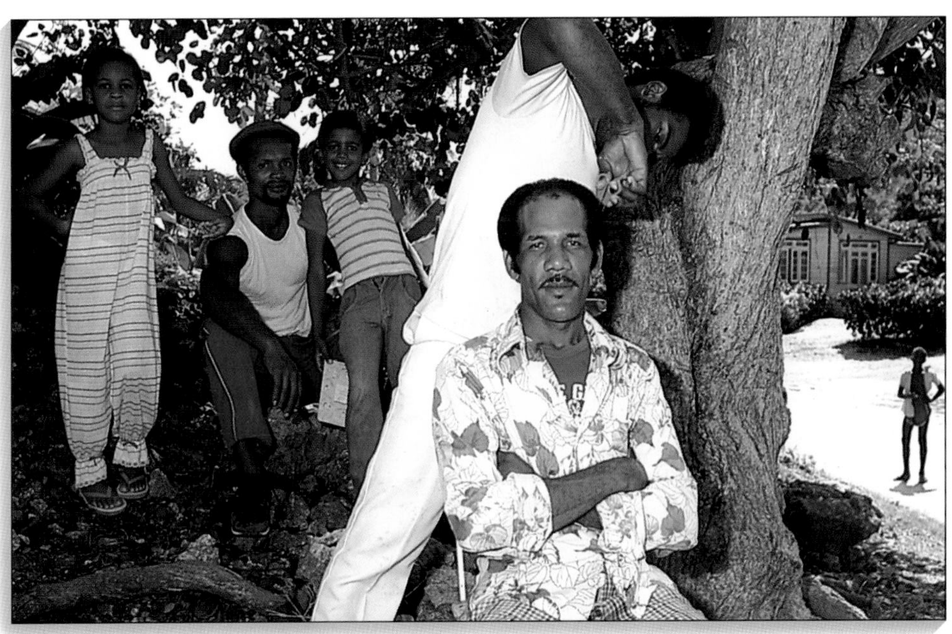

LEFT: "Every bush is a man". **ABOVE:** "Head en mek for hat only" as two of the many Bajan proverbs go.

Bajan words of wisdom

The surprising turn of phrase and the semantic extension of English words are seen more clearly in the local idioms and proverbs in which old Bajans wrap their folk wisdom to pass on to the youth, like a philosophical baton in an ancestral relay. Unfortunately, the baton is not being passed on quickly enough to many young people, especially those in the city and it is often dropped by the so-called educated.

Below is a sample of sayings which aim to provide guidance in all aspects of life. Grounded in the familiar setting of domesticity, these sayings, often delivered with a caustic wit, evoke laughter, offer advice based on experience and reveal an insightful grasp of universal truths:

REKINDLED PASSION

"Ole stick o' fire don' tek long to ketch back up." (An old love affair can become passionate again.) But "Egg have no right at rockstone dance." (Avoid situations you know you can't cope with.)

- "One bellyful don' fatten a hog."
Success comes after sustained effort.

- "Handsom' don' put in de pot."
Being physically beautiful does not offer any practical benefits.
- "Goat head everyday is better dan cow head only on Sunday."
It is better to be given good treatment every day than excellent treatment occasionally.
- "If greedy wait, hot will cool."
If you wait patiently, you will get what you want.
- "Every bush is a man."
Be careful where you talk; someone might hear.
- "An eyeful en no bellyful."
The pleasure derived from seeing something does not match the satisfaction of owning it (Often said to a man who is admiring a woman).
- "Cut pumpkin can't keep."
Once virginity has been lost, it's not easy abstain from sexual activity.
- "One-smart dead at two-smart door."
There is always someone who is cleverer or more devious than you.
- "De more yuh peep, de less yuh see."
People who try to find out things by underhand means usually remain ignorant, either because they miss the obvious or because others deliberately mislead them.
- "Every skin teet' en a laugh."
Outward signs of friendliness are not always genuine.
- "Head en mek fo' hat only."
Always use your common sense.
- " Mek sure better dan cock sure."
It is better to be sure about something than to assume all is well and be disappointed.
- "Yuh can' wan' it in de glass an' de bottle too."
You cannot have it both ways.
- "Yuh spit up in the air and le' it come back down in yuh face."
You are doing the same thing which you have always denounced.
- "The higher up a monkey climb de more 'e show 'e tail."
The more successful people become, the more they tend to show their true nature.
- "News don' lack a carrier."
There will always be some one to pass on gossip.
- "Tekking you' time en laziness."
Much can be achieved by taking one's time.
- "Pretty pretty t'ings does fool li'l children."
Superficial things impress naïve people.
- "Yuh does rust out before yuh wuk out."
More harm is done to yourself from laziness than as a result of hard work.
- "Talk does mek talk."
There can be no quarrel if you remain silent.
- "Coconut don' grow 'pon pumpkin vine."
Children inherit their parents' traits.
- "Fishermen never say dat de fish stink."
People never give bad reports about themselves even if they are true.
- "High wind know where old house is."
People will take advantage of the weak.
- "Manure can't mek ole plant grow."

No remedy, no matter how good it is, can help a hopeless situation.

● "Trouble don't set up like rain."
Misfortune comes unexpectedly.

● "Yuh cud hide and buy ground but yuh can' hide and wuk it."
It is impossible to hide all of one's actions.

● "Better fish in de sea dan wha' ketch a'ready."
You can always find someone better than the one you have at present. (This is said to anyone who thinks he/she is indispensable).

● "Cat luck en, dog luck."
One person might get away with the type of behaviour for which another might be chastised.

Elegant trappings look out of place on those who are not used to them.

● "De las' calf kill de cow."
Taking the same risks repeatedly and getting away with it does not mean that you will not eventually get into serious trouble

● "Cou-cou never done till de pot tu'n down."
An issue is never settled until there are actual signs of finality.

● "It is not de horn dat hurt' but de echo."
It's not your partner being unfaithful that hurts, but the gossip.

All English speaking visitors to Barbados, whatever their dialect, are advised to "mind" (consider carefully) how they interpret the words they think they have in common with Bajans. But, at the same time, do take the opportunity to savour the symmetry of the Bajan language, its unusual contours of thought and unique turns of phrase.

Since language is the fabric of thought, be sure to take time to explore the lively patterns, to see the cloth this hybrid language has fashioned and find pleasure between the woof and warp of its logic. With an open mind and an attentive ear, any visitor to these shores can become familiar enough with the local lingo to leave quoting the final line of Bruce St John's poem: "*De cook-up is a beautiful soun'*." ❑

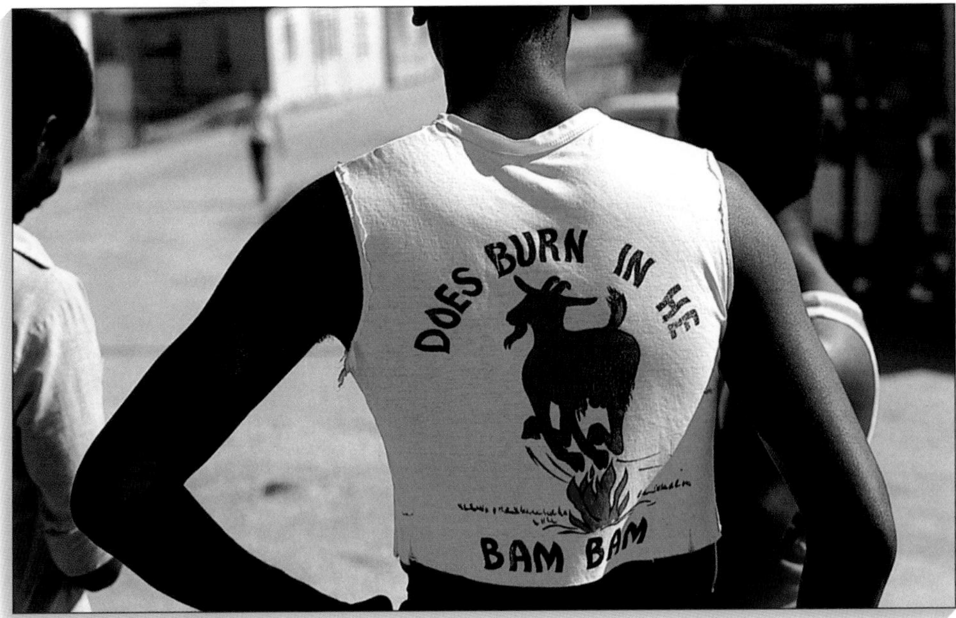

● "Every pig got 'e Saturday."
Everyone has a day of retribution.

● "Hungry mek cat eat salt."
Hardship causes people to do things which they would not normally do.

● "Two smart rats can' live in de same hole."
Two tricksters can't live peacefully together.

● "When hog dance, look fuh nuff rain."
Unusual signs often precede unusual events.

● "De new broom does sweep cleaner but de old broom know de corners."
Both the new and old have their advantages.

● "Gold teet don' suit hog mout'."

LEFT and ABOVE: some helpful advice.

STREET BEATS, STAGE TREATS

There is much more to the performing arts in Barbados than flaming limbo and steel bands playing "Yellow Bird" beside the pool

If all the world's a stage, everyday life in Barbados is high theatre, from the musical pulses and pitches of community gossip to the rhythmic swaying of hips as the calypso beat fills the street during an island festival.

There is much more to the performing arts of Barbados than flaming limbo and a poolside steel band playing *Yellow Bird*. The many local dance performances, plays, concerts and annual festivals are now marketed for visitors. Once you land in Barbados, however, you won't have to go far to experience the theatrical. A walk down a busy street is a drama in itself. Listen to the rhythm and use of the language. The sounds of words, it becomes apparent, are as important as the words themselves; double meanings; expressive folk sayings, stories told with much gesturing and emotion are entertainment without an admission charge. The repartee and haggling at an open-air market easily make co-stars of vendor and customer.

Dancing in the streets

Music is everywhere: at parties, at church, on the mini-buses, at home. Portable radios take music to the streets and to work. It is said that Bajans dance before they can walk – watch any toddler, barely able to walk, hoist himself up, grasp his mother's knee, and stand and sway to the sounds of calypso.

Out of this verve come the performing arts infused with spontaneity and energy. Little wonder that a strong ballet tradition doesn't exist in Barbados, and that most island dance companies are interpretative, modern, ethnic.

From the earliest days of colonialism, there were two dance traditions on Barbados: the more formalised European dances of the planters, and the energetic, spontaneous dances of the slaves, rooted in West African tradition. Both groups loved to dance. Originally, the plantation owners tried to prohibit slaves from gathering to play music and to dance, out of fear that they would organise rebellion. However, the owners quickly realised that the slaves worked more productively if often allowed to enjoy their own form of dance and music.

They "hollered and bellowed in an Antique manner, as if they were all madd," wrote an early observer. "Some dancers would tie rattles to their legs and wrists; others looked on, clapping their hands and chanting 'Alla, Alla!'" A description from 1750 commented on the use of the entire body, which is typical of West African dance, observing that "their bodies are strongly agitated by skipping, leaping and turning around".

An account from 1880 said that "the twistings of the body seem to constitute the supreme excellence of the dance," and went on to describe the dancers' "indecent, wanton, and lascivious" movements in great detail. Today, the West African tradition of pelvic gyrations is still seen in West Indian dance. Bajans call it

PRECEDING PAGES: swirling petticoats.
LEFT: performer at Crop Over.
RIGHT: African rhythms.

"wukkin' up", and you're most likely to see it on dance floors in the nightclubs, on the streets during festivals, in fact, anywhere you hear the infectious sounds of soca and calypso.

Modern dance

Modern dance on Barbados, both abstract and expressionistic, began as a rejection of formalism and sterility. Mary Stevens, founder of the Barbados Dance Theatre Company, introduced it to the island in 1968. One of the island's leading dance groups, the BDTC still conducts training classes, promotes community spirit through dance, and develops greater interest among young people in cultural affairs – a worthy mandate.

Other groups, including Rotana Dance Movement, Dance Experience, Country Theatre Workshop, Tyrona Contemporary Theatre and Youth Creative Expressions (which spawned New Generation and Seitu – Nigerian for artist), have played similar roles.

Of course, no brief history of the performing arts in Barbados would be complete without mention of Yoruba Yard. One of the pioneers in interpretative dance, Yoruba Yard was based in a small theatre in the suburbs of Bridgetown. During the late 1960s it housed a broadly based cultural organisation founded by Elton "Elombe" Mottley, who later became director of the National Cultural Foundation (*see page 110*). Yoruba Yard explored Bajan folk material and researched the island's Caribbean and African past for use in productions. Although financial problems forced the theatre to close, the Yoruba Dancers continued to flourish as a semi-professional group. Nowadays, such traditions are carried on by groups and schools such as Dancin' Africa, Dance Nationale Afrique, Pinelands Creative Workshop, Dance Strides Barbados and Louise Woodbine Dance Academy, and they often perform at dinner shows organised by hotels.

African Inspiration

White witnesses of the African-inspired dances and rituals revealed both fascination and astonishment: after all, they had never seen anything quite like it – they were ballroom dancers.

The first plays

Theatre in Barbados began in the late 1600s, with plantation improvisations called "tea meetings" in which individuals recited passages, presented slapstick skits and gave spontaneous speeches. Just as spontaneous were the alfresco performances given by troupes of actors who pulled into port and presented plays in the shadow of their ships.

The first mention of theatre in Barbados occurred in, of all things, the diary of former US president George Washington. He noted that, on 15 December 1751 when he was staying on the island, he attended a presentation of *The Tragedy of George Barnwell.*

By 1783, a theatre called the Patagonian, complete with boxes, was presenting English plays, including performances of Shakespeare. An advertised billing of *Richard III* notes that the Duchess of York was played by "Miss McIntosh (being her first appearance)" and also included "on the programme, Lady Pentwenzle from Blow-Bladder-Street". The Patagonian Theatre soon received swift competition from another, referred to as the "New Theatre". Comedies and pantomimes drew crowds exclusively from the plantocracy and a newspaper review noted that "no profligate or abandoned women were admitted".

The Green Room Players

Until the early 20th century, the small theatre groups in Barbados were exclusively white. Then, after World War II, the Green Room Players emerged, and began to stage productions of local and international plays. From light farce to serious drama, the Green Room Players' extensive and efficiently produced offerings have pleased several generations of Barbadians and visitors. Among their popular comedies, playing to packed audiences, are *Let's Go Bajan*, *Move Over Mrs Markham*, *Absurd Person Singular*, and *See How They Run*. Their 1978 production of *Colly!* was a celebration of the work of the late Frank Collymore (*see page 108*), a distinguished Barbadian writer of mime, dance, song and poetry.

In the late 1960s, the now defunct Barbados Writers Workshop produced several West Indian plays under the directorship of Earl Warner. Then the non-profit Stage One Theatre Productions, established in 1977, carried on the tradition of producing works relevant to the Caribbean experience aiming to foster greater interest and participation in the theatre.

One of Stage One's most successful productions was Errol John's warm and powerful play *Moon on a Rainbow Shawl*, set in a Caribbean back yard in the late 1940s, which was suffused with raw energy and was the winner in a 1957 competition sponsored by a British newspaper.

Today, Stage One continues to help develop theatre arts in Barbados by organising the annual Stage One Playwriting Contest. The first

LEFT: putting on a show.
ABOVE: Laff It Off Inc. at Queen's Park.

was held in 1998 as part of the company's 21st anniversary celebrations.

Laff it Off

Folk and popular theatre have been developed through the winning efforts of newer island groups. For example, the work of Community Theatre Productions (now Laff It Off Inc.) grew out of a demand for entertaining Barbadian theatre. The company's first event, an improvised folk comedy called *Laff it Off*, premiered in 1984 to packed houses at Queen's Park Theatre, now named The Daphne Joseph-Hackett Theatre – after the Queen's College teacher (1915–88) who was an inspirational force behind the island's theatre movement – still delights Bajans and visitors every year with its amusing, satirical explorations of the everyday goings-on in society. The action takes place in a village rum shop, called "The Nook and Cranny Bar" which is transformed from bar to courtroom to church to parliament to cultural centre to television studio.

Productions such as *Pampalam* (penned and produced by popular columnist and businesswoman Jeanette Layne-Clark) and *Bajan Bus Stop* feature social and political comment in witty sketches and songs. Quite popular with locals, such productions have also found audiences in Britain, Canada and the US.

Since the early 1990s, there has been a decline in the number of plays staged yearly in Barbados. Upon close inspection, however, one can find dramatic flair and a strong oral tradition manifested during the harvest, Christmas and Easter plays and pageants of the island's many churches and schools.

Heading in the right direction is the expansive WWB Productions, a company formed in 1986 with a "developmental focus" encompassing the whole of the Caribbean. A registered charity, WWB has hosted a number of theatre workshops, such as acting, mime,

Drama at Holders House

If you'd like to experience opera Bajan-style, head for the hills. That is, Holders Hill, St James, for The Holders Opera Season held in the grounds of Holders House. Founded in 1993 by John and Wendy Kidd, who also set up the Holders Performing Arts Centre, this major production is a unique blend of classical opera, local music and theatre. The cast has included performers such as the world famous Luciano Pavarotti and Lesley Garrett and Bajan celebrities John King and The Mighty Gabby. The productions, one of which is the home-grown opera *Inkle and Yarico*, have received international critical acclaim. For details, call 432-6385.

directing and the use of indigenous materials in costume and set design, inviting instructors from Jamaica and Trinidad. WWB is committed to learning from and with other Caribbean islands by swapping actors, producing work from around the region, inviting neighbouring theatre companies to produce plays in Barbados and vice versa.

DRIVING FORCE

Daphne Joseph-Hackett (1915–88) was a driving force behind the development of the island's theatre movement in the 1970s and 1980s and organised drama workshops throughout the Caribbean.

With no membership, casts are picked from an ever-increasing pool of talent on the island and around the Caribbean.

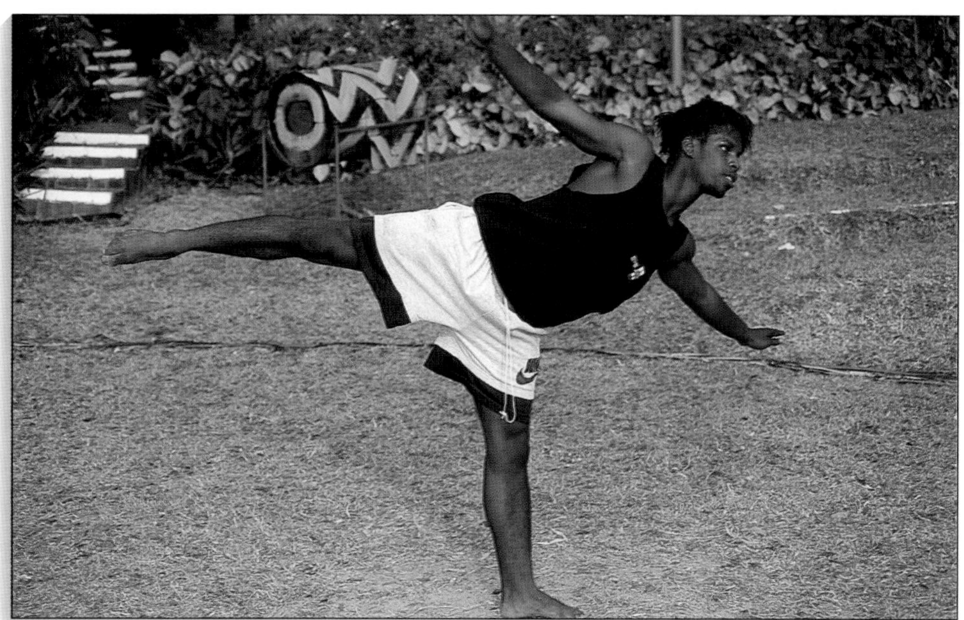

Into the millennium

With the appointment of a Cultural Officer for Theatre Arts in1998, the NCF aims to channel energy into developing drama in Barbados. Already a Theatre Arts curriculum is being drawn up with teachers to be used in all schools and colleges. Also the formation of a National Theatre Company is on the cards to be based at the soon-to-be refurbished Empire Theatre in Bridgetown. The aim, says Cultural Officer Kofi Akobi, a founding member of the Barbados National Theatre Workshop in the 1970s alongside Daphne Joseph-Hackett, is to produce new generations "who understand the importance of theatre in our unique culture. Theatre is also important in the self-development of our young people who are under pressure to conform to North American and other cultures."

LEFT: acting out the past.
ABOVE: warming up for the Holders Season.

Performance poets

While not a theatre group, VOICES: Barbados Writers Collective (*see page 109*) contributes greatly to the local drama scene by providing the arena for live, provocative performances of poems and prose from guests and members each month at the Barbados Museum.

Poetry combined with music is also big on the local arts scene today and has received much attention since the 1970s, mainly due to rhythm poets Adisa Andwele, Winston Farrell and Ricky Parris. Their strongly syncopated styles have evolved into the offerings of "performance poets" who can be heard during Interludes: Poetry and Jazz, a six-week poetry and music series held at The Waterfront Café in Bridgetown during April and October.

For details of these events and many others, it's best to look regularly in the local press.

Weekend entertainment abounds in Barbados. Both *The Nation* and *Advocate* newspapers feature Entertainment and Arts sections. And the weekend editions are packed with what's on, from concerts featuring local, regional and international artists to dances generally known as fetes, brams, bashments or jump-ups.

Dinner shows are tailor-made for visitors, often presenting entertaining demonstrations of Bajan history and mores in a colourful extravaganza. *1627 And All That* portrays the folk culture of the island in music and dance at the Barbados Museum on Thursdays. And many of the hotels present cabaret acts and contemporary dinner shows that are open to non-residents, for instance *Skitsomania* is a farcical production, featuring a handful of the island's most promising young actors, and *Tim's and Anne's Wedding* has an experienced and talented cast.

FOLLOW THE BAGPIPES

At the Celtic Festival in May you can attend a Tartan Ball, Haggis Night, Highland Games, a rugby tournament and a Celtic wedding when couples really get married.

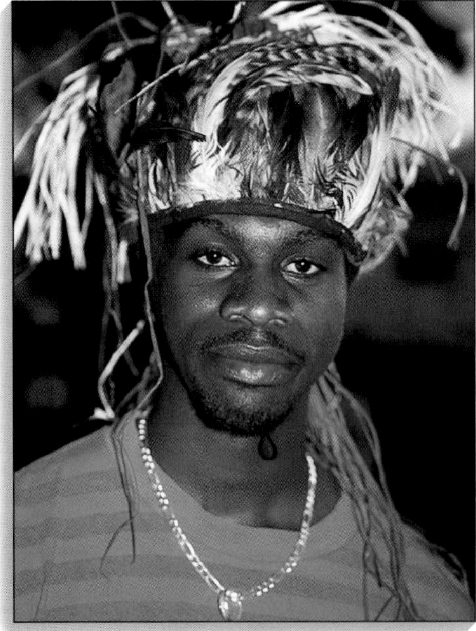

Living theatre

Festivals are living theatre and Barbados offers many of these special celebrations and events. The Barbados Tourism Authority (BTA), recognising the appeal of culture and entertainment to those visiting the island now markets some of these events as The Magnificent Seven, although in fact there are more. The NCF contributes to all of them, even the ones produced by other organisations. Here we take a look at a few which, though marketed locally and internationally, through glossy ads and trendy TV commercials, have lost none of their "homespun" charm.

The dynamism of Bajan culture radiates out of these cultural extravaganzas. For example, the Holetown Festival, held in February, commemorates the landing of the first European settlers in 1627. Now in its 24th year, the week-long festival is a cultural potpourri of music, literary readings, beauty contests, dancing, parades, "practical art" displays and stalls.

Oistins Festival coincides with the Easter weekend and celebrates the fishing community of the town and its contribution to the island's development. For three days, the unofficial capital of the South Coast is brought to more colourful life as people converge there to enjoy music, dancing, fish-boning competitions, a Coast Guard Exhibition, food stalls, arts and crafts, singing and road races.

Those of Celtic origin can make merry at the Celtic Festival scheduled for the end of May. Conceived in 1995 the festival commemorates the role played by Celts in the development of the island.

Street revellers

And in the summer there's Crop Over (*see pages 134–35*), the island's largest festival and produced by the NCF – a month-long celebration inspired by what was once the island's main economic event, the harvesting of the sugar cane crop. Today, Barbadians from all over the world return to dance in the streets, sing with the calypsonians and dress up in magnificent creations.

At the NCF's National Independence Festival of the Creative Arts (NIFCA), held in November as part of the island's Independence Day celebrations, talented artists of every genre compete for gold, silver and bronze medals and lucrative awards for excellence. ❑

LEFT: an extravagant attire.
RIGHT: making music at Holetown Festival.

WUKKIN' UP IN THE STREETS

Everyone loves a street festival and in Barbados they've got it down to a fine art with their spectacular parades full of music and colour

Crop Over, De Congaline Carnival and Independence Day are the three main festivals when The Rock seems to vibrate with the music and dancing in the streets, as thousands of Barbadians and visitors join in the merry-making. Gyrating, sunsoaked revellers follow the parades of magnificent costumes swaying to the pulsating calypso rhythms, and it's impossible not to be swept along with the sweet and infectious beat. There is plenty of wukkin' up to be done too at the Holetown Festival in February and Oistins Fish Festival at Easter.

CROP OVER FEVER

The most colourful event in the Barbadian calendar, Crop Over starts in June with the calypso competitions and climaxes on the first Monday in August at the Kadooment Day parade. Traditionally a celebration of the end of the sugar cane harvest, this vibrant festival is an integral part of the island's culture.

The ceremonial delivery of the last canes by a brightly, decorated donkey and cart to a designated plantation, heralds the official opening and from then on calypso music reigns supreme at such events as the Decorated Cart Parade and Cohobblopot, when costumed kings and queens vie for the supreme Crop Over title, until the grand finale on Kadooment Day.

▷ **A BIRD'S-EYE VIEW**
Stilt walkers are atraditional feature at festival time, skillfully dancing and performing acrobatic stunts alongside the parades.

△ **CONGALINE**
Thousands of dancing revellers match up their colours in a T-shirt parade, the highlight of De Congaline Carnival.

◁ **SOLEMN NOTES**
On Independence Day the mounted police don their ceremonial attire and join the parade before the dignitaries.

◁ **GRAND FINALE**
On Kadooment Day, the judging starts at 8am and then the costumed masqueraders take to the streets, jumping up until the final fireworks display.

△ **BURN MR HARDING!**
The burning of this effigy, symbolises a hope for an end to hard times, a ritual that has survived from the original crop over festival.

PIC O' DE CROP: A CALYPSO CROWN

The Pic-o-de-Crop calypso competition plays a major role in Crop Over bringing the best out of songwriters, arrangers and calypsonians all aiming for the coveted Calypso Monarch title.

Social commentary is the order of the day and it is not unusual to hear songs attacking the politicians or commenting on the state of the economy.

Tents, or venues, are set up around the island throughout the season where more than 100 calypsonians are judged in the first round. Then 18 go on to the semi-finals when seven are picked to compete against the reigning monarch on finals night.

Seldom does this competition not end in controversy, as the debate rages for days afterwards about who should have been the Pic o' de Crop. Ironically this all adds to the excitement of the competition and fans cannot wait for another Crop Over season to begin.

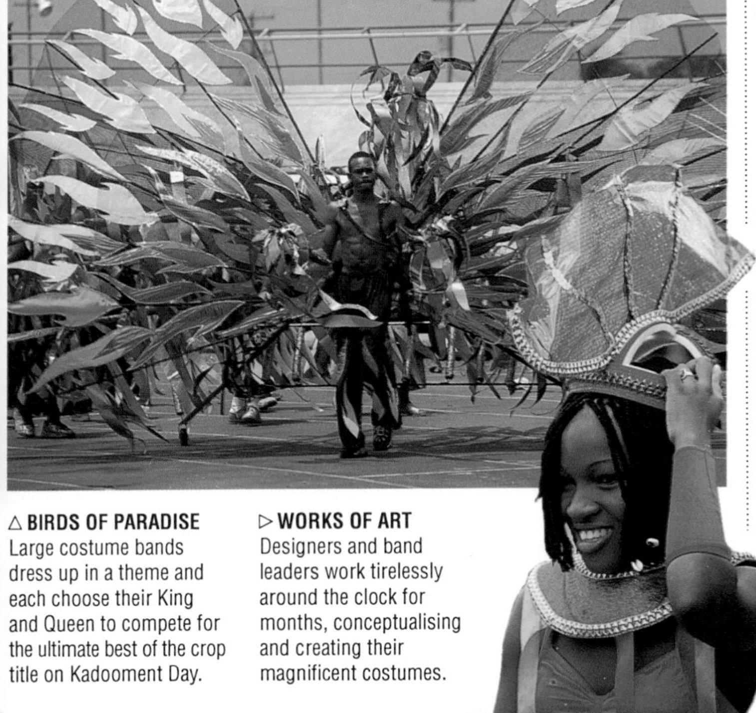

△ **BIRDS OF PARADISE**
Large costume bands dress up in a theme and each choose their King and Queen to compete for the ultimate best of the crop title on Kadooment Day.

▷ **WORKS OF ART**
Designers and band leaders work tirelessly around the clock for months, conceptualising and creating their magnificent costumes.

BARBAD
miles long and a

RIDING DE RIDDIM

The rhythms of Barbados have permeated the rest of the Caribbean in a Bajan invasion and the island today is in a constant state of musical expression

Pump me up with de music, pump me up
'cause you know I'm addicted,
Pump me up with de music, pump me up
start me whole body pumping
Pump me up with de music, pump me up
all me nerves just a jumping.
—*Pump me up*, Krosfyah (1995)

Hailed as the new music capital of the Caribbean, this little island has a musical feast to offer that is capable of satisfying the most insatiable appetite. Whether your tastes are for the sultry sounds of contemporary jazz, honey dipped reggae, delightful and inspiring gospel, rhythm and blues or calypso, with its younger offspring soca and its many hybrids, or classical opera, Barbados serves up a healthy portion of each genre.

Even so, it is practically impossible to sample the music of Barbados, or Bajan music as it is more commonly called, without first taking a look at calypso and its progeny soca – a blend of calypso and soul – for it is this rhythm, this artform, which has dominated the musical landscape for centuries – and still does.

Calypso gossip

The origins of calypso can be traced back to the 17th century, when the African slaves started arriving in the Caribbean, bringing with them two types of song – work songs and witty songs of commentary. The work songs, sung as they toiled beneath a bitter and unrelenting sun, were usually laments on the daily hardships they suffered and served as fuel to lift their weary spirits while helping to pass the time on the plantation. Surprisingly, the slaves rarely attacked their masters in song but created lyrics and tunes for the spread of local gossip.

By the end of the 1640s, there were almost as many Africans as there were British colonists. Barbados gained the name "Little England" as social and cultural life was patterned after and reflected that of the mother country England. Therefore, it was of no surprise that the colonists viewed the Africans' culture – their music, dance, dress, food, languages and religious rituals – as pagan and barbarous and sought to stifle any form of expression of it.

Rebellious drumbeats

In 1649, using the lively music of horns, drums and conch shells to rouse each other into battle, the indentured servants and Africans rebelled against the white landowners. After another uprising was preempted in 1675 a slave code was passed banning the beating of drums. And in 1688, when slaves outnumbered the colonists by three to one, a law was made stipulating that any drums or loud instruments that were discovered had to be burned.

In response, the slaves hid away their African customs, carefully preserving them to hand down to younger generations. Even after Emancipation in 1838, any vibrant expression

PRECEDING PAGES: dancing on the beach.
LEFT: getting into the rhythm.
RIGHT: feeling the beat.

of African culture was deemed as dangerous, hence indigenous music was forced to remain in a subterranean state and survived as folk music in the small villages and tenantries.

My calypso, is my weapon, and I will
use 'em,
'Cause it will liberate me one day of that
I am very sure...
Calypso, sweet sweet calypso...
—*Calypso*, Mighty Gabby (1982)

Issues of the day

In the early 20th century, the calypso that had developed in Trinidad began to influence Barbadian folk music and helped revive the calypso traditions. The songs from Trinidad influenced not only the melodies of Barbadian songs but more importantly, the lyrics.

Themes widened beyond gossip and scandal to include satire and social commentary, but it took many years before calypso became an influential vehicle of musical expression in Barbados. For, despite being free for over a century, in the 1930s black Barbadians were still in a state of mental slavery and were now preoccupied with achieving British standards of respectability. The more closely an individual approached the British in his manner and

The Mighty Gabby – A Calypso Great

The Mighty Gabby burst on to the calypso scene in 1965 when he was still a teenager and he has been there ever since, evolving with the times and remaining a trendsetter at the forefront of Bajan music.

He won his first Calypso Monarch crown in 1968 and then, after the competition had been incorporated into Crop Over in 1974, he won it again in 1976, 1977, 1985 and 1997, his winning songs speaking for the people. Gabby has become to Barbadian calypso what Bob Marley was to Jamaican reggae and what Sparrow means to Trinidad's calypso. Folksinger of the Year in 1977, 1978 and 1979 further illustrates the place Gabby has carved out for himself as a Bajan musician. And he's still at the top – albeit in a different guise.

In 1982 Gabby joined forces with international reggae star Eddie Grant who had set up a recording label in Barbados called Ice Music, and from then on he produced a string of hits reflecting the new forms of calypso, such as *Gimme Soca*, *Gisela*, *Pow Pow* and *Debra*, leading the way for Grant's Young Brigade (*see page 145*).

The *pièce de résistance* came in 1994 when Gabby recorded *Dr Cassandra* in the new Ringbang sound, focussing on the rhythm rather than the melody, which swept through the Caribbean and is still going strong…

speech, the more cultured he was considered. Thus the singing of calypso was frowned upon and early calypsonians were seen as jokers. They functioned like strolling minstrels, wandering from rum shop to rum shop and from street corner to street corner. Mothers would pull their children indoors and forbade their daughters to talk to them.

Yet calypso pioneers persisted and it was calypsonians like the Mighty Charmer, Mighty Sugar, Frank Taylor and DaCosta Allamby who kept the calypso embers aglow during the 1940s, 1950s and early 1960s. Still ironically, it was a group of white middle-class men called The Merrymen who gave Barbados calypso international recognition in the 1960s and early 1970s and kept Barbadian calypso alive.

By independence in 1966, a new crop of performers had entered the calypso arena, including the Mighty Gabby – who went on to become the high priest of calypso – and the charismatic Sir Don, Lord Summers and Lord Deighton, who like Lord Radio had the uncanny ability to compose and sing songs instantly on any topic to a live audience. Sadly, this art, called ex tempo or picong, is seldom heard today.

These men and others helped calypso reclaim its rightful position as the real music of the people and in 1968 and 1969 there were major calypso competitions which attracted wide public attention. Then as fate would have it, a new sound came on the scene and drove calypso underground once again.

DE BAG

In 1979 Stedson Wiltshire became Red Plastic Bag – De Bag or RPB for short – and hit the calypso scene, where he has stayed at the top as a "conscientious king of social commentary".

FAR LEFT: Red Plastic Bag, Mighty Gabby's rival.
LEFT: Calypsonians can sing their mind.
ABOVE: John King's lyrics are philosophical.

Spouge – a new sound

The new music was spouge. A cross between reggae and calypso, it was originated by Barbadian Jackie Opel who had started out in the early 1960s as a calypso singer. He migrated to Jamaica, where he was succesful as a ska and rock-steady singer, but when Jamaica started turning to the reggae sound in 1968, Opel returned home to introduce his calypso-reggae hybrid.

Opel and spouge dominated the Barbados music scene from 1969 to 1974, although Opel himself died in a car crash in early 1971. The Draytons Two, Sandpebbles, Troubadours, Blue Rhythms Combo and the Outfit all cut original spouge records, which filled the airwaves until the Crop Over Festival was revived in the 1970s and calypso really came back to life.

Calypso platform

Crop Over (*see pages 134–35*) not only provides calypsonians with the opportunity to showcase their talent but also to compete for cash and prizes at the Pic-O-De Crop, Tune-O-De Crop or Party Monarch competitions. Each year, during the months of June, July, and early August, calypso lovers flock to various venues called calypso tents to have their fill of social commentary from top calypsonians such as the Mighty Gabby, Red Plastic Bag, Romeo and John King who, to an infectious calypso rhythm, will sing about anything from the performance of the Government, the economy, or society as a whole.

Not surprisingly, this is not a time that politicians look forward to with relish, and general elections are timed to fall well out of the way of the acerbic songsters.

Some calypsoes are almost religious in nature, like the youthful Edwin's *Voice in my Head*, which speaks about God being present and communicating with him at all times. Others are philosophical like John King's *How Many More* about the pains of war.

POLITICIANS BEWARE!

General elections have been carefully timed not to be held around Crop Over time so as to avoid the acerbic tongues of the calypsonians.

Of course, comedy also plays a big role in the calypso tents and at the turn of the millennium it was the comedy group MADD who were getting all the laughs. Yet despite being funny, MADD are able to blend serious issues with their brand of comedy, getting the message across in their own unique and rhythmic manner.

The Bacchanal Time calypso tent, House of Soca, Conquerors and the Untouchables are but four of the many tents where calypso can be experienced at its very best.

New rhythms

With De Congaline Carnival in late April, dubbed "the World's Greatest Street Party" and Crop Over a few months later, it is of no wonder that party music reigns supreme. It is against this backdrop that calypso has undergone a major transformation.

The popularity of reggae in Barbados during the early 1990s encouraged calypso arrangers like Nicholas Brancker to experiment. By fusing calypso or soca with reggae, a new rhythm was created; raggasoca. This rhythm, characterised by its bouncy bass line, is faster than reggae but slower than up-tempo soca and took off in 1993 with Red Plastic Bag's mega-hit, *Ragga Ragga*, bringing the calypsonian from St Philip international fame.

The raggasoca groove

Indeed, it is the raggasoca groove which is more readily accepted in non-Caribbean territories and is favoured ahead of hardcore soca because of its slow to medium tempo rhythmic beat, lyrics and melodies.

Ringbang is yet another fusion of soca – soca and tuk. A lively, quick, pulsating, almost military rhythm, tuk has been around for well over a century. With the emphasis on the kettle drum and the bass drum, this music has been played at picnics and on public holidays and it is difficult to stop your foot from tapping when a tuk band strikes up.

However, there is still some controversy surrounding the ringbang beat for, on one side of the fence, we have the international recording singer and arranger Eddy Grant claiming to be the creator, while other Barbadians, none more vocal than Wayne "Poonka" Willock, a calypsonian and exponent of the tuk rhythm, argue that ringbang is simply another name for tuk. It's a debate that looks set to run and run.

Tuk or ringbang, whichever you choose to call it, this rhythm is now the most widely used beat in today's soca and is guaranteed to make you get up and dance or "wuk up" as the locals would say.

Today, thanks to the input of youthful arrangers and performers, Barbadian calypso and its many hybrids is alive and well. Gone are the days when a calypso singer was ostracised or when less indigenous music kept it underground. Calypso is an indispensable component of contemporary society, providing the people with a clear mirror image of the land they live in.

Calypso is my culture, like a river
it will always keeping flowing...
—*Calypso* Mighty Gabby (1982)

LEFT: a tuk band on parade.
ABOVE: Arturo Tappin giving his all.

Paint It Jazz

Jazz has been a growing musical force in Barbados since the cultural festival Carifesta was staged in Barbados in 1981. This was when the Caribbean jazz greats of today such as Barbadian saxophonist Arturo Tappin and bassist/keyboardist Nicholas Brancker came to the fore in the many jamming sessions staged throughout.

Now each year around early January, these indigenous artists take part in a kaleidoscope of colourful jazz at The Barbados Jazz Festival, also known as Paint It Jazz. Like a giant tropical magnet, Barbados has also been able

SAX PLAYER EXTRAORDINAIRE

Barbados-born jazz musician Arturo Tappin has been a prominent figure at jazz festivals around the Caribbean for many years performing his own, unique brand of reggae-jazz that he is famous for. The talented saxophonist, who names the legendary Grover Washington as his mentor, started his musical journey as a violinist, but soon discovered his love for the sax while still a teenager.

Drawn to jazz through an appreciation of classical music, Arturo soon recognised the role Caribbean rhythms could play in his music. His blend of reggae and jazz in his compositions and those of Bob Marley have been described as "awesome".

to attract the crème de la crème of the world's best jazz musicians to its shores since it started in 1994. From the soulful saxes of Kenny G and Grover Washington Jr, to the sensual vocals of Roberta Flack and Patti LaBelle. From the contrasting guitar styles of George Benson and Marcus Miller to fiery and energetic bands like Earth Wind and Fire and Spyro Gyra.

MUSIC IN EVERYTHING

The versatile steel pan was first discovered in Trinidad in the 1930s when someone realised the musical potential of a discarded oil drum.

Brancker, Tappin, fellow saxophonist Andre Woodvine and flautist Ronald Lashley are just a few of the top Caribbean artists that impress with their own brand of jazz – a blend of Caribbean rhythms like reggae and calypso – and yet are versatile enough to improvise and fuse these ethnic beats with the more contemporary styles of the great players of today.

Jazz has now infiltrated Barbados to the core and can be sampled daily at hotels, restaurants and pubs across the island.

Steel pan – a distinctive sound

To visitors the sound of a steel band plays a major part in the Caribbean picture, the gentle ringing tones of the steel pans seem to waft in the air from when you get off the plane – there's a band at the airport to greet every flight – to when you leave. Wherever you are in the tourist areas – hotel, restaurant, beach or pool – a steel band is sure to strike up, playing anything from classic calypsos to popular classics. And visitors love them.

But steel pan is not as popular with the locals and, to keep alive this artform that originated in the oilfields of Trinidad on empty oil drums, the instrument is being taught in schools. Now large high-quality steel orchestras are coming out of schools such as St Lucy's and the Garrison.

Spreading the word

Churches also contribute to the music of Barbados. Born of a fusion of African spiritual traditions and formal Christian worship, gospel music plays an important role in the lives of many church goers. For years, village churches around the island have been resounding to the vibrant rhythms of harmonious voices and tambourines as they joyfully praise the Lord.

At the end of the 1960s, Joseph Niles emerged from one such church in St Simons to become the pioneer of gospel music across the region and, with his unique voice and style, remains the "Godfather" to this day. Joined by Sister Marshall they have revolutionised the genre and brought it to a wider spectrum of people by fusing it with calypso (creating yet another hybrid called gospelypso), reggae and spouge. More importantly, they have inspired a new generation of bands such as Promise and top choirs such as the Nazarene Silvertones, along with Zoe and other solo artists.

In 1993, the first annual Gospelfest was staged in Barbados. And now, at the end of every May, top singers from North America and the Caribbean congregate for a showcase of foot stomping, hand clapping devotion. Stars such as Dr Bobby Jones, Jeff White and Ron Kenoly have all graced the Gospelfest stage.

Much like the Barbados Jazz Festival, Gospelfest affords local singers the opportunity to promote their talent and is a major event for gospel music lovers.

Calypso, reggae, jazz, soul, gospel, steel pan and even an international opera season at Holders House (*see page 130*) should leave few visitors' tastes uncatered for ❑

LEFT: songs of praise.

The Young Brigade

In 1995 "HE" announced his arrival on the local calypso scene by becoming the first person to capture all three major Crop Over music titles, winning the coveted Pic-O-De Crop calypso monarch, the Tune-O-De Crop title and the Party Monarch crown. In New York City 1998, "HE" was crowned Soca Monarch of the World, winning the title from a field of the world's finest soca artists.

In 1996 "SHE" became the first woman in the history of Barbados calypso to win the Tune-O-De Crop. In 1997, "SHE" convincingly captured both Tune-O-De Crop and Party Monarch titles.

"HE" is Edwin Yearwood, lead singer and songwriter for the band Krosfyah. "SHE" is the one-time demure teenager Alison Hinds, who is now the raunchy lead singer of the band Square One. Together they head The Young Brigade, signed to Eddy Grant's label Ice Music, and are the front runners of the fête or party scene.

It was not too long ago when the solo calypsonian ruled the soca arena. Today, bands like Krosfyah and Square One, led upfront by these youthful, energetic and dynamic performers, dominate the airwaves as well as the parties, nightclubs and concerts.

Aggressive lyrics and singing, complemented with catchy rhythm patterns and pounding bass lines, hallmark the success of Barbados' two premier soca bands, as they are able to produce hit song after hit.

Spectacular dancers, Edwin and Alison enjoy mass appeal throughout the Caribbean and, once on stage, when their respective bands break out into a favourite song of their many fans, the dance floor sizzles with gyrating bodies.

Notable Krosyah hits are, *Pump me up*, *Sweating*, *Peace Sign*, *Yardie* and *No Behaviour*. Square One has to its credit *Aye Aye Aye*, *Sugar*, *Faluma*, *Turn it Around* and *Raggamuffin*. In fact it was the hit *Raggamuffin*, a high energy party song, that gave Alison the nickname "Raggamuffin Queen".

Buoyed by the success of Yearwood and Krosfyah, along with Alison and Square One, several more young people and quite a few more bands have now jumped on the soca bandwagon, appealing to thousands of party animals.

It is noteworthy that the majority of The Young Brigade, including Alison and Edwin, are all graduates of *The Richard Stoute Teen Talent Show*, a junior talent TV show conceptualised and started by local singer Richard Stoute back in 1977. Thanks to the exposure gained from this show, such people as Terencia Coward, Rupert Clarke, Adrian Clarke, Rameses Brown as well as the full Square One band are now contributing successfully to calypso, soca and ringbang in Barbados.

Right: Alison Hinds – the Ragamuffin Queen.

Lil Rick, another member of The Young Brigade, is almost as popular as Edwin and Alison and is sometimes a featured guest on stage with both bands. His creative themes and picturesque use of the Bajan dialect as well as his penchant for "wukking up", has established him as a perennial favourite both on and off stage.

With stalwarts like Gabby, Red Plastic Bag and Romeo still around, as well as the annual advent of The Young Brigade, who seem enthusiastic and willing to learn, the future of Barbados calypso appears safe, sound and prepared for the new millennium. ❑

SOUVENIR

THE LAND OF FLYING FISH AND COU-COU

Bajan cooking is the result of a cultural heritage filtered down through the generations and full of delicious tastes

After a while off The Rock, the affectionate name for Barbados, a Bajan is always glad to come home to some "sweet food". The word sweet has nothing to do with sugar but it refers to the wonderful herbs and spices, a large variety of delicious vegetables, some of the best fish and pork in the world and the traditional creative talent of good Barbadian cooks.

The many influences which have shaped Barbadian life are perhaps nowhere as apparent as on the dinner table. Bajan cooking is a culinary hybrid, drawn from African and English traditions along with Amerindian, Spanish, French, Chinese, Indian, American and Caribbean cooking techniques.

Out of Africa

The Bajan national dish, cou-cou and salt fish is African inspired. Cou-cou is a cornmeal and okra pudding, a relative of a basic African foodstuff of crushed starchy vegetables called "foo-foo" in Ghana. It is ladled with gravy and served with a salt fish stew. Cou-cou in the making is a wonderful sight, and a challenge: much energy is put into the stirring, for if any lumps are allowed to form, it is considered a failure. The finished mixture is packed into a bowl and then turned out on to a plate. The centre of the mound is sunk with a spoon and a light gravy ladled into the centre and around the golden mound.

Also delicious with steamed flying fish, a tomato-and-onion butter sauce or a "sweet" Bajan beef stew, cou-cou can be made with breadfruit that has been boiled soft with herbs and salt meat, or potato, yam and even banana. Traditionally served on Fridays, many of the restaurants frequented by locals can be relied upon for a tasty one.

PRECEDING PAGES: a Bajan family meal.
LEFT: every Friday at Oistins, women cook fish Bajan-style over open fires in buckpots.
RIGHT: fruit for sale.

Bounty of the seas

Salt fish is a food originally imported to feed slaves as it was an inexpensive, easily stored source of protein. The slaves developed delicious amd inventive ways of preparing the

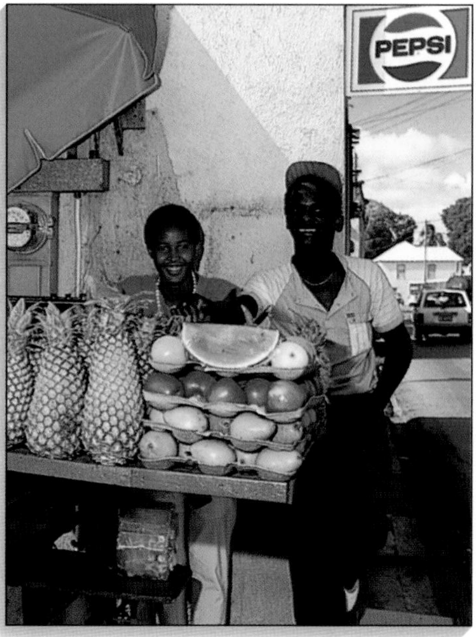

seemingly unappetising salted cod, such as fried salt fish balls and fish cakes which are now considered a delicacy and are served at parties and festive occasions.

Barbados is probably most famous for flying fish. These silvery blue specimens, 7–9 in (18–23 cm) long, abound in clear warm waters in many parts of the world. Yachtsmen and passengers on ships have often reported seeing schools of 50 to 1,000 flying fish suddenly leap from the water, and glide through the air for up to a distance of about 75 ft (23 metres).

The women of Oistins and other fishing villages have the intricate skill of de-boning them down to a fine art – perfected and passed on down the generations. Flying fish are most plentiful and cheap from December through June when they are caught in large quantities and stored in freezers. But they are undoubtedly best when bought fresh and boned in the fish markets.

Other fish on Bajan menus include barracuda, kingfish, snapper, tuna, chub and dolphin (dorado). You can buy these frozen from the supermarkets but it is far better to go to Oistins and buy a piece fresh from the fish market. There is usually someone there who will fillet your purchase beautifully with their razor-sharp cutlass for a few extra dollars. Unfortunately, there are not enough of the locally fished spiny lobsters to fill the demand but there are certain restaurants that have a regular supplier so it is worth checking around for.

The roe of the white sea egg, or urchin, caught on reefs around the island is a much sought after delicacy but they have also been over fished and the Government has declared a temporary ban on them. The yellow roe is picked from the shells and piled into other cleaned shells and then topped with a sea grape leaf rolled into a cone before being steamed. Small fish such as sprats, jacks and fray, usually seen in the mornings at markets, are skilfully

Where to Find Real Bajan Cooking

When in Rome... so the saying goes, so why not in Barbados? That is, eat authentic Bajan cooking. Many more people nowadays have become adventurous in their tastes and are willing to try new flavours and textures. The top restaurants are using local ingredients in their menus, but very few truly specialise in local dishes and, in the mainstream hotels, international cuisine seems to be the safest bet.

You haven't experienced the real Barbados until you have dined Bajan style and there are several restaurants around the island that serve authentic local food, such as Brown Sugar in Aquatic Gap, Waterfront Café on the Careenage and David's Place at St Lawrence Gap. All of the restaurants – Atlantis Hotel, Round House, Bonito Bar & Restaurant, Barclays Park and Edgewater Inn – along the wild and windy East Coast serve good local cooking, especially on a Sunday when they provide a Bajan Buffet. (It is essential to book – *see Travel Tips on pages 341–343*). Most hotel restaurants also do a weekly Bajan buffet but it is usually tempered to less adventurous tastes. However, with live steel band music and plenty of rum punch, a good time is had by all.

Oistins has become famous for its outdoor fish fry on Friday nights where you can watch the sizzling fish being cooked in large buckpots by the village women. And there is another more low-key fish fry by Six Men's Bay.

transformed into tasty favourites. One of the secrets to preparing fish is soaking it in water with a generous amount of lime and salt.

Nothing is wasted

An island of small livestock farmers, Bajans are pork lovers, too. It is often said that the only part of the pig which the Bajan cannot convert into a tantalising dish is the hair. The prized joints are roasted for Sunday lunch, first soaked in lime and salt, washed and then scored and laced with generous amounts of Bajan seasoning (*see page 152*). The skin is then rubbed with more lime and salt to make it "crackle" which is aided by having a very hot oven for the last half an hour of roasting.

> **PIGGING OUT**
>
> It is often said that the only part of the pig which the Bajan cannot convert into a tantalising dish is the hair.

Saturday is "pudding and souse" day. This is an old island dish still made everywhere. The pudding is made from grated and well-seasoned sweet potato which is stuffed into the cleaned pig's intestines called "belly", which is then steamed. The cooked pudding looks like a long dark sausage which is cut into slices and served with the "souse" – pig's head (features), feet and flesh cooked until tender, cut into slices and "soused", or pickled, with lime juice, onion, hot and sweet peppers, salt, finely-chopped cucumber and parsley. The health conscious make souse with the leaner cuts of pork.

The black belly sheep – it looks very similar to a goat – is unique to Barbados, and the distinctive flavour is highly prized by many overseas to whom it is exported. It is not widely available locally as the cheaper lamb from New Zealand is used for "stewing down" weekly. The few cuts of black belly that do make it to the meat section of the supermarkets are snapped up very quickly.

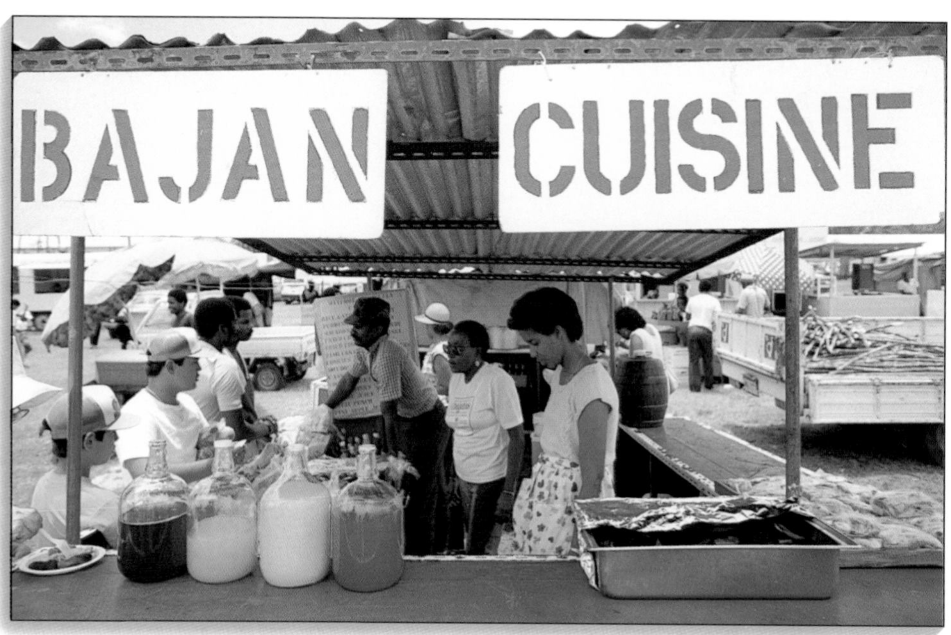

Fast food Bajan-style

The American fast food joints have not really made their presence felt in Barbados. Bajans are not generally keen on hamburgers. However, there are plenty of fast food outlets selling fried chicken, which is consumed in very large quantities and has the distinction of being stuffed with Bajan seasoning.

Rotis are another fast food item served throughout the island. Originating in India, the flat, unleavened bread wrapped round a stuffing of a spicy meat or vegetable curry mixture, was

LEFT: sea eggs have been over fished.
ABOVE: Bajan cuisine at the roadside.

introduced to Barbados from Trinidad, which has a large Asian population, and is so popular that it has come to be considered a Bajan food.

From the country

The diversity of the Barbadian root crops, vegetables and fruits also helps create a unique and healthy cuisine. Yam, sweet potato, eddoe, cassava, plantain, green banana and breadfruit are the starches served with Bajan meals in addition to the familiar rice, pasta and English potato. Hotels usually include sweet potato and sometimes pickled breadfruit in their Bajan buffets but you will probably have to visit a Bajan home to savour most of the other unusual ground provisions.

One reason is that yam needs to be served soon after cooking or it tends to discolour. It also can cause itching when being peeled so needs to handled with caution. Visitors don't usually like the look of the slimy appearance of eddoes, but there's nothing better than an eddoe with a dash of Worcester sauce or a hot slice of white yam with Bajan butter sauce.

Imported and local vegetables are sold in supermarkets but the hucksters in the markets have the best quality produce: sun-ripened tomatoes; small cucumbers, which are best eaten peeled, sliced and "dressed" with fresh lime, salt, white vinegar and a small amount of finely-chopped onion and fresh hot pepper; home-grown pumpkin with green and white skin and bright orange flesh that's boiled and made into creamy pumpkin fritters or into a soup with a freshly-made chicken stock, herbs and onions. Plantain is a member of the banana family that is unpalatable raw. It is fried, boiled in the skin or cut into 1-inch (2.5-cm) pieces, wrapped in streaky bacon and baked for about 30 minutes in a moderate oven. Christophene, a small green prickly pear-shaped vegetable is nicest peeled, cored like an apple, sliced, blanched and baked in a light cheese sauce. The

Seasonings and Sauces

Bajans are rightly proud of their spicy seasonings and hot pepper sauces which make a tasty, sometimes fiery, addition to a dish. Bajan seasoning, a paste of onions, shallots, clove, garlic, fresh Scotch Bonnet pepper, herbs, spices and lime juice, is kept in the fridge and used for coating fish or meat half an hour before cooking.

Barbados' own special pepper sauce consists of Scotch Bonnet peppers, fresh turmeric, shallots, dry English mustard, onions and vinegar. It is fiercely hot and should be used cautiously. Pepper wine, a tradition of the plantocracy's dining rooms, is a combination of sherry and fresh peppers and used sparingly in soups.

local varieties of avocado, referred to as pears, are very large, fleshy and tasty.

Breadfruit – a staple

For nearly two centuries, breadfruit has been a staple in the Bajan diet. It is a large, round starchy fruit, white in the middle with a bright green skin, that grows on trees all over the island. The breadfruit tree originally came from Tahiti and was brought to Barbados in 1793 by the British Captain Bligh, on his second attempt, after the infamous mutiny on the *Bounty* which was caused by orders to give the breadfruit suckers water and not the men. Nutritious, breadfruit is peeled, boiled and served in a variety of ways: lathered in a rich butter sauce of onions, tomatoes, garlic, parsley, lime juice, salt and pepper; cold with a pickle of cucumber, onion, parsley, lime and salt; mashed with butter and salt meat into a cou-cou; baked in a cheese sauce; or fried in thin slices to make chips.

> **A BAJAN CREATION**
>
> The grapefruit was created in Barbados in the 18th century by crossing a sweet orange with a shaddock, a bitter citrus fruit brought over from Polynesia by a Captain Shaddock.

Peas and rice is a popular main dish. Rice is cooked with one or several kinds of peas, including green or dried pigeon peas, black eye and split peas, cow peas or lentils. Salted pig tails or other salted meats and fresh herbs are often cooked with the rice to season it.

The revered pigeon pea is also the basis for jug jug, a Christmas dish of mashed peas, guinea corn flour, salt meat and herbs, which is a corruption of the Scottish haggis, introduced to Barbados by the Scots when they were exiled here after the Monmouth Rebellion of 1685.

Weird and wonderful fruit

Dunks, fat porks, Bajan gooseberries, Bajan cherries, guavas, golden apples, mangos, passion fruit, water melons, ackees, hog plums, chilli plums, Jamaica plums, tamarinds, sugar apples, mammee apples, sapodillas and cashews. These are the fruits that generations of Bajan children have been conquering difficult tree limbs to enjoy but are often hard to find commercially. The hucksters sometimes sell them but in the supermarkets it is easier to buy English apples and Florida oranges than the island's delicious golden apples, passion fruit and Jamaica plums.

Mangos are imported from neighbouring

FAR LEFT: rotis make a good Bajan snack.
LEFT: breadfruit has been a staple for two centuries.
ABOVE: liquid lunch on the beach.

islands, the most popular being the sweet, medium-sized "Julie" and the very large "Imperial". The small green limes are very juicy and gloriously pungent. Locally grown water melons, musk melons and fragrant pawpaws are everywhere.

LEAD PIPE

A rock-hard, 6-in (15-cm) long, cylindrical sweet bread known as lead pipe is sold in rum shops throughout the island and is a Bajan institution.

Exotic sweets

The clean, golden, well-defined crystals of Barbados sugar have a good full flavour, ensuring that preserves such as orange marmalade, guava jelly and green mango chutney are of a very high quality – the cottage industry brands, apparent by their simple labels, tend to be the best. The wide range of exotic confections, available in the bigger supermarkets and the Women's Self Help, include guava cheese, coconut sugar cakes, tamarind balls and chocolate and peanut fudge.

Traditional desserts, such as bread'n'butter pudding, lemon meringue pie, apple pie, apple crumble, jam puffs, coconut pie and chocolate pudding, hearken back to English nurseries but with a Caribbean touch – often in the way of a large dash of vanilla essence which is available in large bottles everywhere, albeit not in its pure form but nonetheless smelling wonderful. The rich fruit cake served at Christmas and weddings is a very old and outstanding recipe, needless to say, laced with rum. There are a couple of variations available commercially well packaged for travel and you can even buy the cake mixture in a jar.

Popular drinks

There are many refreshing drinks to choose from and they don't have to be expensive either; the tap water is naturally filtered through the island's coral limestone, and chilled in the fridge, it is pleasant to drink. Fresh coconuts are sold by the roadside for their almost clear coconut water. The vendors will skilfully hack off the tops with a cutlass and pour out the cool, slightly earthy liquid for you. You can ask to have the drained coconut cut in half and for a "spoon" to be made from the husk to scoop out the jelly inside.

With so many lime trees, limes are usually plentiful and you will never want to drink bottled squash again after making it with fresh lime juice, syrup and sparkling water. Lemonade is the same but made with flat water.

Wherever you go, you will be able to order a rum punch (*see pages 206–207*) and although the basic recipe is the same – one of sour (lime juice), two of sweet (syrup), three of strong (Barbados rum) and four of weak (water or fruit juice), five dashes of bitter and nutmeg spice, served well chilled on plenty of ice – at each establishment it will be different. Some mix it with falernum, a local rum liqueur, which can be a killer. A delicious alternative is to squeeze a whole lime, place the juice and skins in a cocktail shaker with a measure of old rum, half a measure of syrup, and enough ice to fill a glass.

Mauby is a traditional drink made from boiling pieces of a bitter bark with spices and essences. It is then strained and sweetened, and can be brewed to make it frothy like beer. A very refreshing drink, it is also said to have medicinal properties. Sorrel is prepared from the fresh and dried red bracts of the sorrel plant, a relative of the hibiscus family and served at Christmas time. Caribbean ginger beer is usually still, strong and served chilled. Made from green or dried root ginger, the drink is mixed in a similar way to sorrel. ❑

LEFT: old-time mauby seller.
RIGHT: fresh produce at Cheapside Market.

HERBAL CURES AND ITALS

Traditional folk medicine has been passed down through the centuries and the use of natural remedies are as popular today as they ever were

Nature was Barbados' first pharmacy, or "doctor stop". While "modern" medicine has superseded traditional folk cures throughout most of the island, ancient herbal remedies are once again attracting a following among Bajans.

Folk cures seem to have sprung from three diverse sources on the island. The original Amerindian inhabitants probably used indigenous plants and herbs in teas and "cures". It is also likely that African folk cures and bush medicines made their way to Barbados with the island's African inhabitants. More recently, the development and growth of the Rastafarian movement has spurred a resurgence of interest in nature cures: Rastafarians look mainly to nature for their needs; they have initiated research and experimentation with non-traditional teas and cures, and in doing so have extended that range of Barbadian folk medicines to modern life.

Unfortunately, much of the open pasture where many wild plants and herbs once thrived has been cleared for housing or cultivation. Some bushes have been overused and are very difficult to find. A good example is a bush called finger grow; it has very sharp thorns and reportedly is an aphrodisiac for men. (You may therefore guess which "finger" it helps to "grow".) Of course, some bushes still thrive all over the island, such as Christmas bush, cure-for-all and circee.

Groundnuts and coconuts

The Rastafarians have revived the use of groundnuts (primarily peanuts) and coconuts. They call these foodstuffs "itals", a derivation of "victual". On almost every street corner, Rastafari brethren trade in coconuts.

Coconut water is praised by most as a preventative and cure for illnesses of the bladder and kidneys. Coconut oil is also a long-standing cold remedy: it may be rubbed into the head to break up a cold. It is also used on the scalp a day or two before washing the hair to help loosen dandruff flakes. And, as well as making a refreshing beverage, coconut water is a sterile liquid and so pure that it can be used as

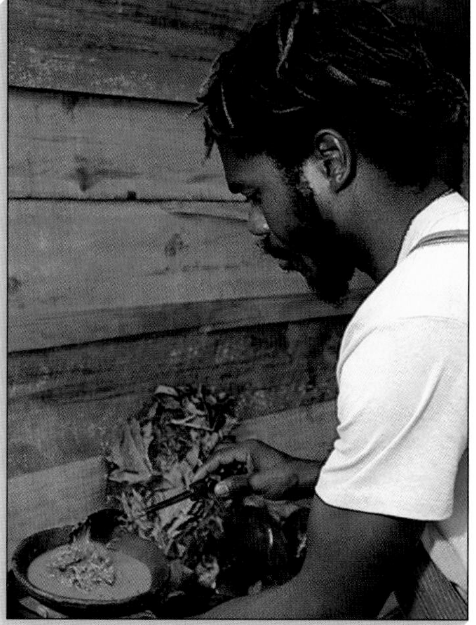

plasma in dire surgical circumstances. The ever useful coconut inspired this ditty:

Coconut woman is called out
An' everywhere you can hear her shout
"Get your coconut water
Man it good for yuh daughter
Coco got a lot of iron
Make you strong like a lion..."

The song goes on to advocate "if you tired and feeling down/Get coconut water an' little rum." A perfect pick-me-up for the end of a long hard day.

Peanuts are another Bajan "health" food. Barbadians have always eaten them raw for general health; and in large quantities peanuts

PRECEDING PAGES: a tray of hibiscus flowers.
LEFT: shinning up a palm tree for a curative coconut.
RIGHT: a Rastafarian serves up some "itals", an all-natural vegetarian stew.

are supposed to stimulate sexual desire or increase sexual prowess. For this purpose, the nuts are soaked in milk, gin or beer for one night or for as long as one week, depending upon the potency desired.

Brings the blood down

A melon-like fruit called pawpaw, or papaya as it is known elsewhere, is put to many uses in a Bajan home. The fruit itself is delicious and it is often puréed into a beverage as well. Either way, it prevents constipation or, as the Bajans say, it helps to "keep the bowels moving".

WONDER-OF-THE-WORLD

Chewed with a pinch of salt, Wonder-of-the World is supposed to bring relief from mild asthmatic attacks. Others believe a bowl of green-lizard soup will do the trick.

Green pawpaw is reportedly useful for reducing the effects of hypertension, or high blood pressure; it "brings the blood down," goes a local expression. The pawpaw for this purpose is taken one or two ways, either as two small cooked slices of green pawpaw, or in an elaborate concoction that involves grated nutmeg, candle grease and an optional few drops of coconut oil.

This versatile fruit is also used to prevent infection from cuts and boils. Two or three thin slices are placed over a cut and bandaged for two or three days to promote rapid healing without infection. Pawpaw is used in this same way in parts of Africa, with excellent results.

No part of the pawpaw is wasted: the many black seeds inside are good for gently getting rid of worms and the latex from the trunk of the tree can do the same job but with a more purgative effect.

Cool and soothing gel

The cactus-like aloe plant is another Bajan all-rounder. For colds, itching throats and constipation, the outer skin is removed and a small piece of the inner pith is swallowed with a pinch of salt to reduce the bitterness. A thin "inside" slice of aloe can also be bandaged on to cuts to aid healing and it is a well-known first-aid remedy for scalds and over exposure to the sun. Simply split open a succulent grey-green leaf, squeeze out the cool, soothing aloe gel and rub over the sunburn.

The green brew made from the circee bush, is also a bitter medicine; it is used to help reduce fever and relieve the symptoms of influenza. Some people refer to the circee bush as "miraculous bush", as a tribute to its healing powers. A cousin, in name at least, to the miraculous bush is the "wonder-of-the-world" plant (pronounced wonda-worl') which, when chewed with a pinch of salt, is supposed to bring relief from mild asthmatic attacks. Others believe in a bowl of green-lizard soup to get rid of asthma.

Creative cures

Some Bajan herbal teas and home cures have merit, while others are definitely doubtful to the modern mind. For example, a child with asthma would be taken to a young pawpaw tree and made to stand upright against the trunk. A nail would be driven into it just above the child's head. People believed that, as the tree grew, the illness would gradually disappear.

For a child afflicted with worms, a piece of bitter wormwood would be steeped in rum and the liquid fed to the child for nine consecutive mornings. If that failed to work, raw aloe in milk was administered instead. Hiccups mandated a different "cure": a match stick was pushed into the child's hair, or a small piece of brown paper was moistened with saliva and then placed on the child's forehead. ❑

LEFT: bringing home the sorrel.
RIGHT: coconut water is the perfect pick-me-up.

MAXI PRIEST

BARBADOS

PLACES

A detailed guide to the entire island, with principal sites clearly cross-referenced by number to the maps

Barbados is divided into 11 parishes: the southern half of the island is a rich region of fertile plantations, resorts and industrial centres where you'll find areas full of unique features that reflect the historical, geographical and social heritage of the island. The parish of St Michael embraces the capital and its environs; Christ Church hogs the vibrant South Coast with requisite resorts; St George harbours a rich valley of working sugar plantations and Great Houses; St Philip hides two world-famous resorts with fascinating pasts; and St John, described as "behind God's back", climbs up into the hills above the East Coast where there's an amazing panorama at every turn, complementing the turquoise calm of the Caribbean on the West Coast beaches of St James.

No matter how addicted you are to sea and sand – and it does have a special allure in Barbados – it's worth tearing yourself away and renting a car or Mini-Moke to see the rest of the island for yourself. The parish of St Thomas, occupying the heart of the island, is full of natural wonders. Driving on, you discover the "other" Barbados on the east and north coasts. Here, the scenery is stunning: rugged hills and gentle slopes are bordered by a stretch of narrow coastline with sweeping bays and some spectacular views. The Atlantic crests over treacherous reefs and pounds on to the shore, mangling the huge rock formations on the beaches. In this beckoning region, you'll see the colourful chattel houses of St Lucy, the green rolling hills of the Scotland District in St Andrew and St Joseph, the two contrasting coastlines of St Peter – the rough and the smooth.

Of course you'll get lost – that's part of the fun. Road maps are a good guide to the island's seven main highways but, with 800 miles (1,300 km) of paved roads in a country 14 miles (23 km) wide and 21 miles (34 km) long, it's best to relax and enjoy the adventure. You'll never be more than a 20-minute drive from one coast or the other – and don't hesitate to ask for directions. However, Barbadians do not refer to their roads by highway numbers, they give directions using village names, which can be confusing…

To help you find your way around and discover more of its hidden delights, we've grouped the parishes into regions, leading you through each one. You may want to "go an' come back," visiting one place at a time. Or you can explore a fair portion of the island in a single excursion – "one time" as the Barbadians would put it. ❑

PRECEDING PAGES: windswept coast; St Philip beach; colourful chattel house.
LEFT: a friendly smile.

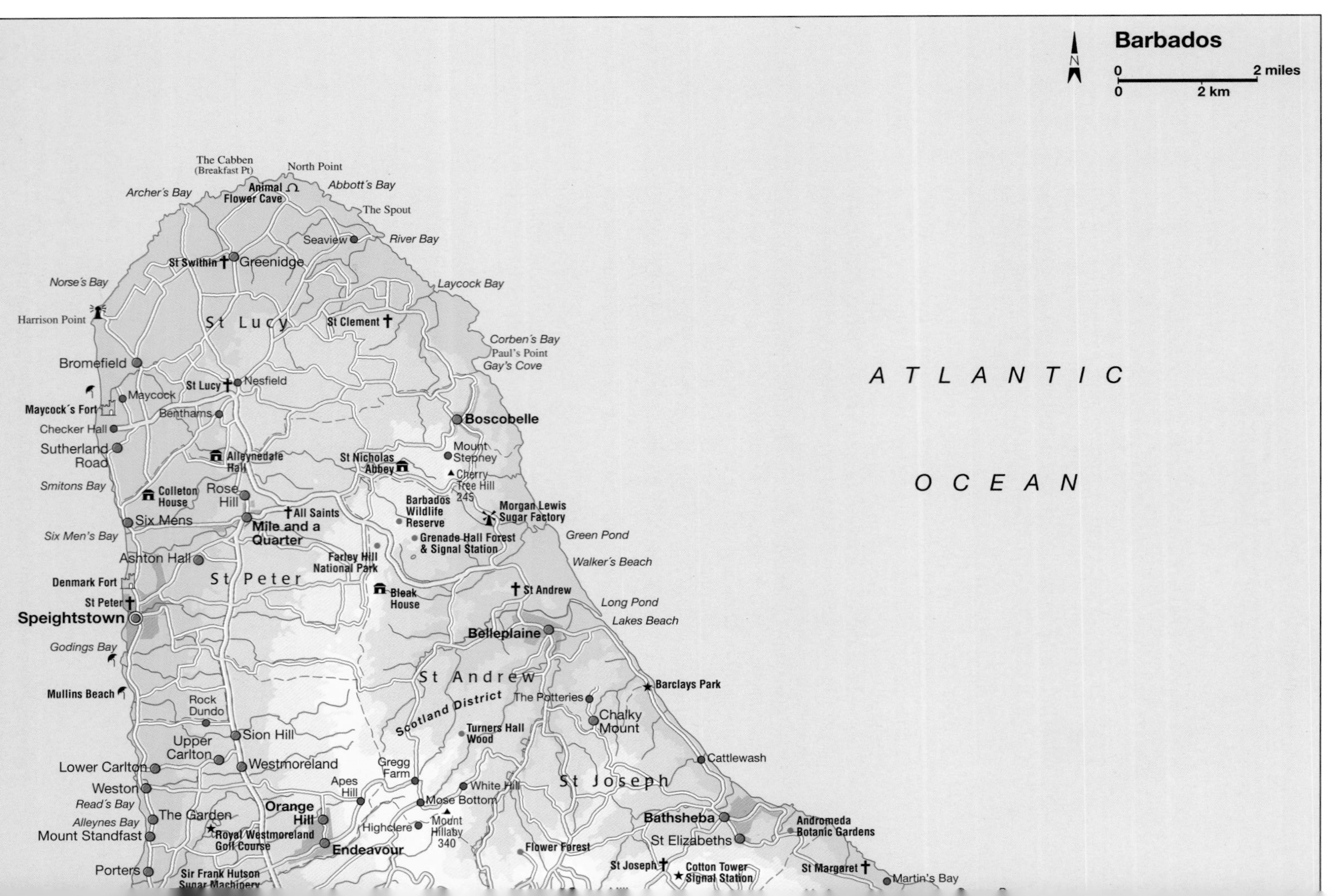

Barbados
N
0 2 miles
0 2 km
ATLANTIC
OCEAN
The Cabben (Breakfast Pt)
North Point
Archer's Bay
Animal Flower Cave
Abbott's Bay
The Spout
Seaview
River Bay
St Swithin
Greenidge
Norse's Bay
Laycock Bay
Harrison Point
St Lucy
St Clement
Corben's Bay
Paul's Point
Gay's Cove
Bromefield
St Lucy
Nesfield
Maycock
Maycock's Fort
Benthams
Boscobelle
Checker Hall
Sutherland Road
Alleynedale Hall
St Nicholas Abbey
Mount Stepney
Cherry Tree Hill 245
Smitons Bay
Colleton House
Rose Hill
Barbados Wildlife Reserve
All Saints
Morgan Lewis Sugar Factory
Six Mens
Mile and a Quarter
Six Men's Bay
Grenade Hall Forest & Signal Station
Green Pond
Ashton Hall
Farley Hill National Park
Walker's Beach
St Peter
Denmark Fort
Bleak House
St Andrew
St Peter
Long Pond
Speightstown
Lakes Beach
Belleplaine
Godings Bay
St Andrew
Barclays Park
Mullins Beach
Rock Dundo
The Potteries
Scotland District
Chalky Mount
Turners Hall Wood
Sion Hill
Upper Carlton
Cattlewash
Lower Carlton
Westmoreland
Gregg Farm
Apes Hill
White Hill
St Joseph
Weston
Read's Bay
Mose Bottom
Orange Hill
The Garden
Bathsheba
Andromeda Botanic Gardens
Alleynes Bay
Mount Hillaby 340
Highclere
Royal Westmoreland Golf Course
St Elizabeths
Mount Standfast
Endeavour
Flower Forest
Porters
Sir Frank Hutson Sugar Machinery
St Joseph
Cotton Tower Signal Station
St Margaret
Martin's Bay

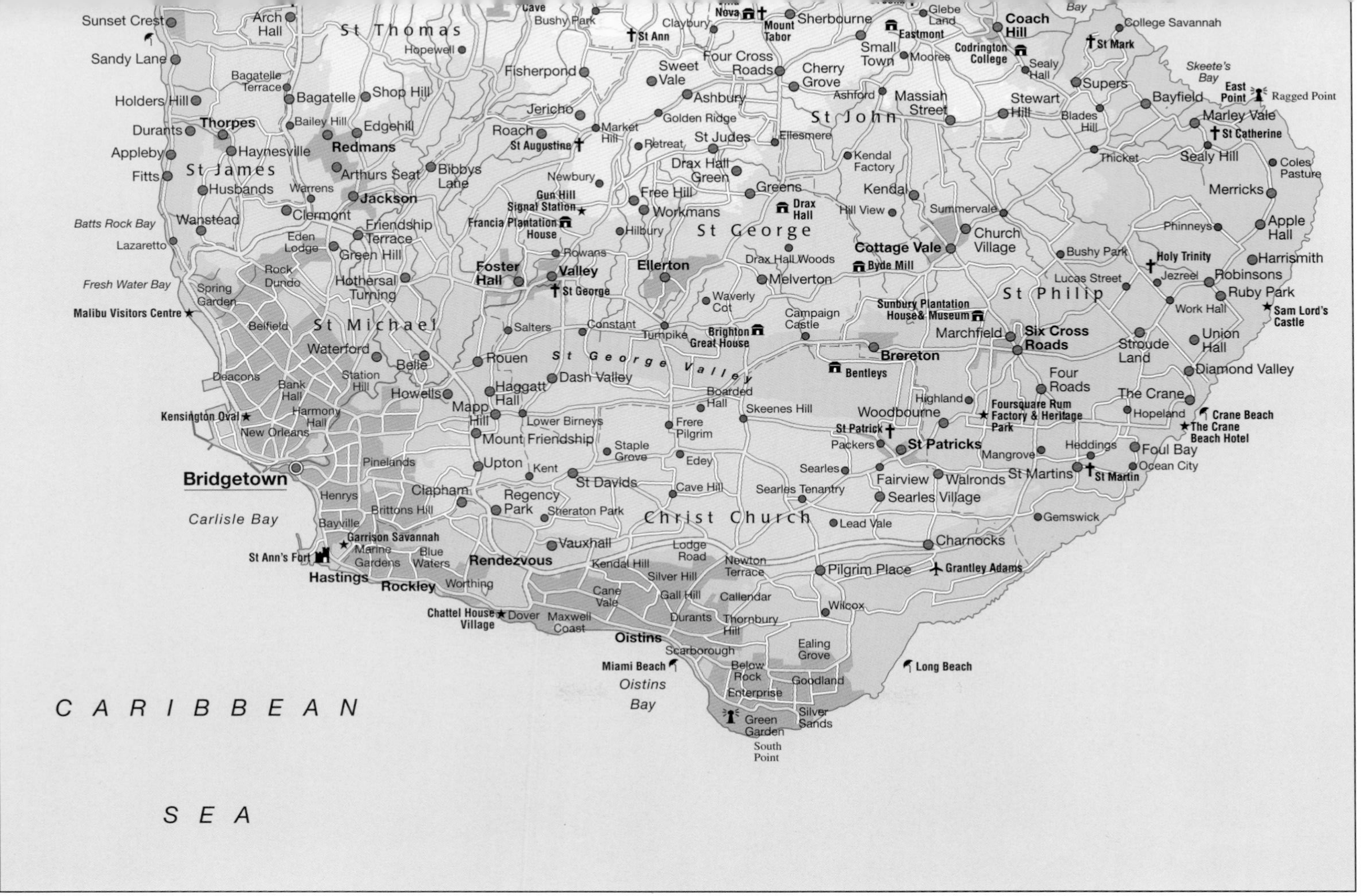
CARIBBEAN SEA
Bridgetown
Carlisle Bay
St Michael
St James
St Thomas
St John
St George
St George Valley
St Philip
Christ Church
Oistins Bay
Fresh Water Bay
Batts Rock Bay
Skeete's Bay
Ragged Point
East Point
South Point
Sunset Crest
Sandy Lane
Holders Hill
Durants
Appleby
Fitts
Lazaretto
Malibu Visitors Centre
Kensington Oval
Spring Garden
Deacons
New Orleans
Harmony Hall
Bank Hall
Belfield
Rock Dundo
Eden Lodge
Clermont
Warrens
Redmans
Arthurs Seat
Jackson
Friendship Terrace
Green Hill
Hothersal Turning
Waterford
Station Hill
Belle
Howells
Mapp Hill
Bagatelle
Bagatelle Terrace
Bailey Hill
Haynesville
Husbands
Wanstead
Thorpes
Arch Hall
Edgehill
Shop Hill
Hopewell
Bibbys Lane
Fisherpond
Roach
St Augustine
Jericho
Market Hill
Newbury
Gun Hill Signal Station
Francia Plantation House
Rowans
Foster Hall
Valley
St George
Salters
Rouen
Haggatt Hall
Dash Valley
Constant
Lower Birneys
Mount Friendship
Upton
Kent
St Davids
Staple Grove
Regency Park
Sheraton Park
Vauxhall
Rendezvous
Clapham
Brittons Hill
Pinelands
Henrys
Bayville
Garrison Savannah
Marine Gardens
Blue Waters
Hastings
Rockley
Worthing
St Ann's Fort
Chattel House Village
Dover
Maxwell Coast
Cane Vale
Kendal Hill
Silver Hill
Gall Hill
Durants
Oistins
Miami Beach
Scarborough
Thornbury Hill
Callendar
Newton Terrace
Lodge Road
Below Rock
Enterprise
Green Garden
Silver Sands
Goodland
Ealing Grove
Wilcox
Pilgrim Place
Lead Vale
Searles Tenantry
Searles
Long Beach
Grantley Adams
Charnocks
Searles Village
Fairview
Walronds
St Martins
St Martin
Gemswick
Mangrove
Heddings
Ocean City
Foul Bay
The Crane
The Crane Beach Hotel
Crane Beach
Hopeland
Diamond Valley
Union Hall
Stroude Land
Work Hall
Jezreel
Ruby Park
Robinsons
Sam Lord's Castle
Harrismith
Apple Hall
Coles Pasture
Merricks
Sealy Hill
St Catherine
Marley Vale
Bayfield
College Savannah
St Mark
Supers
Blades Hill
Thicket
Phinneys
Holy Trinity
Bushy Park
Lucas Street
Six Cross Roads
Four Roads
Foursquare Rum Factory & Heritage Park
St Patricks
St Patrick
Woodbourne
Packers
Highland
Marchfield
Sunbury Plantation House& Museum
Brereton
Bentleys
Campaign Castle
Skeenes Hill
Boarded Hall
Frere Pilgrim
Edey
Cave Hill
Brighton Great House
Waverly Cot
Turnpike
Ellerton
Melverton
Drax Hall Woods
Cottage Vale
Byde Mill
Hill View
Kendal
Summervale
Church Village
Coach Hill
Sealy Hall
Stewart Hill
Codrington College
Glebe Land
Eastmont
Moores
Massiah Street
Small Town
Ashford
Kendal Factory
Sherbourne
Mount Tabor
Cherry Grove
Ellesmere
Drax Hall
Greens
Four Cross Roads
Ashbury
Golden Ridge
St Judes
Drax Hall Green
Retreat
Free Hill
Workmans
Hillbury
Sweet Vale
Claybury
St Ann
Bushy Park

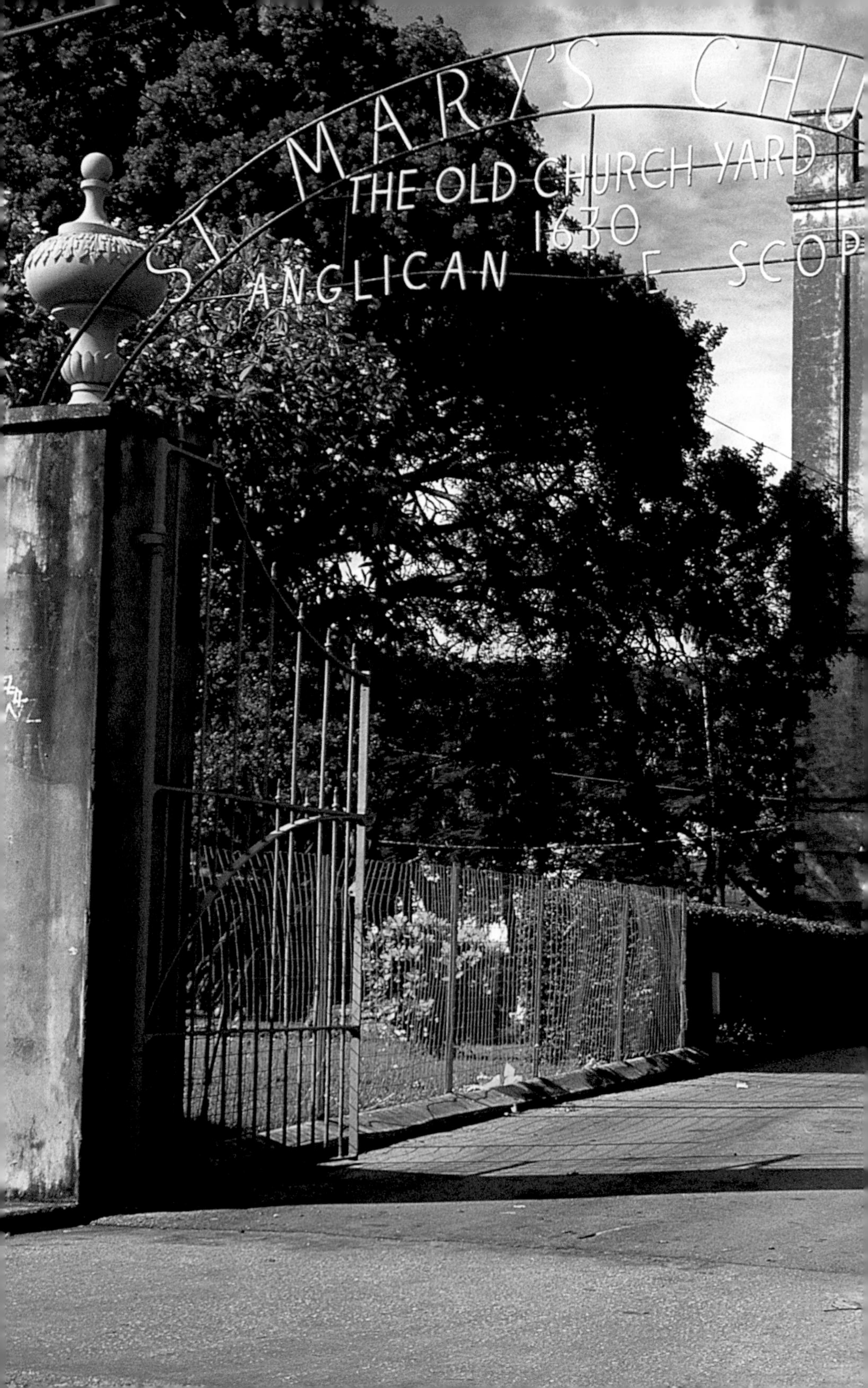
ST MARY'S CHU
THE OLD CHURCH YARD
1630
ANGLICAN
E SCOP

HURRICANE
SHELTER

BUSTLING BRIDGETOWN

With major changes taking place, the colourful capital of Barbados is a haven for shoppers and a showcase for colonial architecture

Map on page 176

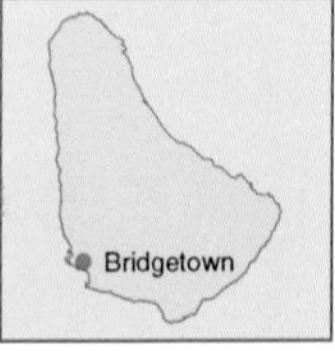

Despite its small size, the centre of Bridgetown pulses with all the energy of a major Caribbean capital – and with something that is uniquely Barbadian. In brilliant sunlight, and in the shade of colonial buildings and modern offices, the city hustles and bustles to an ageless quick tempo; women bearing baskets hurry to market: curbside vendors, or hawkers, sell their wares; well-dressed business people head for their office buildings. It is easily one of the most thriving and colourful capitals in the region with a history that spans almost four centuries.

And the Government is in the process of implementing plans to beautify Bridgetown and its environs and to preserve buildings of architectural and cultural interest, in order to give the city a new and improved image. With the rapid expansion of the international business community, schemes – under the eagle eye of the Barbados National Trust which is concerned that nothing of historical value is lost in the process – are being put in motion to redevelop the waterfront and pedestrianise Broad Street, the main shopping thoroughfare, spicing up the city to attract not only new commerce but residents too, as well as stimulating an after office hours social scene.

PRECEDING PAGES: St Mary's Church offers shelter.
LEFT: Crop Over fun.
BELOW: fishing boats in the Careenage.

Rival settlers

Bridgetown was founded on 5 July 1628 when Charles Wolverstone was sent with 64 settlers by the Earl of Carlisle, who had been given the legal right to settle Barbados by Charles I. Wolverstone soon had the whole island under his power, including the Powells who had arrived the year before.

The presence of a small river which was actually an arm of the sea undoubtedly led the new arrivals to choose this site. However, it was not without its drawbacks. The Royalist and historian Richard Ligon commented in 1647 that Bridgetown was "a town ill situated, for if they had considered health, as they did convenience, they would never had set it there". A primitive bridge built by the Indians to span the waterway meant that the town was called Indian Bridge, Indian Bridgetown or just simply The Bridge until it was eventually named Bridgetown.

The lower reaches of the river, known as the **Careenage** Ⓐ, form a natural basin or port – an important facility at a time when the sea was the only means of travel and international trade. Visiting ships and schooners could be careened here, hence the name, while they were cleaned and painted and the area soon became the centre of trading and news for the island. Today, although the blue and yellow wooden fishing boats sometimes still depart from here, you will not find the cargoes of bananas,

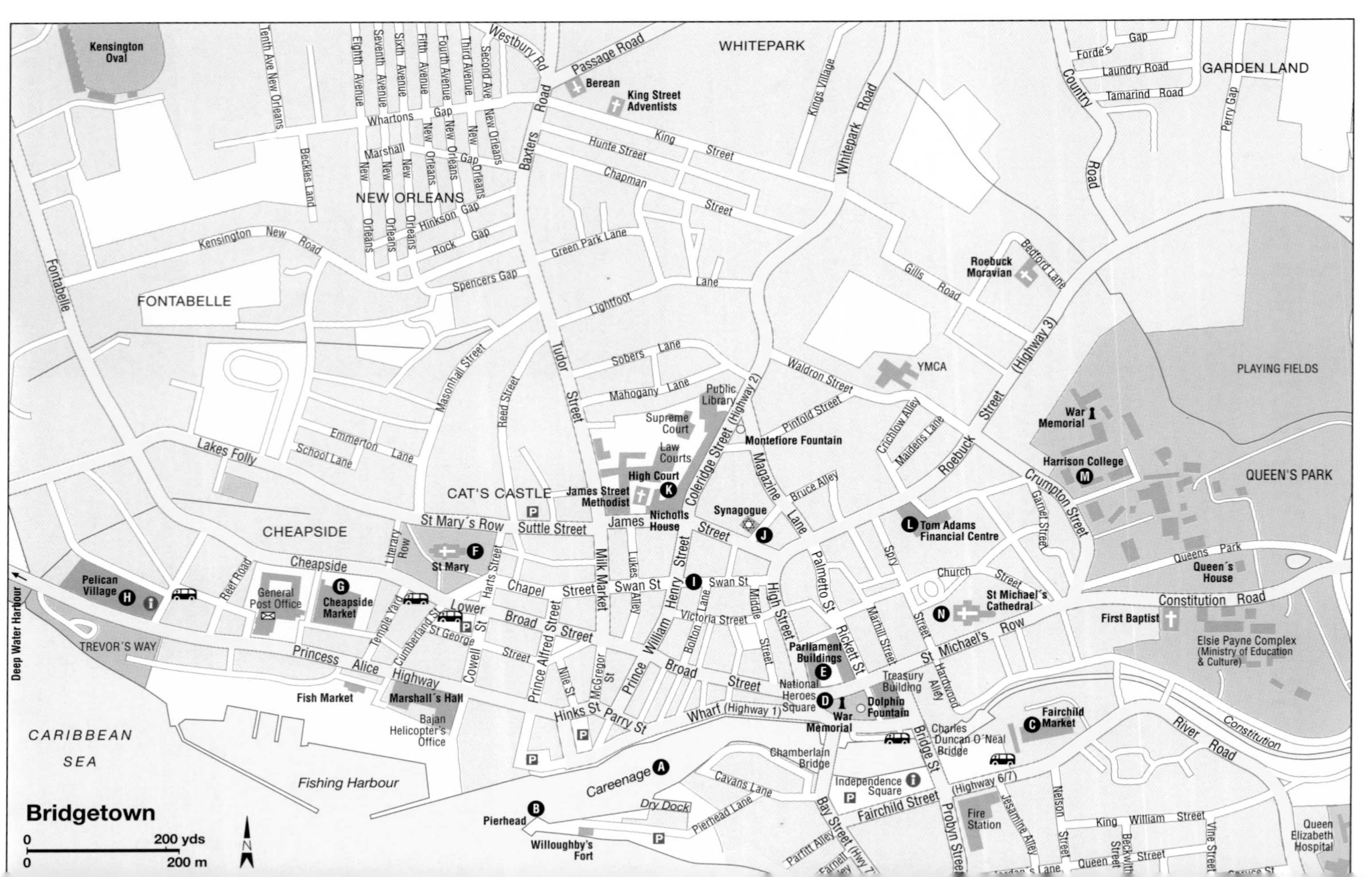
Bridgetown
CARIBBEAN SEA
Fishing Harbour
Careenage
Deep Water Harbour
TREVOR'S WAY
Pelican Village
Fish Market
Marshall's Hall
Bajan Helicopter's Office
Cheapside Market
General Post Office
CHEAPSIDE
CAT'S CASTLE
St Mary
James Street Methodist
Nicholls House
High Court
Law Courts
Supreme Court
Public Library
Synagogue
Montefiore Fountain
Parliament Buildings
National Heroes Square
War Memorial
Dolphin Fountain
Treasury Building
Independence Square
Fire Station
Fairchild Market
Charles Duncan O'Neal Bridge
Chamberlain Bridge
St Michael's Cathedral
Tom Adams Financial Centre
YMCA
Roebuck Moravian
Harrison College
War Memorial
First Baptist
Queen's House
Elsie Payne Complex (Ministry of Education & Culture)
Queen Elizabeth Hospital
QUEEN'S PARK
PLAYING FIELDS
GARDEN LAND
WHITEPARK
NEW ORLEANS
FONTABELLE
Kensington Oval
King Street Adventists
Berean
Pierhead
Willoughby's Fort
Dry Dock
Constitution Road
River Road
Roebuck Street (Highway 3)
Coleridge Street (Highway 2)
Tudor Street
Milk Market
Baxters Road
Whitepark Road
Country Road
Bay Street (Hwy 7)
Wharf (Highway 1)
Bridge St
Probyn Street
Fontabelle
Kensington New Road
Lakes Folly
Princess Alice Highway
Broad Street
Swan St
High Street
Magazine Lane
Palmetto St
200 yds
200 m

mangoes, plantains and other fruits being loaded on to the boats as years ago. These have been replaced by a wide array of vessels and slender-masted yachts berthed here by their wealthy owners, and it is the main departure point for exotic deep sea fishing trips, catamaran cruises and a host of other marine activities designed for the visitor intent on having a good holiday. A good place to sit and watch the marine world at play by day or night is at the **Waterfront Café**, where you can have a drink, lunch or dinner either in the cool interior or on the pavement European style, looking across the Careenage to the Wharf, the Parliament Buildings and the Dolphin Fountain. At night you can listen and dance to live jazz. Close by in Bridge House you can have an elevated view from **The Rusty Pelican**, another lively restaurant.

Restoring the Pierhead

Both establishments set the scene for the new **Pierhead** **B** development project behind, covering an 11-acre (4.5 hectare) peninsula on the south bank of the Careenage. Here are the old coral-stone warehouses that grew up due to the rum and sugar trade from the port nearby. Now, those not already converted to modern day use are to be faithfully restored and used for housing, shops and entertainment recapturing the historic maritime atmosphere. Also earmarked for preservation is the "screw dock", a fine piece of Victorian engineering built between 1889 and 1893, which is believed to be the only dry dock of its kind in the world.

At the tip of the Pierhead is **Willoughby Fort** built by a William Withington, who was paid some 80,000 lb (36,300 kg) of sugar for the job. It is not generally known that the fort once occupied an islet called Little Island. Used in recent

Map on page 176

TIP

In Bridgetown, Barbadians traditionally adhere to a conservative dress code. Skimpy clothing is regarded as unseemly for the nation's capital.

BELOW: shoppers in early 20th-century Bridgetown.

See de women
How dey calling,
singing:
Come for your bread-
fruit,
Come for your corn,
Come for de apples –
fresh as de morn.
Come for your guava.
Your guava, your guava
–THE MIGHTY GABBY
Bridgetown, Early
Saturday Morning

years as the headquarters of the Barbados Coast Guard, the site, now connected to the mainland, is planned to become a Naval Heritage area with a water-taxi reception centre close by.

An independent spirit

Across Bay Street sprawls **Independence Square**, a car park by day, a meeting place by night – and sometimes the venue for political rallies. Here you are likely to be accosted by enthusiastic car washers, but be firm if your car doesn't need a clean, otherwise the going rate is about BDS$5. On the other side of the square, next to the Charles Duncan O'Neal Bridge, part of the one-way system out of the centre, is the city's main **bus station** where commuters and minibuses jostle at almost any time of day. Next door is **Fairchild Market** Ⓒ, one of the two big public markets in this city.

In bygone days, the public markets were a riot of colour and full of gaiety, especially on Saturdays when people from all over the island came to shop for the week's supply of food. Yams, potatoes, breadfruit, lettuce, cucumbers and tomatoes still spill out from the stalls and, although the markets do not fill the central role they did before the existence of more modern day conveniences, they are still a vital and lively part of Bridgetown life.

The **Charles Duncan O'Neal Bridge** is named after an eminent Barbadian who dedicated his life to spreading socialist principals among the masses during the mid 1920s and 1930s. O'Neal (1879–1936) trained as a doctor in Britain but later returned to his homeland and began campaigning for better representation for every class, compulsory education, old age pensions, workers' compensation and a whole host of reforms that would form the charter for the working-class

BELOW: a wide variety of shopping in Bridgetown.

movement. He was one of the founding members of the Democratic League and the Workingmen's Association. These organisations are recognised as the forerunners of democracy and trade unionism on the island. O'Neal's achievement is remarkable as it was virtually unheard of for a man of his background, class and education to devote his life so completely to the lot of the ordinary people.

Bridge Street crosses **Fairchild Street** that runs along the south side of the square and is named after a prominent citizen who lived there in the mid-18th century. Colonel John Fairchild was a member of the Assembly and was appointed Chief Justice in 1752. The street crosses Nelson Street in front of the market, bordering a rough residential neighbourhood and one of the city's red light districts, once known as Racoon Quarters. The origin of the name remains unclear, but racoons were considered to be vermin in Barbados and this neighbourhood was probably a haven for these creatures at some time. Nearby lies **St Ambrose Church** which was consecrated on 1 January 1858. On 14 March 1857 *The Barbadian* newspaper noted that "The place known as Rebitt's Ground had in it an amount of spiritual destitution startling in the extreme, and was covered with a pall of darkness too deep to be fancied."

The great cholera epidemic

In the 19th century a devastating cholera epidemic swept through the island at astonishing speed. On 14 May 1854, a resident of Fairchild Street died under suspicious circumstances and within three days similar deaths had occurred in and around Nelson Street. By mid June the epidemic had spread throughout the island and by 6 August the known death toll was 15,243. When the

Map on page 176

FAIRCHILD STREET BUS TERMINAL

Catch the bus for the south coast here.

BELOW: a quick haircut in Nelson Street.

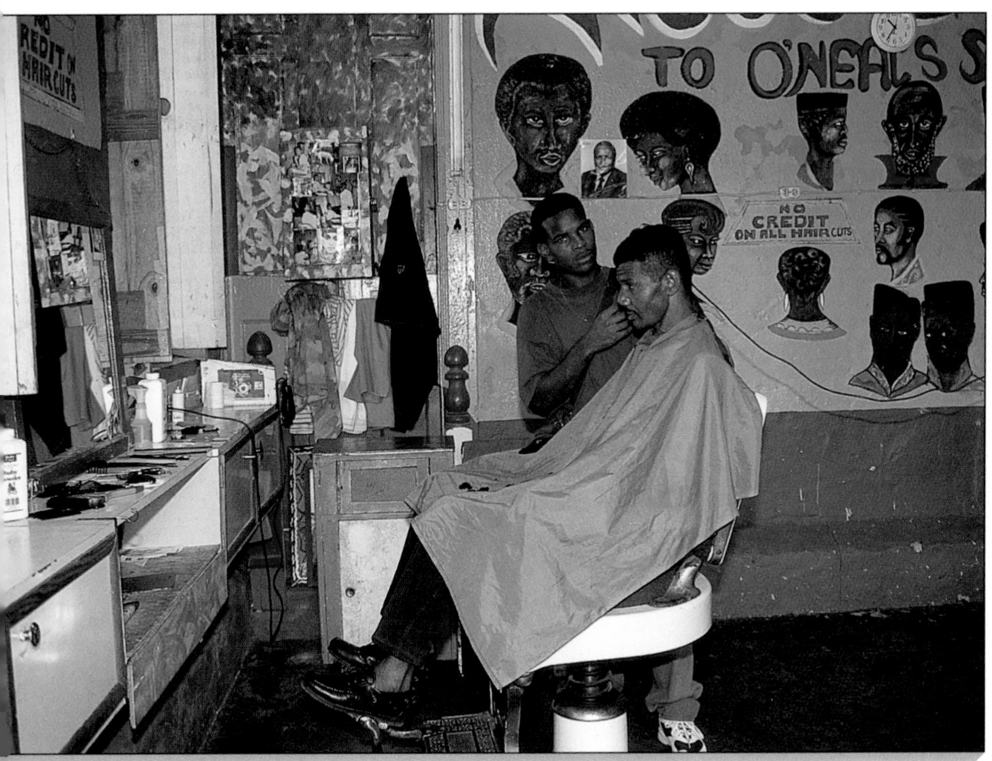

Enjoy a bird's eye view of Barbados with a trip in a helicopter, which starts at the end of the Wharf on the north side of the Careenage. Call Bajan Helicopters for a flightseeing tour on 431 0069.

pestilence finally ended, between 18,000 and 20,000 people had died. A Moravian minister who lived though the epidemic reported that the disease "increased in town steadily… until it reached 340 per diem… In the most erratic manner it went from street to street omitting one or two in its course and returning to them when the resident thought they had escaped, and taking off more in such cases than in the street first visited".

Across Chamberlain Bridge

Back on Bay Street at the main entrance to Bridgetown, **Chamberlain Bridge** separates the inner basin from the Careenage. Originally a swing bridge, visitors and locals would stop and watch it swing back to allow boats to pass through. Several other versions of the bridge have gone before this one, which was finally rebuilt after the hurricane of 1898. It was named the Chamberlain Bridge after British Colonial Secretary Joseph Chamberlain (1836–1914), as a symbol of gratitude to the British Government who awarded a generous grant for the island's rehabilitation after the destruction wrought by the hurricane. However the bridge swings no more; mechanical problems finally forced the Government to make it a stationary structure.

The road over the bridge leads into the heart of Bridgetown which, for nearly 200 years, was called Trafalgar Square. In the centre, the statue of Lord Nelson has caused much controversy as many islanders consider him a British hero rather than a Barbadian one and want him moved. Others say the statue, which has stood in the square since 1813 (preceding Nelson's Column in Trafalgar Square, London, by 17 years), is an important part of the island's heritage and should remain. On 28 April 1999, the Prime Minister Owen Arthur renamed the

BELOW: Chamberlain Bridge makes a grand entrance.

Map on page 176

square **National Heroes Square** (*see pages 46 and 48*) and suggested that the statue be replaced with one of Errol Barrow, the Father of Independence, fuelling the debate. Since then, the Prime Minister has indicated that Nelson may move to the Naval Heritage site to be developed at Willoughby Fort (*see page 177*).

Lord Nelson, and the flagship *HMS Victory* accompanied by other ships of his fleet, arrived in Barbados on 4 June 1805. When news of his death in the Battle of Trafalgar reached the island later that year, patriotic citizens dedicated the square to his memory. However, from as early as 1833, people have petitioned to have Nelson's statue – sculpted by Sir Richard Westmacott ("the first castor of bronze in the Kingdom") – removed. It has been an object of ridicule and a platform for protesters against colonialism prompting calypsonians such as the Mighty Gabby to sing "Take down Nelson and put up a Bajan Man".

East of the square across a small garden, the **Dolphin Fountain**, built in 1865, commemorates the introduction of piped running water to Bridgetown in March 1861. The **War Memorial** Ⓓ here was erected in honour of the many courageous Barbadians who fought in World War I (1914–18). The decision was made to erect the monument just six months after the Armistice and the memorial was unveiled on 10 May 1925. The names of those who died in that war are listed on three bronze panels. A fourth panel, bearing the names of those who died in World War II (1939–45), was added in 1953.

The Government seat

Dominating the northern side of the square are the neo-Gothic facades of the **Parliament Buildings** Ⓔ, which house many of the island's public records and accommodate the Houses of Parliament. In fact, Barbados has the third

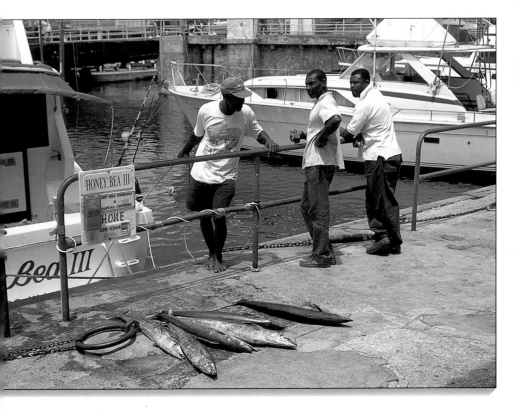

ABOVE: Barbados' national flag. **BELOW:** bringing home the catch.

oldest parliamentary body in the Commonwealth, after Bermuda and Britain, founded in 1639. Yet it wasn't until the latter part of the 19th century that the present Parliament Buildings, known until recently as the Public Buildings, were constructed. For years the House of Legislature met in people's homes and public places and even in taverns.

Eventually, in 1856, John Glasgow Grant introduced a bill to the Assembly for the construction of Public Buildings. The west wing of the present building, used for offices, was finished in 1871, and the east wing, where Parliament sits, was ready for occupation in 1874. The House of Assembly was elaborately done up, with a Speaker's chair and mace, Government and Opposition benches, and a stained-glass window representing the English monarchs from James I to Victoria. Interestingly, the stained-glass window carries the image of Oliver Cromwell, the Great Protector, despite the staunch Royalist sympathies of Barbadians during the English Civil War (*see page 34*).

The Parliament Buildings clock and bell were imported from England in 1875 and were installed in the south tower of the West Building nine years after their first home in the East Building began to sink under their weight.

Shopping in Broad Street

Bridgetown's main thoroughfare and the centre for duty-free shopping outside the ports, **Broad Street** starts northwest of the square by the traditional Bajan, 18th-century coral-stone building, with an overhanging balcony, which houses the **Women's Self Help Association**'s shop that sells delicious home-made guava jelly and hot pepper sauce.

Broad Street contains a mixture of architectural styles: old colonial buildings, such as the regal Victorian Mutual Life Assurance building (now Barclays Bank), DaCosta's and Harrison's, struggle to retain their old-world charm amidst the steady proliferation of more modern neighbours. As part of the Bridgetown

BELOW: colonial-style Parliament Buildings.

Redevelopment Scheme, plans are afoot to smarten up the busy thoroughfare making it a pedestrian zone.

All along the street are fine stores selling duty-free goods. The ornate pink **DaCosta's Mall** and **Cave Shepherd** department store, specialise in designer fare from clothing, jewellery, perfumes and cosmetics to crystals, chinas, cameras and leather goods. Opposite, the **Verandah Art Gallery** (open Mon–Fri, Sat am; free) has a new home above Collins Pharmacy. Run by artist and teacher Indriani Wittingham, the gallery exhibits paintings by new and leading Barbadian artists. Trading in Broad Street goes back to the mid-17th century. In a statute of 1657, the street was declared reserved "for a market-place and other publique uses of this island". At that time it was known as Cheapside, but today only a small district to the west still bears that name. During the latter half of the 17th century, the Merchants' Exchange was situated here.

Shelter from the storms

Broad Street leads into Lower Broad Street and after about 350 yards (300 metres) is **St Mary's Church** **F** which doubles up as an official hurricane shelter. Surrounded by gardens, the Georgian solid-walled church remains the neighbourhood's most dignified figure. It was completed on 15 July 1827, to accommodate the overflow from St Michael's Cathedral, but it was the original site of St Michael's before it was rebuilt at the other end of the city (*see page 188*).

Probably the most famous local figure laid to rest here is Samuel Jackman Prescod (1806–71). In June 1843, Prescod became the first coloured man to be elected to the Assembly and with a keen journalistic talent he made his views against class legislation known far and wide. His vigorous style made him a

Map on page 176

TIP

Remember to bring your passport and ticket with you when you go shopping in Bridgetown, to buy things duty-free. You can take your purchases straight away now, except for alcohol which will be sent to the airport for you to collect on your departure.

BELOW: a timely reminder in Broad Street.

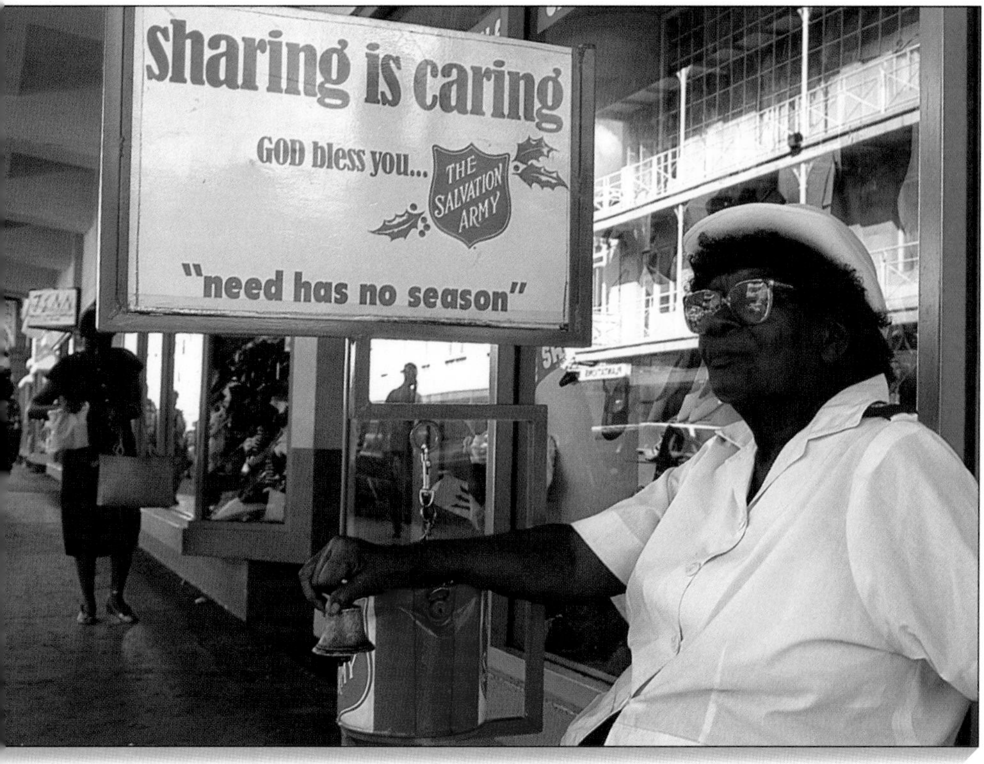

Baxters Road at the northern end of Tudor Street is renowned as the Street That Never Sleeps. Here you can sample Bajan roadside cooking to the throb of raggasoca until 4 or 5am.

formidable statesman and probably one of the greatest Barbadians. When he died, *The Barbados Times* referred to him as "The Great Tribune of the People" who could not be induced to "swerve one jot or tittle from his allegiance to the cause of right and justice".

Temple Yard and Cheapside Market

South of the church, the **Lower Green Bus Station** services all routes to the north of the island and is supplemented by the Jubilee stand and a number of privately owned minibuses at **Temple Yard** a little further on. Temple Yard was once the site of an old naval hospital but it was later acquired by the Ancient Masons who converted it into a lodge known as the Temple. Today it is a Rastafarian stronghold where, from a cluster of ramshackle stalls, these artistic and talented people sell their crafts, mainly leatherwork, jewellery and art. The location was originally provided for the Rastafarian market by the Government because the vendors had erected stalls all over the city, often on busy sidewalks, causing congestion.

Cheapside Market Ⓖ is the second of the city's two public markets where you can find a wide selection of items from fresh produce to clothing. The bustling scene behind the concrete facade on Saturday mornings, when there is a fruit market, is typically Caribbean.

Next door is the **General Post Office** which was finally completed in 1984. Originally the postal services were housed in what was then called the Public Buildings with the Senate and the house of Assembly and which are now the Parliament Buildings. It took more than 40 years for plans to construct a separate building to reach fruition.

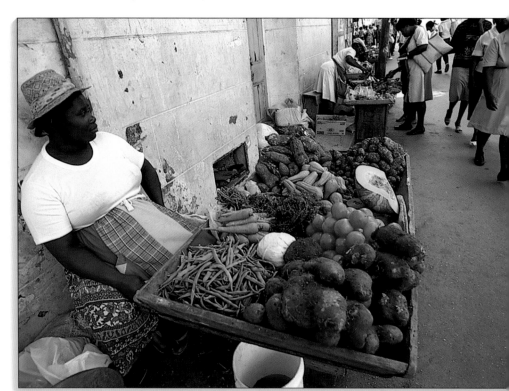

BELOW: vegetables from the country for sale in Cheapside.

Pelican Village and Deep Water Harbour

Behind the Post Office on the sea front, a scenic strip of parkland runs along the Princess Alice Highway to the gates of the Deep Water Harbour. Maintained by the National Conservation Commission, the park, called **Trevor's Way** after a young man who was killed in an accident nearby, gives passers-by a glorious view of the stunning blue of Carlisle Bay.

Opposite the park, **Pelican Village** (H), named after a small island that once existed offshore, is a network of small shops and galleries specialising in local handicrafts from clothing, jewellery and paintings to pottery, baskets and straw mats. After having been given a considerable facelift and more modern premises to cater for the growing number of cruise ship passengers arriving at the port nearby, the village was reopened in 1999. Pelican Island was used as a quarantine station up until the 1950s and was later joined to the mainland on construction of the Deep Water Harbour.

Deep Water Harbour was officially opened in 1961 after more than 60 years of debate. The issue of the new harbour centred on the method of shipping sugar. Traditionally, sugar had always been shipped in bags but competing countries now favoured shipping in bulk. The subject was discussed among Barbados' sugar magnates and finally a new bulk sugar store with a capacity of 81,280 tons was constructed. Today, sugar arrives at the bulk store from the island's three remaining factories and is carried via conveyor belts and underground channels to loading towers. There, at peak times, it is discharged into ships' hatches at the rate of 508 tons an hour.

The harbour provides 1,700 ft (518 metres) of quay space and about 2,700 ft (822 metres) of protective backwater for ships. It has four groups of berthing

At the Caribbean Cigar Company's factory, near Pelican Village, you can watch Cuban tobacco being rolled into cigars by hand. The company produces about 500,000 mild premium cigars a year and exports worldwide. (Tours Mon–Fri; free; tel: 437 8519).

BELOW: docking after a day out at sea.

areas, can take in eight ocean-going ships, and can easily provide simultaneous bunkering for five vessels. As a result, this has become an ideal facility for the island's blossoming cruise ship industry which brings at least 500,000 passengers to these shores a year and is rapidly increasing. Arrivals are strongest, about 3,000 visitors a day, during the winter season from November through to April. The modern Cruise Terminal is well equipped with over 20 duty-free stores, banking and postal facilities. It is easy to tell when a cruise ship is in port as a long line of taxis appear at the Harbour gates from early on to carry visitors into the centre.

The heart of Bridgetown

Back in Broad Street, if you walk northwards up any of the streets between Milk Market and the Parliament Buildings you come to **Swan Street ❶**, a busy but shabby back street crammed with shops, several of them with overhanging balconies still standing from the 19th century. Here, and in Roebuck Street around the corner, is where Barbadians come to shop and where most things are cheaper than in expensive Broad Street. Here you can catch a colourful glimpse of city life where curbside sermons fill the air and a constant tide of shoppers ebb and flow around the myriad stalls lining the roadway that sell everything from sunglasses to coconuts and local fruits. The street is particularly well known for its wide selection of textiles which are snapped up by the island's many seamstresses and is named after John Swan, a surveyor and sea captain who brought some of the first settlers to the island. He is purported to have laid out many of the principal streets in Bridgetown.

ABOVE: duty-frees at the Cruise Terminal. **BELOW:** alternative shopping in Swan Street.

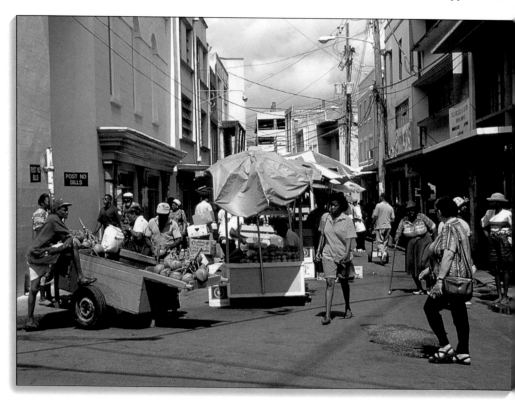

By cutting north up Whites Alley you arrive on James Street opposite the

Synagogue ❶ (open Mon–Fri, 9am–4pm; donations) whose entrance is on Synagogue Lane. Beautifully restored by the Barbados National Trust during the 1980s, the first synagogue – one of the two earliest in the Western hemisphere – was thought to have been built on this spot in around 1654, although the oldest gravestones in the cemetery date from the 1630s. In 1831 the building was destroyed by a hurricane, and this one was completed two years later. However, owing to many turning to Anglicanism and a fall in sugar prices causing an exodus of much of the Jewish community, the building fell into a state of disrepair and decay. In 1929, the Synagogue was sold, only to be bought back by the new Jewish community in 1983 with the help of the National Trust, winning many awards for the restoration work. The Synagogue today is one of the finest examples of its type in the West. It now gleams brightly and is once again in full use. Particularly impressive are the four brass chandeliers hanging above the carved prayer benches, the originals of which are in a Delaware museum in America.

Map on page 176

The Montefiore drinking fountain in front of the public library in Coleridge Street was endowed in 1864 by a Jewish businessman. It bears the inscriptions: "Do wrong to no one", "To bear is to conquer", "Be sober-minded", "Look to the end".

The High Court

Continuing westward along James Street, you quickly come to a crossroads with Coleridge street leading up to the right. On the opposite corner is the 17th-century **Nicholls House**, an early architectural example of Dutch influence in the Caribbean through the slave trade. Alongside is the site of the **High Court** ❸, believed to be on the first piece of land owned by the Barbadian Government. It was purchased on 5 December 1682 by the Governor, Sir Richard Dutton, to build a new public warehouse. This was duly constructed in 1683 but demolished in 1728 to make room for a single structure to house the

JEWS IN BARBADOS

The first Jewish people to arrive in Barbados are believed to have settled in the 1650s, although it is thought that some may have come even earlier. Escaping from the Spanish Inquisition, Sephardic Jews first found refuge in Dutch Brazil, where they played a major role in the cultivation of sugar and the slave trade. But when Portugal took over, they were expelled.

Many moved back to Europe but others remained in the Caribbean, where the Puritan leader Oliver Cromwell, not usually considered a man of tolerance, granted them asylum in Barbados. With them, the Jews brought their sugar cane knowledge, making an important contribution to the island's early prosperity. Mostly merchants, their trading centred on Swan Street, known as Jews Street, where they lived over the shop.

Although Barbados had an official policy of religious tolerance, Jews, Catholics and Non-conformists were discriminated against until 1831, when they were given equal rights. However, many left when the sugar industry took a dive and by 1926 there was one practising Jew left. Just prior to World War II, some Polish Jews started to arrive pre-empting the horrors to come and, since the end of the War, a thriving community has been established.

BELOW: the gleaming interior of the Synagogue.

Legislature, the Law Courts and the jail. Placing a Town Hall in the same compound as a jail was an anomaly, and the source of many wry comments from visitors to the island. The prison was finally closed in 1878 by order of the Governor, Sir John Pope Hennessy. Today, the buildings house the Law Courts, the Magistrates' Courts, the Public Library and the Police Station.

Roebuck Street – full of character

Back on **Roebuck Street**, which has many overhanging balconies and 200-year-old traditions reminiscent of the days of the mule and cart, this characterful central artery of Bridgetown has been marked as one of the areas for restoration by the Government. Once a thriving commercial centre with a lively concentration of shops, it went into decline in the latter half of the 20th century becoming rundown and shabby in appearance. The street got its name from a tavern called The Roebuck, established by Thomas Noell, a London merchant, who sold it in 1659. The tavern continued to flourish for many years as the favourite meeting place of the Barbados Council and the General Assembly.

The women selling a small range of sweets, chewing gum and peanuts from a tray are called hucksters, while hawkers are roving traders who set up their own stalls often selling farmers' fruit and vegetables.

Out of character with the rest of the street is the modern **Tom Adams Financial Centre** Ⓛ, housing the Central Bank of Barbados. At 11 storeys high, it is the tallest building on the island and cost more than BDS$60 million to build in 1983–86, causing quite a stir among taxpayers. A staunch supporter of the arts, the Central Bank hosts art exhibitions in the **Grande Salle**, and the building is also home to the **Frank Collymore Hall**, one of the island's most important cultural centres. Seating 490, the hall has the latest stage equipment for theatre, concerts and conferences and, in November, as part of the Independence Day celebrations, holds the **National Independence Festival of Creative Arts** (NIFCA).

BELOW: an entrepreneur on every corner.

Roebuck Street continues northeastwards for nearly 200 yards (180 metres) before Crumpton Street turns off to the right, leading to **Harrison College** Ⓜ, once a prestigious boys' school and now a successful co-ed. On the site of the old Harrison Free School, founded by Thomas Harrison in 1733 to provide free education for indigent boys, the central buildings are now in line for preservation.

St Michael's Cathedral

Crumpton Street joins St Michael's Row to the south which leads westwards to **St Michael's Cathedral** Ⓝ. Although first constructed in 1628 where St Mary's Church is, the cathedral was rebuilt on its present site in 1665 only to be destroyed by the 1780 hurricane. The coral limestone structure we see today was built several years later with the help of lottery money, ironically lending a Church blessing to gambling. The Greek classical-style cathedral is supposed to have one of the widest unsupported expanses of roof in the world, the oldest manual organ in the Caribbean and a 200-year-old single-hand clock still in working order. The font bears a Greek inscription that is a palindrome – it reads the same backwards and forwards – which translates as "Wash my sins, not only my face". In the cemetery are several governors and two former political leaders – Sir Grantley Adams and his son, Tom Adams. ❑

The Story of Rachel Pringle

Bridgetown's history has had its lighter moments. One of them involves an infamous Barbadian hotel owner of the 1700s named Rachel Pringle.

Rachel was the mulatto daughter of a Scottish schoolmaster, William Lauder, and his African slave mistress. According to legend, Rachel grew up into a beautiful young woman who was badly treated by her dissolute father.

She was able to escape his cruel hand, however, with the aid of one Captain Thomas Pringle, a British naval officer. Pringle paid an exorbitant price to Lauder for Rachel, and set her up in a house in lower Bridgetown. In gratitude to her benefactor, Rachel adopted Pringle's surname.

Much to Pringle's dismay, his liaison with Rachel was barren. In order to maintain Pringle's affections, Rachel "borrowed" a baby while Pringle was away at sea and presented it to him as their own when he returned to Barbados. Nevertheless, her ruse was revealed, however, when the rightful mother arrived to claim back her baby. Captain Pringle left the scheming Rachel in disgust, but it did not take long before she found herself another wealthy "protector" in the name of Polgreen.

At some time in 1780, Rachel managed to open the island's first modest hotel, starting a Bridgetown tradition of taverns that were run by black or mulatto women, who were the favourite paramours of influential men, be they planters or naval officers. By this time she had grown into a woman of very large proportions and could be seen sitting outside her door in her favourite chair.

Rachel's hotel (on what is now St George Street) quickly became a popular haunt with the British Royal Navy. One night in 1789, a visiting party of Royal Naval officers, led by Prince William Henry (who later became King William IV in 1830) who had sailed into Carlisle Bay on the frigate *Pegasus*, paid a visit to Rachel's hotel.

The Prince and his companions had their fill of what we might assume was Barbados rum, and, in a spree of drunken horseplay, proceeded to smash the place up, breaking furniture and shattering glassware. Crowds gathered outside to see what the commotion was all about and witnessed the unruly Prince's parting shot of capsizing Rachel's chair and sending her sprawling onto the ground. Throughout the whole incident, the outsized proprietor remained remarkably quiet and composed.

The next day, just before the ship sailed with the royal vandal on board, Rachel sent the Prince an itemised bill for £700 – a princely sum indeed. He paid the bill promptly and Rachel restored her hotel in a more sumptuous style, renaming it the Royal Naval Hotel.

Regrettably, her hotel was destroyed by fire in 1821, but her story lives on in Bajan folklore and she has been immortalised in a cartoon (1796) by Thomas Rowlandson (1756–1827) which takes pride of place in the Barbados Museum and Historical Society's art gallery (*see page 195*). ❑

RIGHT: Rachel Pringle in her favourite seat, caricatured by Rowlandson.

Banks
Xactly!

Banks
exactly!

AROUND BRIDGETOWN

On the outskirts of the capital, explore the historic Garrison with an enlightening art gallery and museum, see how the island's favourite drinks are made and admire the pretty houses in Belleville

Maps on pages 194/199

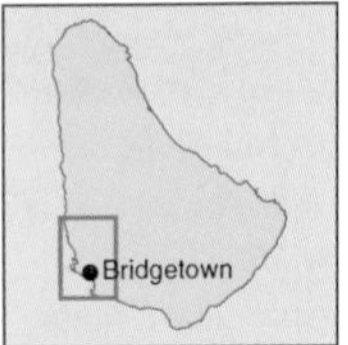

The capital city of **Bridgetown** ❶ lies in the parish of St Michael, encompassed by the ABC Highway to the north and east. It is a highly developed and densely populated area – the hub of Barbadian culture and commerce. This parish, more than any other perhaps, has witnessed the most significant change since the island's early years. A traveller describing the area in 1672 said it "hath a commodious road for ships, is a place well frequented and traded unto, and is strongly defended by two powerful Forts." Gone are the old military defences that hark back to days of Colonial rule and in place of the once grassy pastures and marshlands is a sprawling fusion of residential and commercial districts.

Today, some of Barbados' major industries are located in St Michael on the outskirts of Bridgetown. They include the Caribbean Broadcasting Corporation, the island's only television company; Barbados Dairy Industries, which produces local pasteurised milk, and many government institutions such as the Barbados Telephone Company and Barbados Light and Power Company.

St Michael is also the centre for Barbados's burgeoning offshore industry that fosters many financial services including international banks and insurance and investment management companies. International businesses flocked to the island in the latter part of the 1990s due to its low tax status achieved through a network of international treaties (mostly with the United States, Canada, United Kingdom and some European countries). This has given a vital boost to the economy and has had a positive impact on many associated areas servicing the sector, from accounting and legal firms to property management, rental companies and the construction industry. A fine example is the international business centre that's been developed at Warrens on the north arm of the ABC Highway.

The days of musket and cannon

In its heyday the **Garrison Savannah** Ⓐ, about a mile (1.5 km) south of the town centre on Highway 7, was often described as one of the finest parade grounds in the West Indies. Even today, lined on one side by old naval cannons, it is easy to imagine regiments of brightly-uniformed soldiers marching across it. Since the withdrawal of British troops in 1905–6 the Savannah has been used mainly for recreational rather than military purposes. These 50 acres (20 hectares), surrounded by historic buildings, provide a green open space that is ideal for all types of sporting activities including football, rugby, cricket and basketball. And at Easter it is the site of the annual kite flying competition – a colourful tradition.

Home of the **Barbados Turf Club**, the Garrison is

PRECEDING PAGES: Congaline revellers at the Garrison Savannah.
LEFT: on show at the National Stadium.
BELOW: The prestigious Gold Cup.

The National Cannon Collection in front of the Main Guard is considered to be the most outstanding collection of 17th-century iron guns known to exist in the world.

perhaps best known throughout the Caribbean as a top-class horse-racing track. On race days, such as the prestigious **Sandy Lane Gold Cup**, contagious excitement fills the air and the Garrison is transformed into a circus of activity. The Turf Club, which is responsible for the upkeep of the Savannah, has done a fine job. It has recently not only added a new stand for race enthusiasts but is responsible for the addition of a paved track to the oval which is popular with early morning and evening joggers.

On 30 November, the island's Day of Independence is celebrated in full pomp and splendour when the colourful regiments of the armed forces and the mounted guardsmen in red waistcoats and white tropical helmets go on parade on the Savannah. Here the Barbados Defence Force, the Royal Coast Guard, the Cadets, Girl Guides, Rangers and anyone else who wears a uniform gather to march before the assembled dignitaries.

Among the many fine buildings that surround the Savannah, few can match the stately beauty of the **Main Guard** Ⓑ on the southwest corner, with a distinctive cupola tower and clock, which has been the subject of many paintings and photographs. Formerly the guardhouse of the British Regiment and the venue for the grim business of court martials and subsequent penalties, after the British military left, the building became the Savannah Club, where members of "high white" society met for a drink on the wide verandah, or came for lunch or dinner and to play tennis.

The clock tower bears the date 1803 and the building itself was probably completed a few years later. Now the headquarters of the Barbados Legion, the Main Guard is also an Information Centre, set up by Major Michael Hartland, the former Garrison Secretary of the Regiment – who also created the impressive

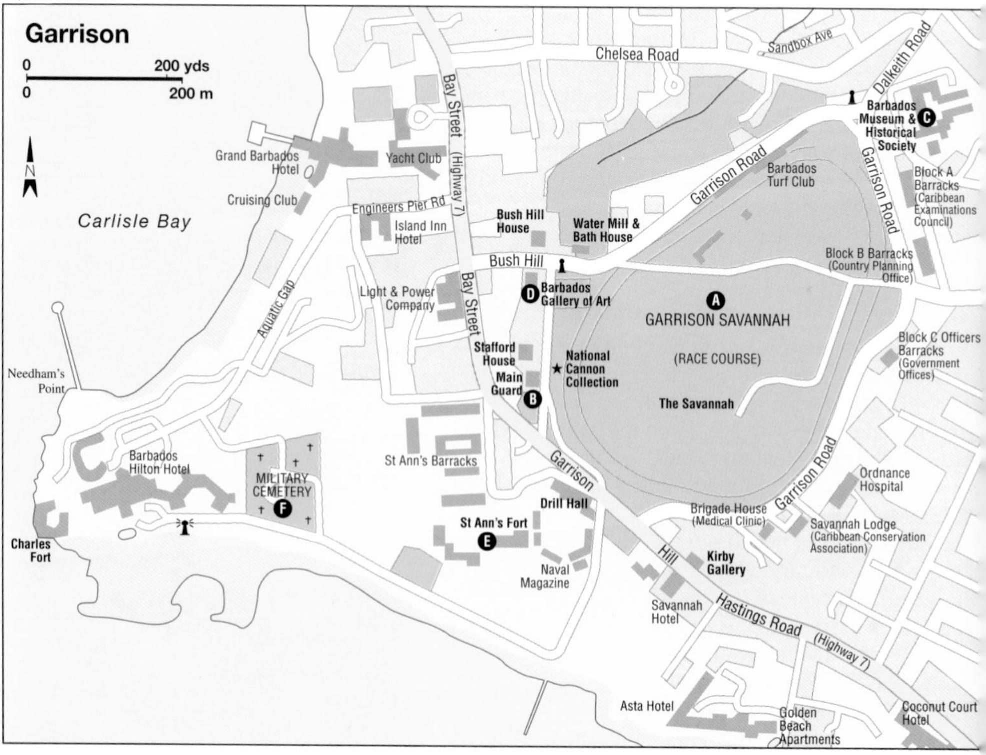

Garrison

0 200 yds
0 200 m
N
Carlisle Bay
Chelsea Road
Sandbox Ave
Dalkeith Road
Barbados Museum & Historical Society Ⓒ
Bay Street (Highway 7)
Grand Barbados Hotel
Yacht Club
Cruising Club
Engineers Pier Rd
Island Inn Hotel
Bush Hill House
Water Mill & Bath House
Garrison Road
Barbados Turf Club
Garrison Road
Block A Barracks (Caribbean Examinations Council)
Block B Barracks (Country Planning Office)
Bush Hill
Light & Power Company
Ⓓ Barbados Gallery of Art
Ⓐ GARRISON SAVANNAH
(RACE COURSE)
The Savannah
Aquatic Gap
Needham's Point
Stafford House
Main Guard Ⓑ
★ National Cannon Collection
Block C Officers Barracks (Government Offices)
St Ann's Barracks
Garrison Hill
Barbados Hilton Hotel
MILITARY CEMETERY Ⓕ
Drill Hall
Brigade House (Medical Clinic)
Garrison Road
Ordnance Hospital
Charles Fort
St Ann's Fort Ⓔ
Savannah Lodge (Caribbean Conservation Association)
Kirby Gallery
Naval Magazine
Savannah Hotel
Hastings Road (Highway 7)
Asta Hotel
Golden Beach Apartments
Coconut Court Hotel

National Cannon Collection in front – as part of an ambitious redevelopment project for the Garrison.

The Barbados Museum & Historical Society

Across the Savannah in the northeastern corner, the **Barbados Museum & Historical Society** ❸ (open Mon–Sat and Sun pm, closed pub. hols; entrance fee; tel: 427 0201) is the former military prison of the British Garrison. Established in 1933 by a group of public spirited individuals, led by E.M. Shilstone, the museum is considered one of the best in the Caribbean. The building is a fine example of Georgian architecture with a pleasant courtyard used for cultural activities and a café shaded by trees. The two wings at the back were built between 1817 and 1821, and the main block was completed in 1853.

The beautifully presented collection is laid out in a series of mostly wheelchair-friendly galleries, many of which were once prison cells, relating the history of Barbados from the Amerindians through to the first settlers, the days of slavery and the development of the island until the present, with portrayals of modern everyday life. Exhibits include reconstructions of a plantation house room and a prisoner's cell, and a fascinating collection of old maps includes one by Richard Ligon, dated 1657. The Children's Gallery allows younger ones to experience history hands on and see the toys and games from bygone days. The curators have not forgotten the island's natural history either: fish of the surrounding seas, native plants and birds are all represented here and there is a Museum Shop well stocked with West Indian books, reproductions of prints and paintings in the museum and Barbadian crafts and jewellery.

Every Thursday evening the Pinelands Creative Workshop puts on a show in

Map on page 194

TIP

The Barbados Museum's Research Library has archives of rare West Indian material including maps, photographs and genealogical records (open Mon–Fri am; tel: 427 0201).

BELOW: Barbados Museum – once a military prison.

Amerindian art in the Barbados Museum.

BELOW: *Palm Sunday* by local artist Vanita Comissiong.

the courtyard called **1627 And All That**, a colourful folkloric production of song and dance illustrating the island's history, and which includes a tour of the museum, a buffet dinner with drinks and transport to and from your hotel (call 428 1627 to make a reservation). In early December, the museum organises a Fine Craft Festival of local art and crafts.

Barbados Gallery of Art – a non-commercial enterprise

Garrison Road runs down the northwestern side of the Savannah for a couple of hundred yards, past the Barbados Turf Club and into Bush Hill. On the left stands the **Barbados Gallery of Art** (**BGA**) **D** (open Tue–Sat, closed pub. hols; entrance fee; call 228 0149 for tours). Since 1988, the BGA has gathered together a 300-strong permanent collection of paintings, sculptures, prints, drawings and other mixed media works from the Caribbean, South America and the United States. There is a special emphasis on Barbadian art – featuring the likes of Ras Ishi, Alison Chapman-Andrews and Stanley Greaves – which are rotated in six annual exhibitions.

The BGA seeks to preserve, research and exhibit important works and is the only non-commercial gallery of its kind on the island that is dedicated to the visual arts. Director and curator Rodney Reynolds says in *Simply Barbados*: "I like to think about objects on view in an exhibition like a well-written chapter in a book. It should all fit together… The Gallery staff and volunteer tour guides function like dictionaries to help us if we get stuck." The BGA also runs a four-week National Summer Art Camp for children.

Opposite the Gallery is **Bush Hill House** on the site where, according to extensive research carried out in the early 1990s, it was established that George

Washington stayed when he visited Barbados in 1751. Reputedly it was the first US president's only trip to a foreign country. According to his diary, he and his half-brother Lawrence stayed in a house that belonged to Captain Crofton, who was the Commander of James Fort. Lawrence suffered from tuberculosis and had come to Barbados hoping to be cured by the tropical climate. George had the misfortune to contract smallpox, the scars of which he bore for the rest of his life. Some historians suggest that Washington's illness was not entirely bad luck. By surviving the disease in Barbados, he developed an immunity which kept him alive and at the head of the rebel forces throughout the American Revolution, while smallpox ravaged his troops.

Map on page 194

St Ann's Fort and the Military Cemetery

Back across Highway 7 stands the long, thin Victorian **Drill Hall** that was built on the foundation of one of the ramparts of **St Ann's Fort** Ⓔ. Although construction of the fort began in 1704, it was never completed. Now only the main ramparts survive from that period, indicating the grand design once envisaged. The fort today is of a much simpler style with walls ranging from 4 ft–20 ft (1–6 metres) thick and inside are the store rooms, armoury and powder magazines as they were at the end of the 18th century. Nowadays, the Barbados Defence Force is headquartered here, carrying on some of the same drills and duties that were a familiar sight within these walls more than 100 years ago.

It was the threat of French invasion during the American War of Independence that led to the establishment of the first garrison of British troops on Barbados. As the size of the military establishment grew, Barbados became the headquarters of the British forces in the Leeward and Windward Islands. But it was

BELOW: coconuts for sale on a typical Bajan street.

Brown Sugar in Aquatic Gap is one of the few restaurants that serves Bajan cuisine daily and in a traditional tropical setting. The staff are trained to help people with disabilities and the menu is available in Braille. Visit their website: brownsugar restaurant.com, or call 436 7069.

tropical diseases, not the French, that killed the British recruits. One report states that, of 19,676 soldiers sent to the West Indies from England in 1796, 17,173 died before 1802.

Many of the soldiers who died after 1800 were buried in the area directly behind St Ann's Fort. The earliest burials seem to have been near the shore adjoining the property that is now the Barbados Hilton Hotel. Some time in 1820, The Garrison discontinued burying its dead here and began to use a new site close by which is now known as the **Military Cemetery** **F**. It is still used for the burial of service personnel, active or retired, and their families.

To reach the **Barbados Hilton** at the end of Aquatic Gap, you continue towards Bridgetown along Bay Street (Highway 7) for 400 yards (365 metres) and turn left by the Island Inn Hotel, which brings you into Aquatic Gap and past an ugly oil refinery. The Hilton is undergoing major reconstruction and modernisation due to be completed by 2002, but it shares lovely **Needham's Point** where you will find silent old cannons pointing out to sea – relics of **Charles Fort**, the largest of the defences built during the prime of the British Regiment. Here is a picturesque stretch of beach that is a popular spot for Bank Holiday picnics and a centre for the island's sailors. The **Grand Barbados Hotel** which borders the other end of the beach spills on to a picturesque pier. It was first built in 1925 as the Aquatic Club with a cinema and an elegant dance floor.

Sunset on the Esplanade

Continuing towards Bridgetown centre along Bay Street you come to a sudden gap in the buildings along the sea front. This is the **Esplanade** which has a bandstand and a splendid view of the calm waters of Carlisle Bay. It is an

BELOW: sunset on Carlisle Bay.

ideal spot from which to watch the sun set behind the numerous yachts moored off the coast. At one end, sleepy fishermen laze in hammocks in the shelter of the afternoon sun. Plans have been put forward among government circles to extend this 100-yard (90-metre) or so walkway so that pedestrians may enjoy this sea view clear into Bridgetown.

Opposite the Esplanade are the **Government Headquarters**, which house the offices of the Prime Minister. At the front of the circular driveway, bordered on all sides by poinsettias, begonias and hibiscus flowers, stands a bust of Sir Grantley Adams, the island's first Premier, sculpted by the eminent artist Karl Broodhagen who also created the Emancipation Monument (*see page 201*).

Just past the Esplanade continuing towards Bridgetown are two nightclubs – **Harbour Lights** and **The Boatyard** – popular with young Barbadians and visitors alike and within half a mile (1 km) of each other. Both offer live bands, drinks included in the entrance fee, and dancing on the beach to the early hours. The Boatyard also has a restaurant that is open for lunch and at the end of May hosts the annual **Mount Gay/Boatyard Regatta** (*see pages 240–41*).

Queen's House and Park

Turn right, away from the coast, just after The Boatyard, head towards the **Queen Elizabeth Hospital** which has a 24-hour accident and emergency department, and continue northwards over the roundabout to **Queen's Park ❷**, a short distance away. Set in the elegant park grounds, **Queen's House** (1780) is a fine example of Georgian architecture and was once the official residence of the Commanding General of the Imperial Troops. After the British forces left the island in 1905, the Government acquired the land and house and in 1909 the

Map on page 199

No Catholic priest was allowed to live on the island until 1839, when Irish soldiers stationed here demanded one and St Patrick's Cathedral in Bay Street was built. To this day their flags and crests adorn the walls of the church which was rebuilt in 1897 after a fire.

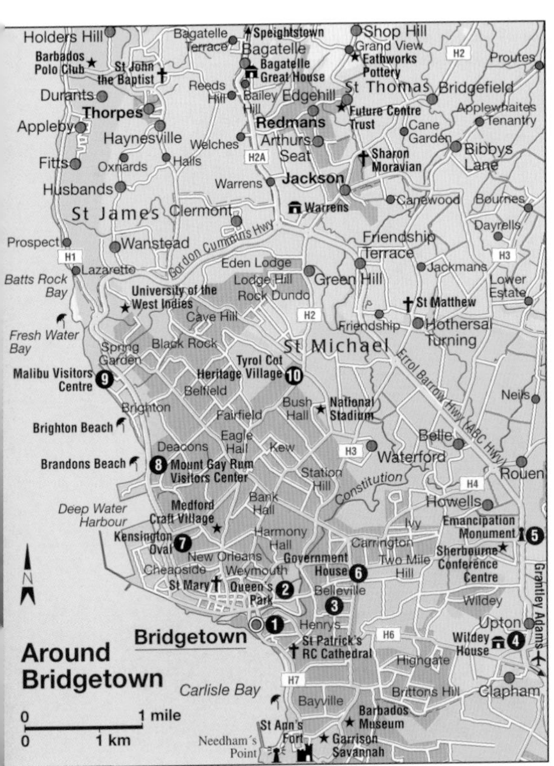

BELOW: stained glass at St Patrick's Cathedral.

The giant baobab tree, which shades the playground in Queen's Park, is a mystery – it is more than 1,000 years old, yet it is native to Africa not the Caribbean.

BELOW: Wildey House, home of the National Trust.

park, landscaped by the Governer's wife Lady Gilbert Carter, was opened to the public and is often used for cricket matches. Today, the ground floor of the house, which has a magnificent wooden verandah, is now used for exhibitions of local art, while upstairs is the **Daphne Joseph-Hackett Theatre**, named after the island's influential dramatist (1915–1988).

The beautiful suburb of Belleville

Travelling eastwards along Constitution Road and into Belmont, you come to the picturesque suburb of **Belleville** ❸ whose 11 avenues are lined with fancy Barbadian-style Victorian villas. The well laid out area was designed in the 1880s by Sam Manning who owned a nearby residence called Erdiston. Although many of the wooden structures have been renovated for modern use, these houses largely retain their original architectural lines and 19th-century grace but they are increasingly being used as business premises.

Turning left at the roundabout south of Belleville, you soon come to an industrial area called **Wildey** where the Barbados National Trust (*see page 205*) has its headquarters in the magnificent Georgian **Wildey House** ❹, built on a ridge looking out to sea between 1760 and 1780. Meticulously restored in 1997, and decorated with the help of John Chandler of Fisherpond (*see page 290*), this traditional Great House, once in the middle of acres of swaying sugar cane, is a showpiece for the Trust's comprehensive collection of antique furniture, which can be seen as part of the Open House scheme (*see Travel Tips on page 343*).

Hitting the ABC Highway a little further east you come face to face with the large satellite dishes of BET, Barbados's telephone company. Behind is the **Garfield Sobers Sports Complex**. In 1992 Barbados acquired its first totally covered sports hall with a capacity for 4,000 spectators and named it after local cricketing legend and Barbados National Hero Sir "Gary" Sobers (*see page 90*). The complex is a centre for a wide number of sports and leisure enthusiasts, including walkers, joggers and skaters and is also a regular venue for musical entertainment. The grounds include tennis courts and the headquarters of the Barbados Lawn Tennis Association; the Aquatic Centre equipped with an Olympic-sized pool and a state-of-the-art astroturf hockey field.

TIP

Bajans are very proud of their award-winning home brew, Banks Beer, developed in 1961 and now sold worldwide. Tours of the Wildey brewery are on Tuesday and Thursday at 10am and 1pm; the entrance fee is donated to charity. Call 429 2113 to book.

Two Mile Hill – fit for a president

Driving north along the ABC Highway, turn left down **Two Mile Hill** back towards Bridgetown at the next roundabout where the stately **Emancipation Monument** ❺ stands (*see below*). Not far down the hill on the left is the **Sherbourne Conference Centre**, a world-class conference facility fully equipped with state-of-the-art high technology. Opened in 1994, it was beamed around the world in 1997 when US President Bill Clinton attended a Caribbean/USA summit here. The main hall seats up to 1,200 people theatre-style and there is ample floor space to house large exhibitions.

Conveniently, the house next door, **Ilaro Court**, is the official residence of the Prime Minister of Barbados, which was designed in 1919 by Lady Gilbert Carter, the American wife of Sir Gilbert Carter, the Governor of Barbados from 1904 to 1911. Built mainly with coral stone, it combines many luxurious and varied architectural features, including Ionic columns and an enclosed swimming pool. Purchased by the Government in 1976, the grounds are opened to the public only for charitable events, such as **Carols by Candlelight**, an outdoor family concert held each Christmas.

BELOW: Bussa – a symbol of freedom.

THE STORY OF BUSSA

The Emancipation Monument or "The Freed Slave" was erected in 1986 and is the masterpiece of Karl Broodhagen, one of Barbados' best known sculptors. It represents an African slave called Bussa, who led a rebellion against the local planters in 1816.

Now a National Hero (*see page 46*), Bussa was an intelligent, able man and a ranger on Bayley's Plantation in St Philip. Although his position afforded him relative comforts compared to regular slaves he became dedicated to the fight for freedom. As news filtered to Barbados of significant steps towards liberation from overseas, the slave population grew increasingly bitter and discontented.

Inspired in part by the brutal slave uprising of 1791 in St Domingue and suspicious of the virulent reaction by the planter class against the proposed Slave Registry Bill, local slaves were spurred to action on Easter Sunday 1816. The uprising started at Bayley's and soon spread to the other plantations across the island. However, it was soon to be mightily quashed by troops from St Ann's Fort. Bussa was among the hundreds of slaves killed during the short-lived rebellion but lives on as a symbol of freedom.

Glendairy Prison on Station Hill is the only prison on the island. Built for 350 inmates by William Farnum in 1855, it has been subject to overcrowding despite Barbados's low crime rate. The death penalty is still the ultimate punishment but it hasn't been given since 1983.

At the bottom of Two Mile Hill, on the northern boundary of Belleville, stands the imposing **Government House** ❻, which has been the official residence of the Governor General – the Queen's representative to Barbados – since the mid 18th century. This sturdy mansion has been sited here since 1702 and has survived several hurricanes. Originally called Pilgrim House, it was purchased by the Government in 1736 from John Pilgrim, a Quaker. The house incorporates many of the typical features of Barbadian Great Houses: shady verandahs, arched porticoes, jalousied windows, parapet roof and circular driveway. The house and grounds, where there is a magnificent specimen of a cannonball tree (its fruit look just like cannonballs) are also only open to the public for charitable events, such as the **International Women's Fair** in February.

Cricket, lovely cricket

North of Bridgetown centre, tucked almost completely from view off Fontabelle, is **Kensington Oval** ❼, a Barbadian shrine to cricket and the site of many an exciting international Test Match. Dating from 1882, the Oval and surrounding area is a hive of activity when a cricket match is being played and people from all walks of life become united by their mutual love for the game. The crowds pack the stands and dress up in fancy clothes, bringing picnics, beer and rum punch and create a noisy carnival atmosphere as they loudly cheer on their team – the spirit runs even higher when the West Indies are playing against England their former mother country.

Food stalls and T-shirt salesmen crowd the road outside the entrance to the cricket ground and all stay close to their radios to keep in touch with the score (*see Cricket – A National Religion on pages 89–92*).

BELOW: broad-casting a cricket match to the nation.

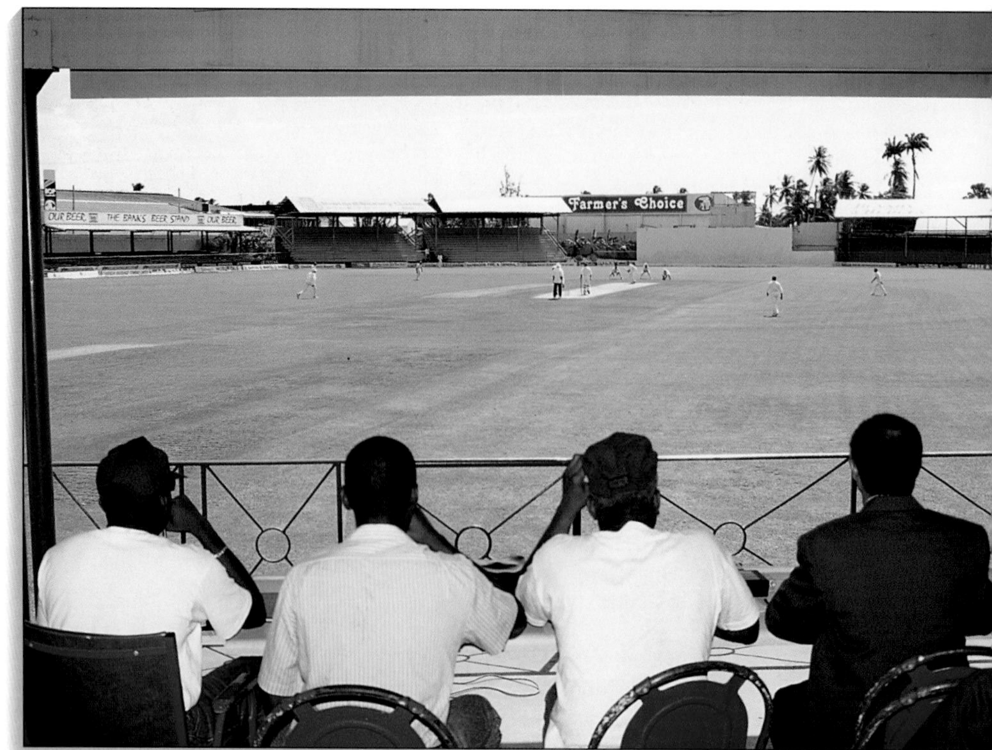

Tall Ships in Shallow Draught

Just north of the Oval a few minutes away on the coast is an inlet of sea called **Shallow Draught** which is a popular departure point for all types of fun tours and sailing adventures. Visitors can take the notorious ***Jolly Roger*** pirate ship complete with rope-swinging, plank-walking and lots of rum punch. The spacious ***MV Harbour Master*** has a capacity for about 600 passengers on its four decks and on occasion hosts dinner, theatre and other special events. There is also a wide selection of catamarans for more intimate cruises, with lunch provided and snorkelling stops, around the island. The **Atlantis Submarine** departure point is at Shallow Draught and transfer boats to one of the world's first recreational submarines leave from here on the hour every hour (9am–6pm).

In **Indian Ground**, an area between Deacon's Road and Westbury Road, is a little known monument that was erected to commemorate the tercentenary of the first landing of the English on Barbados. The monument bears the date 1605, but the event really occurred in 1625, when the English landed at Holetown (*see page 217*). Since the mid 1980s, this area has developed considerably and is a mixture of residential and commercial enterprises.

Map on page 199

Fun and rum on the Jolly Roger.

Rum and more rum

Spring Garden Highway skirts Shallow Ground as it heads northwards away from Bridgetown. Close by is the **Mount Gay Rum Visitors Centre** ❽ (open Mon–Fri and Sat am; entrance fee; tel: 425 9066), where you can discover the fascinating history of Mount Gay's award-winning rum – claimed to be the oldest in Barbados and probably the world – and learn how it is made. There is certainly evidence of a rum-making operation dating back to 1703 on the Mount

BELOW LEFT: piling up the rum barrels.
BELOW: cruising on a catamaran.

At Fairfield Crossroads just south of Tyrol Cot, in an old syrup boiling house, is Maggie Bell's Red Clay Pottery and gallery. Call 424 3800 for a tour.

Gay estate in St Lucy. There is an impressive audio-visual presentation, a gift shop, and an opportunity to sample the rum, straight up or in a cocktail.

A little further along the coast in Brighton is the **Malibu Visitors Centre** ❾ (open Mon–Fri; no tours 11am–noon: last tour 3.45pm; tel: 425 9393), where you can see how the popular coconut-flavoured rum-based drink, sold around the world, is made. At the beachside centre, where you can stay all day, you can go on a tour of the distillery, watch a video presentation and enjoy a free tasting! Malibu also offers a variety of packages that allows you to delve into a delicious Bajan buffet luncheon and take part in all manner of activities, from non-motorised watersports such as kayaks and aquacycles to beach games like volleyball, football and paddle tennis. An all-round Caribbean fun day.

Travelling back towards Bridgetown on Spring Garden Highway, take a left at the major intersection with traffic lights and you soon reach the **Medford Craft Village** (open Mon–Fri and Sat am; tel: 427-3179). Mr Reggie Medford, who has honed and perfected his own techniques for producing local wood artworks set up this workshop and showroom in 1988. And here you can watch wood carvers creating masterpieces from the trunks and roots of mahogany trees that you can see growing around the island, but only offically felled or fallen trees are used, and no part is wasted.

Tyrol Cot – historic home

An enterprise of the Barbados National Trust, **Tyrol Cot Heritage Village** ❿ (open Mon–Fri and Public Holidays; entrance fee) was the home of Sir Grantley Adams, the island's first premier (*see page 45*). The house was built by a prominent local builder William Farnum in 1854 and it was the home of the Adams family – their son Tom was the island's second prime minister after Independence – from 1929 until Lady Adams' death in 1990. On Codrington Hill, the Heritage Village is a living museum created by the National Trust in landscaped gardens portraying Barbadian life in the 1930s. It includes a restored slave hut, a blacksmith's shop and a rum shop with craftsmen working as you look on.

Below: mahogany art has a Caribbean flavour.

Not far to the east of Tyrol Cot stands the **National Stadium**, which opened in 1970. Inter-school and Caribbean track and field events are held here along with Division One football (soccer) and cycling. In need of an upgrade, plans are in place to improve the track surface and add a warm-up track. With a seating capacity of 5,000 and standing room for 2,000 more, it is the largest gathering place on the island and the magnificent Crop Over costumes are judged here on Grand Kadooment Day (*see pages 134–35*).

Just over a mile (1.5 km) north of Tyrol Cot on the ABC Highway, a massive building project is under way. **Warrens International Business Centre** is providing nearly 1 million sq. ft (93,000 sq. metres) of new office space to service offshore and international companies and aims to be the best in the Caribbean. Originally planned to be a new town centre, Warrens will include residential areas, a shopping centre and recreational facilities, part of which are forming the Millennium Project. ❑

The Barbados National Trust

Travelling around the island, it won't take you long to appreciate the importance of the Barbados National Trust. This charity was set up in 1961 with the aim of recording and preserving Bajan history by acquiring properties and opening them to the public. Not only was the Trust concerned to conserve the island's fragile environment wherever possible, but it also wanted to rescue some of its architectural treasures from terminal collapse. For over 40 years, it has stepped in to buy and restore a wide range of buildings, including Great Houses, signal stations, a windmill and a synagogue.

The brains behind the Trust's foundation was Ronald Tree, a self-styled Anglo-American businessman and British MP. He was a friend and associate of Winston Churchill, serving in his War Cabinet. Tree remembered how during World War II Churchill and friends would shelter in his English home, when the German bombing raids aimed at the Prime Minister's residence came too close for comfort. After the War, he came to the Caribbean and fell in love with Barbados. Heron Bay Villa (*see page 221*), which he had built, was frequented by his many rich and famous friends.

With the founding of the Trust, Tree was able to make the most of these contacts, and his fund-raising efforts were soon rewarded when the Government agreed to pay half the purchase price for Welchman Hall Gully (*see page 274*), with the Trust providing the balance. Since then, successful fund-raising has been a regular feature of the Trust's activities, enabling it to diversify the sorts of properties it owns and manages. The Bridgetown Synagogue (*see page 187*), for instance, was a tumbledown warehouse listed for demolition until the Jewish community, led by the Altman family, worked with the Trust to raise the renovation funds.

Ronald Tree's death in 1976 led to a fresh influx of donations from friends around the world. These enabled the Trust to buy its first owned headquarters in 1983, in a Victorian villa in Belleville. It is mostly individual bequests and donations that make the Trust's work possible. The Andromeda Botanic Gardens (*see page 262*) were bequeathed by avid horticulturalist Iris Bannochie in 1989, while the elegant Georgian Wildey House, the Trust's current home, was left by Edna Leacock in memory of her son. Perhaps the most unorthodox gift came from Lawrence Bannister, who decided to donate some land around the historic Morgan Lewis Sugar Mill (*see page 306*). Climbing to the top, he threw a pebble, saying that where it landed would mark the limit of the land attached to the mill.

There is nothing stuffy about the Trust and its activities. It works with schools to encourage tree-planting programmes, co-sponsors weekly hikes throughout the island and even runs an Adopt-Your-Beach campaign. Private houses sometimes open their doors to the public through the Trust where you can buy publications on local heritage. ❑

● *See page 343 for details about the Open House Scheme, Heritage Passport and hikes.*

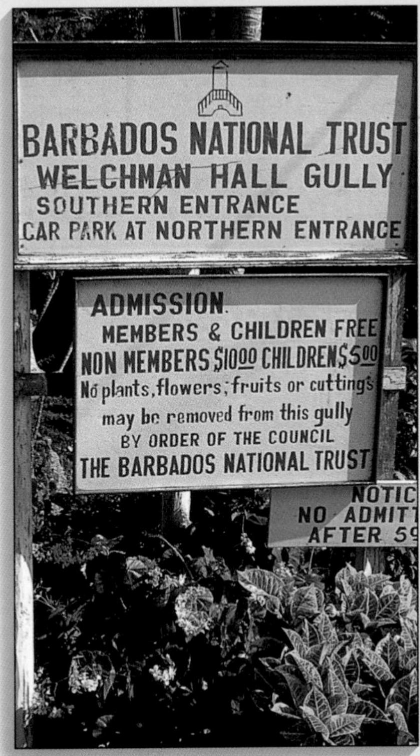

RIGHT: Welchman Hall Gully was the National Trust's first project.

LEH WE FIRE ONE ON DAT...

The national drink of Barbados, with a rum shop on practically every corner, rum plays an integral part in the island's culture

Unquestionably, rum is the social drink of Barbados today and an excuse can always be found to "fire one" (have a drink). A by-product of a booming sugar industry, the first batches of native distilled spirit were already in circulation in the 1640s and were referred to in a document as "Rumbullion, alias Kill Divill…a hot, hellish and terrible liquor". It is likely that the word "rum" was first coined in Bridgetown's waterfront taverns, where over indulgence of the potent liquor, being loaded aboard ships for the crew and export, encouraged rumbustuous behaviour which often ended in a "rumbullion", an old English word for a brawl.

Rum shops sprang up all over the island and today not only sell liquor, but double up as a village store and informal community centre

LIQUID GOLD

Of all alcoholic drinks rum is one of the most natural as it is made directly from molasses, a dark sticky residue left over in the production of sugar. A pure water supply, a result of filtering through coral limestone, has also been credited as distinguishing Barbados rums from the rest. After fermentation the liquor is distilled and blended for flavour. It is the only liquor that comes in two distinct colours – white, or clear (unaged, or kept in stainless steel barrels) and dark, or golden brown. Dark rums get their colour through aging in old oak casks and become smoother and mellower as they mature. A fine 10-year-old rum can achieve the same complexity as quality cognac.

▷ FIRE WATER
Bajans are said to drink rum like water – amounting to 250,000 cases a year (almost a case per person).

▷ FUN AND RUM
Never the two be parted! Present in every aspect of life, Barbados' rum producers provide sponsorship for major sports events and festivals.

△ REAPING THE SWEETS
It didn't take long to find out that a forceful fiery liquor could also be made from sugar cane adding to the planters' prosperity.

△ HIGH SPIRITS
In the rum shops tongues are loosened, politics discussed, rumours spread and fierce games of dominos played, but women are not welcome.

▷ NAVAL TRADITION
Lord Nelson himself is believed to have been preserved in a cask of his favourite rum when he died aboard ship at the Battle of Trafalgar.

SWEET FUH DAYS –

Rum is the chameleon of the drinking world with humble beginnings among seafarers yet savoured today by the sophisticated. Usually shared among friends, rum is drunk neat straight from the bottle, in small snap glasses, or "on the rocks" with plenty of ice. White rums such as ESAF are believed not to give hangovers and blend well in the dozens of rum cocktails available, from daquarís of rum, lime juice, sugar syrup and banana, to Pina Colada, a pineapple concoction, to Malibu, a coconut-flavoured rum made in Barbados. But the classic Caribbean drink must be Rum Punch, made to a recipe handed down through the generations in the rhyme: One of sour (lime), Two of sweet (sugar syrup), Three of strong (dark rum) and Four of weak (water) and five drops of bitters.

◁ **RUM STOP**
About 1,200 rum shops dot the landscape, at least one at the heart of every community.

▽ **SUNDOWNERS**
George Washington, Lord Byron and Paul Revere are said to be among the world's more famous rum lovers of the past.

THE PLATINUM COAST

Sophisticated hotels and luxurious villas hide in coconut groves along the Caribbean-kissed West Coast, where you can play golf on world-class courses, watch polo and go to the opera

Map on page 212

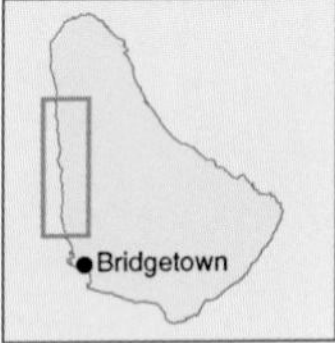

This gentle piece of coastline must have been a welcoming sight to the shipload of English mariners who stopped off where Holetown now stands on their way back from Brazil in 1625. They claimed the island in the name of the King and set plans in motion to make it a British colony. Now the 7½ miles (12 km) of white sandy beaches, that were covered by thick forest when the explorers first set eyes on the island, are worth more than US$3 million an acre as the rich and famous from all over the world have made them their holiday idyll and earned them the epithets "platinum" and "gold".

Stretching from Bridgetown to Speightstown, almost all the luxurious hotels on the island are in the parish of St James, with several being in St Peter, as the belt extends gradually northward – most of them right on the edge of the clear, glittering Caribbean Sea and some of the island's finest beaches. Here, luxurious homes, many hidden behind long, tree-lined driveways and high walls, rival stately plantation Great Houses and plush hotels. These establishments exist side by side with their humble neighbours, the gaily painted chattel houses (*see pages 282–83*) just across the narrow Highway 1 coast road.

Since the mid–1990s, the West Coast has seen an unprecedented construction boom – more and more luxury residences are being built and beach front property is at a premium. Gated communities are on the rise too – the golf course at Royal Westmoreland, the marina at Port St Charles (*see page 301*) and British tennis personality David Lloyd's Sugar Hill "lifestyle resort" are all multimillion-dollar property developments with restricted public access.

Several of the smaller hotels have joined the fray and found themselves with a new lease of life. The Tropicana Hotel on the border of St James and St Peter used to be a rather rundown establishment offering rooms for as little as BDS$50 night and catering primarily to low-end package tour operators. Many millions later it emerged in 1998 as Reed's House, a luxury apartment/penthouse block offering one-bedroom units at more than US$500,000. A little further north in Roadview, St Peter, the King's Beach Hotel is expanding to become another village oasis of luxury accommodation where a one-bedroom townhouse sells for around US$200,000.

PRECEDING PAGES: dusk on the beach at Mullins Bay.
LEFT: running for cover at the Colony Club.
BELOW: hobie cats ready and waiting.

Beachcomber's paradise

Thanks to a Barbados law that doesn't allow beaches to be privately owned, you can stroll along miles of uninterrupted white sand beach either just to take in the natural beauty of the coastline and gentle azure sea, or to check out the other sights of a St James' beach: a vacationing movie star, local craftsmen selling their wares, fishermen drying their nets, a lively

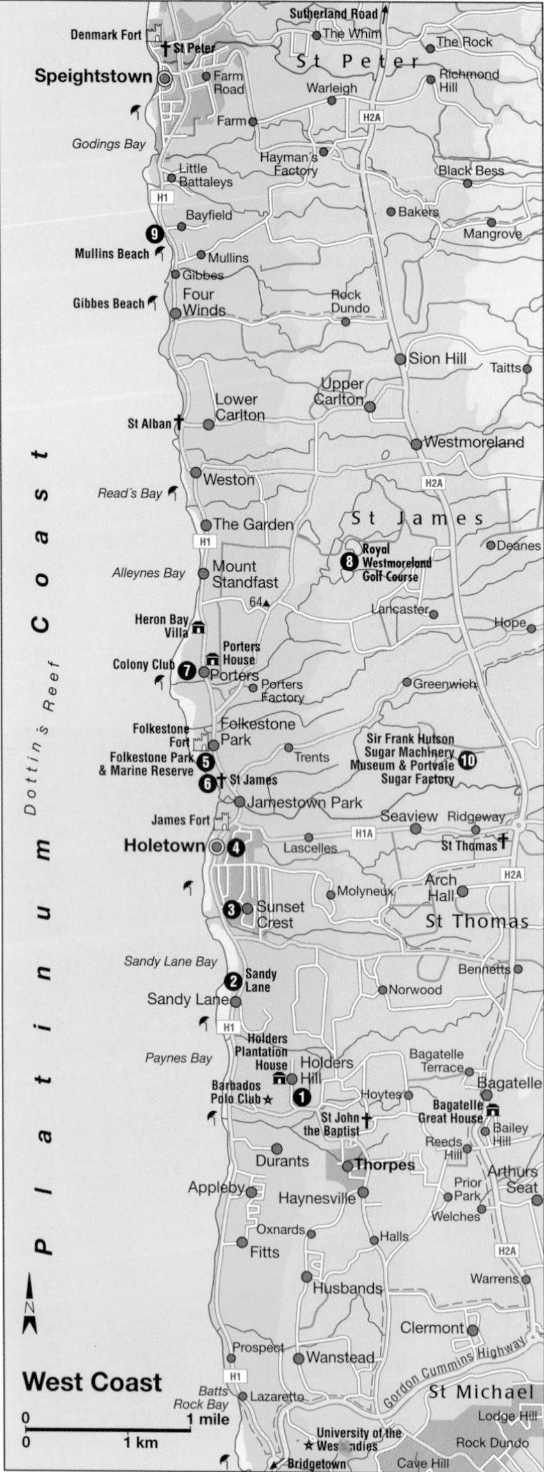

game of beach cricket, people roasting breadfruit and flying fish over an open fire, a family picnic, and pause to sip rum punch at a hotel beach bar. A variety of watersports are available on most of the beaches, either from the dive shops dotted along the coast or from independent operators who approach you with offers of banana and tube rides, jet-skiing and parasailing.

Up the coast road

Highway 1 starts its journey northwards from the ABC Highway just below the campus of the **University of the West Indies** (UWI), which was established in 1948 and is one of the Caribbean's top educational centres. Buried in the grounds and marked by a huge concrete wicket, erected in 1995, are the ashes of Sir Frank Worrell, batsman *extraordinaire* of the late 1950s.

Following the coast, the road pens in luxury hotels such as **Crystal Cove** and, further on, **Coconut Creek**, perched on a coral cliff. The beaches are smaller and more difficult to get on to due to erosion at this southern end but, as you move on into the hotel belt, they become wider and busier and are dotted with sun loungers, parasols and scurrying hotel waiters attending to their charges. Rather elegant in nature and differing slightly from hotel to hotel, the beaches still retain a few things in common – calm blue sea, fine sand, and a gentle breeze. Through windows to the sea between the hotels, public footpaths are marked down to the shore.

High class entertainment

Entertainment is top quality and it comes in a variety of forms with such a well-heeled clientele to compete for. Most of the hotels have something on every night, ranging from polished dance performances to the ubiquitous flaming limbo dancers, or music by a steel band.

But hotel-hopping does not have to be the norm. Close to the bottom of **Holders Hill ❶** is **Crocodile's Den**, a spacious and popular bar with pool tables, air hockey, video games, occasional live music and satellite TVs. Built in the style of a chattel house, its owner/operator is Barbadian ex-jockey Harry Hinds, aka "the Croc", who has amassed an incredible collection of peculiarities from public auctions that can be seen strewn throughout the bar; over 12,000 LPs reside in the DJ booth. No one is sure whether it is his island-wide reptilian reputation or the fact that the bar stays open until the wee hours of the morning that accounts for its popularity. Either way popular it is, especially at weekends, and is a haunt of Julian Lennon, Joan Collins and John Cleese when they are in residence.

Around the corner, half way up Holders Hill is the **Barbados Polo Club** (tel: 427 6022). Look for a turning on the left marked Polo Ridge – turn in here and follow the road around to the left and on to the field. The club house has a well-stocked bar, a roof-top stand and serves tea and cucumber sandwiches. Parking is available along one side of the field and many opt for deckchairs and a picnic from the boot of the car. Matches are normally held on Sundays and start at 4.30pm, and may feature teams from as far away as South America and England. Most fixtures take place in the early part of the year but there are exceptions so it's worth giving the Club a call.

Overlooking the polo field **Holders Plantation House** is the site of the annual Holders Season. The grounds and gardens of this 18th-century plantation house come alive for two weeks in March with theatre, opera, jazz and classical music. There is always a Shakespeare production and curiosity or two such as classical Calypso. The tenor Luciano Pavarotti performed here in 1997 and other well-known performers from the classical and pop music scene have included Lesley Garrett, Willard White, Simon Williams and Kylie Minogue.

The wreck of the Stavronikita *sits upright in 135 ft (40 metres) of water not far offshore from Fitts Village. Sunk intentionally in 1978, this 356-ft (110-metre) Greek freighter ranks among the world's top 10 wreck dives.*

BELOW: sinking the *Stavronikita.*

Film director Michael Winner has aired his views on the rebuilding of Sandy Lane loud and clear in the British press.

Back on Highway 1, a short distance northwards is **The Coach House**, an English-style pub that has thrown off its wild and wacky mantle to go upmarket by transforming the bar into a sports bar, creating an art gallery in the restaurant and offering live music in the garden every night – of the acoustic variety rather than the electric that used to wow the punters every Thursday night.

The new-look Sandy Lane

But it is **Sandy Lane** ❷ that set in motion the invasion of many of the world's rich and famous when its doors were opened in 1961 as a simple, but luxurious hotel. Ronald Tree (1897–1976), an Anglo-American who was once an adviser to Churchill's government and was joint founder of the Barbados National Trust (*see page 205*), built the now world-famous hotel for his friends to stay in after he chose to settle in Barbados. He wanted a place where they could vacation in luxuriant tropical surroundings, while maintaining the habits and standards of English upper-class life.

He spared no expense in the original construction of Sandy Lane, travelling far and wide to ensure that only the finest materials and workmanship would be used. Portuguese masons were brought in to create the bathrooms and Tree designed much of the original furniture himself. The hotel's fame grew and people such as Princess Margaret, Claudette Colbert, Jacqueline Kennedy Onassis, David Niven, Tom Jones and Mick Jagger have passed through its porticoes and several, such as British film director Michael Winner, became regulars.

Many of Tree's friends purchased property and built houses around the hotel and its golf club. Now, the exclusive 380-acre (154-hectare) Sandy Lane Estate has around 140 luxury homes in its grounds.

BELOW: on a romantic honeymoon.

A Tropical Wedding

A wedding in paradise is how the travel brochures and advertisements describe getting married in Barbados, and they are not far from the truth. What could be more romantic than tying the knot in warm sunshine by a white sandy beach, surrounded by tropical flowers and palm trees and then sealing it with a kiss in the warm shallows of the Caribbean Sea at sunset?

Most hotels along the West Coast can provide such a setting, as can several in the south. But that's not the only type of romantic venue on offer in Barbados: you can have your "special day" among the orchids at Orchid World (*see page 290*) or tropical plants and trees at Andromeda Gardens (*see page 262*) or the Flower Forest (*see page 276*) high up in the hills. Or you can have a historical wedding surrounded by antiques in a Great House such as Fisherpond (*see page 290*), Sunbury (*see page 252*), or Palmers (*see page 259*). You can even take your vows under water, with fish as witnesses, in *Atlantis Submarine* (*see page 203*).

A photographer, minister, banquet and all the trimmings can be provided by wedding coordinators and specialists on the island, so all you have to do is arrive on time. See *Travel Tips* page 334 for details of marriage regulations.

After a long association with Trust House Forte, Sandy Lane was purchased by the Granada chain. The liaison however was short-lived and, in December of 1996, the hotel was bought by Irish-born financiers John McManus and Dermot Desmond for the none-too-trifling sum of £38 million US$60 million). Much to the consternation of its regulars, who loved it for its Bajan character, the new owners razed it to the ground promising to "construct the most magnificent resort hotel in the world" with 112 guest rooms and a brand new 30,000-sq. ft (2,790-sq. metre) spa spanning three levels. However, many of the original features that the hotel was renowned for, such as the pillared portico and crescent terrace, are being recreated in the new edition which, after many constructural hiccoughs, has had its grand millennium opening delayed.

Sandy Lane's golf course, nine holes of which were built in 1962 and another nine added 10 years later, is being expanded too. Around 600 acres (240 hectares) of land adjacent to the Sandy Lane Estate were bought up by the hotel for two brand new 18-hole courses, designed by Tom Fazio, the USA's leading golf course architect. Another 50 building plots will add to the steady increase of exclusive luxury homes in this area.

Sunset Crest – tropical shopping

A little further up from Sandy Lane lies **Sunset Crest** ❸, a sprawling complex of villas, apartment buildings and shopping centres which is a particularly busy area just before Holetown, always bustling with both visitors and residents. Originally designed and built in the late 1960s, many of the businesses here, not to be left out of the building boom, were upgraded in the late 1990s. **Super Centre** has initiated an on-line grocery shopping service (*see Tip*), the

Map on page 212

TIP

If you are self-catering in a villa or an apartment, you can save time by shopping for groceries on-line at www.supercentrejbs.com and they will be delivered free.

BELOW: Methodist church overlooking Paynes Bay.

A monument erected in 1905 in memory of the first landing of the British on the island bears the wrong date of 1605. This was rectified in 1975.

first in the Caribbean, the Bridgetown department store **Cave Shepherd** has opened a huge new duty-free shop stocking the very latest in designer wear and fragrances, and **West One** offers a fully equipped gym and fitness centre.

The **Chattel House Village** opened here in 1998 and like its sister in St Lawrence Gap (*see page 233*) consists of a dozen or so brightly painted chattel house shops. There is a truly international deli, a café, stationery shop, a hair salon, plus an array of gift shops and a small farmer's market where Bajan ladies sell locally grown fruits and vegetables – good for snacks. Depending on the season, they sell avocados, which Bajans call pears, pawpaws, which are Bajan for papayas, and mangoes, soursop, passion fruit and a great variety of vegetables. To the rear of the village are several floodlit tennis courts which are available for hire both day and night.

Over the main road, the **Inn on the Beach** is a small hotel that serves flying fish cutters (sandwiches) right on the beach on every day the sun is shining. But beware of the hot sauce, it is one of the spiciest you will find anywhere. **The Europa**, **Golden View** and **Travellers Palm** all have reasonably priced accommodation along the shore, while the stylish **Baku Beach** has a brasserie, beach bar *and* **The Casbah Nightclub**, another popular venue on the West Coast party scene. With an exotic Moroccan decor, The Casbah is a large air-conditioned club with a lively atmosphere and dance floor. Soak up live jazz or a Bajan Floorshow with dinner at the brasserie and then after hours move through the Moroccan door for a night of dancing until 4am. As with most of the establishments along the West Coast, the club tends to attract a more mature, chic crowd than its South Coast counterparts, due in part to the predominance of the more upmarket hotels in the area.

BELOW: seeking solace from the sun.

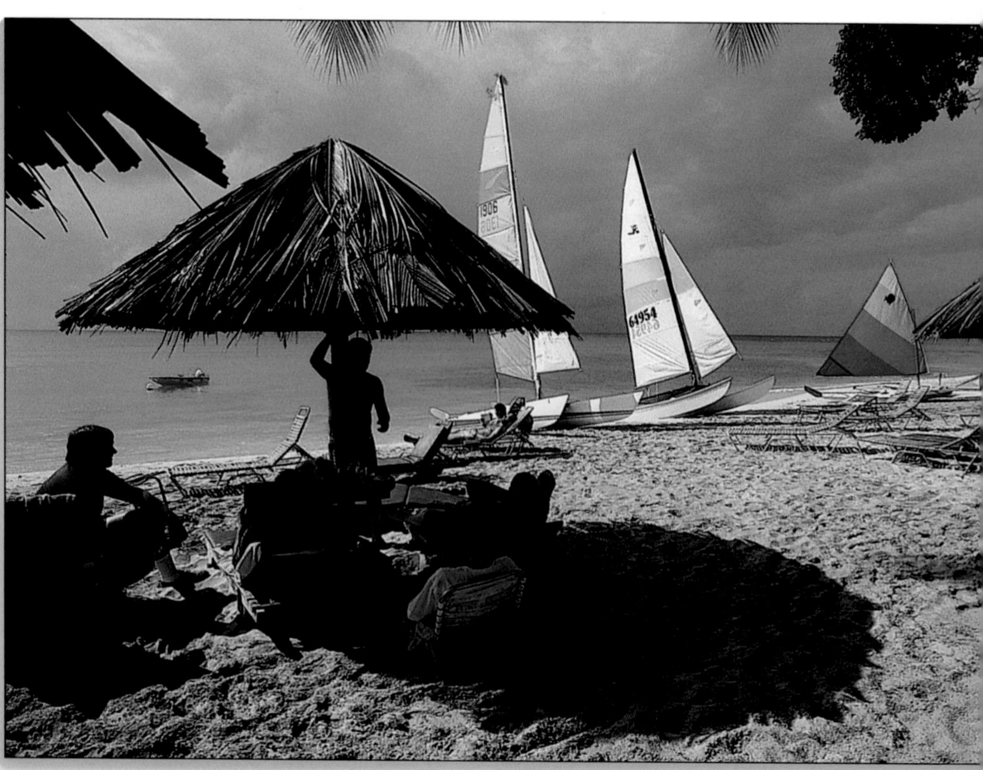

Holetown – the first settlement

Sunset Crest blends into **Holetown** ❹, the site of the first settlement in Barbados. This was where Captain John Powell and his crew landed on 14 May 1625, and claimed the island in the name of King James of England, who unknown to them had died while they were at sea. They named the area St James' Town, but it was later changed to Holetown because the shallow-draught ships could enter the river at this point, reminding sailors of The Hole on the River Thames.

Two years later, on 17 February 1627, the *William and John* landed with 80 settlers and 10 African slaves captured from other ships on the way over from England. Mid-February, every year, the **Holetown Festival** celebrates the discovery of Barbados by the British: streets are filled with stalls selling local food and crafts, music is heard everywhere, and you can see dance performances and stilt shows.

First and **Second Streets** have a high concentration of bars and restaurants that make Holetown a lively nightspot. The dozen or so restaurants that are packed into this small area offer a stunning variety of fare and ambience. **Olives** and **The Mews** are sophisticated and popular with the "in crowd", while **Raggamuffins** in a chattel house and the vividly painted **Angry Annie's**, run by an English couple, are more down to earth, quirky, and quite unique. **The Sitar** offers Indian food, **Sakura** does Japanese, and the world's most populous nation is well-represented by **Mins** and **Tams Wok** for a Chinese takeaway.

The Holetown restaurants have enjoyed a good reputation for many years and any one of them is a good bet. Two of the more popular local bars here include the **Rum Barrel** and the TML bar, which incidentally has great karaoke on Saturday night. Set back from the main road just south of Olives, **Indigo**, a

Map on page 212

ABOVE: bikes of all kinds for hire.
BELOW: banana riders having fun.

The Art Foundry West (open daily, Sat until 2pm), opposite The Cliff, sells more commercial art than its more avant-garde sister at the Rum Factory & Heritage Park (see page 246)*. Call 420 1366 for information on art events.*

late-night weekend watering hole with a comfortable bar and spacious restaurant, is co-run by one of the island's top chefs Nick King, who has previously cooked at The Cliff, Sandy Lane and The Mews.

Dining out in St James

In addition to the plethora of restaurants in Holetown, all along the St James coast an assortment of dining establishments range from the casual to the super-sophisticated. **Fathoms** at Paynes Bay offers local delicacies served on a beach-front terrace and **The Rose** in Prospect specialises in seafood and is well known for its lobster. Both have a casual and informal atmosphere. **Nico's Champagne and Wine Bar** at Derricks offers dining in a tropical garden and at the **Carambola** in Prospect tables nestle along a cliff directly above the sea.

In fact many of the West Coast restaurants offer waterside dining, including the two perhaps most sought-after and talked about culinary venues on the island; The Cliff and The Lone Star. **The Cliff** is an elegant coral-stone building located at Derricks, near Holders Hill, overlooking a small secluded beach. Dining is on three levels, the lowest being literally on the cliff top. *Flambeaux* (gas torches) burn on the cliff edge and add to the atmosphere. **The Lone Star** is further up the coast in an area known as The Garden. It was originally a garage and sits adjacent to the former home of Lady Belinda Robertson, of Robertson's jam fame. A sushi bar and cocktail lounge occupy the upstairs floor while the main bar and dining area are at the water's edge below. Both these restaurants offer superb food, attract the rich and famous, and between them offer such treats as caviar, Cuban cigars, and BDS$5,000 bottles of wine. Traditional international tastes are catered for by **Il Tempio** at Fitts Village,

BELOW: steel bands often play in restaurants.

which offers Italian food, and **Ile de France** at Settlers Beach specialising, not surprisingly, in French cuisine. The seafood specialist is **Neptunes**, at the luxurious Tamarind Cove Hotel. Many of the West Coast hotels have their own in-house restaurants including the Coral Reef Club, Sandpiper, Colony Club, Royal Pavilion and Glitter Bay.

Folkestone – an underwater park

Behind the Holetown post office and police station are the remains of **James Fort**, which once protected this coastal area until after the Napoleonic Wars. Not much of it is left today, except for part of a wall and one gun. This area was landscaped by the Barbados Rotary Club, which included a playground and tennis courts. Two popular beach bar/restaurants can be found here: **Surfside**, just behind the police station, and **Cocomos** 100 yards (275 metres) to the south.

Close by, **Folkestone Park and Marine Reserve** ❺ houses an interpretive Visitors Centre (Mon – Fri 10am–5pm; entrance fee) which includes a marine museum and saltwater aquarium. Offshore is a marked "recreational zone" where snorkellers can follow an underwater trail around **Dottin's Reef**, a 7-mile (11-km) long reef just a short way out to sea. Scuba divers can hire boats to go to the many diving spots along the reef, a habitat for sea anemones, man-sized fans, soft corals and sea lilies. Those who are not so adventurous can view the active marine life from a glass-bottomed boat.

Next to Folkestone Park is the **Bellairs Research Institute** where studies of the marine biology of the island are made. Set up in 1954 as an affiliate of McGill University, Canada, the institute's goals are to improve the agriculture

Map on page 212

Although it is illegal for jet-skis to come within 150 ft (45 metres) of the shore, this has proved difficult to enforce. Snorkellers should mark their location with brightly coloured floats tied to their waist or foot.

Below: an underwater world.

This stained-glass window in St James Church is the work of renowned Barbadian artist Bill Grace. An example of his sculpture can be seen in Sandridge Hotel, north of Holetown.

BELOW: a relaxing moment.

and fisheries of Barbados, as well as to investigate and cultivate new sources of food from the sea.

Settlers in the graveyard

Close by is **St James Church** ❻, erected on the same site almost 250 years after the original church was built. The first St James Church was built in wood in 1628, not long after the first settlers arrived, and then it was replaced by a stone church in 1680. In 1874, after being severely damaged in the 1871 hurricane, the building was rebuilt and extended and arches and columns were added; in the 1980s, it was restored to what it is today. Several of the original settlers are buried here and the original font from 1684 and an old bell, dated 1696, with the inscription "God Bless King William" have survived to this day.

In the church is a mural of Sir John Gay Alleyne (1724–1801), the Speaker of the House of Assembly in the late 1700s. He was called an aristocrat and a radical, but undeterred by criticism, he succeeded in making the Barbados Parliament a much more effective instrument of government. At the opening of every session, he claimed for society members the privileges claimed by the English Parliament: freedom of speech, freedom from arrest and free access to their representative in government.

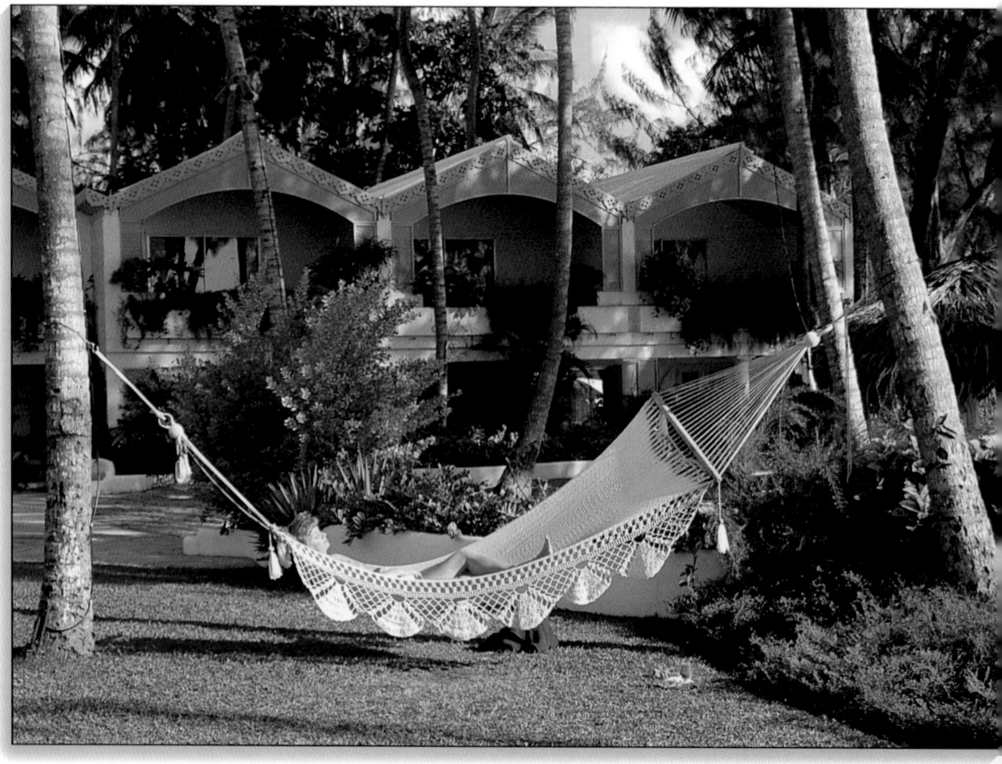

Sir John owned one of the plantation Great Houses in St James – **Porters House**, less than a mile (1.2 km) further north, opposite the Colony Club Hotel. Porters, hidden among the mahogany trees, is one of the few remaining plantation houses constructed in the early period of the island's history. The oldest part dates back to the 1700s, but it has not been preserved entirely in its original form. Sections were added in the 1800s. The house is furnished with Barbadian antiques, including a large mahogany dining room table and mahogany four poster beds which can be seen by the public occasionally through the National Trust's Open House scheme (*see page 205*).

Map on page 212

Stately mansion on the beach

The **Colony Club** ❼ and its southern neighbour the Coral Reef are examples of the many West Coast hotels which have earned world-wide reputations for excellence. The Colony Club has a series of lagoon swimming pools and waterfalls meandering through the property. Many of the rooms open on to a small private patio with steps leading into a semi-private pool. It has a lovely beach shaded by graceful casuarina trees and a seaside terrace for lunch or a rum punch at sunset. The **Coral Reef** is delightfully English in that it upholds a tradition of serving afternoon tea and yet remains thoroughly Caribbean in the way that dinner is served in the open air by a moonlit sea.

On the northern side of the Colony Club, where there is public access to the beach, is the stately **Heron Bay Villa**, a house designed along the lines of an Italian palazzo. Taking several years to build, the Palladian mansion was started in 1947 by Ronald Tree (*see page 214*) and Patrick Leigh Fermor described it in his book *Traveller's Tree* in 1950 as being "assembled in an architectural formula alien to the island, but which, by the same brilliant conjuring trick, seemed astonishingly appropriate and harmonious." Set in 20 acres (9 hectares) of parkland, Heron Bay includes in its grounds a small lake filled with mullet, a coconut grove and a citrus orchard and can be visited as part of the National Trust's Open House scheme. However, you can see the similar-styled gazebo and some of the grounds from the beach.

Ronald Tree became a Conservative MP in 1933 and served as Parliamentary Private Secretary to the Minister of Information during World War II. Winston Churchill was a regular visitor to his home but, when Tree lost the election in 1945, he moved to Barbados.

Below: Heron Bay Villa – Ronald Tree's first Bajan home.

Barbadian Maureen Edghill's award-winning shell works of art are for sale at the Shell Gallery (open Mon–Sat; closed Sat pm) in her home in Carlton – just follow the seahorse sign from St Alban's Church on Highway 1.

A high-tech golf course

In competition with Sandy Lane is the similarly exclusive **Royal Westmoreland ❽**. In the winter of 1994 the first nine holes of the new course opened 2 miles (3 km) inland from Alleynes Bay just up from the Glitter Bay and Royal Pavilion Hotels. Nine more were opened in August 1995 and there are a further nine to go. Designed by Robert Trent Jones Jr, who has referred to it as "one of my best", the 27 greens will eventually be surrounded by some 270 luxury coral-stone villas, many of which are already home to golf celebrities such as Ian Woosnam and veteran tennis stars Virginia Wade and David Lloyd.

The world's best golfers regularly play on the perfectly tended grass which is irrigated by computer, with rainwater collected in tanks and ponds, and fed with environmentally friendly fertilisers. The ponds are an attraction to an assortment of birds passing through.

Continuing along Highway 1 towards Speightstown for less than a mile (1.5 km), you pass the villages of Weston and Carlton and arrive at **Gibbes Beach** (also known as Gibbs), a spacious and beautiful stretch of sand just over the parish border in St Peter. Hidden from the main road and fronted by large private residences, it is often missed by the masses and is a quiet alternative to neighbouring **Mullins ❾**, which is popular and gets quite crowded at the weekends. The great draw here is the atmospheric **Mullins Beach Bar and Restaurant** whose covered wooden verandah stands on stilts at the water's edge.

Right: time for a cocktail. **Below:** winding down at Mullins Beach Bar.

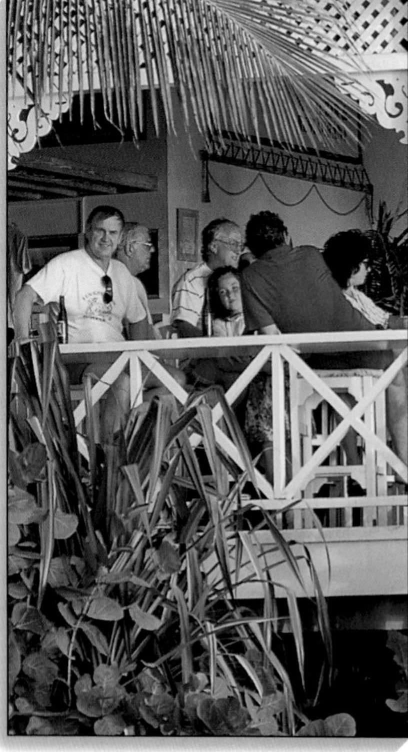

A sugar manufacturer's legacy

Travelling inland for a mile (1.5 km) or so on any of the roads branching off Highway 1, you reach Highway 2A passing only cane fields interspersed with small villages, mostly situated around plantations such as Orange Hill, Westmoreland and Bakers. A mile (1.5 km) or so to the north of the St Thomas parish church (*see page 280*) and directly east of Holetown, but still within the boundaries of St James, is the **Portvale sugar factory** and the **Sir Frank Hutson Sugar Machinery Museum ❿** (open Mon–Sat; entrance fee), which is managed by the Barbados National Trust. Hutson was a skilled engineer whose expertise lay with sugar machinery. He was responsible for a number of pioneering developments within the industry and it was his vision and dedication that led to the creation of the museum.

Housed in the original stone-walled boiling house, which was built around 1880, display boards give a comprehensive history of the sugar industry and include many period photographs from the plantation era. The machinery exhibits are well laid out and clearly marked and include many unusual pieces.

The adjacent working factory can be toured during the cane-grinding season which usually lasts from February to May. A mix of state-of-the-art technology and older more traditional machines are used inside the factory, some pieces dating from the 1920s. The sheer scale is mind-boggling and the dust, heat and noise create an unparalleled experience. The inland road takes you back through fields of sugar cane down to Bridgetown 4 miles (6 km) to the south. ❑

Gaastra Sails

THE LIVELY SOUTH COAST

Vibrant by day and night, this affordable part of Barbados is for those after a slice of the action, with world-class windsurfing, hot nightspots, beautiful beaches – and a bird sanctuary

Map on pages 228–29

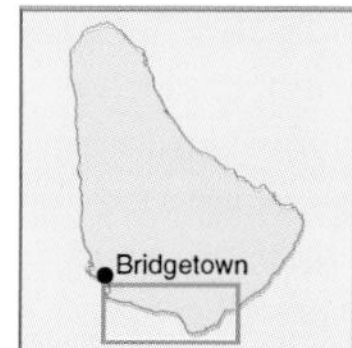

Strung along the 4-mile (6.5-km) stretch of beautiful southern coastline in the parish of Christ Church are the areas of Hastings, Worthing and Dover, poignantly named after the English seaside towns the homesick settlers had left behind. Fringed with sandy beaches and wonderful surf, it is difficult to tell where Hastings ends and Worthing begins as, since the early days of Barbados' tourist industry in the 1970s, the population along here has grown at such a steady pace that this coast is now the most built-up on the island.

The entire South Coast strip from the Garrison to the far end of St Lawrence Gap has been developed and an empty lot is a rare sight indeed. A mix of small hotels and apartment blocks, shopping malls, restaurants and bars line both sides of the road, and day or night the strip is always busy. The construction boom of the late 1990s has affected this region too, although lack of available space has meant that many businesses have upgraded rather than expanded.

Hotels typically are smaller and cheaper than their west coast counterparts and many offer a mix of self-catering and in-house restaurants. The Oasis Hotel and the Woodville Beach Hotel in Worthing are good examples of the small, modern hotels that proliferate the South Coast. At the other end of the scale are the larger hotels that began appearing along with the construction boom such as the Accra Beach Hotel in Rockley, and the brand new Bougainvillea Beach Resort on the Maxwell Coast Road, both of which have more than 100 rooms.

PRECEDING PAGES: windsurfing off South Point.
LEFT: sand gets everywhere.
BELOW: beauty on the beach.

North American influence

The whole area has taken on a new and polished look and one could be forgiven for thinking that you were in fact in a Miami suburb, not in a developing Caribbean nation. Fat Andy's, a 1950s theme diner, and Bubbas Sports Bar, with 12 televisions and three 10-ft (3-metre) screens showing live sports action from around the globe, are recent US-style additions to the strip. At night the South Coast hums with the sounds of partying emanating from a wide choice of clubs, discos and bars. This part of the island is not the place to come for some peace and quiet.

The entire Christ Church tourist belt is serviced by Highway 7, which runs parallel to the sea from Hastings to Oistins where it swerves up Thornbury Hill and heads northeast toward the Grantley Adams International Airport. In the southernmost tip of the island a more peaceful scene emerges of genteel residential areas backing on to a rocky shore interspersed with sandy beaches but battered by a rougher sea – here the Caribbean Sea clashes with the turbulent Atlantic Ocean and the windsurfers take advantage.

The other major artery through Christ Church is

The 500 seat air-conditioned Vista Cinema at the bottom of Rendezvous Hill has a 48 ft by 22 ft (14 metres by 6 metres) screen and a full digital surround-sound system. Open seven days a week, it usually features a double bill starting at 7pm.

Highway 6, which passes through the middle of the parish and across the farmlands behind the coastal razzmatazz. From the roundabout at Graeme Hall, the Tom Adams Highway goes directly to Grantley Adams International Airport.

Because the Christ Church coast has gained a reputation as the island's premier tourist playground, many forget that it also has many sugar plantations. These estates, with names like Bentleys, Grove and Newton, dominate the north of the parish as much as hotels, apartments and guesthouses do the south.

Chic battle for Hastings

Leaving Bridgetown on Highway 7, you enter Christ Church at **Hastings ❶**, an area that, as its name suggests, is steeped in military history. A number of old red buildings lining the left side of the road were once barracks for St Ann's Fort (*see page 197*). Once humble soldiers' quarters, they are now the chic residences of private tenants – and the envy of many, since the waiting list for these apartments is very long. A military hospital and surgeons' quarters also graced Hastings in the fort's glory days. Nearby, the American diner **Fat Andy's** cocks a snook at the remnants of British colonialism.

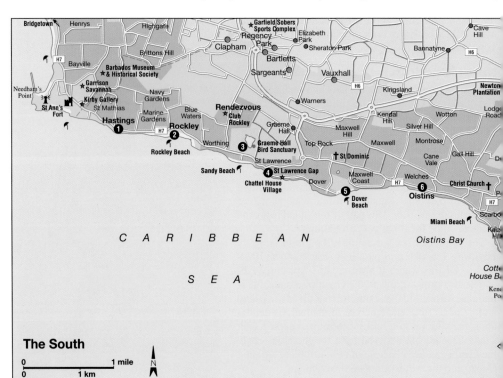

Across from the **Savannah Hotel** – the beautifully restored and renamed Sea View Hotel, which was a popular holiday spot during the 19th century – is the inspirational **Kirby Gallery** (open Mon–Fri, Sat until 2pm). Opened in 1997 in a renovated traditional Barbadian house with 2,000 sq. ft (186 sq. metres) of floorspace, it is the largest commercial gallery on the island. The emphasis is on works on canvas although there are small showings of watercolours, mixed media and photography. As well as hosting some of the Caribbean's most talented artists, the gallery exhibits work by visiting artists who come to study and work in the region (*see A Living Art on pages 97–101*). Not far, in Pavilion Court is the **Mallalieu Motor Collection** (open daily; entrance fee; tel: 426 4640), a fascinating selection of vintage cars, including a 1947 Vanden Plas Drophead, a 1937 Chevrolet and an Austin A90, each with a story to tell.

Map on pages 228–29

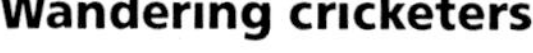

Wandering cricketers

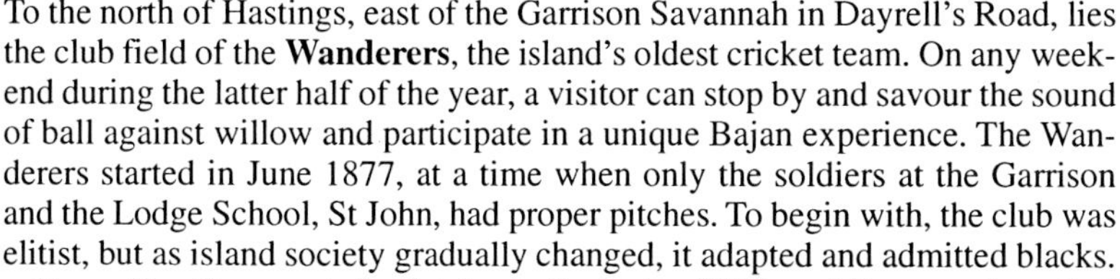

To the north of Hastings, east of the Garrison Savannah in Dayrell's Road, lies the club field of the **Wanderers**, the island's oldest cricket team. On any weekend during the latter half of the year, a visitor can stop by and savour the sound of ball against willow and participate in a unique Bajan experience. The Wanderers started in June 1877, at a time when only the soldiers at the Garrison and the Lodge School, St John, had proper pitches. To begin with, the club was elitist, but as island society gradually changed, it adapted and admitted blacks.

Bruce Hamilton wrote in *Cricket in Barbados*: "If the soldiers may be called the missionaries of modern cricket in Barbados, and Lodge the pioneers among the local people, to Wanderers must certainly be given the credit of setting the game on a permanent footing and keeping it there."

Shopping on the beach.

Busy beaches

The coastal stretch from Hastings to Oistins has some of the finest beaches in the island and, despite the pollution that inevitably accompanies fast-growing development, some of the healthier reefs. Any stress to the reefs has been limited to those less than 100 yards (90 metres) from the shore, which has caused some erosion to the beaches. However, since the mid 1980s, the Government has been committed to preserving the beaches and marine habitat through the con-

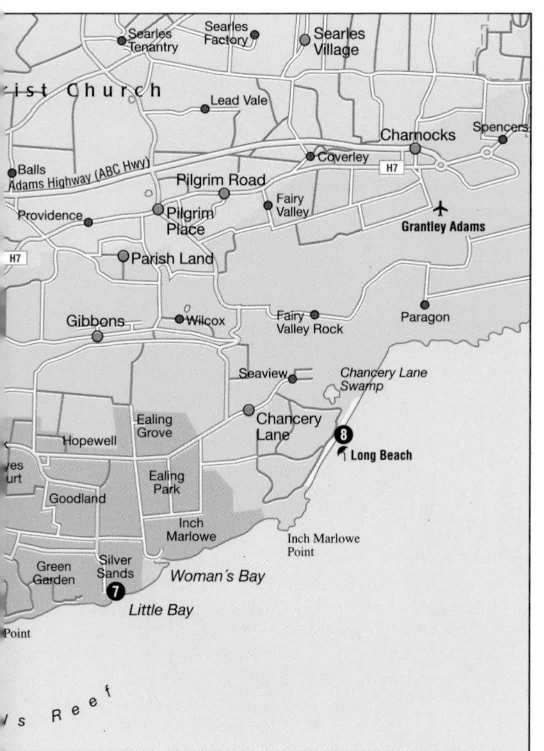

BELOW: let's be friends.

struction of new sewage treatment plants and has erected offshore groynes and submerged breakwaters made of limestone boulders – which have become encrusted with coral developing into an artificial reef – to minimise sand loss.

Not yet in the lee of the island, the beaches along this coast have a lively swell rolling into shore. Not too much to prohibit safe swimming, but enough to make body-boarding a viable option. As with anywhere on the South Coast the beaches are busy all day, every day. Beach vendors, food kiosks, restaurants and bars sit at the water's edge and snorkelling gear, kayaks, hobie cats and chairs are among the many items available for hire. **Rockley** ❷ (also kown as Accra), opposite Bubbas Sports Bar, and **Dover**, 2 miles (1.5 km) further along, are probably the most popular and crowded of all the beaches.

In between, at **Worthing**, is **Sandy Beach**, a large flat expanse of sand with a shallow lagoon. Not quite as hectic as its neighbours, it is a good choice for those in search of a little more peace and quiet and is perfect for young families. The popular **Carib Beach Bar** offers a welcome escape from the midday sun and has a good selection of food and drinks.

Barbadian sculptor Bill Grace lives and works just a few minutes from Rockley Beach. Working primarily in glass, ceramics and natural stone his pieces focus on the reef system from which the island is built. His work is regularly exhibited at both the Art Foundry at Foursquare Rum Factory & Heritage Park (*see page 246*) and the Art Foundry West (*see page 97*), and can be viewed by appointment (call 435 6398) at his studio.

Just inland **Club Rockley** provides inclusive sporting holiday packages along with a nine-hole golf course that is open to non-residents at a more affordable price than those on the West Coast.

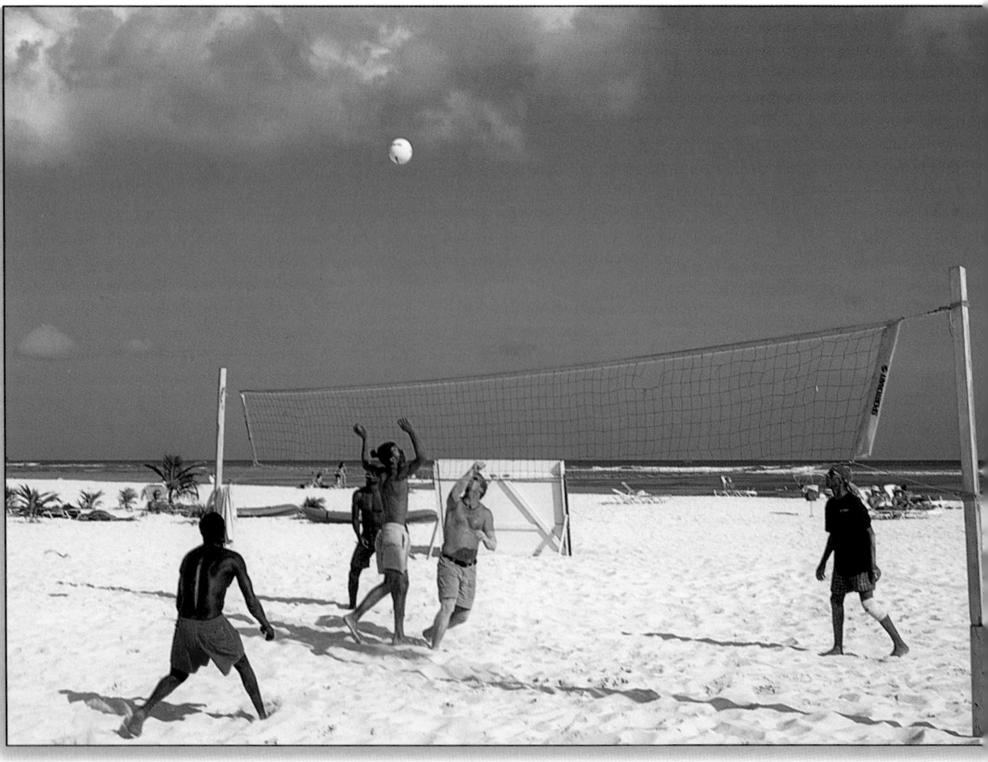

At Graeme Hall Bird Sanctuary are intricately carved wooden replicas of birds like this green heron (above) *by Barbadians Geoffrey and Joanie Skeete and their family. Call Wild Feathers Bird Art on 423 7758 to view more of their impressive collection.*

BELOW: playing volleyball on Sandy Beach.

Beautiful bird sanctuary

In contrast to the ceaseless urbanisation that typifies this area, there is one oasis of calm down a left-hand turning just before St Lawrence Gap – **Graeme Hall Bird Sanctuary** ❸ (open daily, 7am–6pm; donations; tel: 435 7078), a development aimed at preserving the natural environment rather than building on it. For years, it was a swamp used by hunters and fishermen, lost and forgotten by most of the population. The last remaining area of natural wetland on the island (some 92 acres/37 hectares in total) it has provided a convenient resting place for migratory birds en route from the eastern United States to the South American mainland for hundreds of years.

A large brackish water lake is bordered by dense mangrove swamps and freshwater streams, providing a habitat for hundreds of species of aquatic flora and fauna. Years of neglect and misuse have taken their toll on this fragile ecosystem and its very survival has been in doubt. On the recommendation of local environmentalist Dr Karl Watson, 40 percent of the swamp area was purchased by Peter Allard, a Canadian philanthropist, in the mid 1990s. The remaining 60 percent still belongs to the Government but is leased and looked after by Allard. Revenue from guided tours will be put towards the upkeep of the sanctuary and it is hoped that a greater public understanding of this unique ecosystem will emerge.

Over 150 species of migratory birds have been recorded in Barbados, including many rare and unusual specimens. The last two sightings of the now extinct Eskimo curlew were logged in Barbados in the 1960s, and the first ever sighting of a purple heron in the western hemisphere was made at Graeme Hall in early 1999. Among the more common visitors to the swamp are shore and marsh

Map on pages 228–29

BELOW: white egrets roost on the trees at Graeme Hall Bird Sanctuary.

For a resplendent Caribbean night out, reserve a table at The Tropical Spectacular Dinner Show at The Plantation Restaurant (tel: 428 5048) in St Lawrence. Buffet dinner, unlimited drinks and transport are part of the deal.

birds such as plover and snipe, and birds of prey like the osprey and peregrine falcon. The island has some 40 species of resident birds of which almost half can be found living at Graeme Hall. These include the yellow warbler, the green heron, the yellow crowned night heron and three species of egret: snowy, white and cattle. The latter has bred in great numbers and descend upon the swamp in their hundreds every evening to roost.

The lake itself contains over 40 species of fish including tilapia, snook and several huge tarpon. Two large walk-through aviaries house birds from the Caribbean region and South America.

After dark in the Gap

To top off a day of surf and sand, many people enjoy the South Coast's lively and varied nightlife. The action heats up at the major nightspots clustered along **St Lawrence Gap ❹**, which branches off Highway 7 by Worthing Police Station. Each club is unique, with its own ambience and following. Some of the names to know are The Ship Inn, After Dark, The Reggae Lounge and B4 Blues. **The Ship Inn** features local bands nightly and attracts a young, primarily English crowd, while **B4 Blues** is about the only place on this calypso-crazy island where you can hear Barbados blues bands live.

After Dark, on the other hand, is the island's answer to a North American club for young urban professionals, and it's popular with locals and visitors alike. On weekends it's jammed with men and women in their late 20s and early 30s. **The Reggae Lounge** next door attracts a more "rootsy" crowd, and is a favourite hang-out for Rastafarians and dub aficionados. The vast majority of the clientele are local and, like After Dark, The Reggae Lounge features DJ

RIGHT: enjoying a cool Banks beer.
BELOW: another good day's surfing.

music. On Friday and Saturday nights, the Gap is jam-packed and traffic is reduced to a crawl. The Ship Inn has a large car park for patrons at the rear, otherwise just keep driving until you find a place to park at the side of the road and walk back. However, be sure to lock your car as the Gap attracts its fair share of opportunists. With Government plans in the pipeline to smarten the area up, St Lawrence Gap is also where you will find many of the island's better restaurants – from the American cuisine of **Boomers** to the Mexican treats in **Café Sol** to the international menu of **Josef's**, specialising in local fish and produce with Thai and Japanese flavourings. **Pisces**, located at the water's edge, features seafood and drinks in a romantic setting. But if you prefer a singsong or karaoke, **McBride's**, an Irish pub, is the place.

During daylight hours the Gap is a lot quieter and a leisurely stroll from one end to the other is a good way to while away some time. It is popular with street vendors and all manner of local arts and crafts can be found here. At the southern end, just before Dover Beach, is the **Chattel House Village**, a cluster of brightly painted shops in replica chattel houses (*see pages 282–83*) surrounding an open courtyard. In addition to a good selection of arts, crafts and clothing, there is a Visitor Information Centre and a café that does a great English breakfast, inside or out.

Doing the Conga

On the other side of St Lawrence Gap, pretty **Dover Beach** ❺ hoves into view, and on the village playing field during the last week of April the Congaline Village is set up as the focal point of the six-day **Malibu De Congaline Carnival**. First introduced in 1994, the carnival features live entertainment nightly

Map on pages 228–29

Promise of a good night out.

BELOW: twilight stroll along the water's edge.

Barbadian-style fast food.

and exhibits of local arts and crafts during the day, accompanied by lots of good local food. The climax of the carnival is a May Day parade from Independence Square in Bridgetown right the way down Highway 7 ending at the Top Rock roundabout at Dover. Thousands of revellers jam the road to make the region's longest Congaline as they gyrate behind flatbed trucks carrying live bands belting out Carnival tunes.

Leaving Dover on Highway 7 you join the **Maxwell Coast Road** where there is more nightlife and good dining on offer. A residential area with a more restrained character, the restaurants here include **The Mermaid**, **Jeremiah's Bistro**, **Gideons** and **Water's Edge** and the **Welcome Inn**, which also serves meals to non-residents. Also along here is the Club Mistral home of the **Barbados Windsurfing Club**, where the conditions are perfect for the learner and intermediate windsurfer with good sea breezes but quieter water, as opposed to the challenging sea at Silver Sands (*see page 237*).

Oistins – the island's fishing capital

Half a mile further along Highway 7 is the fishing town of **Oistins** ❻. It got its name from a cantankerous early settler called Austin (which people pronounced Oistin) and is important not only for its large fishing fleet but for its history.

It was at Oistins in 1652 that the Charter of Barbados, or articles between the Royalist supporters in Barbados and Oliver Cromwell's naval forces anchored in the bay, were signed in a tavern called Ye Mermaid's Inn. Onerous to the Royalists, these articles pledged the islanders to loyal obedience to Cromwell and his Commonwealth Parliament in return for continued self-government and free trade. Unfortunately, the historic tavern no longer exists.

BELOW: fishing boats at Oistins.

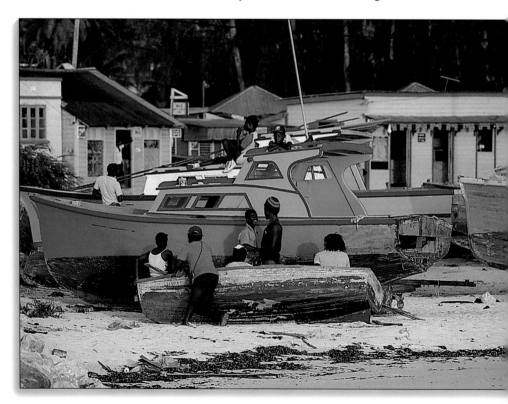

Map on pages 228–29

Oistins is better known as the island's fishing capital. For generations, Bajans have travelled to Oistins Bay, on foot or by bus, to buy all types of fish caught out at sea, but it has undergone quite a change in the past 25 years.

The transformation began in the early 1970s when the cinema at Oistins was torn down to make way for a modern shopping plaza at the eastern end of the town, on the corner where Highway 7 swings northeast up Thornbury Hill. Over the years, Oistins Shopping Plaza has housed a launderette, Barclays Bank, a supermarket, disco, boutique, video club and electronics shop. Then competition, in the form of Southern Plaza, sprang up at the western end of town. Its lure for one-stop shoppers has always been a branch of **Super Centre**, one of Barbados' largest supermarket chains.

The Government then modernised the fishing industry by building a BDS$10 million fisheries terminal occupying over 4 acres (1.5 hectares) of land, most of which was reclaimed from the sea. Boats were fitted out with cold storage equipment so that fishermen could stay out at sea longer. Although necessary, the new building has not added to the charm of Oistins, but the catch is the same: dolphin, shark, barracuda, snapper, kingfish and, of course, the ubiquitous flying fish. At times, shoppers can find Old Wives, a succulent fish that is not as large as a shark or barracuda but can be prepared in the same way. In the old days, before the fish terminal, women selling fish stood at the roadside calling out "Fish! Fish!" and the day's prices. Today, vendors may well approach you in the car park even before you leave your car, to entice you to their stalls.

The best time to go to Oistins for fish is around 4pm when the day's catch is being brought in and the filleting, which is fascinating to watch, is at its peak. In times of plenty, flying fish sell as cheaply as eight for BDS$1. Out of season

Filleting flying fish is an art.

BELOW: Christ Church parish church.

THE GREAT COFFIN MYSTERY

On the ridge overlooking Oistins is Christ Church Parish Church and the site of the renowned "great coffin mystery", which occurred in the Chase Vault in the church's graveyard.

George Hunte, in his book on Barbados, wrote: "The trouble at the Chase Vault began on 9 August, 1812. When it was opened for the interment of Colonel Thomas Chase, two leaden coffins inside were discovered by workmen to be in an unusual position, while the coffin of an infant, Mary Ann Chase, had been moved from one corner of the vault to another. Twice in 1816 and again in 1817 a state of confusion was found when the vault was opened for burial of other members of the family. The Governor of Barbados, Viscount Combermere, was present on 7 July 1819… he made impressions with his seal on the cement which masons had put on the outside of the entrance."

Nine months later, Viscount Combermere checked that the seal was still intact and commanded a man to go inside the vault: one huge coffin was upright against the middle of the stone door and the infant's coffin was lying at the far end where "it had been thrown with so much force it had damaged the wall of the vault". The family removed the coffins and the vault remains empty.

TIP

The Barbados Golf Academy and Driving Range at Balls, northeast of Oistins off the ABC Highway, offers family golf with an 18-hole mini golf course (daily 10am–10pm), a public driving range (daily 7am–11pm) and expert coaching. Call 420 7405 for details.

(during the months that don't end in "r"), you might be asked to pay as much as BDS$2 for just four fish.

The area has also become a lively Friday night hot spot: the **Oistins Fish Fry** as it is now known started quietly and has now grown to a major weekly event. So much so that fairy lights depicting fish are permanently strung above the road between telegraph poles. Women at roadside stalls serve freshly cooked fish, chicken, pork and other Bajan delicacies accompanied by the usual complement of drinks, both alcoholic and soft.

A larger, longer and more potent version of the Friday night fish-fry takes place every April in the form of the **Oistins Fish Festival** which seeks to highlight the contribution made to the country by those involved in the fishing industry. Local arts and crafts are on display, food and drink are in plentiful supply and there are several unique competitions such as Moses racing – a wooden rowing boat race – net throwing and fish-boning.

Clues to slave life

To the northeast of Oistins, 1¼ miles (2 km) inland along Lodge Road, lies **Newton Plantation** where, in the 1970s, the excavation of a large slave burial ground revealed valuable information on slave life and conditions in early Barbados. The 17th-century, privately owned plantation still reveals a pattern similar to that used in the days of slavery, with the manager's house on an incline overlooking the yard. Professor Jerome Handler, the American who supervised the expedition, and Dr Fred Lange reported their findings in the book *Plantation Slavery in Barbados: An Archaeological and Historical Investigation.*

They wrote: "Newton and its slave population typified medium to large-size

BELOW: searching for the best spot.

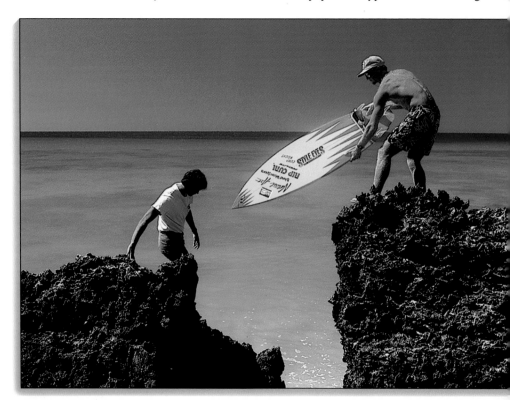

Barbados sugar plantations. Because Newton, as a plantation, so well reflected island-wide characteristics, and because its slave community also seems to have typified the Barbadian pattern, we assume that in their mortuary beliefs and practices Newton's slaves also displayed characteristics that were found elsewhere. In general, we believe that the findings of the archaeological investigations at Newton's slave cemetery can be extended to indicate patterns that also existed in other Barbadian communities."

The National Cultural Foundation (*see page 110*) has recognised Newton's historic value by making it the venue of the ceremonial delivery of the last canes at the end of July every year, so launching the Crop Over Festival (*see pages 134–35*). Generally the plantation is not open to the public.

Windsurfing at Silver Sands

Back at Oistins if, instead of following Highway 7 up Thornbury Hill, you take the **Enterprise Coast Road** along the coast, you will be heading towards the southernmost tip of the island. This area of land, which bulges out at the bottom of the island, providing a perfect perch for the South Point lighthouse, contains a number of large middle- and upper-class housing developments beginning on the coast and spreading inland.

First stop along this road is **Miami Beach**, a favourite with the locals and to where you can also walk from Oistins' harbour in five to 10 minutes. This lively spot is edged by a row of shady casuarina trees and has good body-boarding waves. The road extends southeast through a number of residential districts that have sprung up within the past 20 to 30 years and which are criss-crossed with a network of roads that can be quite confusing. Eventually **Silver Sands** ❼

Map on pages 228–29

ABOVE: South Point lighthouse.
BELOW: Silver Sands beach during a windsurfing competition.

Map on pages 228–29

TIP

Frederick Forsyth's best-selling novel *The Fist of God* (1994) tells the factual story of Gerald Bull and his research in Barbados – and what happened afterwards…

hoves into view which, after a few wrong turnings, feels miles from anywhere. Here are two hotels: a large, family resort called **Silver Sands** and the **Silver Rock Hotel** which recently reopened after extensive refurbishment as an Adventure Sports Centre. Both are popular with windsurfers, the latter being the site of world-ranked native windsurfer Brian Talma's new **Windsurfing Academy**. Talma, whose influence in the area has turned it from a fishing village to a windsurfing village, also has a shop here which is where you will find him when he is back on the island during the winter months.

Each year the beach at Silver Sands plays host to the world's best windsurfers who gather here for the first leg of the PWA World Cup tour; 1999 saw local sailor O'Neil Marshall twice beat out a field of 60 competitors to take first place in both the Ultramanoeuvre and the Free Ride competitions.

Chancery Lane discoveries

Continuing eastwards around the point you come to **Inch Marlowe** which was once swampland and connected to the **Chancery Lane Swamp** beside it. The Inch Marlowe Swamp was drained to make way for tourist development, which many felt was ideal because of the sandy Long Beach that runs alongside.

Long Beach ❽ stretches for about a mile (1.5 km) from Inch Marlowe Point to the cliffs below Paragon (an area to the south of Grantley Adams International Airport). A desolate spot, often forgotten by the populace at large, the entire beach and swamp once belonged to the Chancery Lane Plantation.

In the early 1970s, an ambitious scheme for a Holiday Inn resort was brewed for Long Beach which never came to fruition. But now there are new developments afoot with plans for a community of 380 houses, shopping and recreational facilities.

Right: the sky's the limit. **Below:** waiting for a friend.

Long Beach and Inch Marlowe are generally perceived as out of the way, the "outback" of Barbados and, until recently, the area was used as a shooting range by hunters.

In 1966, archaeologists unearthed the remnants of Amerindian settlements near Chancery Lane. It was an exciting discovery, for the pottery they found was very different from any seen before on the island. It led them to believe that the first inhabitants of Barbados were agricultural people, and that they settled on the island in about AD 600. Subsequent excavations, notably those at Port St Charles on the North Coast (*see page 301*) and Hill Crest at Bathsheba (*see page 264*) on the East Coast, have indicated that in fact there was a pre-ceramic culture in Barbados some 4,000 years ago. This date will probably recede further as new discoveries are made and more modern techniques such as carbon-dating employed.

At the top end of Long Beach near **Paragon** are two huge rusting cannons and an abandoned wreck of a DC3 aircraft. In the 1960s, a series of experiments named HARP (High Altitude Research Project) was started here which entailed creating a gun that could shoot projectiles to a height of 100 miles (160 km) and more through the atmosphere. The project was the brainchild of Canadian Gerald Bull, who was mysteriously murdered in 1990. ❑

SURF, WIND AND THE DEEP

Water is life, so the saying goes, and no more so than in Barbados where the Caribbean and Atlantic provide ideal conditions for watersports.

The crystal clear tropical waters surrounding Barbados change from deep blue to bright turquoise, from gentle swells to roaring breakers creating conditions to suit most watersports. On the Caribbean beaches, hotels, dive shops or individuals offer one-man watersports such as water-skiing, parasailing and jet skis, and fun rides on giant bananas pulled by power boats.

The northeasterlies power the Hobie cats and Sunfish boats (also available for hire on the beaches), and attract "yachties" to the international races from all over the world. Windsurfers also take advantage of the trade winds that whip around South Point. Under the sea, PADI diving instructors can introduce beginners to the wonders of the coral reefs. Or, a trip in a submarine gives a window on this magical world.

SURFING SAFARI

The powerful Atlantic provides surfers with perfect waves all year round at the Soup Bowl at Bathsheba on the East Coast. And world class surfers flock here each November for the International Surfing Championship, renting a small "bay cottage". But winter storms can transform the West Coast, pushing monster swells into normally flat calm bays that can lower a beach by 4–5 ft (1–1.5 metres) in a couple of days. Batt's Rock, Sandy Lane, Tropicana, Gibbs, Maycocks and Duppies are some of the better West Coast surfing spots.

▷ **REGATTA FINALE**
The Caribbean yachting season ends in a week-long jamboree at the Mount Gay/Boatyard Regatta at the end of May.

△ **RIDING THE WAVES**
The steady northeasterly trade winds blow around South Point whipping up the waves and filling the sails of the windsurfers.

◁ **BATHING BEAUTY**
Protection from the hot sun's rays is all-important when you're on, in, or by the water, so don't forget the sunscreen…

△ **DOWN UNDER**
An underwater trail aroun the shallow-water reefs of Folkestone Marine Reserv reveals a fascinating scenario of tropical fish.

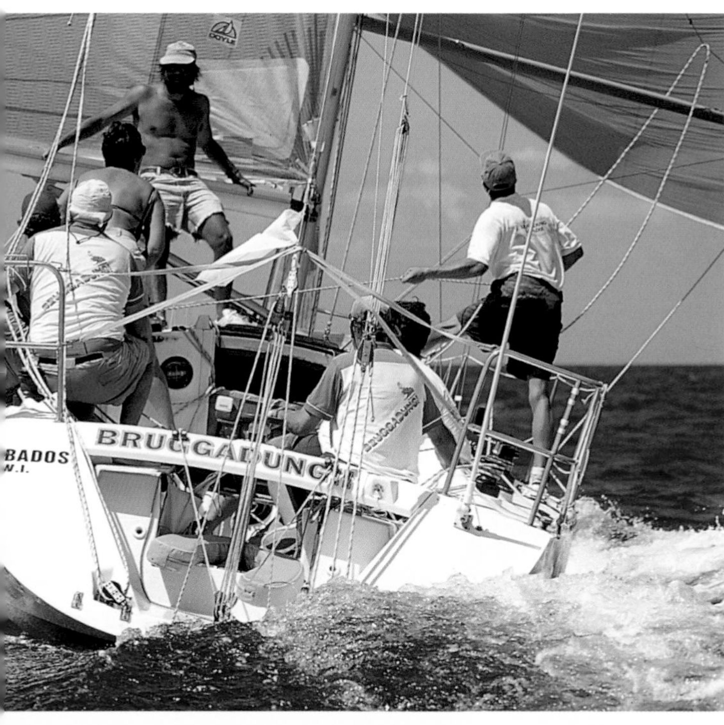

△ **EXPLORING THE DEEP**
Divers can explore three shipwrecks over which corals, sponges and anemones have formed an elaborate patchwork.

◁ **SCUBA CENTRES**
Several dive shops not only provide diving equipment and qualified instructors but they organise night dives too.

△ **FLYING HIGH**
For a truly different view of the island why not check out parasailing? Higher than your hotel and cheaper than a helicopter, it's a thrilling experience.

THE ONE THAT DIDN'T GET AWAY

A game fisherman's dream, this 910 lb (400 kg) blue marlin is a record breaker and a life-size replica hangs in the arrival hall at Grantley Adams airport. Barbados has around 20 game fishing boats available for charter. Typically they fish around 5 miles (8 km) out to sea but may venture as far afield as 40 (65 km) during competitions. You can expect to catch barracuda, kingfish, dolphin (also known as mahi mahi or dorado), marlin, wahoo, tuna, sail and billfish. Charters are typically full or half day and can be shared. Most of the fish is sold or eaten and underweight fish released. Each spring the International Game Fishing Association holds the Barbados leg of the annual circuit that stretches from Guadeloupe to Trinidad with a prize of $50,000 for the record-breaking fish.

THE BREEZY SOUTHEAST

A beautifully preserved Great House, a modern rum factory and art gallery, historic hotels and some spectacular beaches can be found on this cool, windswept corner of Barbados

Map on page 246

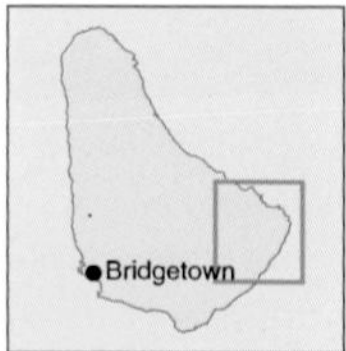

The flat expanse of land sprawling across the southeastern corner of the country is in St Philip, the largest of the 11 parishes. On coral rock, the last part of the island to be reclaimed from the sea half a million years ago, this area has retained an isolated feel – windswept and battered by the waves determined to get their own back. Periodically along the low-slung jagged coastline, the sharply pointed rocks give way to stretches of soft, white sand and tiny shells where the waves roll in and create ideal conditions for body boarding, often with few others to share it with. On the pastureland, sweeping back from the cliffs but still within the sound of the sea, new houses dot the landscape between grazing cows and the goat-like black belly sheep.

In the past, due to poor agricultural land and the distance from Bridgetown, St Philip was regarded as a bit of a backwater but, since the beginning of the 1990s, it has emerged as one of the most productive and fastest growing parishes. Because of the availability of low-cost land here, many Barbadians have been building their dream homes with their hard-earned savings, after returning from the United States, Britain or neighbouring islands, where they have spent most of their working lives.

PRECEDING PAGES: the Atlantic at Ragged Point.
LEFT: an empty beach.
BELOW: bringing up the crude.

True "Philipians", who are distinctive even in their manner of speech, have developed an unusual homogeneity because of their parish's isolation. This communal feeling among the people of this area is especially strong during the Crop Over calypso competition, when they support their home-grown calypsonians, particularly their champion "Red Plastic Bag" (*see page 135*).

Highway 5 is one of the main roads into St Philip which has been greatly improved, and at **Six Cross Roads**, 9 miles (14.5 km) from Bridgetown, each direction leads to somewhere interesting. Highway 6 also meets up here, entering the parish from Christ Church and running through St Philip's oil fields.

Black gold

Oil production in Barbados goes back to the 1870s after oil seeps prompted exploration in the Scotland District. Before then the island had been producing bitumen (manjak) since the early days. The West Indian Petroleum Company was formed in 1896 and sunk more than 60 wells – machine-drilled and hand-bored – which by 1910 had produced over 25,000 barrels of oil. It was not until 1966 that the **Woodbourne Oil Field** was discovered in St Philip by General Crude, and in 1982 it was nationalised and run by the Government-owned Barbados National Oil Company. Today, the monster-like pumps painted in the blue and yellow of Barbados' national colours raise enough oil for about a third of the island's energy requirements

This chattel house at Six Cross Roads is typical of many in the parish of St Philip.

and oil reserves are estimated at around 3.1 million barrels. Costs are very high and there are plans for privatisation.

Modern rum distillery and heritage park

About half a mile (1 km) further on you reach Foursquare and the **Rum Factory & Heritage Park** ❶ (open daily; Fri and Sat until 9pm, Sun pm; entrance fee; tel: 420 1977). The idea of local rum producer David Seale, the park opened in November 1996 on 7 acres (3 hectares) of a 300-year-old sugar plantation. The park has the most modern rum distillery in the world, which you can see in action in the converted 17th-century sugar factory. Also the first environmentally friendly distillery in the Caribbean, the factory produces ESA Field White Rum, Doorly's and Old Brigand and you can watch the rum being bottled – the old way by hand as it was 100 years ago and the high-tech way by computerised machinery at a rate of 25 miniatures a minute.

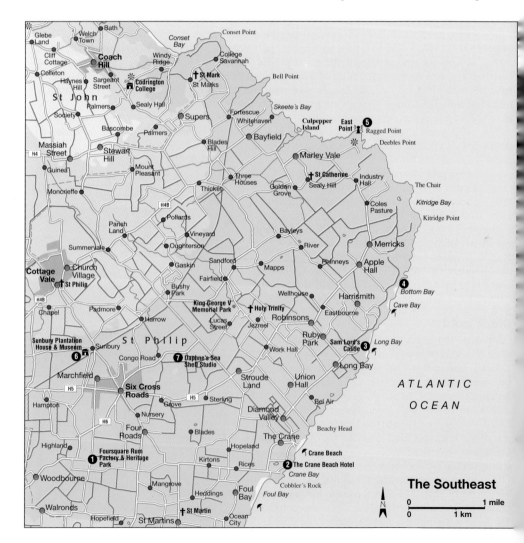

The residual water from the distillation process is then used to irrigate the

Map on page 246

surrounding gardens, planted with tropical flowers, fruits, shrubs, vines and trees, all comprehensively labelled. The old cane pit, where the harvested sugar cane used to be tipped when it arrived at the factory by mule and cart, has been converted into a 250-seat amphitheatre where shows and concerts are regularly produced. The outbuildings, including the cane weighing station, of the original sugar factory, which finally closed its doors in 1984, have been turned into shops and craft studios making baskets, pottery and jewellery. Street carts roam the park offering sweets, coconuts and ice creams, and children can play in the largest playground in Barbados.

A 300-year-old, two-storey building with the original coral-stone walls, in which you can still see the shapes of the coral, has been home to the Art Foundry (*see page 97*). Upstairs in a cavernous room, adorned with old sugar factory relics, non-commercial exhibitions of contemporary art by renowned Caribbean artists have been arranged. A print-making operation runs on the ground floor and in the courtyard are a selection of sculptures on permanent display.

Sea grape trees (Cocoloba uvifera) *grow alongside many beaches and can be seen at Foul Bay.*

About 2½ miles (4 km) east of Foursquare, through Kirtons and past the turning for the Crane Beach Hotel, is a beautiful beach incongruously named **Foul Bay**. The bay earned its name because it was a "foul" or bad anchorage for sailboats from Bristol and London in the early days.

The Crane – a famous beauty spot

Perched on top of a craggy cliff is **The Crane Beach Hotel** ❷ (entrance fee for non-residents redeemable at the bar or restaurant). To leave Barbados without experiencing the view from here would be a crime, especially at sunrise or sunset when the colour of the pink sand beach intensifies – you may already be familiar

BELOW: playing dominoes in the shade.

The Crane Beach Hotel's welcoming sign.

with the hotel swimming pool, graced by neo-classical columns, as it has provided the setting for many a fashion shoot in a glossy magazine. Barbadians have been coming here since it opened as a hotel in 1887 to enjoy the beautiful situation and take the curative sea air refreshed by the luxuriant trade winds.

The eroded steps built into the cliff have been replaced by a new safer staircase leading down to the beach of very fine, pinkish sand and a surf that provides excellent waves for body-boarding (boards can be hired on the beach). In the coconut grove behind the beach, plans are afoot for a beach restaurant, and hammocks strung between the trees will offer respite from the tropical sun.

Canadian Paul Doyle bought the 18-room hotel, with 35 acres (11 hectares) of adjacent land, in 1989 and has been running it with his wife since 1996. Plans are under way to expand by constructing 160 new apartments in three three-storey blocks overlooking the sea along the Crane's southeast-facing cliff top. They are being built in traditional Barbadian style in order to blend in with the historic charm of the original hotel.

The Crane got its name from the massive crane at a pier in the bay in the 18th century, which was used to load and unload the boats that plied daily between here and Bridgetown delivering goods and carrying the sugar back. An opening in the Cobbler's Reef protecting the bay allowed the small freighters access to this part of the island. In 1881, a railway was built from Bridgetown to Sunbury Plantation (*see page 252*) – later continuing on to Bathsheba and Belleplaine – which stopped off at the Crane and eventually led to the demise of the port. When the hotel opened six years later, horse-drawn trams would be sent to fetch the guests from the station. In 1921, the hotel's magnificent ballroom was added making it very popular "night spot" with the island's élite.

BELOW: modelling at the Crane's pool.

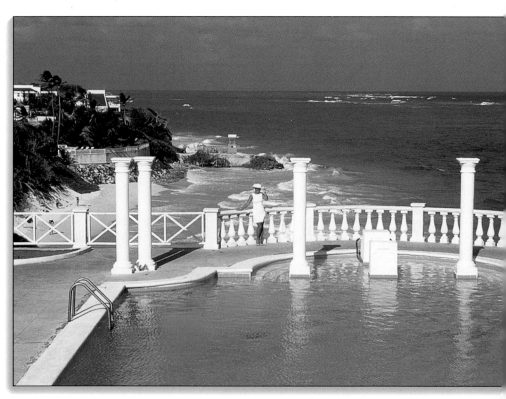

Tales of extravagance and piracy

About 1½ miles (2.5 km) eastwards along the coast, **Sam Lord's Castle** ❸ (open daily; entrance fee to non-residents) lies above the spacious, white sandy beach of **Long Bay**. Steeped in history and folklore, the splendid Georgian-style mansion is now the central part and reception area of an all-inclusive luxury hotel owned and run by Grant Hotels.

The original owner was the notorious Samuel Hall Lord (1778–1844), a planter who had lavish tastes and apparently felt no qualms about spending money he often did not have. His ostentatious house took three years to build from 1830 and he imported craftsmen from Italy to decorate the ceiling with stucco work and sought the advice of the architect Charles Rutter who had been involved in the decorative work at Windsor Castle. He then filled it with expensive furniture, a lot of which can still be seen in the hotel, including his four-poster bed, mahogany wardrobe and sofa, crystal chandeliers and huge mirrors. With traditional thick walls, the house has survived many a hurricane – during one such storm the scaffolding around it set up for some light repair work was ripped off and found 3 miles (5 km) away in a field.

He is best remembered for the way in which he chose to pay for his extravagant lifestyle: it is said that he used to invite the Harbour Master frequently to his sumptuous dinners and ply him with the island's best rum and fare, after which the wily host would question his honoured guest about the arrivals of vessels. Sam would then put lanterns in the palm trees on the beach at night to fool the captains of the passing ships that they had reached the safe harbour in Carlisle Bay. When the ships were wrecked on the rocks, he would plunder them. Rumour has it that Sam Lord's treasure is buried somewhere in the

Map on page 246

Non-residents wanting to visit Sam Lord's Castle can buy a pass which varies in price according to choice and can include use of all facilities, drinks at any bar, meals and admission to theme night entertainment.

BELOW: Sam Lord's Castle – built with ill-gotten gains.

At Wild Feathers, near Sam Lord's Castle, woodcarver Geoffrey Skeete has put together a family tree that traces the bloodline history of the modern thoroughbred race-horse back to the three original Arab stallions in the 17th century. Call him on 423 7758.

grounds of his castle, but whether this is actually the case is anybody's guess, especially as he died with a debt of £18,000.

One of the most well-known characters of Bajan folklore, Sam Lord has been the subject of several books (one being *The Regency Rascal* by Lt Col Drury) as well as a record produced by Barbados' renowned old-time calypso group, The Merrymen. James H. Stark, in a guide to Barbados published in 1903, describes the mansion before it was changed into a hotel: "Within a hundred yards from the sea, stands a large house known as 'Long Bay Castle', or as 'Lord's Castle'. The building is of a pretentious style, the rooms are large and lofty, and the tall mahogany pillars of the dining room have a fine effect. The house is too large, and its situations too remote for the wants of most Barbadian families, therefore, it has been unoccupied for years and is slowly going to decay."

Some time after Stark's visit, the property was bought by the Cooke family, distant relatives of the 19th-century novelist Anthony Trollope, who apparently did not take to Barbados when he visited in 1859. In 1942, they sold it to some Bajan businessmen who turned it into a hotel, converting the north and south open porches into castellated wings. Since then the castle has changed hands three times and more not-so-attractive additions have been made in the grounds.

Opposite the hotel's entrance, in the car park, taxi drivers waiting for a fare slam down their dominoes in heated games, often for stakes, under the trees. Huddles of men like this can be seen all over the island clustered around tables in the shade playing the game which has won the Barbadians the domino world championship title many times. In 1998, a 29-member team went to the domino world championships in St Kitts and beat off all opposition from the rest of the Caribbean, Canada and the United States.

Below: basketball is a popular sport. **Right:** peaceful, picture-book beach at Bottom Bay.

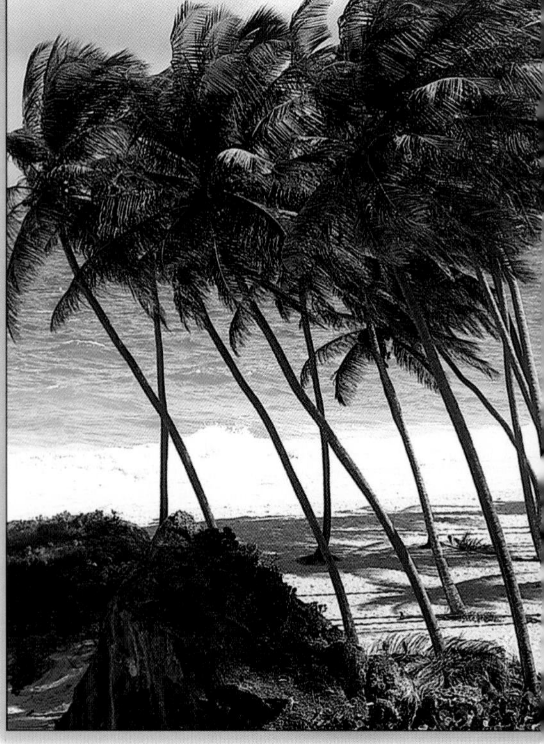

Castle Close behind is a private estate which has holiday villas surrounded by beautiful gardens to rent and the residents can use the hotel's facilities.

Ragged beauty

The 4-mile (6-km) stretch of coastline, from Long Bay to Ragged Point at the easternmost part of the island, is indented with peaceful coves and bays hewn from the dark coral limestone cliffs and include the beautiful and often deserted beaches of **Harrismith**, **Cave Bay** and **Bottom Bay** ❹ – one that is easily recognisable from countless photographs and postcards. Here the only noise is the crashing of the waves, which can make swimming rather a challenge for those with a nervous disposition.

At the spectacular **Ragged Point** ❺, the scenery becomes more desolate as the cliffs get higher and are pounded by the Atlantic Ocean, and from the still-functioning **East Point Lighthouse**, which is not open to the public, there is a magnificent view. Just off the coast about 1½ miles (2 km) north of the lighthouse is what Barbadians consider as their own colony – **Culpepper Island**. No more than 7,875 sq ft (732 sq metres) in area, it is about 20 ft (6 metres) above sea level. A channel of about 35 yards (32 metres) wide separates the island from the coast but it is too deep to wade out to it. People have been known to swim it. In *Exploring Historic Barbados*, Maurice Hutt wrote: "On the island one has that sensation of being in a small world of one's own, reached by one's own physical efforts, not by some mechanical contrivance, which is always rewarding. And as in all intimate contact with wild nature, one feels a close kinship with the natural forces of the earth which is beyond the price of rubies."

Just around the corner lies **Skeete's Bay**, where a quiet fishing village hugs

Map on page 246

The Barbados Rally Club operates from its purpose-made race track at Bushy Park, St Philip, suitable for both go-kart and saloon racing. The highlight of the year is the Texaco International in May. Fax: 438 7068 for more information.

BELOW: desolate, craggy coastline at Ragged Point.

Map on page 246

TIP

Sunbury's "Planter's Candlelight Dinner" is an opportunity to experience dining as the wealthy planters did when the notorious Sam Lord came to call. For reservations, call 423 6270.

RIGHT: young Philipians planning a ride. **BELOW:** a planter's drawing room restored.

the beach, untouched by time. From here, the Highway 4B heads westwards through Thicket for about 4 miles (6 km) until it reaches **St Philip's Church** and the more fertile region of the parish.

Plantation relics at Sunbury

A road at the western end of the church's graveyard leads southeast for about 1½ miles (2 km) through the cane fields to **Sunbury Plantation House and Museum** ❻ (open daily; entrance fee), a superb example of a Barbadian estate which was opened to the public in 1983. More than 300 years old, the Great House has survived several hurricanes and a major fire in 1995, which closed it for a year. Some of the original features were saved, such as the old-fashioned jalousies over the frame sash windows, fitted with storm shutters, and a turned mahogany staircase. The 2½-ft (76-cm) thick walls of the house date back to the late 17th century when flint and other hard stone used in the construction were brought over from England as ballast for schooners.

The only plantation house on the island with all the rooms on view, Sunbury is full of antiques, china, glassware and has an extensive collection of old prints. After the fire, pieces that had escaped the flames were joined by furniture purchased from other plantation houses and one Barbadian family, who had moved to Florida, sent back some of their items for the museum. In the cellars, which used to store yams and sweet potatoes grown on the plantation, is a range of antique kitchen equipment and other relics from the plantation era, plus a unique collection of horse-drawn carriages.

Outside in the beautifully landscaped gardens is a 200-year-old mahogany wood, the first teak tree to be planted on the island in 1799 and another tree referred to as the Graveyard Tree, as underneath it are buried two children, believed to be members of the Barrow family who lived at Sunbury in the 18th century. It is said that they were both accidentally suffocated by their father while sheltering from a hurricane in the cellar.

A descendant, John Barrow, was a colonel in charge of the militia in 1816 when the Easter (also known as the Bussa) Rebellion started at a neighbouring plantation (*see page 201*). One of the slave leaders belonged to him and the plantation suffered BDS$4,000 of damage.

After a tour of the house you can stay on for refreshments in the Courtyard Restaurant and Bar.

Sea shell craft

If you return to Six Cross Roads a mile (1.6 km) away and take the adjacent road to the left, after about the same distance you come to the Congo Road Plantation and **Daphne's Sea Shell Studio** ❼ (tel: 423 6180). In a converted cow pen at the back of the 320-year-old plantation house, which has a coral-stone arch at the entrance, Daphne Hunte and her daughters, Carolyn, Roberta and Gina, create beautiful gifts decorated with shells, from shell mirrors and hand-crafted shell jewellery to shell-encrusted ceramics and frames. They also have a shop in Holetown and have branched out into handpainted clothing. ❑

THE WILD EAST COAST

A world apart from the beaches of the west and south coasts, the unspoiled Atlantic side of the island offers spectacular views at every turn, a cliffside garden and ideal surfing conditions

Map on page 258

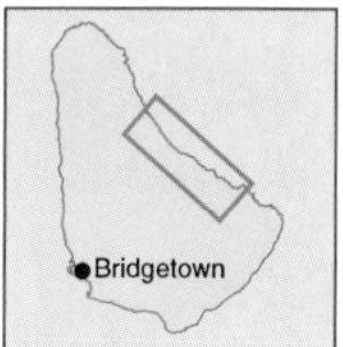

The East Coast on the opposite side of the island is just that – the opposite. There are no deluxe hotels here; no crowds; no shopping complexes; no calm sea. The only sound that dominates the coastline of the parishes of St John, St Joseph and St Andrew is from the large Atlantic waves rolling on to long, golden beaches, which during the week are deserted. As you drive eastwards across the island the roads become narrower and steeper, the sugar cane fields give way to large areas of banana trees growing on hillsides, peppered with tiny villages. Every now and then an avenue of towering cabbage palms proclaims the site of a plantation house hidden from view and, all of a sudden, a magnificent panorama reveals miles of wild and windy coastline where sculptured rocks jut from the foaming sea and wind-blown sea grape trees hug the deserted sandy beaches.

There are several ways of approaching the East Coast, and be prepared to lose your way: Highways 3 and 3B enter the region either side of **Hackleton's Cliff** which rises 1,000 ft (300 metres) above the sea offering spectacular views from Pico Teneriffe in the north to Ragged Point in the south. The cliff is a coral limestone escarpment which was once battered by the sea and dominates the northeastern section of the lush and hilly parish of St John. History buffs, nature enthusiasts and those who like to chat with residents of small fishing villages will enjoy these parts.

PRECEDING PAGES: the road to a bay in St John.
LEFT: royal palms line the driveway to Codrington College.
BELOW: a Martin's Bay resident.

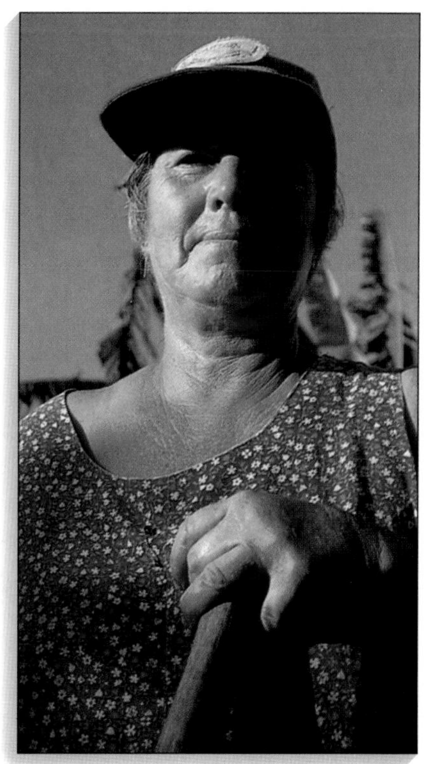

Codrington College – a perfect setting

From the south the road enters St John via St Philip and after about half a mile (1 km) you see the long, majestic drive lined by tall Royal Palms leading to the arched entrance of **Codrington College** ❶ (open daily; entrance fee). Set in a beautiful campus with lush and peaceful grounds, the complex of coral-stone buildings stands on a cliff 360 ft (110 metres) above the sea, looking out over **Conset Bay**.

Still an active theological college, it was founded in 1710 by Christopher Codrington III (1668–1710), who left £10,000 for the "Society for the Propagation of the Gospel in Foreign Parts" to establish an educational institution on the island of Barbados. His will stipulated: "a convenient number of Professors and scholars maintained there, all of them to be under vows of poverty and chastity and obedience, who shall be obliged to study and practice Physics and Chirurgery as well as Divinity, that by the apparent usefulness offered to all mankind they may both endear themselves to the people and have the better opportunities of doing good to men's souls, whilst they are taking care of their bodies."

Also responsible for the establishment of St John's Lodge School, Christopher Codrington came from a

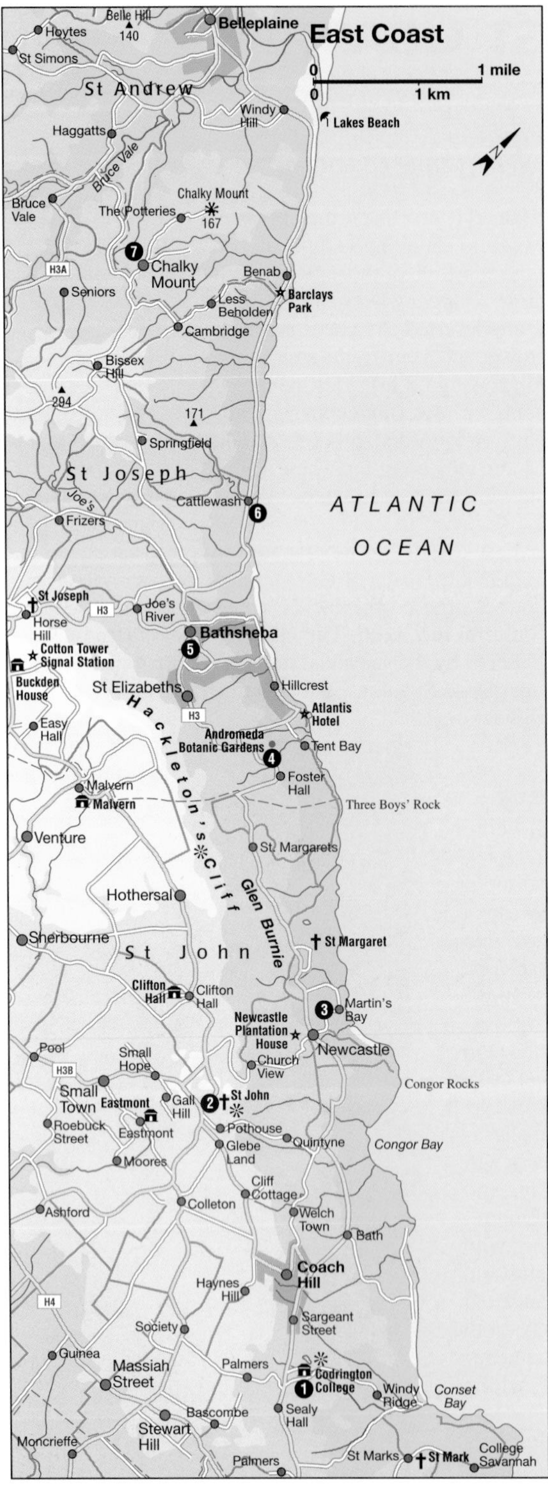

long line of Codringtons who owned land in St John. The first Christopher Codrington came to Barbados from England in 1642 and his son, also called Christopher, went on to become Deputy Governor of Barbados in 1668. The Codrington of Codrington College fame was *his* son, who served a stint as Governor of the Leeward Islands based in Antigua and Barbuda. He had attended All Souls College, Oxford, and later studied law at the Middle Temple in London. He was made a fellow of All Souls College because of his outstanding intellect.

Despite Codrington's best and most pious intentions, his will was contested by his family in England. The court case laboriously dragged on for several years until the society eventually won. The college, however, was not started until 1748, nearly 40 years after his death. Then there was the problem of finding men of the right calibre who would be willing to live under monastic vows. Eventually, by 1760 the first deacon of Codrington College, Philip Harris, had been ordained.

A 300-yard (275-metre) well-marked nature walk to the northwest of the buildings starts by the ornamental lily pond and passes through the primeval vegetation of Codrington Woods, where giant trees such as mahogany and kapok grow alongside the thorny macaw palms and imposing cabbage palms. The trees and plants are identified in a brochure available from the ticket office.

Bajan safari

You can experience the view of the coast from the college first hand, if you turn left out of the grounds and left again down a steep hill to the picturesque beach at **Conset Bay**. This road is notoriously winding, so prepare yourself for an adventure, something like a safari. The overhanging trees are home to a number of wild green monkeys, one or two of which are likely to bound across the road in front of any car that drives through their territory. The narrow beach at the bottom is not an ideal spot for a swim but the colourful fishing boats pulled up on the beach make it a pretty sight.

Back on the road heading north past the college, take the right turning that meanders down a hill to **Bath**. Although Bath was a thriving plantation in the days when "sugar was king", it is now a park where Bajans come to picnic on public holidays and adjoins a beach where many a cricket test match has been reenacted. It is safe to swim here when the lifeguard is in attendance and there is a car park with toilet facilities and a snack bar.

A Byzantine tomb

Continuing north you soon come to a left turning which leads steeply up to the historic **St John's Church** ❷, set upon a splendid cliff and overlooking both coastal St John and the Atlantic Ocean.

Although a stone version of St John's Church was built as early as 1660, it was destroyed by fire and the next church on the same spot was totally destroyed by the hurricane of 1831. The present building was constructed in 1836 and the wooden pulpit here, made from six different kinds of beautiful wood – ebony, locust, mahogany and manchineel from Barbados and some imported oak and pine – was all that was rescued from the original church fire. Also inside is an interesting sculpture depicting the Madonna and Child with the infant St John carved by Sir Richard Westmacott, the sculptor of the controversial Lord Nelson statue, and a beautifully carved circular staircase to the gallery and panelled ceiling. Plaques on the walls and bizarre inscriptions on the gravestones in the cemetery outside nourish the imagination.

One tomb belongs to Ferdinando Paleologus who lived at Ashford Plantation,

Map on page 258

Palmers, near Codrington College, is a beautifully restored plantation house with a small restaurant in the grounds and a chapel which can be hired for weddings. Call 423 1604 for information or if you would like a tour.

BELOW: inside the highly positioned St John's Church.

A much-needed road sign.

about 2 miles (3 km) away to the west, from 1649 to 1670. A descendant of the brother of the last Byzantine Emperor, Constantine the Great, Paleologus fought as a Royalist in the English Civil War and fled to Barbados as a refugee. For several years he was warden of St John's Church. At first his tomb was in a vault under the choir in the church and according to Greek Orthodox custom his body was placed with his head pointing to the west and his feet to the east, but after the 1831 hurricane it was moved to the churchyard. Some years later, nearly 200 years after Paleologus died, the rector of the parish (apparently curious to find out whether the story about the coffin's arrangement was true) ordered the lead coffin to be opened. All scepticism about the nature of Paleologus' burial was put to rest when his skeleton was found inside embedded in quicklime in accordance with the Greek funeral custom.

Along Hackleton's Cliff

Three historic Great Houses strategically surround St John's Church. About a quarter of a mile away as the crow flies lies **Eastmont**, a private house that is significant architecturally as the prototypical 19th-century Great House, and which has symbolic importance. Miller Austin, a mulatto blacksmith, broke the monopoly of the white plantocracy when he bought Eastmont in 1895, and it has remained in his family ever since. His daughter, Lucy Deane, inherited the estate and her son, Bernard St John QC, MP (now Sir Harold), became the third Prime Minister of Barbados in 1985.

Clifton Hall, a little further to the north, is another private residence which stands on the top of Hackleton's Cliff, named after a man who committed suicide by riding his horse over the edge. With an arcaded verandah on three sides

BELOW: unusual Anglican church.

and a double staircase leading to a central porch, this house is a prime example of Georgian architecture, but not open to the public.

On the eastern side of the church, on the way down to the coast, you pass the ruined **Newcastle Plantation House** hidden by a wood. Norma Nicholls, who once lived at Newcastle, paid stirring tribute to her former residence in an article that appeared in the August 1977 edition of the now defunct magazine *The Bajan*: "Memories of Newcastle where I spent most of my holidays as a child, come flooding back. Newcastle in the morning, the smell of almonds – West Indian almonds – of roses and the sea. Blowing up from Martin's Bay, the sea breeze brought with it the aroma of burst almonds in the driveway and my aunt's roses which grew in a small bed just below the drawing-room window. Pungent, refreshing, exhilarating, I would take deep breaths and drink it all, as I sat on the window-sill of the front bedroom, looking down at the horses as they nuzzled away at their oats and corn in the long concrete trough which stood nearby, the sunshine rippling on their flanks, their tails swishing in contentment." In the same article she referred to a gardener at Newcastle named Thomas, who was "a descendant of the Scottish political prisoners banished to the West Indies in the 17th century: his eyes were as blue as the seas and he always had a tale to tell."

Map on page 258

The dramatic heliconia is used in hotel arrangements.

Glen Burnie – wild and unspoiled

The road plunges down the escarpment to **Martin's Bay** ❸. A fishing village known for lobster catching, the beach has rock pools perfect for a refreshing dip. Towards the end of the 1800s and until it ceased operation in 1938, the old Barbados railway (*see page 267*) passed by here. The road just above Martin's

RED LEGS OF GLEN BURNIE

Legend has it that the pejorative term "Red Leg" was used by the English to describe Scotsmen working in the sugar fields because the kilts they wore exposed their legs to the sun. But for generations in Barbados it has been a term for the poor whites who settled "below the cliff" in Glen Burnie, St John and along the East Coast through St Andrew as far north as St Lucy.

These poor whites were in part descendants of the losers in the Monmouth Rebellion in 1685 who instead of being hung drawn and quartered were sent to Barbados for 10 years by the choleric Judge Jeffreys as indentured servants. Others were descendants of another group of indentured servants brought to the island in the 17th century. Some escaped, some completed their indentures, others were treated so badly by their plantation masters that they ran away to the caves of Glen Burnie and created villages such as Martin's Bay. Here they kept themselves to themselves, becoming inbred. They were an oppressed and ill-treated group who eked out a living by fishing and hunting turtles and land crabs.

As the island's economy strengthened after 1960, most poor whites improved their situation and today, for the most part, they have integrated into Barbadian society.

BELOW: a quiet walk by the sea.

A specimen of the calabash tree can be seen growing in Andromeda Botanic Gardens. Believed to be introduced by Amerindians, the dried gourds of 4 in (10 cm) to 12 in (30 cm) are still used as bowls and maracas.

Bay, which runs along the coast, today more or less follows the train's path. A hiker can follow the path from the bay along the coast and into the parish of St Joseph. Aside from the abandoned train tracks, this region, known as **Glen Burnie**, remains a wild and rugged place, unspoiled by civilization.

Glen Burnie is regarded by the local naturalists as one of the last areas on the island with original tropical scenery. When Tom Adams was Prime Minister he designated the whole of the East Coast between Ragged Point in St Philip and North Point in St Lucy as a nature conservation area. There have been plans to establish a Tom Adams Memorial Park in memory of the late Prime Minister who died suddenly on 11 March, 1985.

Mythological gardens

Following the road north along Glen Burnie for 2 miles (3 km), you come to **Andromeda Botanic Gardens** ❹ (open daily; closed pub. hols; entrance fee), named after the maiden in Greek mythology who was chained to a rock, and just inside the parish of St Joseph. The island's foremost horticulturist, Iris Bannochie (1914–88), started the gardens in 1954 and named them after Andromeda because they are situated on a cliff on a site littered with large fossil-encrusted boulders which form the backdrop to the plants and link one area to another.

Mrs Bannochie acquired plants for her gardens from all over the world through gifts from friends and from her travels and when she died she willed them to the Barbados National Trust, of which she was a founder member. A tiny stream that dries up during the dry season bisects the 6-acre (2-hectare) profusion of exotic flowers, plants and trees, which include many varieties of orchids, bougainvillea, hibiscus, heliconias, anthurium, cacti, succulents, ferns and shade-

BELOW: a lily pond in Andromeda Gardens.

Map on page 258

loving plants. Also in the garden is a magnificent specimen of the bearded fig tree (*Ficus citrifolia*), which reputedly gave Barbados its name when the Portuguese stopped off in the 16th century and named the island Os Barbados – the bearded ones.

Below Andromeda is **Tent Bay** – one of the few places along the rugged St Joseph–St Andrew coast where fish are landed. Barbados has 25 landing areas in all – so it's unusual to see such a long stretch of coastline so bereft.

A bearded fig tree that many say gave Barbados its name.

A writers' retreat

Overlooking Tent Bay, down what must be the world's steepest driveway, is the renowned **Atlantis Hotel**. A simple, pleasant place, with a run-down look about it and a reputation for good Bajan food, it took its name from the legendary continent of Atlantis, said to have occupied what is now the North Atlantic.

Atlantis is one of the oldest hotels on the island and opens out on to the beach, with balconies and sunlit rooms looking out over the dazzling blue ocean. The island's famous novelist, George Lamming, whose best known book *In the Castle of My Skin* encapsulates simple village life in Barbados before Independence, stays at the Atlantis when he is on the island. Travelling for most of the year, he enjoys the tranquillity of the spot, and new writers and artists are beginning to come here to look for his kind of inspiration. Lunch on the terrace, especially at the Sunday Bajan buffet, is a memorable experience: cooling winds caress you as you savour delicious Bajan fish or chicken and gaze out at the colourful fishing boats and the sea. Be sure to try the coconut pie. Every morning at dawn, guests can watch the fishing boats manoeuvre through a dangerous S-shaped channel in the bay before heading out to sea.

BELOW: cutting up the catch.

TIP

In the Round House, a restored 19th-century house at Bathsheba, you can dine on the deck overlooking the ocean to live music on Tuesday, Wednesday and Saturday nights. Call 433 9678 to book.

Surfing at Bathsheba

In the next bay is **Bathsheba** ❺, a fishing village where many families have lived for generations, and a number of wealthy folk from other parts of the island own beach houses. Highway 3 from Bridgetown descends from **Horse Hill** at the northern end of Hackleton's Cliff, once one of the steepest roads in Barbados, now a well-graded highway that cuts through an abundance of banana, mango and soursop trees: the overhanging greenery creates a welcome coolness on hot days. In the centre of the bay in front of the village is Bathsheba's **Soup Bowl** – so named because the surf there is very foamy and the waves are big and long providing ideal conditions for surfing.

In November when the winds blow from the south, the waves get even better and the Soup Bowl's surfing competitions generally held at this time always draw large crowds (*see pages 240–41*). Perched on the cliff above on the overhanging balcony of the **Edgewater Inn**, you can watch the island's surfing elite at work. This is another hotel that provides a good Sunday lunch Bajan buffet and, down by the beach, the **Bonito Bar and Restaurant** goes a step further by offering one every day of the week.

A Bajan legend at Joe's River

Going back towards Horse Hill you reach **Joe's River**, where The National Conservation Commission is currently marking out footpaths in the 85 acres (34 hectares) of tropical woodland there – a project that has been on the back boiler for many a year. The river is barely a trickle in the dry season but fills up for a while when it rains. At **Joe's River Plantation**, a Bajan legend finds its home. According to local historian Edward Stoute: "At some period during the 18th

BELOW: defying the Atlantic rollers.

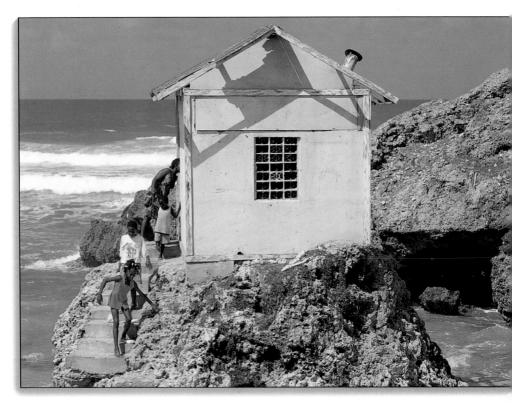

century, the owner of the property died leaving an infant son as heir. He left the child's uncle to see after the estate and to take care of the child. The uncle was a schemer and desired to possess the estate for himself… One fine day the child and his nurse disappeared and could not be traced.

"In due course the wicked uncle died, and it is claimed that two pairs of horses which were put in succession to the hearse refused to draw it, and that he was eventually buried on the estate. After the death of the uncle, this mansion became known as a 'haunted house', for it was claimed that the ghost of the nurse and child were frequently seen walking around.

"It is also claimed that during alterations to the house a very thick wall was removed, and to the surprise of everyone, two skeletons, one of a child and the other of an adult were discovered. These were given a decent burial and the ghosts were never seen again… this old mansion was demolished around the turn of the 20th century."

St Joseph's – a church with a view

On top of Horse Hill, with far-reaching views over to the Scotland District, is the **St Joseph's Church**, rebuilt in 1839 after the original was destroyed in the 1831 hurricane. Fraser and Hughes in *Historic Churches of Barbados* relate an amusing tidbit about its history: "The story goes that the Vaughn family and the Blackman family were competing to donate land for the new church. The Vaughn family won because they demanded only a single family pew, rent free, in perpetuity, while the Blackman family had demanded two pews!"

From the coast, a left turn at Horse Hill off Highway 3 leads to **Cotton Tower**, another site that offers a panoramic views. The tower at the end of Hackleton's

Map on page 258

Cotton Tower on Hackleton's Cliff is an old military signal station restored by the Barbados National Trust, but it is kept closed.

BELOW: surfers at the Soup Bowl.

The fastest growing coral is Finger Coral, which grows at a rate of 1 in (2.5 cm) a year. The average rate of coral growth is around ¾ in (1–2 cm) in 10 years. Slow-growing coral increases by 2 in (5 cm) in 100 years.

Cliff was one of six old military signal stations used by the British during the colonial days when communication was difficult. It was restored by the Barbados National Trust but is not open to the public. Other stations that can be visited are at Gun Hill (*see page 288*) and Grenade Hall (*see page 307*).

The spectacular East Coast Road

The East Coast Road from Bathsheba stretches northwards for 4 miles (7 km) hugging the most spectacular part of coastline and following the exact path of the old railroad from Bridgetown to Belleplaine. Officially opened in 1966 by Queen Elizabeth II, it has now been renamed the **Ermie Bourne Highway** after the first woman to be elected to the Assembly in 1951 – the first general election with adult suffrage. Along the back of the beach – punctuated by large boulders, remnants of the Pleistocene epoch – between the sea grape trees and wind-blown coconut groves are quaint beach cottages, or bay houses, which can be rented by vacationers and have been used as holiday homes by Barbadians for decades. This area is called **Cattlewash** ❻, where the vigorous trade winds make the surf beating against the wide golden beach particularly violent and hazardous to swimmers. However, at weekends and holidays when the Barbadians flock here with their body-boards – grandads and children alike – safe areas for swimming are marked out and lifeguards patrol the beach. At low tide, the beach and exposed coral reefs are ideal for exploring. On weekdays, it is quite likely that it will be only you on this wild and wonderful beach and the invigorating sea air and the feeling of being so close to nature can inspire the most sedentary people to jump up and run…

Across the road once stood the Kingsley Club, a delightful old traditional hotel which sadly was demolished in 1998 to be replaced by modern condiminiums – a harbinger of things to come?

Below: on the road to St Joseph.

Chalky Mount

Further along the beach the road enters the parish of St Andrew at **Barclays Park**, a 50-acre (20-hectare) park with a shaded picnic area, snack bar and toilet facilities, created by Barclays Bank in 1966 as an Independence Day gift to Barbados.

Behind the park, **Chalky Mount** (550 ft/167 metres), a hill made of clay, looms over the coast. Nearby, **Chalky Mount Village** ❼ has been home to generations of potters living mostly in wooden houses on the hillside close to one of the largest reserves of clay on the island, where they made functional cookware such as "connerees", special pots for preserving meats, "pepperpots", in which stews can last for weeks as more is added each day, and "monkeys" water jugs that kept drinking water cool. Surnames such as Devonish, Harding, Springer and Cummins can often be found on pots that were made here. However, only four potters are left now, others having gone to the more lucrative and accessible potteries near Bridgetown, where the Barbadian pottery tradition is flourishing. A narrow road that should be negotiated carefully and is often subject to land slippage meanders along ridges up to the village. ◻

All Aboard For Bathsheba

An excerpt from *The Bridge: Barbados* by Patrick Roach encapsulates the effect of the railway line from Bridgetown to Belleplaine in the early 20th century.

"Barbados had a train that operated from 1881 up to 1938 and was a wonderful means of transport, linking many beautiful scenic places such as Bath, Martin's Bay, Atlantis Hotel, Bathsheba, Kingsley, Dan and Belleplaine. In those days the roads left much to be desired, and most of the motor cars in Barbados were incapable of ascending the terrific hills. If one took a chance and drove down to Bathsheba it was essential to leave well before sunset to get over the hills.

"Bathsheba and Bath were not then served by buses and when one went on holiday, which many families did, it meant going for a month or two. This necessitated packing up and bringing down by train suitcases with clothes, bed linen and pillows, large quantities of canned goods such as salmon and condensed milk, PY canned salt butter and hundreds of pounds of Wallaba wood in bags to be fed into the old wood and coal cookers. Ice was always brought down 200 pounds at a time and this had to be got up to the house and into the ice box.

"Yes, it was quite an undertaking to pack up and go to Bathsheba by train in those days. The train used to leave Bridgetown on afternoons around 4pm and frequently there were heavy landslides in the Consets cutting or Bath section which meant that a crew had to be summoned to work shovelling the earth from off the train lines. This sometimes took two or three hours and, of course, mothers always had to have emergency rations easily available for the children so that if a serious delay was encountered there would be a picnic meal to keep everyone happy. The train station in Bridgetown was located in what is now the Fairchild Street Market and the journey from there through all of the intervening stations to Bathsheba took around three to four hours. When the train came puffing around the Beachmount Hill corner it always gave three loud hoots of triumph and all the people at Bathsheba would flock to the station to welcome it. My favourite was No. 3, which was a very powerful engine, and we knew all of the guards by name. Sometimes letters or messages or packages used to be sent down by these guards and they knew who was in every house. Very few people ever shut doors or windows in the houses and stealing was non-existent.

"Yes, there was a train in Barbados and it was loved and looked forward to all day. During August Bank Holidays special excursions left Bridgetown about 6 or 7am and 15 or 16 carriages would be filled with holidaymakers with their picnic baskets visiting Bathsheba for the day, and, of course, there were always a few who got rather tipsy and did most amusing things. These excursions were known as outings and were very popular with Sunday School excursionists and other groups. Around 4pm the train began to hoot and they would all flock back into the carriages and the train then pulled out puffing loudly." ❑

RIGHT: the popular narrow-gauge railway engine.

INTO THE HIGHLANDS

A trip through a subterranean wonderland, a walk in a tropical ravine or flower forest, or horse-riding over the hills of the Scotland District – there's plenty to do and see away from the beaches

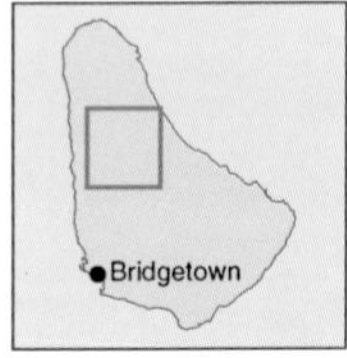

A journey into the rich, agricultural heart of the island crosses the parish of St Thomas, where the countryside lies like a patchwork quilt, decorated at intervals with tenantries, small clusters of houses on the peripheries of plantations. Gradually the road climbs up into the somnolent hills of St Andrew from where the views over the East Coast are spectacular. The dramatic landscape and bizarre rock formations reminded early Scottish settlers so much of their homeland that they named the region the Scotland District.

Completely different from the mainly flat limestone cap that covers the rest of Barbados, today these rugged highlands are threaded with steep and uneven roads which make for an adventurous drive, winding round the last remnants of genuine rainforest and through sleepy villages where cows and sheep can be seen tethered in the yards. This region consists of folded and faulted sedimentary rocks – sands, clay, shale and conglomerates. The rocks that were to become the bottom layer of Barbados were probably formed 60 to 70 million years ago when the area was just a muddy sea. Earth movements then caused them to sink deep beneath this sea. A second layer of white, clay-like rock built up over the top and a final layer of coral then grew on top of that and the island emerged from the sea. During prehistoric times, tidal waves which beat upon the eastern side of the island gradually removed the coral cap there, exposing the sands, clays and shale of what is now the Scotland District.

PRECEDING PAGES: a view across the Scotland District to the East Coast.
LEFT: exploring on horseback.
BELOW: old-time donkey cart.

A right turn at the baobab tree

In the heartland of Barbados, there are many fascinating places to visit – most have a restaurant or café attached – where you may want to spend several hours, making it necessary for more than one trip. Highway 2 wends its dramatic way northeast across the island to Belleplaine. It starts at Eagle Hall just outside Bridgetown and crosses the ABC Highway at the **Warrens** roundabout, named after an old plantation house built in 1686 nearby. A fine example of what the wealth of sugar harvests could bring planters in the 17th century, the house has lent its name to the new business park (*see page 204*) that is springing up around it. Close by stands the second-oldest baobab tree on the island. This massive-trunked tree is about 250 years old but is still small fry compared with the one in Queen's Park in Bridgetown (*see page 200*).

About a mile (1.5 km) further along stands the **Sharon Moravian Church** ❶, built in 1799 by the Moravians, who settled on the island in 1765. Arriving from Germany, they were the first missionaries to bring Christianity and education to the slaves, and the first in Barbados to admit slaves to their congregation. Sharon Church is one of the few 18th-century

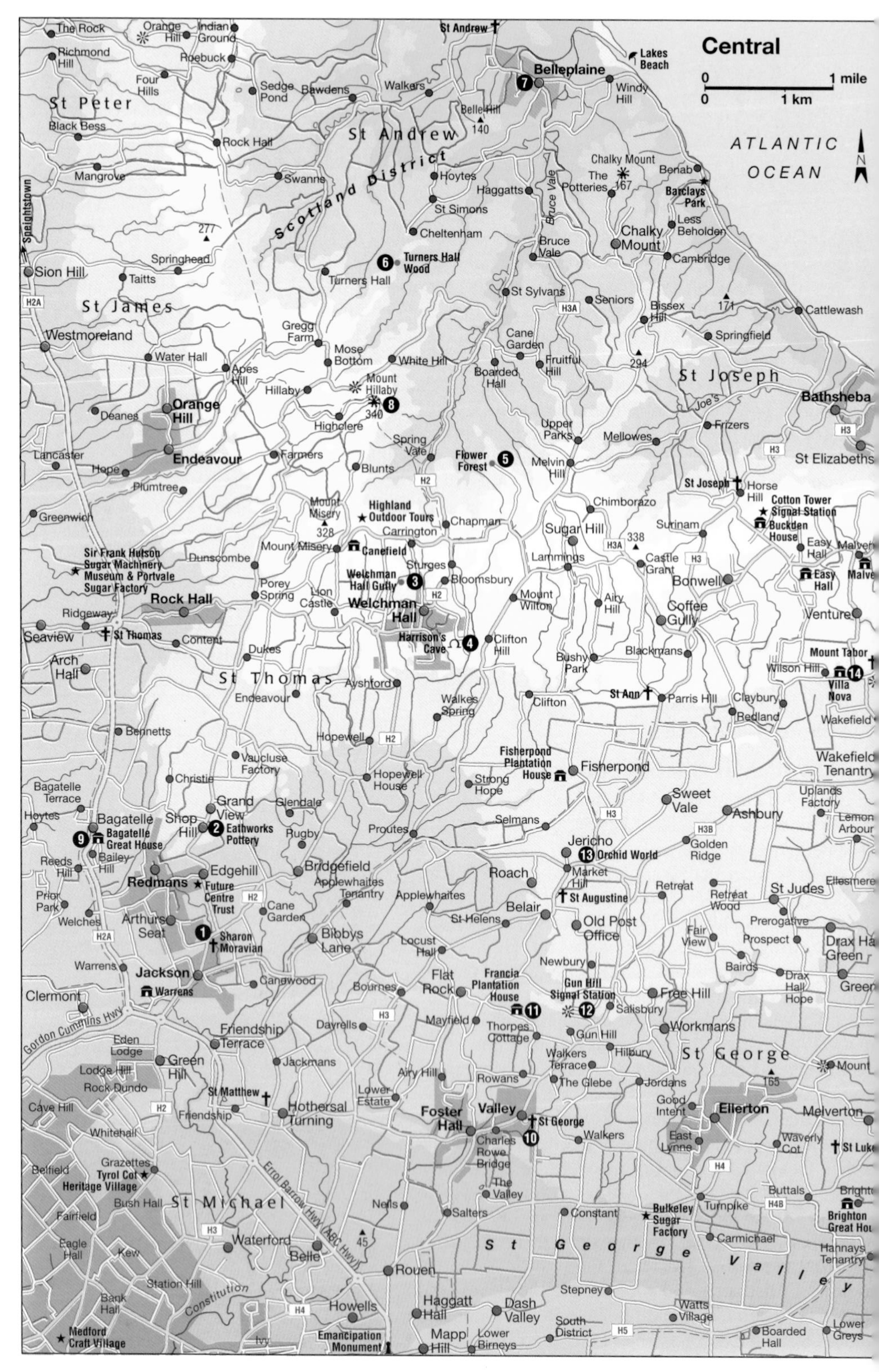
Central
0 1 mile
0 1 km
ATLANTIC OCEAN
N
St Peter
St Andrew
Scotland District
St James
St Joseph
St Thomas
St Michael
St George
St George Valley
The Rock
Orange Hill
Indian Ground
Richmond Hill
Roebuck
Four Hills
Sedge Pond
Bawdens
Walkers
St Andrew
Lakes Beach
Belleplaine
Windy Hill
Belle Hill 140
Black Bess
Rock Hall
Mangrove
Swanne
Hoytes
Haggatts
Bruce Vale
Chalky Mount
The Potteries 167
Benab
Barclays Park
St Simons
Less Beholden
Speightstown
277
Cheltenham
Chalky Mount
Cambridge
Sion Hill
Taitts
Springhead
Turners Hall Wood
Turners Hall
St Sylvans
Seniors
Bissex Hill
171
Cattlewash
H2A
H3A
Westmoreland
Gregg Farm
Cane Garden
Springfield
Water Hall
Apes Hill
Mose Bottom
White Hill
Fruitful Hill
294
Boarded Hall
Mount Hillaby
Hillaby
Joe's
Bathsheba
Orange Hill
Deanes
340
Highclere
Upper Parks
Mellowes
Frizers
H3
Lancaster
Endeavour
Farmers
Spring Vale
Flower Forest
Melvin Hill
St Elizabeths
Hope
Blunts
H2
Plumtree
St Joseph
Horse Hill
Cotton Tower Signal Station
Buckden House
Highland Outdoor Tours
Mount Misery
Chimborazo
Greenwich
328
Carrington
Chapman
Sugar Hill
Surinam
338
Easy Hall
Malvern
Mount Misery
Canefield
H3A
Sir Frank Hutson Sugar Machinery Museum & Portvale Sugar Factory
Dunscombe
Sturges
Lammings
Castle Grant
Welchman Hall Gully
Bloomsbury
Bonwell
Easy Hall
Porey Spring
Lion Castle
Mount Wilton
Rock Hall
Welchman Hall
Airy Hill
Coffee Gully
Ridgeway
Venture
Seaview
St Thomas
Content
Harrison's Cave
Clifton Hill
Blackmans
Mount Tabor
Arch Hall
Dukes
Bushy Park
Wilson Hill
Villa Nova
Ayshford
St Ann
Parris Hill
Claybury
Endeavour
Clifton
Walkes Spring
Redland
Wakefield
Bennetts
Hopewell
Wakefield Tenantry
Vaucluse Factory
Fisherpond Plantation House
Fisherpond
Christie
Hopewell House
Strong Hope
Uplands Factory
Bagatelle Terrace
Sweet Vale
Grand View
Glendale
Ashbury
Hoytes
Bagatelle
Shop Hill
Selmans
Lemon Arbour
Bagatelle Great House
Earthworks Pottery
Proutes
H3B
Rugby
Jericho
Golden Ridge
Reeds Hill
Bailey Hill
Orchid World
Edgehill
Bridgefield
Market Hill
Ellesmere
Redmans
Future Centre Trust
Applewhaites Tenantry
Roach
Retreat
Retreat Wood
St Judes
Prior Park
Applewhaites
St Augustine
Welches
Cane Garden
Belair
Arthurs Seat
St Helens
Old Post Office
Prerogative
Sharon Moravian
Bibbys Lane
Locust Hall
Fair View
Prospect
Drax Hall Green
Warrens
Newbury
Bairds
Jackson
Flat Rock
Francia Plantation House
Gun Hill Signal Station
Free Hill
Drax Hall Hope
Green
Clermont
Warrens
Canewood
Bournes
Salisbury
Dayrells
Mayfield
Workmans
Gordon Cummins Hwy
Friendship Terrace
Thorpes Cottage
Gun Hill
Eden Lodge
Green Hill
Jackmans
Walkers Terrace
Hilbury
Lodge Hill
Airy Hill
Rowans
Mount
Rock Dundo
St Matthew
Lower Estate
The Glebe
Jordans
165
Cave Hill
Hothersal Turning
Foster Hall
Valley
Good Intent
Ellerton
Melverton
Friendship
St George
Whitehall
Charles Rowe Bridge
Walkers
East Lynne
Waverly Cot
St Luke
Belfield
Grazettes
Tyrol Cot Heritage Village
H4
The Valley
Buttals
Brighton
Errol Barrow Hwy (ABC Hwy)
Bush Hall
Nells
Salters
Constant
Bulkeley Sugar Factory
Turnpike
H4B
Brighton Great House
Fairfield
Eagle Hall
Kew
45
Carmichael
Waterford
Belle
Hannays Tenantry
Rouen
Station Hill
Constitution
Stepney
Bank Hall
Howells
Haggatt Hall
Dash Valley
Watts Village
H4
South District
H5
Boarded Hall
Lower Greys
Medford Craft Village
Ivy
Emancipation Monument
Mapp Hill
Lower Birneys

buildings unspoiled by alterations and additions. Its stately tower and hand-crafted windows reflect the staunch faith and hard work of the Moravians. Admired by visitors, the church shows a marked architectural influence from the Low Countries of Europe, the birthplace of Moravianism.

Map on page 272

Back to the Earthworks

At the next left, a detour of about a mile (1.5 km) leads past **Edgehill Great House** (open daily; entrance fee), the base of the ecologically minded **Future Centre Trust** (*see page 274*), to the innovative **Earthworks Pottery** ❷ on Shop Hill. Set up in 1975 by art teacher Goldie Spieler, the pottery has gone from strength to strength and now in partnership with her son David their distinctive, hand-finished range, which includes tableware, vases and lamp bases in the rich blues, greens and golds of the Caribbean, are works of art in their own right. Originally, Goldie started Earthworks to prevent the island's waning pottery industry centred on Chalky Mount (*see page 266*) from disappearing. After funds were made available for the revival of the traditional potteries, she encouraged other artists to share her studio space. Today the pottery is the holder of two awards and much in demand worldwide.

Pottery with a Caribbean touch.

Next door, the Spielers have created a gallery in **The Potter's House** (open Mon–Fri and Sat am; free) displaying work of other Bajan artists and craftsmen and where you can stop for a bite on the café verandah and marvel at the view.

Returning to Highway 2, after about 3 miles (5 km) you come to **Ayshford Bird Park** (open daily; entrance fee) whose many different breeds of chicken, three ostriches and collection of emus are a delight for young children, but not quite so riveting if you are not a fowl fancier.

BELOW: roadside poinsettias.

Christmas Candles flower in Welchman Hall Gully.

Welchman Hall Gully – a tropical preserve

Next along this route – right at the roundabout and follow the signs – is the exotic **Welchman Hall Gully** ❸ (open daily; closed pub. hols; entrance fee; tel: 438 6671) where tropical plants and trees abound, highlighting the lush natural wonder of this three-quarter-mile (1.2-km) ravine. The gully is actually a crack in the coral limestone cap covering most of the island, which revealed a cave and is part of the network at Harrison's Cave (*see page 275*) close by. The area is named after a Welsh general, Asygell Williams, an early settler and the original owner of the land, who fought on the Royalists' side in the English Civil War and was banished – or "barbadosed" – to Barbados when they lost.

Around 1860, one of his descendants cleared a portion of the gully and planted fruit and spice-bearing trees, adding to the already plentiful tropical growth. But the gully was allowed to grow wild again soon after, and became a dense tangle of trees, interlaced with a profusion of fruits and flowering plants. For over 50 years it remained private property and was visited by only a few curious and adventurous souls. In 1962, the Barbados National Trust, spearheaded by the then Director of Agriculture for Barbados, C.C. Skeete (1900–83), turned it into a delightful place to stroll through and soak up the sights, sounds and smells of a tropical forest.

The Trust left much of the gully in its natural state, adding only a few flowering plants and benches. Winding paths lead you through the dense green shade of palms and ferns, past colourful flowering plants and exotic herbal treasures such as cinnamon and nutmeg. In the morning, you may sometimes meet chattering groups of wild Barbados green monkeys (*Cercopithecus sabaeus*). As you walk through you can see the stalactites, one of which has formed a mas-

BELOW: sitting under the stalactites.

THE FUTURE CENTRE TRUST

Set on a hillside in St Thomas, Edgehill Great House is home to the Future Centre Trust (tel: 425 2020), a non-profit, non-governmental organisation whose mission is to discover ways of safeguarding the environment for the future, encouraging sustainable economic growth, and enhancing the quality of life in Barbados, while "treading lightly" on this planet.

The "spark plug" behind the Centre is agricultural scientist Dr Colin Hudson, a passionate environmentalist who moved to Barbados nearly 40 years ago. Living and working in harmony with nature is crucial to his *modus operandi*. He leads the "Stop and Stare" hikes in conjunction with Barbados National Trust (*see page 205*) every Sunday when he can share his amazing knowledge of Barbados' geology, history, fauna and flora.

Run mainly by volunteers and financed by donations, the Centre was opened in 1998 and operates the western hemisphere's largest organic tyre garden, growing 52 varieties of vegetables, fruit and herbs that are used in the restaurant. A children's interactive centre, with ponds and playing areas, is being developed along with a simulated walk under the sea. Projects developing small business opportunities have also been created.

sive pillar 4 ft (1.2 metres) in diameter by merging with a stalagmite making it one of the largest in the world. At the northern end is a gazebo from where there's a spectacular view over the Scotland District to the Atlantic.

Map on page 272

Subterranean splendour

Close by is **Harrison's Cave** ❹ (open daily, last tour 4pm; entrance fee) a subsurface phenomenon said to be the only one of its kind in the Caribbean. A special tram takes you for nearly a mile (1.5 km) through the amazing limestone caverns, where you can witness nature's work of art, carved by the slow but steady passage of underground streams over the centuries.

The existence of the cave network had been known for more than 200 years when they were described by an English visitor in 1796 and they were also believed to have been used as a hideout for runaway slaves. But it wasn't until 1970 that a Danish speleologist (cave specialist) named Ole Sørensen discovered a new and interesting section of the cave, the **Crystal Cavern**. Heavy rains had caused severe flooding in several areas of the island, and a large quantity of ground water found its way into the underground system where its force eroded a small entrance into this unknown and parallel cave. Through this opening, Sørenson found other small passages leading to a large room about 250 ft (75 metres) long by 100 ft (30 metres) wide, and 100 ft (30 metres) high.

The Barbados National Trust paid the expenses for Sørenson to map the cave and encouraged the Government to open it to the public, and today indirect lighting enhances the magnificent subterranean scenery, adding a special aura to the thousands of gleaming, actively growing stalagmites and stalactites. In the depths of the cave is a 40-ft (12-metre) waterfall into a blue-green lake.

TIP

Before you visit Harrison's Cave give them a call on 438 6640/41/43/44 to reserve a place on the tram. It can get very busy, especially when a cruise ship is in.

BELOW: the splendours of Harrison's Cave.

The poker-like flower of the red ginger lily which can be seen in the Flower Forest.

Flower Forest – on the top of the world

High on a hill in St Joseph, not far off Highway 2 – it is well signposted – sprawls the **Flower Forest** ❺ (open daily; entrance fee) flourishing naturally in a beautiful landscaped setting and commanding glorious views across to the Atlantic Ocean. Carefully planned paths weave around the 50 acres (20 hectares) of tropical flowers, plants and trees. Bright red ginger lilies pierce the greenery, the artificial-looking anthurium and heliconia, a familiar sight in extravagant hotel arrangements all over the world, astonish in their natural surroundings and an assortment of palms create a welcome sunshade.

A visitor-friendly forest, there are no rules against walking on the grass and you are actively encouraged to touch or smell the different plants. Walking sticks and umbrellas can be supplied and seats are strategically placed to allow you to soak up the atmosphere – if you are quiet enough you may spot a humming bird, a monkey or a mongoose.

Nutritious cherries

If you wish to explore more of the remote rural countryside of St Joseph, instead of returning to Highway 2, keep left out of the Flower Forest and continue northeastwards. Tiny lanes disappear to the right and left to villages like Sugar Hill, Chimborazo, Spa Hill, Fruitful Hill and Cane Garden until you get back on the main road just south of the **Government Agricultural Station** on the old **Haggatts** estate. The headquarters of the Soil Conservation and Rural Development Scheme in the Scotland District, started in 1957, the station is renowned for its research into fruit tree production, forestry development, fish farming and the role it plays in the prevention of soil slippage and erosion.

BELOW: something to contemplate.

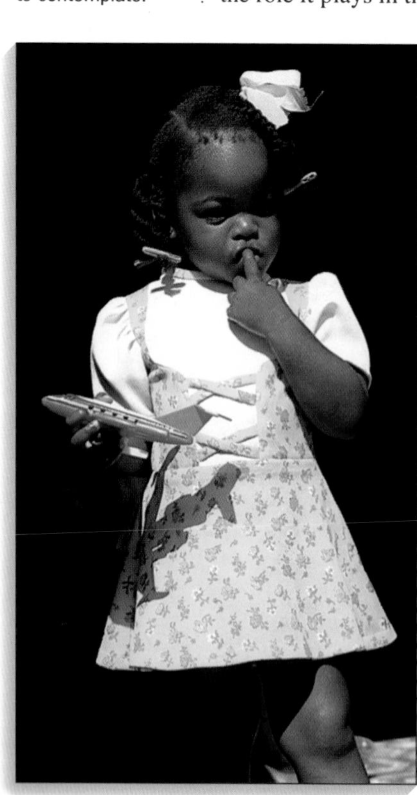

Haggatts is actually in a valley in the parish of St Andrew, bordered by the hills of St Simons and Mount All on the west and Chalky Mount on the east, and is dominated by Haggatts' extensive orchards that produce such fruits as mango, citrus and the world-famous Barbados cherry (*Malpighia glabra*).

The cherry is well known for its high vitamin C content. Just one Barbados cherry supplies a day's requirement for the human body. It also contains riboflavin, niacin and thiamin and, under ideal conditions, the tree can fruit up to 10 times a year.

By Haggatts the road forks to the left and the tiny village of **St Simons**, where the Caribbean's foremost gospel singer, Joseph Niles, grew up, and Turner's Hall Wood at the end of the cul-de-sac.

Primeval forest

Turner's Hall Wood ❻, on the slopes above St Simons, is the last remnant of the dense forest that carpeted Barbados before it was settled in 1627. Here you can see what those early adventurers must have found when they first set foot on the island. The area of thick tropical foliage, including cabbage palms up to 130 ft (40 metres) tall, covers 46 acres (19 hectares) and runs in a northeasterly direction from Mount Hillaby, at heights ranging from about 600–800 ft (180–240 metres) above sea level. Thankfully, the wood has not been developed and remains relatively unspoiled, complete with a glorious overhead orchestra of birds and monkeys. The early colonists of Barbados set to cutting down trees such as those found today at Turner's Hall Wood (including Spanish oak, beef wood, fustic, candlewood and silk cotton) very quickly for agricultural purposes. In 1631, Barbados was still "so full of woods and trees" that one Sir Henry Colt was unable to train 40 of his musketeers. Historian Richard Ligon reported in 1657 that the first English settlers found a landscape which was "so grown with wood as there could be found no champions [open spaces] or savannahs for men to dwell in."A hole in the ground inside the woods which leaks out natural gas and can be lit with a match indicates that the land is also rich in minerals.

Map on page 272

Belleplaine – the end of the line

A couple of miles (3 km) to the northeast, the village of **Belleplaine** ❼ has a long-standing place in Barbadian history and folklore because it was at the end of the old railway route. In bygone days, Bajans who were uninitiated in the wonders of the Scotland District delighted in going on the lively train excursions from Bridgetown to Belleplaine (*see page 267*).

One modern researcher relates that: "A string band consisting of guitar, violin, mandolin and saxophone accompanied the revellers. The excursionists danced to the lively tempo of the band at various sites en route. Two wooden horses (crudely built merry-go-rounds) were operated at Belleplaine and provided a singular attraction at the end of the train journey."

Though the train has stopped running since the 1930s, these rides to Belleplaine have been preserved for ever in a popular Bajan folk song about the ever-resourceful Bromley, a government sanitary inspector of the day, who also

BELOW: a stop to marvel at the view on a Sunday hike in St Andrew.

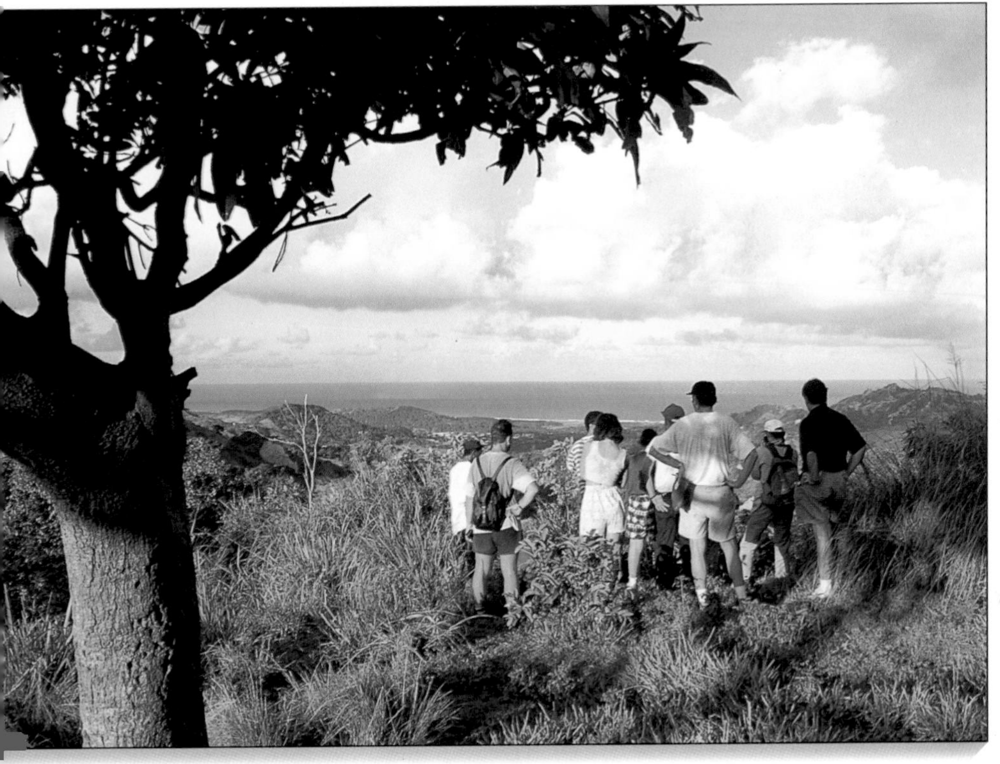

St Andrew's Church, just north of Belleplaine, was one of the few churches to survive the 1831 hurricane. However, it had fallen into disrepair by 1842 and was completely rebuilt in 1846.

owned a horse-and-buggy taxi service and operated a brass band. He occasionally sponsored free train rides from Bridgetown to Belleplaine that were gala occasions. In the song, Bromley denies a young lady's request for more than one kind of free ride:

Yuh hear what Bromley tell de gal,
Yuh never go down Belleplaine outa me...
Yuh never wear dat gol' ring outa me...

Turn back towards the West Coast and travel past the Walkers sand mine and into the spectacular scenery along the ridges of the Scotland District towards Mount Hillaby.

Highest point on the island

To reach the summit of **Mount Hillaby** ❽ at 1,115 ft (340 metres) above sea level, drive into **Mose Bottom**, a point which offers a splendid view of the deep ravine on the northern side of Mount All, Haggatts in the valley, and the eastern reaches of St Andrew and St Joseph, and then up to the top. There is no fanfare here, at the highest point on the island – no park benches, no snack bar; in fact "The Mount", as the people of Hillaby call it, is deserted most of the time.

The summit itself is actually a chalk hill with a dirt cap. On top of it is a stump of cement with the simple inscription:

Inter-American Geodetic Survey
Do Not Disturb
Hillaby 1953

And the order is obeyed – for here it is breezy but quiet. The view to the south includes rolling fields of agricultural land with the telecommunications

BELOW: a game of draughts outside a rum shop.

antennae at Sturges and Mount Misery furthest away. To the north, are the villages of White Hill and Gregg Farm, and the land slopes up on the west to St Peter's eastern ridge. To the east is the most spectacular view of ravines and hills.

Map on page 272

Discovering the hidden Barbados

A wonderful way to view this region is on horseback, especially in the early morning, just at sunrise, when the freshness of the earth saturates the air and envelops you. At Canefield, just north of Welchman Hall Gully, are the headquarters of **Highland Outdoor Tours** (tel: 438 8069/70) which offer well-organised treks around Mount Hillaby, Turner's Hall Wood and places of historical interest off the beaten track and deep in the heart of the Scotland District. Tours can vary in length from two hours to a whole day either on horseback, mountain bike or on foot and guides lead 5-mile (8 km) excursions through previously inaccessible lands, much of it privately owned, all the way down to the East Coast (*see pages 257–66*). After a well-deserved lunch of Bajan cooking, a lift back to base is provided. For those with a taste of adventure but without the wherewithal, a two-hour bumpy tractor-drawn jitney ride can give you a taste of the surrounding countryside and then take you back for refreshments at the bar.

An abandoned sugar mill in the highlands.

On the northwestern slopes of Mount Hillaby, with views over the Caribbean and the Scotland District, the West Coast is encroaching with a new luxury development planned for Apes Hill. Paul Altman, Managing Director of the Barbados real estate company Alleyne Aguilar & Altman, describes the development in *Simply Barbados* (1999) as "a golfing community similar to Royal Westmoreland and Sandy Lane. The difference at Apes Hill will be a large inland hotel with conference facilities, as well as villas."

BELOW: a rural scene.

Here and there in St Thomas are fields of Sea Island cotton, grown for export to Japan and the US. Once grown by the Amerindians, the high-quality cotton – often bugged by the pink bollworm – is still picked by hand, although efforts are being made to use machinery.

Right: a traditional chattel house.
Below: entrance to Bagatelle Great House.

Back on Highway 2A, heading south, after about a mile (1.5 km) you come to the indomitable **St Thomas Church**, which has been the victim of more hurricanes than any other institution on the island. Destroyed by the hurricane of 1675, it was rebuilt five years later. Damaged in 1731, it was completely demolished again by both the great hurricanes of 1780 and 1831.

First free village

A mile or so inland from the roundabout by St Thomas Church is **Rock Hall Village**, an old settlement of great significance to Barbadians. This was the first black freehold village in the country, and possibly the first in the entire West Indies. The Rock Hall story unfolds in 1820 before Emancipation, when the area was part of Mount Wilton Plantation owned by Reynold Alleyne Elcock. This young white planter, a man with moral values well ahead of his time, recognised the plight of the slaves and was determined to improve their lot. He made a will in which he bequeathed £5 sterling per year to each of his 120 adult male slaves, making additional provision for the repairs of their quarters. Somehow, news of the will and its contents leaked out, with tragic consequences. Unwilling to wait for his master to die a natural death before reaping the rewards, Elcock's valet, Godfrey – it is not known whether he was alone or part of a conspiracy – cut the throat of the 32-year-old Elcock while he slept.

Godfrey was apprehended at nearby Hangman's Hill and subsequently paid the ultimate penalty for his crime. Because of the murder, the slaves at Mount Wilton had to wait a further 17 years, until the Emancipation Act came about in 1838, to reap the fruits of their generous master's will. They used the money to purchase plots of land at the Mount Wilton Estate and the village, now Rock Hall, was known as Cut-Throat Village.

Other white planters willed their plantations to their mulatto children, born to slave mothers. Among these were William Ellis, Henry Simmons and George Hewitt. Ellis's son, Thomas, was one of the first coloured men to be elected to the Barbadian House of Assembly in the mid-19th century.

Gambling debt

Another 2 miles (3 km) south on Highway 2A lies **Bagatelle Great House** ❾ which has a restaurant and small art gallery and is one of the oldest houses on the island along with St Nicholas Abbey (*see page 309*) and Drax Hall (*see page 293*). The original owner was the first Earl of Carlisle who was once the proprietor of the entire island. In 1651, the property was handed over to Lord Francis Willoughby of Parham and its name was changed to Parham Park House. In 1877, the property was gambled away and its name changed to Bagatelle.

A little further south is **Welches House,** owned by artist Jill Walker and her husband Jimmy. The plantation buildings have been converted into the administrative offices, screen-printing studios and stockroom for the **Best of Barbados**, their family company that produces Jill's lovely paintings on crafts and gifts, depicting quaint aspects of the island in Jill's charming and distinctive style. ❑

CORAL STONE AND CHATTELS

Classical English styles, the tropical climate, sheer necessity and the whim of local artisans have all left their mark on Barbadian architecture

The first homes the English settlers built were of wood, utilising the timbers felled to make way for sugar cane. Stick and brush gave way to wattle and daub – branches and twigs plastered over with mud – thatched with long grasses, sugar cane or palm fronds. Coral stone was soon discovered to be sturdy building material and during the 17th-century sugar boom was used by many planters for their Georgian Great Houses. Later, Palladian features became popular.

After Emancipation, wooden chattel houses were developed for the plantation workers, designed so they could be taken apart and moved with them when they changed jobs. A Barbadian creation, chattel houses are still being built today, although many people are opting for the more practical but less attractive concrete or "wall" houses. Modern day architecture is for the most part becoming more sympathetic to the past, retaining many Caribbean features.

CLIMATIC CONSIDERATIONS

Although loyal to their British heritage, the planters still had to take the tropical climate into account when building their homes. Jalousie windows were added for protection against storms and to keep out the sun, and air circulation was improved with tray ceilings that were raised above the level of the walls. A fishpond roof caught and funnelled rainwater into storage tanks to be used and a parapet was often added to protect the house from hurricanes.

▽ **ANY OLD IRON**
Light and inexpensive, corrugated iron is used in great quantities by chattel house owners for fencing ("paling"), and for roofing.

▷ **CLASSIC CHATTEL**
Smarter chattel houses have all the trimmings – a covered porch, jalousies, window pelmets and delicately sawn, wooden "gingerbread" fretwork.

△ **MODERN DELUXE**
West Coast hotels imitate colonial architectural features with open archways and verandahs to admit the cooling sea breezes.

▷ **ROOM WITH A VIEW**
Simple airy construction features in this chattel house overlooking Martin's Bay in St. John.

◁▽ **KEEPING COOL**
Jalousies, old and new, can be adjusted to increase airflow, and keep out the rain or sun. And shopkeepers live upstairs in the shop houses whose galleries shade the street.

▽ **SUBURBAN BEAUTY**
Each house in the 19th-century suburb of Belleville has its own individual touch, be it a Palladian staircase or ornate gallery.

◁ **SOLAR POWER**
More new holiday complexes are being planned with concern for the environment, such as Port St Charles.

▷ **HOME SWEET HOME**
The neo-Gothic Parliament Buildings are an architectural oddity – the clock tower was built with an English church in mind.

COLONIAL LEGACIES

Furniture imported by the planters in the 19th century was quickly and skilfully copied by local craftsmen who continue to produce Victorian replicas to this day. Original Victorian antique furniture is still used in the Great Houses and private homes but rarely seen in the island's antique shops. Most of what is available today comes from the Edwardian era. The favourite wood was, and still is, locally grown mahogany, although supplies are being depleted. West Indian Cedar, Cordia, and Samaan are also used to make furniture. Planters or "Berbice" chairs (above) are a colonial innovation and much sought after. Cane-backed furniture is still popular especially in the hotels. The open canework is cooling.

ST GEORGE VALLEY

A drive through the "sugar cane country" provides a glimpse of life in a plantation Great House, a colonial communications system and an impressive collection of orchids

Map on page 272

The fertile St George Valley cuts across the southern part of Barbados from Bridgetown to St John in a swathe of sugar cane. Undulating fields of green stretch as far as the eye can see punctuated by avenues of cabbage palms that lead to clumps of trees concealing a sturdy plantation Great House. Although one or two have been converted into holiday apartments or a hotel – indicating the spread of the tourist industry inland – many of them still remain the hub of working sugar estates lived in by the families who have farmed them for generations.

Thousands of Barbadians still depend on the sugar industry for their livelihood, but the days when sugar production rose to over 200,000 tons – 1957 and 1967 were the record years – are long gone. Today the small farmers together with the large plantations produce just a quarter of that amount. The worldwide sugar market is suffering from overproduction, so Barbadian producers depend on European Union import quotas. At the moment, usually all of the Barbados crop is exported to Europe at fixed prices, while domestic consumption is met by the import of cheaper sugar from Central America.

Highway 4 crosses the Errol Barrow Highway on the eastern side of Bridgetown, near Haggatt Hall, passing through the working-class neighbourhoods of My Lord's Hill, Ivy and Salters where it divides. The road branching off to the left takes you through the hillier parts of this normally flat parish to St George Church and Gun Hill, providing extensive views across the valley below. The Salters area is actually what Bajans call "but an' boun'", meaning that it straddles two parishes: part of it is in St Michael and the rest is in St George.The southern branch passes through countless tiny villages whose histories are linked to the area's plantation tradition.

PRECEDING PAGES: market women grow the crops they sell.
LEFT: cane fields in St George.
BELOW: going somewhere?

Hurricane survivor

St George's Church ⑩ is about half a mile up the road east from Charles Rowe Bridge. One of the oldest ecclesiastical buildings in Barbados, it was built to withstand hurricanes in 1784 for a mere £600 on the site of an earlier church that had been previously destroyed in a storm and is an architectural blend of Gothic and Georgian styles. After surviving the 1831 hurricane, the chancel and the tower were added in 1923 and 1953 respectively.

Inside the church is an altar painting, *The Resurrection*, by Benjamin West (1738–1820), the first American President of the Royal Academy of Art. There is also a sculpture by Richard Westmacott, who created the controversial statue of Lord Nelson.

Outside, the road becomes steeper, rising up from the valley towards Gun Hill. After about a mile (1.5 km),

The stalwart St George's Church.

you reach a bumpy track which branches off to the left and leads up to **Francia Plantation** ⓫ (open Mon–Fri, closed pub. hols; entrance fee; tel: 429 0474). Lying in a large estate with expansive views, this Great House is relatively modern compared to many of the others on the island, being built only in 1913 by René Mourraille, a planter with French and Brazilian links. He came to Barbados on a business trip, fell in love with a Barbadian girl, married her and built Francia, where his descendants still live.

Mourraille imported Brazilian timber for the panelling and furnished it with English and French antiques, which included a magnificent chandelier with etched hurricane shades that still hangs over a finely polished mid-19th century mahogany dining table. In a collection of original Caribbean maps there is one of the West Indies dated 1522. The successive generations of the family have maintained the house and its contents carefully along with beautiful terraced gardens (*see pages 312–13*) reminiscent of southern Europe.

The British lion on Gun Hill

Back on the main road again and continuing up the hill a short way, the milk-white limestone lion on a cliff you see on the left, gazing across the St George Valley, is the first part of the old **Gun Hill Signal Station** ⓬ (open Mon–Sat, closed major pub. hols; entrance fee) above. Sculpted in 1868 by Henry Wilkinson, the Adjutant-General of the Imperial Forces, and some fellow soldiers stationed in Barbados, the lion stands 7 ft (2 metres) tall and carries two inscriptions carved in Latin in the rock of the base. The first includes the name of the sculptor, his rank and the date he completed the project. Then there is the affirmation: "He [the British Lion] shall rule from the rivers to the sea, and from the sea to

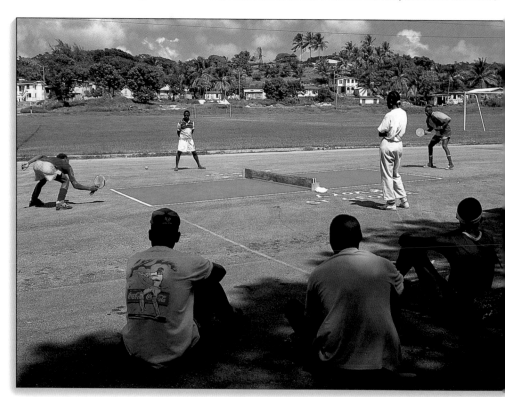

BELOW: a game of road tennis.

the ends of the earth." An inscription to the right of the sculpture lists Wilkinson's four military helpers.

The signal station itself, which can be reached by car through an entrance further up the road on the left, was built in 1818 as part of a chain of signal stations – two of them still exist: Grenade Hall (*see page 307*) and Cotton Tower (*see page 265*) – that operated as an observation system to warn of the approach of enemy ships. The message was then communicated down to the Garrison (*see pages 193–98*) through semaphore. Due to the healthy winds sweeping around Gun Hill (700 ft/213 metres), the station was also used as a place for soldiers to convalesce after illness and they were evacuated here at the first sign of a yellow fever epidemic on the island.

Restored in 1982 by the Barbados National Trust (*see page 205*), the signal station, which now holds a collection of military memorabilia, has been praised by many writers for its incredible view and healthy quality of the air. Historian Robert Schomburgk's description of it in his book *History of Barbados* first published in 1848 (*see right*) holds true today: "The ridge of cliffs, a continuation of those in St John, traverse St George and reach their greatest height near Gun Hill, where there is a signal-post and a convalescent station for the soldiers of the Garrison. The air here is considered very salubrious, and the view from the station, over the rich and fertile valley to Bridgetown and Carlyle Bay, is extensive… no stranger who visits Barbados should omit seeing this spot."

You can stop here for a snack or light lunch in the Fusilier Cookhouse and absorb the magnificent surroundings while wondering whether the soldiers ever felt the same all those years ago when they were scanning the horizon for enemy ships. Or you can move on to Orchid World just over a mile (1.75 km) away.

Map on page 272

Robert Schomburgk's History of Barbados, *published in 1848, is considered to be one of the most important books written about the island and has been reprinted by retired Barbadian banker Tony Thomas. For a copy contact him on 428 4015.*

ROAD TENNIS – A BAJAN GAME

At weekends if you are passing St George's Church you may wonder what the cheering crowds are doing gathered in the car park. They will be supporting their local road tennis team, a sport invented by Barbadians that is similar to table tennis but which is played on any available concrete patch around the island.

Created in the late 1940s, when there were still few cars passing along the roads out in the isolated rural villages and no television to keep youngsters indoors, it became popular as a cheap pastime and was known as "poor man's tennis". The game is played to table tennis rules on a 20 ft (6 metres) by 10 ft (3 metres) area of concrete, marked out with painted white lines and divided by an 8-in (20 cm) high board as a net. All the equipment necessary is a tennis ball and paddle-style wooden bats, the design of which has barely changed over the decades.

In 1976, the Barbados Road Tennis Association was formed and the popularity of the game spread to the towns and to the young and old alike. Now there are tournaments between villages and neighbouring islands with sponsors and stars such as Deighton "Pa" Roach and John "Floats" Cumberbatch. For details, contact the Association's president Phillip Garner on 427 2229/213 2064.

BELOW: Francia's dining room.

At Orchid World, the orchids are watered by hand from a tank capable of holding 30,000 gallons (135,000 litres) of rainwater. The water is then recycled into the streams, waterfalls and fountains.

BELOW: the Bajan blackbird has a distinctive song.

A world of orchids

Orchid World ⓭ (open daily; entrance fee; tel: 433 0306) was opened in 1998 on the site of a disused chicken farm providing an enriching base to create an orchid garden (*see also pages 312–13*). The dream of horticulturist and plantsman Richard Coughlan, who trained at London's Kew Gardens and landscaped the Flower Forest (*see page 276*), Orchid World was developed in a year and the chicken sheds were recycled into shaded houses for the myriad species of orchids many of which were imported from Thailand. Some were donated by local people and several were bought in Barbados too. Also grown outside on pallisades, specimens include those of the Vandaceous family, Phalaenopsis and Cattlyeas, and paths wind around the site which has been landscaped over a geological feature called a raised beach, providing small natural caves in the coral limestone, shady gullies and ponds.

Information boards here and there give facts about the plants and the head gardener and his staff are always around to answer questions. Benches and gazebos – one of which is a wedding chapel (*see page 214*) – are strategically placed around the garden making the visit an unhurried experience.

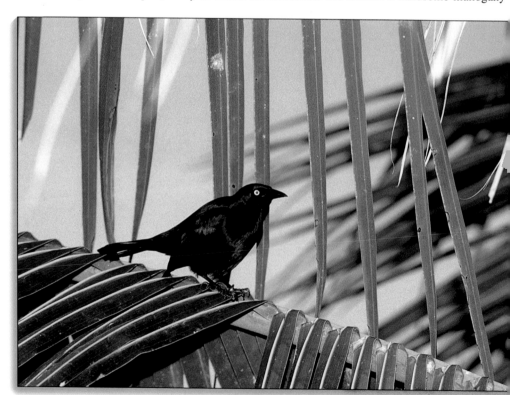

Less than a mile (1.5 km) away to the north (turn next left off Highway 3) stands **Fisherpond Plantation House** (open by appointment only; tel: 433 1754) now owned by Barbadian John Chandler who used to own and manage the Ocean View Hotel in Hastings. After closing the hotel, Chandler bought the Caribbean Georgian-style house, dating back to the early 17th century, which had been standing empty for many years. He quickly transformed the house to its former glory and has filled it with his fine collection of art and antiques, many of which are Barbadian and include a handsome mahogany dining table that when fully extended can seat 24. The story goes that this table was once borrowed for a special function from another plantation house in the 1700s and was never returned. In turn it was loaned to Government House in 1987 for a state banquet for Queen Elizabeth II, but this time it was returned. The wallpaper and fabrics used in the house come from the Barbados National Trust's specially designed collection called the Plantations Collection, which includes designs with evocative names such as "Oistins Fishnet" and "Mount Hillaby Vine". A percentage of the sales goes to the Trust.

Outside in the revived Italian-style garden is a set of coral dripstones, a Barbadian water filter, covered with yellow alamanda.

Villa Nova – a country house hotel

About 4 miles (6.5 km) away in the parish of St John, north of Four Cross Roads, lies the historic Great House **Villa Nova** ⓮ which, from 1997 to 1999, had around £6 million (US$9.6 million) lavished on it by the Swiss company Horizon Resorts, transforming it into a luxurious country house hotel. Built by planter Edmund Haynes after the 1831 hurricane had destroyed the first house, and blessed by the Moravian priest John Gottlieb Zippel in 1834, Villa Nova was at the centre of a 109-acre (44-hectare) sugar plantation.

In 1907, the elegant Great House was separated from the plantation and bought for £800 by the Government for the St John's doctor, who built an operating theatre there. The next owner was the former British Prime Minister, Sir Anthony Eden, the Earl of Avon (1897–1977), who bought the estate as his winter residence in 1965 and, during the following six years, VIP guests included the Queen and the Duke of Edinburgh and Sir Winston Churchill's widow. The

Map on page 272

At Fisherpond Plantation House John Chandler can provide the perfect setting for a private function from lunch for 10 to an 18th-century dinner for 40, or a wedding in the grounds. Call 433 1754 for details.

BELOW: "Snow on the Mountain" tree in full bloom.

A mango tree – a favourite with monkeys.

Earl loved the 14-acre (5.5 hectare) garden, calling it his Garden of Eden, and he especially enjoyed watching the fireflies at night which were apparently introduced to the island in the early 20th century to control root borer and moth borer in the sugar cane.

As a five-star luxury hotel, the original coral-stone house has been restored and extended in the same architectural style, with the distinctive verandahs and timber latticed supports, to make room for 28 suites, four restaurants, a fitness centre and conference facilities, and outside a swimming pool, tennis courts, putting green and a network of paths through old woods have been added.

Nearby, **Mount Tabor Church** has close historical links with Villa Nova. Edmund Haynes supported the Moravians who had come to the West Indies near the end of the 18th century to convert the slaves to Christianity (*see page 82*). He gave the missionaries 4 acres (1.5 hectares) of land and paid for the church to be built, and, when he sold Villa Nova in 1838, a condition of sale was that £60 a year had to be paid for the upkeep of the church. Beside it is the weathered pink building of the old mission school, which became Mount Tabor Primary School and moved into the modern premises behind.

Large sugar estates

Travelling back towards Bridgetown along the St George Valley on Highway 4 you pass through the Drax Hall Estate, which was where sugar cane was first cultivated on the island. The 878-acre (355-hectare) estate is the only plantation in Barbados which has belonged to the same family since the 17th century.

Large estates in the valley, such as Drax Hall, have been major centres of employment and settlement for as long as sugar has been grown in Barbados.

BELOW: Mount Tabor Church – a Moravian enclave.

Through the tenantry system, peasant families rented the land on which they built their houses, sometimes for generations. Legislation, which forces landlords to offer tenants the right to buy, has brought significant improvements to the peasants' quality of life. Now that they have land to call their own, families can build more permanent stone houses, or "wall houses", to replace the traditional wooden, chattel houses which were always built so that they could be dismantled and moved when they moved jobs (*see pages 282–283*).

The names of many villages in Barbados are the names of the plantations they were once a part of. For example, in St George, Boarded Hall is a plantation and a village with its own police station; Drax Hall estate includes the villages of Drax Hall Hope and Drax Hall Green.

Map on page 272

Jacobean gem

A long, narrow driveway goes from the road to **Drax Hall** itself – a private home and not open to the public. James Drax and his brother William built the Jacobean house – one of two in Barbados, three in the West (*see page 309*) – in the mid-1600s, but no one knows the exact date. However, in *Historic Houses of Barbados*, Dr Henry Fraser and Ronnie Hughes write: "There is a length of copper guttering at Drax Hall that bears the date 1653, but this does not prove the date of the present house. The copper drain pipe may have been used originally on an older house and reused on a later house if rebuilding occurred. Architecturally, however, Drax Hall is typically Jacobean, a stately English manor house in a tropical setting. It has steep gables, corner finials, casement gable windows, and an exceptionally fine Jacobean staircase and ornately carved hall archway of mastic wood. These all firmly suggest a pre-1700 date."

BELOW: Drax Hall, one of three Jacobean houses in the West.

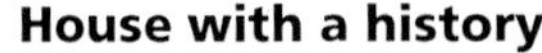

At Constant plantation house, near Bulkeley, is one of the most beautiful gardens on the island. Created by Jean Robinson, it can be seen during the Open Gardens season run by the Barbados Horticultural Society (tel: 429 3254).

RIGHT: the white lion on Gun Hill.
BELOW: a stone picker takes a rest.

House with a history

To the south of Drax Hall, **Brighton Great House** – another private home not open to the public – ranks with St Nicholas Abbey and Drax Hall as one of the oldest houses on the island. It also has the distinction of remaining in the hands of one family (the Piles) for over 150 years. The first owners were the Wilshiers, who had the property from 1638 to about 1800; a marble slab in the outer wall of the south wing with the name "Wilshier" and the date 1652 indicates the time when the house was built. Its roof is supported by mastic columns and 20-ft (6-metre) beams, while its walls are made of a mixture of rubble and corn husks. Arthur Oughterson bought Brighton in 1802 and sold it to John Gittens Archer, the first white Bajan to be convicted for the murder of a slave, two years later. He then sold Brighton to Conrad Pile in the early 19th century.

Several miles further east on Highway 4B, actually on the eastern tip of the parish where it borders St John and St Philip (*see map on pages 170–71*) is the entrance to another of the island's historic plantation houses, **Byde Mill** which dates from just after the 1831 hurricane, and is not open to the public. The first owner of the estate was Joshua Steele, a fellow of the London Royal Society of Arts, who is credited with starting a Barbados Society for the Encouragement of Arts, Manufactures and Commerce in 1781, to help the poor whites better themselves. According to Hilary Beckles in *A History of Barbados,* Steele was concerned that the poor whites were worse off than some of the elite slaves and were a "major social problem". He also owned the adjoining Kendal plantation in St John where Richard Ligon – one of the most quoted historians and earliest social commentators of the island – lived for three years from 1647 to 1650. Ligon's book, *A True And Exact History of Barbadoes*, is the earliest recorded history of the island (*see page 107*).

Middle class on the move

Like its neighbouring parishes – St Philip and Christ Church – St George is rapidly becoming a desirable area for residential development in Barbados, and hence a home for the island's middle classes. Rowans, Fairview and Walker's Terrace are developments on elevated parts of the parish around St George's Church, affording many house owners some magnificent views of the valley.

The western parts of the parish were tagged in the island's physical development plan as areas of "significant population increase" during the 1970s. St George's population grew an average of 23 percent a year for that decade. In comparison, St Michael's population grew by only 0.06 percent, and St John's by 0.4 percent. However, in certain areas the population declined, particularly in the sugar belt above the second cliff in the St George Valley. This was attributed to increased mechanisation in the sugar industry when jobs on the plantations fell from 8,000 to 4,000.

On Highway 4 on the way back to Bridgetown the tall chimney of **Bulkeley Sugar Factory**, one of only three functioning sugar factories (*see page 37*) left on the island looms into view after The Turnpike. **Valley Plantation** further on is owned by a former manager of Drax Hall. ❑

+DOMINABITVR·A·MARI·VS·AD
HEN·IOA·WILKINSON·
CEN·COHPED·IX·BRITAN·
TRIB·CASTR·SCVLPS
A·D·MDCCCLXVI
A FLVMINE V
AD·TERMINOS·ORBI

THE RUGGED NORTH

This is the most remote part of Barbados, where history has been preserved in a quaint old port, a restored sugar mill and an eccentric plantation house alongside nature at its wildest

The northern part of Barbados has a more isolated feel, yet the smart tourist belt of the Platinum Coast has already crept up past Speightstown, the island's second largest town, with the development of Port St Charles, an exclusive marina. The north comprises two parishes and part of another, each with their own individual character despite the small area. St Peter adjoins the sophisticated St James to the south and, spanning the width of Barbados, is blessed with western and eastern seafronts: the calm Caribbean Sea laps gently against the western shores, and the Atlantic batters the parish on the other side. From here the hills of rural St Andrew stretch southward, dominating the eastern wilder fringe and, sprawling across the northern tip of the island, is the rugged and remote St Lucy, affectionately referred to as The Lady, being the only parish with a female name.

In St Lucy you'll find the island's most dramatic scenery: untamed, sparsely populated terrain, still dotted with sleepy villages of old chattel houses and black belly sheep, stretches southward behind a spectacular coastline constantly battered by the powerful, relentless surf of the Atlantic, quietening down as it meets the Caribbean to the west. Bajans call St Lucy's foaming breakers "white horses" and to the northwest The Duppies offer a challenge to the island's most serious surfers. St Andrew climbs steeply into the Scotland District (*see pages 271–280*) and, although it may not be the smallest parish, its population is small – just over 6,500 – so it has managed to keep much of its virgin character. The villagers of the north know one another well and, due to their isolation, have perfected the art of inter-dependence and neighbourly courtesy.

PRECEDING PAGES: stark St Lucy coastline.
LEFT: a solitary moment in St Peter.
BELOW: selling wares on the beach.

Speightstown – historic port

People who live in the north go to the quaint old-time port of **Speightstown ❶**, 4 miles (6 km) north of Holetown) to do their shopping. The character of the old town has not changed much over the past century, even though its face has been revamped with the construction of **Speightstown Mall**. Opened in 1980, it is one of the better shopping areas of the island, with a department store, bank and fast-food restaurant.

Speightstown is unique among the island's four towns because it is the only one to have retained much of its original layout with small streets lined with simple, two-storey shops, many with Georgian-style balconies and overhanging galleries propped up on wooden pillars which are now in line for restoration by the Barbados National Trust (*see page 205*).

The rerouting of Highway 1 has directed traffic away from the centre, making it an ideal place for strolling, especially on Saturday mornings when the

ABOVE: a prize coconut.

"hucksters" sell fresh produce on the narrow streets, and it seems as if all th north has come to shop. In the centre of town are remnants of the **Denmar Fort** and **Orange Fort**, which once mounted 23 cannons between them. Som of the old cannons are still standing on the **Speightstown Esplanade**, whic overlooks the sea. Reportedly named after William Speight from Bristol in Eng land, who was a landowner and a member of one of the earliest parliaments i Barbados, the town at one time was a thriving port shipping sugar produced i the north of the island to Bristol earning itself the nickname "Little Bristol" Until motor vehicles came to the island, schooners would ply between Speights town and Bridgetown taking people into the capital. Today the harbour area i kept alive by the fishing boats.

On the seafront, the **Fisherman's Pub** is a good place to stop for an eco nomical lunch of Bajan cooking. Nearby **Mango's By The Sea** offers evenin meals of fresh fish and Caribbean lobster in a romantic setting. Run by Cana dians Gail and Pierre Spenard, attached to the restaurant is **Mango's Fine Ar**

allery (open Sun–Fri evenings at the same times as the restaurant), which xhibits a fine collection of brightly coloured hand-pulled silkscreens of trop-al scenery by Michael Adams.

Speightstown was twinned with Charleston in South Carolina, USA, in ovember 1997 in recognition of the role Barbadians played in developing the tate in the 1670s (*see page 310*). The tall, 17th-century **Arlington House**, in hurch street, bears a resemblance to the architectural style of historic houses n that part of America and is being restored by Barbados National Bank.

St Peter's Church on the corner of Church and Queen Street was one of the sland's earliest churches, first built in the 1630s. It was rebuilt in 1837, in eorgian style, and then again restored in 1980 after a fire devastated all but its valls and tower. The restoration took three years and cost BDS$750,000.

xclusivity in the north

ust north of Speightstown is **Almond Beach Village**, one of Barbados' largest ll-inclusive resorts and sister to the **Almond Beach Club** in St James. With lmost 300 rooms, it stands on 30 acres (12 hectares) of beachfront property and vas designed around an old sugar plantation by Heywoods Beach. The hotel, ormerly known as Heywoods, was completely renovated and extended in 1994 t a cost of BDS$24 million. The extravagant complex now has several swim-ning pools, a fitness centre and a nine-hole golf course.

At the northern end of Heywoods Beach is **Port St Charles** ❷, an exclusive narina for the seriously rich. Described in the brochure as "the ultimate reward", he marina, which is being developed in five phases, provides luxury living ttached to berths for luxury yachts. The dream of two Barbadian brothers Cow

TIP

The Arbib Nature & Heritage Trail runs hikes from Speightstown into hidden corners of the island. Choose either the 3-hour (for the fit) or 2-hour trail leaving at 9am or 2.30pm (Wed, Thurs, Sat; entrance fee). Call 426 2421 before 3pm the day before to book.

BELOW: messing about on the Caribbean Sea.

A more low key Fish-Fry than Oistins takes place on Friday nights by the beach at Six Men's Bay, where sizzling fish and chicken are served out of a buck-pot and rum is bought by the bottle.

and Bizzy Williams, and Bjorn Bjerkman who has lived in Barbados all hi working life, Port St Charles has been an environmentally friendly project righ from the start. The three businessmen, each with a love of the sea, spent six year of planning and carrying out environmental studies before the building starte in 1996. The lagoon around which the "nouveau Caribbean" style developmen has been built has been designated a marine sanctuary and is home to an eagl ray and two turtles. By early 1998, Port St Charles had won two awards fror the *International Property Magazine* and the following year won three more.

Amerindian discoveries

The development of Port St Charles has also meant that Barbados' history book have had to be backdated by around 2,000 years. While carrying out the initia clearing of the site, a rim of a water pot was spotted in the ground during a cof fee break. This was found to be the type used to create wells by stacking ther on top of each other. As a result of this discovery, Port St Charles sponsore archaeologists from England, led by the renowned Dr Peter Drewett, to excavat the area before each new building phase was started. Other artifacts were du up and found to be around 4,000 years old showing that there had been a larg settlement of Pre-Ceramic fisher/foragers, who had probably rowed from Low land South America, living there. Until then it had generally been believed tha people had lived on the island from around 2,000 years ago.

Another rowing feat was played out at Port St Charles at the end of 199 when the marina was the finishing post for the Atlantic Rowing Race instigate by Sir Chay Blyth, who with Captain John Ridgeway in 1966 rowed from Cap Cod to Ireland in a 20-ft (6-metre) boat in 92 days. Port St Charles promoted an

BELOW: sea-bath for man and beast.

rganised the Challenge in which 29 pairs, including a mother and son, rowed rom Tenerife to Barbados. The race was won in a record-breaking 43 days by Jew Zealand Olympic rower Rob Hamill and Phil Stubbs, a triathlete who adly died a few months later in a light aircraft crash. The next race is scheduled or the end of 2001.

'he remote St Lucy coast

'he fishing communities of Six Men's Bay, Half Moon Fort, Fustic and Checker Iall line the coastal road as it enters St Lucy. The route goes up a steep incline t **Checker Hall** where in the typical Bajan rum shop the men of the village ather to drink the national beverages, engage in heated discussions about politics or cricket and play dominoes or the African game of Warri. **St Lucy's 'hurch**, nearly 2 miles (3 km) away inland, would be far from their thoughts.)ne of the first six churches on the island, the original structure was already in xistence by 1629, and was rebuilt after the 1831 hurricane.

At the top of Checker Hall hill you can see the ugly **Arawak Cement Plant** utting out into the Caribbean, and behind that the beautiful, secluded **Maycock's Bay** beach stretches northward, only reachable by two steep paths. One eads to the ruins of **Maycock's Fort**, where treasure is said to be buried. An)vergrown track on the eastern limits of the Barbados Defence Force base ends p at the **Harrison Point Lighthouse** where on the shoreline below loom large 'ocks that have been so eroded by the sea they assume eerie characteristics.

The Barbados Defence Force base is out of bounds to strangers, and armed oldiers regularly patrol its limits. It used to belong to the US military during and fter World War II, before it was handed back to Barbados in the late 1970s.

When the wind blows from the north, surfers flock to the coast at Crab Hill to ride the 15-ft (5-metre) waves in The Duppies – a Bajan word for spirits. Teenagers sit under a tree chewing cane and watching.

BELOW: surfing at the Duppies.

This seeming flower is narrower at the Discus, or Setting on the leaves, than any flower of that kind. There were strong Appearances of Animal Life; yet, as its Shape, and want of local Motion, classed it among vegetables, I was for some time in Suspense.
– GRIFFITH HUGHES, 1750, *of the animal flowers in* The Natural History of Barbados

Further round the coast is **Archer's Bay** ❸, reached by a road from the Crab Hill police station. Despite being a popular picnic spot with Bajans all that is here is a rocky track to a grassy expanse shaded by a grove of casuarina trees, just a short walk from a cliff which has a magnificent view of the sea. A path winds through the wooded limestone ledge which leads down to a sandy cove.

Moveable homes

Around the northern tip of the island you can see some of the best examples of small wooden chattel houses (*see pages 282–283*) that so characterize Barbados, especially in the villages of **Greenidge** and **Connell Town**, but, as the population's wealth increases, these moveable properties are being replaced by less interesting concrete block bungalows, locally called "wall houses".

Several stone ruins of old peasant dwellings can still be seen around here. Presumably these belonged to folk fortunate enough to own the land on which to build their own homes.

In the 1970s it was believed that they were 19th-century slave huts, but writer Norah Francis, in the May 1974 issue of *The Bajan* magazine, pointed out: "In fact, the houses that slaves lived in are not in existence today. They were small and made of organic materials called wattle and daub. Their roofs as well as those of the stone huts of later date were thatched with materials such as trash or plantation leaves. These houses were usually square or rectangular and consisted of only two rooms, occasionally three."

BELOW: looking out from the Animal Flower Cave.

The last of the animal flowers

Follow the signs to the northernmost point of the island and the wave-eroded **Animal Flower Cave** ❹ (open daily until 4pm; entrance fee), which was named after the tiny sea anemones (sea worms) which once lived in the rock pools: when they opened their tentacles they looked like flowers, but very few, if any, exist now. However, the view out of the huge limestone caverns to the sea is breathtaking.

The land around the entrance to the cave consists of barren rock, much like a moonscape; it's difficult to imagine that sugar cane used to be grown here in the 18th century, when it was known as the Animal Flower Plantation. Today, the Swedish owner, Eva Ward, sells delicious sandwiches, or "cutters", made with freshly-baked salt bread, along with home-made lemonade and other more potent drinks in a bar whose wall and ceiling are lined with business cards.

Continuing eastwards for a mile (1.5 km) around the coast, the road to River Bay passes the abandoned ghost-like **North Point Resort** at Middle Bay, and the remains of some artificial salt lakes which were closed in the 1940s. Water was pumped from the sea, left to settle and then evaporate, leaving the salt.

River Bay ❺ gets its name from a stream that once carved its way to the sea. From the hills above it is a wondrous sight. A popular destination of Bajan bus excursions for generations, the area is full of picnickers on weekends and holidays: but during the week the chances are you'll have this scenic spot, chiselled out of the chalk and limestone rock, all to yourself to explore the wind-eroded landscape and dry riverbed, or to just relax under the casuarina trees. Moss-covered boulders loom out of the shallows, while further out waves break on the reef in laundry-white surf. Now and then a fountain of spray appears from beneath the cliff, and a salty breeze caresses the face of anyone lucky enough to inhale the pure air transported over 2,000 miles (3,220 km) of ocean.

Map on page 300

A point of view

For one of the prettiest coastal spots in all of Barbados, you have to drive away from the sea to **Cove Bay**, or Gay's Cove as it's officially known, following a network of roads for about 5 miles (8 km) through cow pasture and villages such as Hope, Coconut Hall, Spring Garden and Pie Corner, where Amerindian artifacts are said to have been found. But stay on it, and you won't be disappointed, for overlooking the bay and the length of Barbados' Atlantic coastline is a beautiful promontory called **Paul's Point** ❻. In the bay, under the coconut trees, the trade winds are fresh and vigorous.

Towering over the southern end is the **Pico Teneriffe**, an unusually shaped pillar of white cliff which rises from the sea in stark grandeur, guarding the eastern coastline like a sentry and appearing much higher than its 260 ft (80 metres).

Another view of Pico Teneriffe is from the St Peter coast close to the village of **Boscobelle** a little further to the south. George Hunte in his book about Barbados, wrote: "… its pinnacle may be mistaken on a misty day for a sorrowful Madonna gazing out to sea in anxious care of her beloved fisherfolk."

The views are truly spectacular from the top of **Cherry Tree Hill**, just over

BELOW: fishing through a blowhole in the rock.

2 miles (3 km) to the south in the parish of St Andrew. Visible from here is most of the Scotland District, including Belleplaine, Chalky Mount and Hackleton's Cliff in the far south. The name Cherry Tree Hill is a misnomer as the 600-yard (550-metre) long avenue is lined with mahogany (not cherry) trees which form a cool canopy over the road at about 20 ft (6 metres) up.

The type of mahogany tree (above) found on Cherry Tree Hill was introduced to the island around the late 18th and early 19th century. However, their numbers are being depleted due to construction work and they are not being replaced.

A working sugar mill

A steep mile (1.5 km) or so downhill towards the East Coast brings you to **Morgan Lewis Sugar Mill** ❼ (open Mon–Fri; closed pub. hols; entrance fee). It is the only intact Barbadian windmill left on the island and, due to restoration work carried out by the National Trust in 1997 and 1998, its wheel house and points are now in perfect working order. Originally built in 1727, the mill is a good example of the windmills that were introduced to the island by Dutch Jews, who came to Barbados from Brazil (*see page 187*) and pioneered the cultivation and manufacture of sugar cane into sugar, and it was used for grinding sugar cane until 1945. When sugar was "king" (*see page 37*) there were over 500 windmills operating on the island.

The slaves who worked in the sugar mills were specially trained and did not have to work as hard as those in the fields, although it was a dangerous job. The mill gang of about eight men had to feed the canes by hand into the crushing rollers and move the mill points into or out of the wind by pulling and pushing the long tailtree. Heavy wind was just as bad for the grinding of sugar as was a light breeze. Squally wind would rotate the mill out of control and the vibrations could make the entire mill collapse.

Morgan Lewis could produce up to 1,500 gallons (6,800 litres) of cane

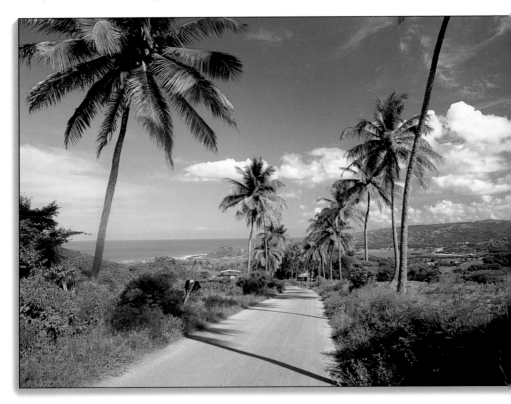

BELOW: view of the East Coast from Cherry Tree Hill.

juice a day which would then go to the boiling house – another dangerous place to work. Now that the sugar mill is operational, the National Trust are hoping to raise enough funds to stage a working exhibition from time to time, to really show how it was.

The road south through Shorey meets Highway 2 less than a mile (1.5 km) away and a right turn takes you along a beautiful stretch, with some wonderful views, to **Grenade Hall Forest and Signal Station** ❽ (open daily; entrance fee includes entry to the Barbados Wildlife Reserve). Restored by the Barbados Wildlife Reserve in 1992, the station formed part of the colonial signalling system in the early 19th century and had visual contact with Dover Fort in the west and Cotton Tower in the southeast (*see page 265*). In the cool, dark tranquillity of the surrounding forest a nature trail winds around a wide variety of tropical trees and plants, boulders of weathered coral rock and small hidden caves. Periodically along the way are boards posing ecological questions – the answers are hidden behind a sliding panel.

Shy monkeys

You can walk from the forest to **Barbados Wildlife Reserve** ❾ (open daily; entrance fee) in a few minutes or you can still use your ticket on another day. The reserve is a project of the Barbados Primate Research Centre in a lush, mahogany woodland with footpaths making it easily accessible. It offers a unique opportunity to observe at close range, in their natural habitat, the green monkeys of Barbados (*Cercopithecus sabaeus*). You'll see young monkeys at play, mothers caring for their babies and older males keeping watch over their territories as they forage for food. An interesting and well written booklet, *The*

Map on page 300

In Shorey, near Morgan Lewis, villagers are so proud of their cricketing hero Conrad Hunte, the West Indies' star opening batsman in the mid 1960s, that they have named their sports club after him. They can be seen playing cricket on the green on any weekend.

BELOW: Morgan Lewis Sugar Mill.

At Pleasant Hall on the road to Mile and a Quarter, there is a cave where it is believed Amerindians once worshipped. The entrance is 10 ft (3 metres) above the ground and hidden by a bush. Inside is a small carved piece of rock shaped like a human head.

Green Monkey of Barbados, provides information on the behaviour of this shy and elusive creature. The booklet, refreshments and gifts are available at the reception centre. Other animals, all free in their natural habitat (except for the python) roam the reserve – tortoises, otters, agoutis, porcupine to name just a few.

A little further along from the reserve on the other side of the road is **Farley Hill National Park** ⓾ (open daily; entrance fee) surrounding the ruins of a notorious Great House. An atmospheric setting for the **Paint It Jazz Festival** (*see page 143*) every January, the beautifully landscaped grounds have dozens of different fruit trees such as mango, soursop, mammee apple and tamarind. And benches on the terrace 900 ft (275 metres) above sea level allow visitors to sit and savour the view of the entire Scotland District to the south.

Farley Hill mansion was built on the grand scale of the 19th-century plantation houses in sections, beginning in 1818. During the late 1800s, it was owned by Thomas Graham Briggs who lived what can only be described as a high life here. Farley Hill gained a reputation as the most lavish of the old Barbadian merchant palaces, and included a billiard room, library, oversized dining room and several reception rooms.

A Hollywood location

After Briggs' death in 1887, the house went into decline enjoying a brief respite when it was chosen as the location for the Hollywood movie *Island in the Sun* in 1956, starring Harry Belafonte. Journalist George Hunte wrote at the time: "For two months in 1956 the crumbling old 'palace' experienced a transformation as 300 persons worked under the supervision of art director John de Cuir from Hollywood and his assistant, Walter Simmons, to convert it into a mansion

BELOW: playing Warri, a game that originated in West Africa.

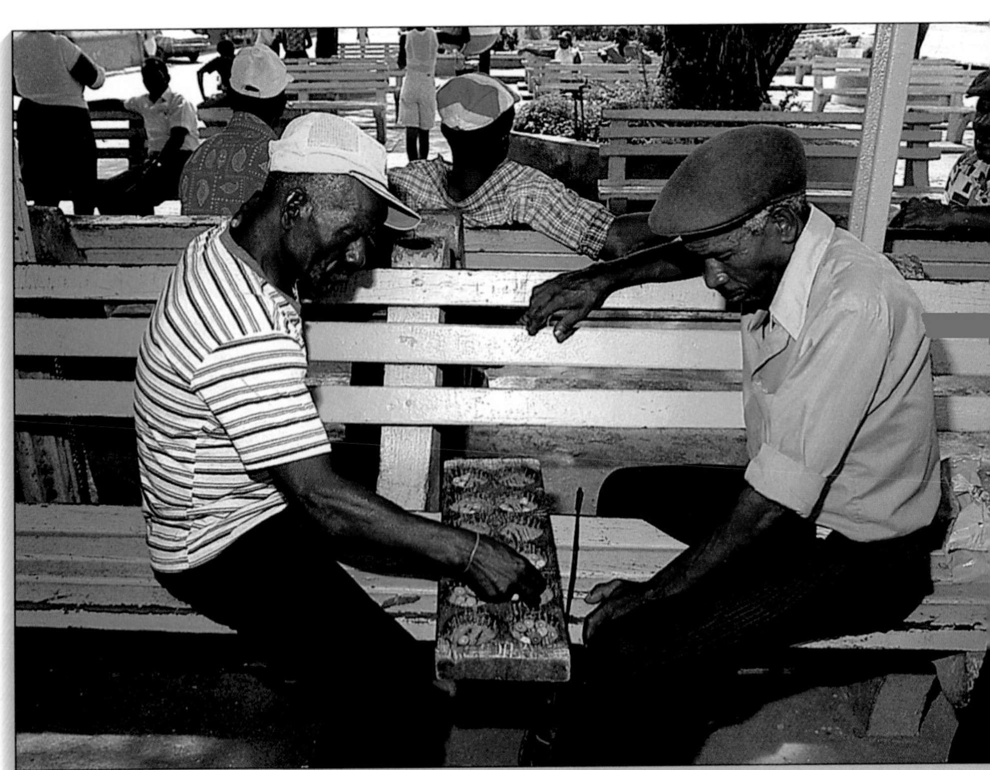

suitable for a sugar baron. A complete new gallery and stairway were constructed to face the lawn. An open verandah was added in front of the main entrance, where a huge *porte cochère* with overhanging roof bordered an artificial lake. The water-works of Barbados had to pump hundreds of thousands of gallons of water into this lake daily for weeks because its bottom was porous. Special paints were flown in from the United States and used to transform ordinary green leaves until they looked through the camera lenses like scarlet flamboyant flowers and magenta bougainvillea blooms.

"One flamboyant tree was delicately cut into numbered pieces at Crystal Springs on the St James coast, transported to Farley Hill and there stuck back carefully together as a single tree growing alongside the *porte cochère*."

However, the large quantities of wool and other flammable materials that were used in the restoration were left by the film crew and a few years later, a fire destroyed everything at the mansion except the walls. In 1965 the Government bought the property and declared it a National Park and it was officially opened by the Queen on 15 February 1966.

Map on page 300

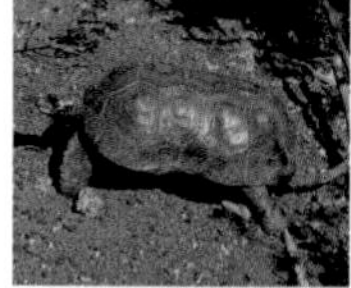

A tortoise at the Barbados Wildlife Reserve.

St Nicholas Abbey – an unusual Great House

A treasured attraction of the north, **St Nicholas Abbey** ⓫ (open ground floor only Mon–Fri, 10am–3.30pm; closed pub. hols; entrance fee) is one of the oldest houses on the island. About 10 minutes to the east along Highway 1, it is one of three remaining examples of Jacobean-style architecture in the Americas, another being Drax Hall in St George (*see page 293*) and the third in Virginia, USA. With the puzzling features of fireplaces (in the upstairs rooms) and chimneys, the stone and wood mansion is said to have been built between 1650 and

BELOW: creative advertising at a repair shop.

An antique "all singing and dancing" planter's chair to be found at St Nicholas Abbey.

1660 by Colonel Benjamin Berringer, a landowner and member of one of the aristocratic families that dominated the social and political life of the island at that time. Soon after his house was built, Berringer was poisoned by his former business partner John Yeamans, who was having an affair with his wife. They married within 10 weeks of Berringer's death and were among the first pioneers who left Barbados in 1669 to settle in the British colony of South Carolina in North America (*see below*).

The house was named after one of Colonel Berringer's descendants, according to local historian Maurice Hutt. Berringer's son John left the house to his daughter, Susanna, who married a man named George Nicholas. It was his name that became attached to the property. No one seems to know how the "Saint" and "Abbey" in the name came about. The present owner, Lieut Col Stephen Cave, who lives here for part of the year, has some old film footage which shows life in Barbados and on the plantation in 1935, which he will show you on request.

In the grounds are ruins of the sugar mill and factory that once ground the cane produced on the estate. The mill crushed the cane until 1889 when it was replaced with a modern steam engine which operated until 1947. Today sugar is still grown on the 420-acre (170-hectare) estate and the cane is sent to the Portvale sugar factory 8 miles (13 km) away (*see page 222*) for processing.

A final resting place

Returning to Speightstown along Highway 1, you reach **All Saints Church** after about 2 miles (3 km). The original church survived hurricanes in 1675 and 1780 but could not withstand the great hurricane of 1831. Another foun-

BELOW: the island's green monkey.

THE CAROLINA CONNECTION

Barbados has close links with the state of South Carolina in the USA. According to Ronald Tree, in his *A History of Barbados*, Sir John Yeamans after purportedly poisoning Colonel Benjamin Berringer, owner of St Nicholas Abbey, so that he could marry his wife Margaret, joined the first expedition of English settlers to South Carolina in 1669.

A leading planter, Sir John Colleton, had obtained with several other noblemen, a grant of land corresponding to the present day Carolinas and he was able to give preference to Barbadians who wanted to emigrate, due to overcrowding on the island or being younger sons with little hope of inheritance. Yeamans and his family settled at Goose Creek near Charleston in 1670 and by 1672 he was Governor of the colony until his death in 1674.

Hundreds followed – it is not known how many – in the next 30 years. They brought their slaves with them and it is said that the coastal dialect of Gullah is very similar to Bajan.

A special friendship between Barbados and South Carolina has remained ever since with the latter sending £785 after the 1766 Bridgetown fire and with the twinning of Speightstown and Charleston in 1997.

dation stone was laid in 1839 and the new church was consecrated in 1843. However, this church barely lasted 40 years before the walls were found to be shaky and it had to be demolished to make way for a new building which was completed in 1884. Despite all the rebuilding, All Saints Church remains on the original site and a number of the old tombstones – including that of William Arnold, who was in the first group of settlers to arrive at Holetown in 1627 – are still present, providing a journey into old Barbados with the names of the prominent planter families of centuries ago. From inside the blue-grey washed chapel you can appreciate the fine stained-glass windows portraying stories of Christ.

On a whim

South of **Mile and a Quarter**, so named because it is that distance from Speightstown, is an exit to the left off Highway 1 into the **Whim Gully**. This is one of the most accessible of the many gullies that dot the island, as the narrow road passes along its floor, and it is part of the route of the Barbados National Trust's **Arbib Nature & Heritage Trail** hike (*see page 301*). The foliage rises up on both sides, and in the centre the road crosses a bridge where the temperature is very cool. In times of heavy rain, water flows over the rocks of the gully's floor and under this bridge. The Whim is notorious to the residents of Speightstown as the source of much of the water which floods the town after particularly heavy rains.

From The Whim, the road connects with **Sailor's Gully**, bordered on the south by a limestone cliff of about 80 ft (25 metres) high which is festooned with thick hanging vines. On the cliff face is the opening of a cave in which the mossy stalactites and stalagmites are visible from the road. ❑

Alleynedale Hall, just north of Mile and a Quarter, is believed to be haunted by a clergyman who cut his own throat at the end of the 18th century. Instead of being buried where four roads met, as was the custom with suicide victims then, he was put in the cellar, but by 1810 the coffin had disappeared.

BELOW: another roadside attraction.

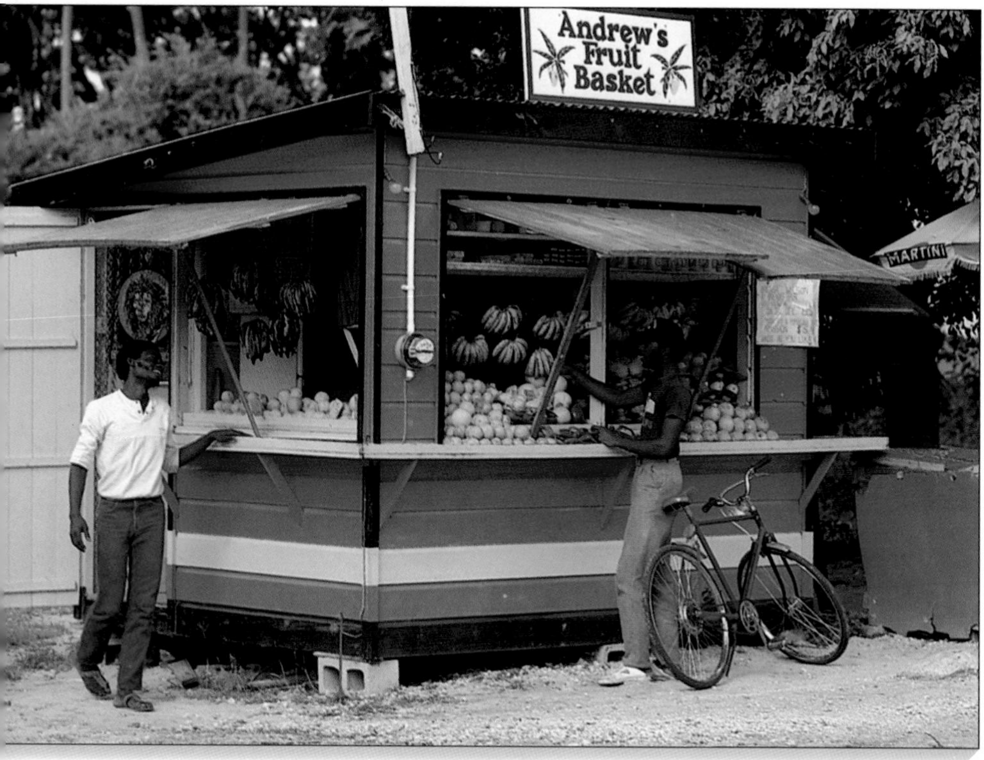

TROPICAL GARDENS OF BARBADOS

A vast variety of colourful flora flourishes all over the island, from the formal gardens of the Great Houses to the natural setting of the Flower Forest

An early historian reported that when the first British settlers arrived in Barbados, the island was "so grown with wood as there could be found no champions (clearings) or savannahs for men to dwell in". But it didn't take long for them to clear it for sugar cane, leaving small pockets of forest in the gullies and on the hills. But there has always been room for gardens and the British love of gardening has remained deep-seated in the island's culture. Brightly painted chattel houses, surrounded by colourful crotons are often dwarfed by enormous breadfruit trees and the owners of the Great Houses take great pride in their gardens, often modelling them on an English country garden.

OPEN GARDENS

Gardens, large and small, exotic or functional, can be seen as part of the Barbados Horticultural Society's Open Gardens season during the winter when owners each show off their pride and joy to the public. And there are many oases of tropical splendour that are permanently open. Hotels, such as Cobblers Cove (*above*), are landscaped stage settings of hibiscus, bougainvillea and palms against the blue Caribbean. Andromeda Botanic Gardens has been created over 40 years on an Atlantic hillside and the Flower Forest blooms in what feels like the roof garden of Barbados. Tropical plants and trees grow in profusion in Welchman Hall Gully and the collection of orchids at Orchid World is magnificent.

▷ PRAYING FOR RAIN
Barbadians are always happy to have some rainy days as they have suffered many droughts in the past – water is a precious commodity.

△ FRANK FORMALITY
The extensive gardens of Francia Plantation include neatly terraced lawns, fountains, ferneries and orchards.

▷ PURE AND SIMPLE
Coral dripstones were once used for purifying water. Fed into the top pot the water slowly filters through to the bottom.

◁ **NATIONAL PRIDE**
The orange and yellow blooms of the national flower, Pride of Barbados, creates a colourful hedge in the Flower Forest.

△ **ABBEY VIEW**
The coral rag walls of St Nicholas Abbey form the backdrop to well laid out gardens that contain a 500-year-old sandbox tree.

△ **ORCHID BEAUTY**
At Orchid World, some of the spectacular blooms are nurtured on palisades, with their roots dangling in mid air.

△ **HONEST TOIL**
With hotels and holiday villas all wanting their gardens to flourish, the gardening workforce is kept busy all year round.

▷ **ANIMAL MAGIC**
Tropical gardens attract abundant wildlife and at Andromeda you may see monkeys, mongooses, lizards, hummingbirds and bananaquits.

AT THE CHELSEA FLOWER SHOW

Every year, members of Barbados Horticultural Society, led by gardeners Audrey Thomas and Jean Robinson, enter their magnificent displays of tropical blooms in England's Chelsea Flower Show at the end of May. And most years they return home with the Gold Medal.

The display is designed nine months ahead to allow time for the plants, such as heliconias, ginger lilies, orchids and anthuriums, to be nursed to total perfection – they have to keep looking fresh for at least two weeks. In the two days before leaving for England, the flowers are picked, inspected and carefully layered in boxes with dry newspaper to insulate them during the long plane flight.

At Chelsea, the team work tirelessly from Thursday until Sunday to arrange their display in time for the judging and Queen's visit on Monday. By Friday, the blooms, now past their best, are snapped up for £1 a bunch to end their days in an English home.

ISLAND HOPPING

Once in Barbados, it's not too far to "go that extra mile" and explore the neighbouring islands – each with a unique character – on a day trip or a two-day special, by sea or by air

Map on pages 318/322

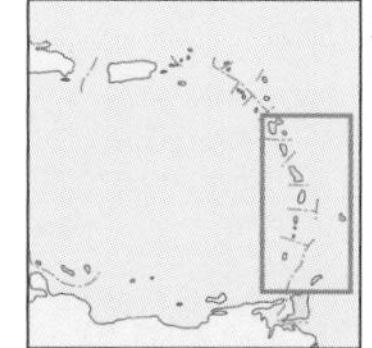

Although Barbados sits 100 miles (160 km) outside the Antillean archipelago, it is still very easy to take a trip and experience another Caribbean island. The immediate neighbourhood, within relatively close proximity, stretches from Dominica, about 160 miles (255 km) to the north, to Tobago, less than 150 miles (240 km) to the south and includes islands of an entirely different nature to Barbados in character and topography. The more mountainous, volcanic islands of Dominica, Martinique, St Lucia, St Vincent and Grenada, whose endemic, tropical rainforests teem with hundreds of species of birds and plant life, many of which are indigenous to these parts, offer a scenery in stark contrast to the rolling cane fields of Barbados.

And there is an impressive variety of ways to get to the islands, ranging from private jet and exclusive yacht charters, to all-inclusive, one-day packages via small, light seven- to 17-seater planes or inter-island ferry services, making it quite effortless to spend a day or two on one, or a few, of these sparkling gems. Depending on the degree of luxury you seek, the amount of time on hand and, of course, your budget, there are many options available through several well-respected local travel companies who make "island hopping" their speciality.

PRECEDING PAGES: Palm Island – all beach and sea.
LEFT: leatherback turtle going strong.
BELOW: a desert island beach.

Companies like **Chantours** (tel: 432 5591) can arrange anything from organised day trips and overnight "escapes" to bareboat (without a crew) or crewed yacht charters and entire luxury villa vacations, in just about any Caribbean island of your choice. **Safari Tours** (tel: 427 5100) offer Two-Night Specials to the islands of Tobago, Grenada, St Vincent, St Lucia, Martinique and Dominica, staying in either small inns, guest houses or superior hotels. Extra night rates are available for longer stays, and car rentals and island tours can be arranged from Barbados before you go. **G & T Tours** (tel: 435 8451) specialise in trips to the Grenadines.

St Vincent and the Grenadines

Just under 100 miles (160 km) to the west of Barbados lies the unspoiled haven of **St Vincent and the Grenadines**. Often referred to as the "Jewels of the Caribbean", comprising more than 30 islands and cays that cover about 150 sq. miles (390 sq. km), this archipelago meanders for about 45 miles (72 km) in a southwesterly arch down to Grenada and offers some of the best sailing waters in the Caribbean. Once you could only get to the Grenadines under sail. Now, small airstrips on Bequia, Mustique, Union Island and Canouan, make these islands within easy reach.

Generally referred to as the Mainland by the locals, **St Vincent** ❶ is the gateway to the Grenadines. There is a very special peace to be found here, close to nature and away from the hustle and bustle of the "real

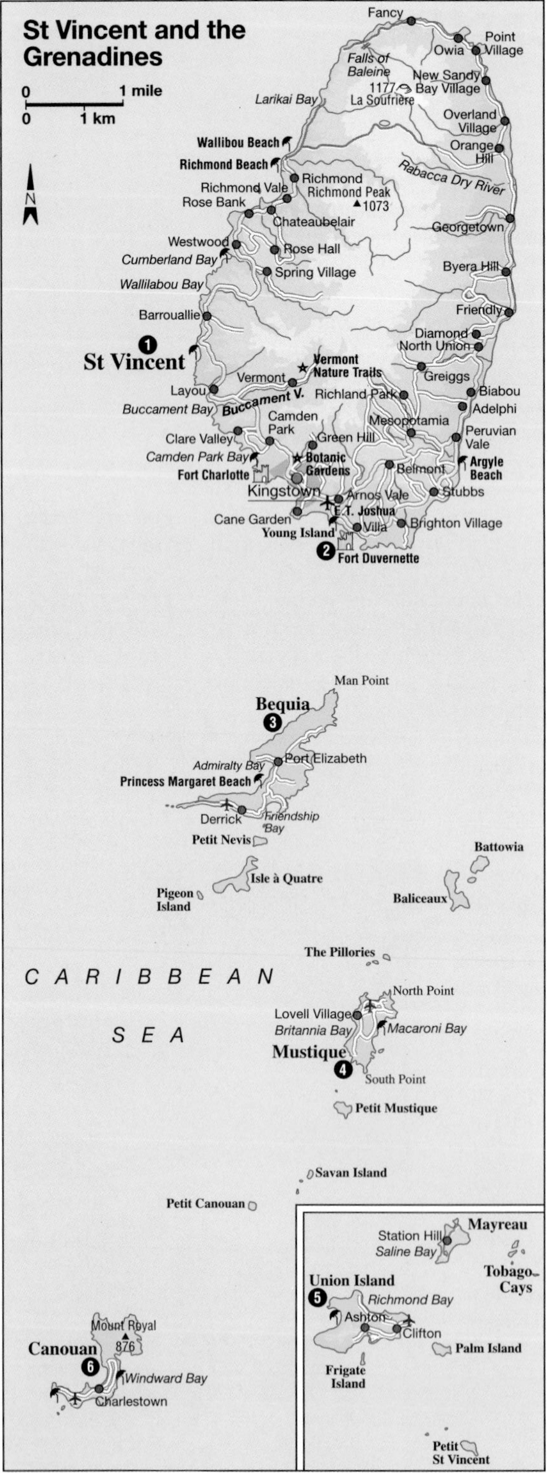

world". **Kingstown**, the island's capital, is not much more than a few dusty blocks carved into a rugged shoreline; just outside to the west lies **St Mary's Cathedral**, a 19th-century marvel incorporating practically every architectural style under the sun. Further on are the **Botanic Gardens** (open daily; free), the oldest in the western hemisphere, with an example of almost every flower and tree that can grow in the Caribbean, including one of Captain Bligh's breadfruit trees brought here on *The Bounty* in 1793.

Further north, you can search for the rare St Vincent parrot in the rainforests along the **Vermont Nature Trails**, or take a boat from Richmond Beach to the **Falls of Baleine** on the northern tip.

Off the south coast of St Vincent, by the town of Villa, is **Young Island** ❷, home to a private, exclusive resort and a challenging swim (about 200 yards/180 metres) across the channel. If you are not feeling that energetic, you can take the Young Island water-taxi. But first it's necessary to call the island from the telephone in the parking area by the dock for permission to visit the resort. Once there you can enjoy a meal or a few drinks – but these won't be at bargain prices.

Bequia – so laid back

The tranquil isle of **Bequia** ❸ (pronounced Beck-way), the second largest island in this chain, lies 9 miles (14 km) to the south of St Vincent and is about an hour's journey from the Ferry Boat Wharf in Kingstown Harbour. Several ferries service the route from St Vincent to Bequia, the main ones being the *MV Admiral I* and *II* which depart twice a day, Sunday to Friday and once on Saturday, and are very reasonably priced. Alternatively, the trip takes about an hour and a half by charter yacht, or a 10-minute hop from St Vincent or Union Island, albeit on one of the small six- or nine-seater islander planes run by Mustique Airways or SVG Air. These operate both as scheduled flights as well as on a charter basis. In fact, chartering a plane can work out to be quite economical if you have several passengers in your party. You can also fly directly in 45 minutes from Barbados.

Bequia is a laid-back island, so full of Caribbean character that you can't help but be bewitched by the atmosphere, which "jumps up" every year at the four-day **Bequia Easter Regatta**. The island itself is simple with just one town, **Port Elizabeth**, in beautiful Admiralty Bay, the main port of entry. With only one road running through the town, it's virtually impossible to get lost. There are a few small grocery stores on and around **Front Street** and a colourful market selling fresh produce brought over daily by farmers on the ferries from the Mainland. Bequians have, for centuries, made their living from the sea as fishermen, sailors, boat builders and whalers and the island still retains these age-old traditions. There is a thriving community of miniature boat builders just past the market and, at **Sargeant's Model Boat Shop**, you can watch these amazing craftsmen at work, using traditional tools and methods.

Admiralty Bay is a hive of activity, and the "Boardwalk" is lined with waterside cafés including **The Frangipani**, a small hotel affectionately referred to as "Frangi". This was the childhood home of Sir James Mitchell, Prime Minister of St Vincent and the Grenadines, and is still one of his favourite haunts. It is a prime spot from where to watch the world go by with a Frozen Lime Daiquiri, and on Thursday nights you can dance under the stars to a live steel band.

Feasting in Lower Bay

A 10-minute water-taxi ride from Admiralty Bay takes you to the peaceful community of **Lower Bay**, and one of the island's finest beaches. Here the tranquil waters are of the bluest blues and crystal clear, making it perfect for snorkelling

Map on page 318

The St Vincent parrot hides in the rainforest.

BELOW: diving in Bequia is superb.

Windsurfing in a beautiful bay.

and swimming – and afterwards there are several good local restaurants just a stone's throw from the beach. At **Theresa's**, set in small, modest surroundings, hosts Theresa and John don't only cook up an amazing feast of local delicacies, but entertain you as well. **Coco's Place** is a lively little restaurant and bar, full of Caribbean flavour well known for their creole Conch Curry.

Dawn's Creole Restaurant, next door, is well known for her local fish dishes and incredible Callaloo Soup and she offers light lunches at reasonable prices with ice cold Hairouns, the local brew, at her snack bar on the beach. **De Reef**, in the middle of the bay, hires out kayaks and can arrange water-skiing and banana boat rides as well as providing snacks of local fish and pickled conch.

Bequia's sea life

Bequia is surrounded by beautiful diving waters, and is a Marine Protected Area with over 30 dive sites many of which are ideal for snorkelling too. There are several good dive companies, including **Dive Bequia** (tel: 784-458 3504) at the Gingerbread Hotel in Admiralty Bay, which offers courses that can get you diving in a day with all the equipment necessary, dive and snorkel tours as well as night dives and sunfish rentals. **Michael's Tours** (tel: 784-457 3116) at **Paget Farm** on the southeast coast, operates a no-frills boat trip over to the deserted islands of **Petit Nevis**, where there's a whaling station, and **Isle à Quatre** to the south. Lunch is often caught on the way and cooked on the beach.

Just outside Paget Farm is Athneal Ollivierre's **Whaling Museum** (open daily; entrance fee). Easily identified by the large whale jawbone archway at the entrance, Athneal delights in recounting his whaling tales to visitors and showing off his memorabilia and relics. Bequia is still very much a whaling community with Aboriginal Whaling Rights allowing them to harpoon two whales a year – the last one was caught in 1992.

BELOW: travel agency in Bequia.

Mustique – an exclusive playground

Mustique ❹, well known as the "playground of the rich and famous", is just under two hours sail to the southeast of Bequia and about 18 miles (30 km) south of St Vincent. The 60-ft (20-metre) catamaran *Passion*, owned and operated by Marty and Heidi Pritchard (and their sailor-dog, Indy), runs day trips from Bequia to Mustique and the Tobago Cays (tel: 784-458 3884). Or you can fly direct from Barbados with Mustique Airways in 45 minutes.

This privately owned, informal, yet refined, island is only 3 miles (5 km) long and less than 2 miles (3 km) wide and is managed by the Mustique Company (whose shareholders are the property owners) and has been a favourite hideaway for celebrities and royalty from around the world, where they can relax in private seclusion. Villa rentals are available at exorbitant prices (tel: 784-458 4621 for details and bookings) and the **Cotton House Hotel** (tel: 784-456 4777) and **Firefly** (tel: 784-456 3414) offer fine up-market accommodation and dining.

The famous **Basil's Bar**, in Britannia Bay, is where it all happens in Mustique. This is where both locals and visitors gather for a bite to eat, a cold beer and to catch up on the local gossip. Basil's is a simple, island-style bamboo bar on the sea, whose guests include the likes of Mick Jagger, Raquel Welch and Prince Andrew, and has been voted one of the world's best bars by *Newsweek*.

Map on page 318

Day trips to the Grenadines

If time is limited, the best way to see the Grenadines is on a day trip with one of Barbados' island hopping travel specialists Chantours, G & T Tours or Safari Tours, who operate a combination of one-day tours to the islands. An early morning departure and a short, 45-minute flight from Barbados takes you to **Union Island** ❺, the most developed of the smaller Grenadines and an established sailing centre. From here, depending on your chosen excursion, you sail by luxury catamaran, or by a traditional 80-ft (25-metre) wooden schooner, through this unspoiled chain of splendid islets and cays, dropping anchor in secluded bays along the way. Some of the islands visited on these day tours include **Mayreau** (*My-row*), only inhabited by 100 people, and the **Tobago Cays**, a group of four miniature, uninhabited islands surrounded by crystal-clear waters and colourful reefs teeming with tropical fish, offering spectacular snorkelling. Two other ports of call are the privately owned islands of **Petit St Vincent** (PSV) and **Palm Island**, two of the world's most enchanting hideaways.

Just to the north of the Tobago Cays is the serene little island of **Canouan** ❻ (*Can-o-wan*), named by Amerindians after the turtles living there, and known only by a privileged few. Chantours and G & T Tours offer an excellent overnight package to Canouan from Barbados. It includes accommodation and meals at the Canouan Beach Hotel, a picnic cruise to the Tobago Cays on their elegant catamaran, return flights, airport transfers and departure tax.

BELOW: sailing between the islands is the best way to travel.

LIAT, the inter-island air company, offers a 30-day ticket deal for exploring the Caribbean islands. Flights arrive at almost all of the islands twice daily, but your ticket does not allow you to visit one twice, except for making connections. Call 434 5428 in Barbados for details.

Grenada – the spice island

Just south of St Vincent and the Grenadines lies the three-island state of **Grenada** ❼ (Gra-nay-dah), incorporating **Carriacou** and **Petit Martinique**. Each of this delightful trio has its own distinctive character, and all share in an extraordinary natural beauty and a warm and friendly people. You can visit for a day, or stay for a few days to dive the *Bianca C*, the largest wreck dive in the Caribbean, or explore the island's 45 glorious beaches, parks, nature reserves and bird sanctuaries. Flying to the tiny island of Carriacou takes just a few minutes with **Airlines of Carriacou** (tel: 473-444 3549) which offers day trips, but if you have time, sailing into the island's natural harbour is very special.

Grenada has quite a history behind her. The British and the French exchanged colonial command on several occasions, each erecting structures and forts in their own unique styles, evidence of which is still apparent today. And incarcerated in the 200-year-old Fort Frederick, above the capital St George's, are the murderers of Maurice Bishop, the charismatic prime minister of the People's Revolutionary Government violently overthrown in 1983, which triggered the "Grenada Invasion" by the United States. To this day, most Grenadians choose not to discuss those tragic events, having put the past behind them and moved on to a course of democracy and stability.

A picturesque capital

St George's is probably the most picturesque capital in the Caribbean. Houses with red and orange tile roofs, churches and forts rise in tiers up the surrounding hillsides. Strolling around the colourful Carenage, or inner harbour, the distinct aroma of spices fills the air. Above the harbour entrance stands **Fort**

BELOW: Tobago Cays and some very explorable reefs.

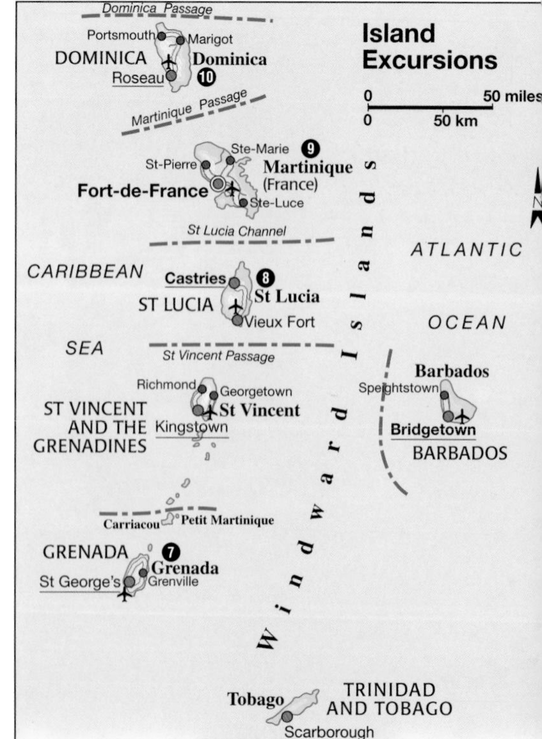

George (open daily), built by the French in 1705 and commanding views of the capital, the beautiful coastline and dramatic mountain scenery.

Both Chantours and Safari Tours offer one-day trips to Grenada, taking in Fort Frederick and the **Laura Spice Plantation** where you can walk down avenues of nutmeg, clove, cinnamon, pimento and bay trees, and see the wide selection of plants used in folk medicine. After lunch, a drive along the East Coast takes you through **Grenville**, Grenada's second town, and on to the Nutmeg Processing Factory. Then the tour enters into the rainforest with a stop at the awe-inspiring Crater Lake in the **Grand Etang National Park**, before descending again to the south for a bite to eat at the **Aquarium Restaurant**, and the return trip to Barbados.

For a longer stay, there are some good hotels in beautiful spots around the island, such as **Secret Harbour Resort** (tel: 473-444 4548) at L'Anse aux Epines, which organises three-day sailing trips to Tobago Cays, and, for a memorable evening out, the award-winning restaurant **Canboulay** (tel: 473-444 4401) overlooks **Grand Anse**, one of Grenada's best beaches, and offers superb local cuisine with an international touch, often accompanied by live jazz.

St Lucia – a treasure island

Known as "Helen of the Antilles", **St Lucia** 8 (Loo-sha), situated to the northwest of Barbados just a 35-minute plane ride away, is a nature lover's paradise. With a dramatic mountainous landscape covered by lush, tropical rainforests, the 238-sq. mile (617-sq. km) island has some spectacular scenery – not least the two majestic peaks, on the southwest coast, called the **Pitons**.

As well as organising bed and breakfast on the island, both Chantours and

Map on page 322

Bright pink bougainvillea make a colourful splash.

BELOW: the old town of Soufrière in St Lucia.

Diving excursions to other islands can be arranged from Barbados. But remember to take into account that you will not be able to fly for 24 hours after a dive.

Safari Tours operate one-day packages to St Lucia – including organised tours, admissions and lunch – designed to give a good overview of the island, its history and cultural heritage.

St Lucia was a much fought over island, actually changing hands 14 times over a 150-year period of battles between the British and French, and was finally ceded to the British in 1814. A strong French influence remains today, and although English is the official language, French patois is often spoken by St Lucians everywhere. The abundance of historic military ruins, combined with the majestic splendour of the Pitons, the intrinsic beauty of the tropical rainforest, volcanic springs, banana plantations, botanical gardens and breath-taking views, make St Lucia a true treasure.

Off the beaten track

The one-day tours are given in open-sided four-wheel drive jeeps, which can get you "off the beaten track" with the greatest of ease (though not necessarily the greatest of comfort!). They start in **Castries**, the bustling, but unattractive capital, and continue south along the scenic west coast through isolated villages. After passing through the **Roseau Valley** banana plantation, the jeep heads off-road, winding upwards, over volcanic hills and deep into the luxuriant tropical rainforest, habitat of the rare St Lucian parrot (*Amazona versicolor*), only now being brought back from the verge of extinction. To the south looms the spectacular sight of **Mount Gimie** (3,117 ft/950 metres), St Lucia's highest point, which you can climb with a local guide on a longer stay.

Back on the main road meandering southward along the West Coast, you pass through the quaint fishing villages of **Anse-la-Raye** and **Canaries** and on

BELOW: fishing boats on the beach in St Lucia.

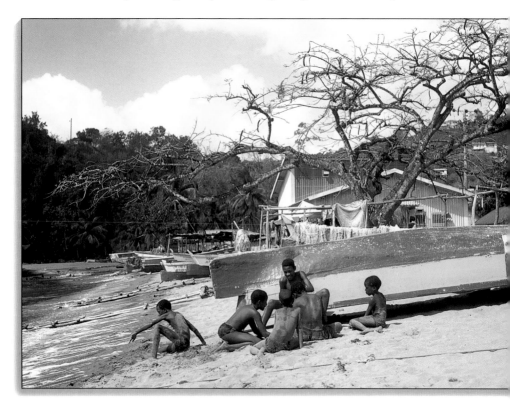

to the rim of the Soufrière Basin. Here the regal splendour of the twin peaks of the **Pitons** almost takes your breath away. **Soufrière** lies on the northern side of Petit Piton and is St Lucia's oldest town, established by the French in 1746, with the oldest surviving architecture on the island. From here you will be taken to the **Diamond Botanical Gardens** (open daily; Sun 10am–2pm; entrance fee), where Louis XVI had bath houses built for his troops to harness the hot spring water; then you can have a refreshing dip at the **Toraille Waterfalls** before going on to **Sulphur Springs** and the world's only drive-in volcano.

After lunch, the tour takes you on a leisurely drive back up the West Coast to **Marigot Bay** for a relaxing afternoon swimming and snorkelling. Marigot was once an essential wartime base where, it is said, a British Admiral Rodney once ambushed the French by camouflaging his fleet with palm fronds. Today, the natural harbour is a haven for luxury yachts and one of the most beautiful anchorages in the Caribbean.

Map on page 322

Martiniquans are proud of their tradition of fine rum.

Martinique – a taste of France

The French island of **Martinique ❾**, an hour's flight away from Barbados, is probably the most cosmopolitan of all the Caribbean islands. Since 1635, with the exception of two short periods of British rule, Martinique has been governed by France, and is officially a fully-fledged *département*. The island still lives up to its Amerindian name of Madinina, Isle of Flowers, with a profusion of tropical blooms flowering in the dramatic mountainous terrain, lush tropical rainforest, along beautiful coastlines and botanical gardens. Combined with a vibrant cultural heritage, Martinique is a real treat to visit.

From Barbados, day trips can be arranged by both Chantours and Safari

BELOW: Fort St Louis in Martinique.

Map on page 322

Tobago, northeast of Trinidad, has tranquil white beaches, rugged coasts and tropical rainforests. It also has a top-class golf course at Mount Irvine Bay – a one-and-a-half hour flight away from Barbados.

RIGHT: dramatic scenery in Dominica
BELOW: Dominica's spectacular Trafalgar Falls.

Tours. There are several alternatives available and tours can even be custom designed to suit each individual's preference.

Parisian shopping

The French influence is quite evident in **Fort-de-France**, the busy capital. With a reputation of being the showcase of Paris in the heart of the Caribbean, almost all products carry a "Made in France" label. Normally stores open from 9am to 1pm and re-open again from 3pm to 6pm Monday to Friday and on Saturday until 1pm, so be sure to plan your shopping accordingly. Although the French franc is legal tender, US currency is readily accepted and very often a 20 percent discount will be given for payment by travellers cheques or foreign currency credit cards.

In the south of the island, just across the Baie des Flamands, lies **Les Trois-Ilets** where Napoleon's Josephine was born, and in **Musée de la Pagerie** (open daily; closed Mon; entrance fee), an elegant little stone building, her childhood bed, letters from Napoleon and several portraits are among the exhibits of her life. Off the south coast by Le Diamant looms the **Rocher du Diamant** (Diamond Rock), once a piece of the British Empire. In 1805, a group of 100 British soldiers took possession of this volcanic rock for just 18 months to control the channel between Martinique and St Lucia.

In the north, the spectacular **Route de la Trace** weaves its way through luxuriant rainforest, passing the **Jardin de Balata** (open daily; entrance fee), a botanical garden with more than 2,000 tropical plants and flowers. In the heart of the island stands **Montagne Pelée** (4,583 ft/1,397 metres) which on 8 May 1902 wiped out **St Pierre** and its 30,000 citizens on the northwest coast in seconds. Now classified a national historic town, St Pierre is today quiet and pretty with resurgent growth.

Dominica – the nature island

The "scrunched up" island of **Dominica** ❿ is well known as the Nature Island of the Caribbean. With an abundance of rivers, waterfalls, mangroves, tropical rainforests, mountains and wildlife, it is a paradise for nature lovers, hikers and dive enthusiasts, so a stay of a few days would be necessary here, or join one of Safari Tours Two-Night Specials (*see page 317*).

An hour and a half away from Barbados by air, there is an excellent choice of hikes ranging from flat, short, easy walks to **Emerald Pool** (bring swimwear) to all-day, uphill endurance tests, which will require guides, such as to the **Boiling Lake** – second largest in the world – and **Valley of Desolation**, a crater-like landscape of bubbling mud pools, steaming vents and sulphur springs: **Ken's Hinterland Adventure Tours** (tel: 767-448 4850) is an established tour operator in Dominica which can help you plan your stay.

The dive sites off the West Coast are among the best in the world and include 1,000-ft (300-metre) drop-offs, hot springs, pinnacles and walls. There are many dive operators – who also organise whale-watching trips – to choose from; ask at the hotel for a recommendation. Several, such as **Dive Dominica** (tel: 767-448 2188), offer packages with accommodation. ❑

INSIGHT GUIDES

TRAVEL TIPS

Contents

Getting Acquainted

The Place

Area: 430 sq. km (166 sq. miles)
Geography: The easternmost island of the Caribbean, Barbados is 34 km (21 miles) long and 22 km (14 miles) wide. It is said that Columbus missed "discovering" Barbados because it was too flat, but the landscape in some locales is hilly, especially toward the north and east along the elevated central plateau, rising to 340 metres (1,115 ft) at Mount Hillaby. On the windward eastern side, magnificent cliffs rise above the Atlantic waves; the leeward west coast is washed by the calm Caribbean Sea, lapping against miles of powdery beaches.
Capital: Bridgetown
Highest mountain: Mount Hillaby
Population: 263,000
Language: English; Barbadian dialect
Religion: Anglican (33 percent); Pentecostal (25 percent)
Time zone: four hours behind GMT
Currency: Barbados dollar (BDS$); BDS$1.98 = US$1, fixed rate
Weights and measures: metric
Electricity: 110 volts A.C. and 50 cycles. Two-pronged US-style plug
National flower: Pride of Barbados
International dialling code: 246

Climate

The climate in Barbados is mild, breezy and sunny all year round. The average temperature is 80°F (27°C), and the warm sunshine – 3,000 hours of it per year – is moderated by a steady Northeast Trade wind. Rain usually comes in quick showers, except occasionally during the hurricane season from June through November (*see box*). Fortunately, these intense tropical storms usually pass by Barbados to the north.

Government

Barbados became an independent nation in 1966, after an unbroken relationship with a single colonial power, Britain, stretching back into the early 17th century. In 1989, Barbados achieved 350 years of uninterrupted parliamentary government.

A Prime Minister and bicameral legislature, consisting of an elected House of Assembly and a 21-member Senate, govern the country. Twelve senators are appointed on the advice of the Prime Minister, two from the opposition party and the remaining seven are chosen to represent the social, political and religious interests of the country. The Prime Minister is the leader of the majority party in the House of Assembly.

The nation retains the British monarch as its official head of state, represented by the Governor-General. However, this could change shortly as plans are underway to make Barbados into a republic. The Queen would no longer be head of state, but Barbados would remain a member of the Commonwealth.

Economy

Barbados is one of the most prosperous countries in the Caribbean. The main areas of economic activity are tourism, financial services, a combination of agriculture and fishing, and light manufacturing. Tourism and international business are the island's main earners.

FOREIGN INVESTMENT

In recent years, Barbados has campaigned to attract foreign investors. The Government – via the Barbados Investment and Development Corporation – is seeking to capitalise on its reputation for political stability in order to capture a greater share of overseas investment market.

Advantages for would-be manufacturers include full

What to Do If a Hurricane Threatens

Hurricanes rarely hit Barbados, passing by to the north, but they are sometimes on track for the island and then they will be closely watched and their progress charted on radio, in TV and newspapers. If one is heading your way, keep calm and follow these procedures:

- **During the storm:** Stay indoors once the hurricane begins buffeting your area. When the eye (the low-pressure area at the centre of a hurricane) passes over, there will be a temporary lull for up to half an hour or more and then it will resume from the opposite direction. Wait for the all-clear from the authorities before venturing out of your shelter.
- **If ordered to evacuate:** Stay tuned to local radio stations for up-to-date information and instructions. Follow designated routes quickly. Take with you blankets, a flashlight, extra clothing and medications.
- **After the storm passes:** Drive with caution when told to return home. Roads near the coast may collapse if soil has been washed away from beneath them. Steer clear of fallen or dangling utility wires. Stay tuned to radio stations for news of emergency medical aid, food, housing and other forms of assistance.

If you have been staying in a rented home, re-enter the building with caution and make temporary repairs to correct hazards and minimise further damage. Open windows and doors to air and dry the house. Be particularly careful when dealing with matches or fires in case of gas leaks.

exemption from corporate taxes for 10 years, exemption on all import duties for parts, materials and production machinery, and unrestricted repatriation of capital profits. Under the International Business Companies Act, overseas firms that do not engage in local trade or investment enjoy an annual taxation rate of just 1–2½ percent. Local regulations regarding offshore banking, foreign ship representation, exempt insurance, and foreign sales corporations have been eased. Low office and industrial space rental rates also contribute to the Government's incentives.

For further information, tel: 427 5350, fax: 426 7802, or write to the Barbados Investment and Development Corporation, e-mail: bidc@interport.net.

The People

The population is about 70 percent black, 20 percent mixed black and white, and 7 percent white; another 3 percent are recent immigrants from around the world. Culturally, despite the long political and economic domination of Britain, Barbadians have fashioned a distinctly Bajan view of life from their country's complex history. With such close relations with the USA and Canada, North American influences on the island's day-to-day life are more and more apparent.

Business Hours

Hours for most banks are 8am–3pm Monday to Thursday, Friday 8am–5pm. A number of banks may also be open 9am–noon on Saturday. The Barbados National Bank in the departure lounge at Grantley Adams International Airport is open every day from 8am until 10pm. Cash machines (ATMs) also offer bank facilities through the day, seven days a week.

In general, stores open between 8 and 9am Monday to Saturday and close between 5 and 6pm Monday to Friday and between 2 and 4pm on Saturday. Most supermarkets open at 8am and close at 8pm from Monday to Thursday. Most are open 8am–9pm on Friday and Saturday. A number of small convenience stores stay open 9am–9pm, Monday to Saturday.

Public Holidays

- New Year's Day: 1 January
- Errol Barrow Day: 21 January
- Good Friday
- Easter Sunday
- Easter Monday
- National Heroes Day: 28 April
- Labour Day: 1 May
- Whit Monday: 8th Monday after Easter
- Emancipation Day: 1 August
- Kadooment Day: 1st Monday in August
- Independence Day: 30 November
- Christmas Day
- Boxing Day

Planning the Trip

Visas & Passports

For travel in and around the islands – including Barbados but not Trinidad and Tobago – it is not always necessary for US or Canadian citizens to bring their passports, although it is recommended (re-entry to the US is almost impossible without a passport). US travellers must, however, have some proof of citizenship – a birth certificate, naturalisation card, voter registration card or affidavit. Canadian citizens travelling without passports should carry a birth certificate as proof of citizenship. Citizens of both countries should also have some form of photo ID.

Citizens from outside North America need to carry a passport. All travellers going to – or even passing through – Trinidad and Tobago must have passports. Visas are usually required only of visitors from Eastern Europe and Cuba. In addition to proper documents, all travellers must have, upon entering the islands, a return or onward ticket, and adequate funds to support themselves for the duration of their stay.

EXTENSION OF STAY

To stay longer than three months an extension of stay can be obtained for a modest fee, but be prepared for a long wait. Take your passport, airline ticket and details of accommodation along with proof of ability to maintain financial support to the Immigration Office, The Wharf, Bridgetown, tel: 426 9912.

Customs

Passage through customs is usually straightforward, if you have nothing to declare. However, all bags are subject to inspection. Agricultural products, firearms, marijuana and narcotic drugs are forbidden. Import duties may be charged for everything except personal belongings including cameras and sports equipment, beyond the following exemptions: 1 litre of spirits, one half-pound (250 g) of tobacco and 50 cigars, or one carton of cigarettes. If you are planning to bring a number of gifts to Barbados, check well in advance with the Customs Department, tel: 427 5940, to determine what charges apply.

A word of caution: do not bring or wear any camouflage clothing because it is illegal in Barbados and will be confiscated.

Animal Quarantine

Barbados has no rabies; entry regulations for animals and frozen meat products are quite strict. Requirements vary depending on the animal and country of origin. On the whole, it is best to leave pets at home. However, if you plan to bring an animal, find out the pertinent regulations by writing to the Senior Veterinary Officer, Ministry of Agriculture and Rural Development, Pine, Plantation Road, Barbados, tel: 427 5073; fax: 429 2143.

TAKING GOODS HOME

Customs regulations for other countries than those below are regularly listed in *The Visitor* and other publications for tourists.

United States

US Customs regulations allow each resident to take home purchases totalling US$400 without paying duty, provided the resident has been out of the country at least 48 hours and has not claimed the exemption within the past 30 days. Family members living in the same household can pool their exemptions. Only one customs declaration form per couple or family travelling together is required. You may also mail home an unlimited number of gifts worth up to $50 each, as long as one person doesn't receive more than $50 worth in one day. However, these gifts may not include cigars, cigarettes, liquor or perfume. For more information, write for the booklet *Know Before You Go*, which is available from the US Customs Service, Washington, D.C. 20229.

Canada

Returning residents of Canada who have been out of the country over 48 hours may bring back C$200 worth of merchandise without paying duty. The merchandise must accompany the resident, and the exemption, claimed in writing, may be taken no more than once per quarter. Canadians who have been abroad more than seven days may bring home duty-free goods worth up to $300 once each calendar year. These goods may be shipped separately, but must be declared when the traveller reaches Canada. Canadians are eligible to take both the $200 and $300 exemptions on separate trips, but the two cannot be combined. Exempt goods may include: 50 cigars, 900 g (2 lb) of tobacco for residents over 16, 40 oz of wine or spirits, or 24 cans of beer, if you meet the age regulations of the province where you arrive.

United Kingdom

The total exemption on goods for residents returning to the UK from outside the EU is £136. In addition, 250 ml (9 fl oz) of eau de toilette, 60 ml (2 fl oz) of perfume, and, for persons over 17, 250 g (9 oz) of tobacco, or 200 cigarettes, or 100 cigarillos or 50 cigars can be brought. Duty-free alcohol is 1 litre (2 pints) of spirits or 2 litres (3½ pints) of sparkling wine, plus 2 litres (3½ pints) of still table wine.

Health

No special precautions are required prior to your trip, although many doctors recommend a hepatitis A vaccination. Barbados has some of the purest naturally filtered drinking water in the world and most tropical diseases were wiped out long ago.

Dengue fever: this disease is a growing hazard. Transmitted by mosquitoes, it commonly presents as a flu-like illness with aching bones (locally known as "break bone fever") and a rash. If you suspect that you may have been infected see a doctor immediately and avoid aspirin. In any case, it is advisable to take insect repellent with you to ward off mosquitos and sand flies.

Sun protection: the sun is perhaps the greatest hazard to visitors, when they underestimate its near-equatorial intensity. Regardless of your skin colour, wear a strong sunscreen, preferably at all times, but especially near water. To avoid serious sunburn, build up a tan gradually, starting with no more than 15 minutes exposure in the early morning or late afternoon. Wear a T-shirt when snorkelling to

Hazards in the Sea

- Certain jellyfish and sea anemones can cause painful injuries. Be sure to contact a doctor if you feel unwell after being stung or bitten.
- Try to avoid stepping on a sea-urchin; if you do, let the spines dissolve on their own rather than trying to pull them out.
- In the crowded waters, snorkelling without a marker can be fatal. Always tie a brightly coloured float such as a plastic bottle to your waist or ankle to alert jet skis and other water traffic of your position.
- However tired you may be, don't hang on to a buoy or anything else covered in a fine green seaweed because the sea lice living in it can cause a very itchy, painful skin reaction.

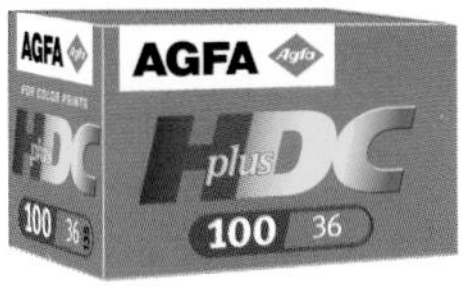

protect your back and shoulders.
Manchineel trees: these grow by the sea and are poisonous. They are usually indicated by red stripes painted on them and a warning notice. The crab apple-like fruit and the resin contain a poisonous substance (the Amerindians used it on their poison arrows) and when it rains they secrete an irritant that burns the skin. Do not touch the fruit or foliage, and do not sit beneath manchineel or coconut trees – falling nuts can cause injury.
AIDS: bear in mind that the incidence of the HIV virus has been increasing and AIDS is becoming a serious problem in Barbados.

Money Matters

Visitors may bring as much foreign currency as they can carry. It is simpler to use Barbadian currency, but US dollars at a fixed rate of BDS$1.98 to US$1 are accepted at most major stores and hotels, and by many taxi drivers. Always find out before you embark on any kind of trip or watersport, such as a catamaran cruise or waterskiing, whether the price quoted is in BDS$ or US$. Exchange rates are listed in the newspaper.

Barbadian paper notes come in denominations of $2 (blue), $5 (green), $10 (brown), $20 (mauve), $50 (orange) and $100 (grey). Coins come in 1, 5, 10 and 25-cent pieces. There is also a silver dollar.

Besides the many banks in Bridgetown and branches on the southern and western sides of the island, there are Barbados National Bank currency exchange booths in the departure lounge at Grantley Adams International Airport, open daily 8am until 10pm, and also at the harbour. Major credit cards and international brands of travellers' cheques (not Eurocheques) are accepted at most (but not all) hotels, restaurants and shops.
Cash machines: ATMs allow visitors with cards that are part of the Visa and Plus system 24-hour-a-day, seven-day-a-week banking. Money can be withdrawn – in Barbados dollars – from the cash machines located at Bridgetown banks and throughout the island. There are also facilities at larger supermarkets such as Julie 'N', on the ABC Highway by the Emancipation Monument, and Big 'B' supermarket, by Worthing in Christ Church.

What to Bring

Books, sunscreens, cosmetics, and sporting goods are expensive in Barbados because of import duties. A small radio will open up a world of local sounds and information.

What to Wear

Light, casual, tropical wear is recommended year-round. Best in the heat and humidity are cotton, linen or other natural fabrics. Evenings can be slightly more formal. A jacket for men and a dress or evening ensemble for women is appropriate at most elegant restaurants, although some require men to wear a jacket and tie. Most nightclubs do not admit men wearing hats or vest tops.

Modesty in dress should be a general rule, whatever you bring. Barbadians are a stylish but conservative people. Bathing suits are unacceptable except at the water's edge. Skimpy clothes look out of place in town, or at banks and shops. Always wear shoes and shirts in public places.

During the winter, the night air can be cool, so a light sweater or wrap will be useful.

Getting There

BY AIR

There are close to a dozen carriers offering flights to and from Barbados' Grantley Adams International Airport, one of the Caribbean's largest, most efficient facilities. The following airlines operate scheduled flights out of Barbados:
AeroPostal, tel: 436 1858. Daily to Caracas, Venezuela, except Thursday and Sunday.
Air Canada, tel: 428 5077. Daily to Canada in winter; four times a week in summer.
Air Caribbean, tel: 436 1858. Daily to Trinidad, except Saturday.
Air Jamaica, tel: 420 1956/57. Three times a week to New York and Montego Bay.
Air Martinique, tel: 436 1858. Four flights a week to Martinique.
American Airlines, tel: 428 4170. Daily to Miami and New York; two daily flights by American Eagle to San Juan.
British Airways, tel: 436 6413. Daily to London; Concorde flies once a week in winter and at peak times in summer.
BWIA, tel: 426 2111 (from Europe, tel: 0181-577 1100; from USA/ Canada, tel: 800-538 2942). Several times daily to Trinidad; once daily to Kingston, Antigua, Miami and New York; three times a week to London; twice a week to St Maarten.

Tourist Offices Abroad

The Barbados Tourism Authority (BTA) can help you plan your visit by providing brochures and information about festivals, tour packages and accommodations. BTA offices abroad are:

- **Canada:**
105 Adelaide Street West, Suite 1010, Toronto 214 9880, tel: 416-214 9882; 800 268 9122, fax: 416-214 9122
4800 de Maisonneuve W, Suite 532, Montreal, Quebec H3Z IM2, tel: 514-932 3206, fax: 514-932 3775
- **UK:**
263 Tottenham Court Road, London W1P 0LA, tel: 0171-636 9448/9449, fax: 0171-637 1496
- **USA:**
800 Second Avenue, New York, New York 10017, tel: 212-986 6516/6518; 800 221 9831 (toll free in US), fax: 212-573 9850
3440 Wilshire Blvd., Suite 1215, Los Angeles, California 90010, tel: 213-380 2198, fax: 213-384 2763.

Caribbean Weddings

Visitors can combine a wedding and honeymoon in Barbados. Tour companies offer complete packages, or you can organise it yourself through a wedding co-ordinator, usually on staff at the larger hotels.

No residential qualification is required to marry on the island and so you can, if you wish, marry on the day or within days of your arrival. As long as both parties are neither divorced nor widowed all that is needed are a valid passport, or birth certificate, and a marriage licence for which you will be charged a modest fee (BDS$150 plus BDS$25 stamp fee). Apply for a marriage licence at the Ministry of Home Affairs in the General Post Office Building, Cheapside, Bridgetown (tel: 228-8950). If either party has been divorced or widowed the original Decree Absolute or death certificate must be produced.

Ceremonies can take place in a church, hotel, on the beach or in any number of venues. Couples have been known to say "I do" on the Atlantis submarine and in the beautiful Flower Forest. For more information contact the BTA office in your home country – see the previous page, *Tourist Offices Abroad.*

Helen Air, tel: 0181-577 1100 (UK/Europe); 800-538 2942 (Canada/USA). Daily to St Lucia.
LIAT, tel: 434 5428; 266-0480 5610 (Antigua Head Office). Daily flights from Puerto Rico, Guyana and Eastern Caribbean.
Surinam Airlines, tel: 436 1858. Once a week to Trinidad and Guyana.
Virgin, tel: 418 8500. Flights three times a week to London.
Several charter airlines also service Barbados:
From the Eastern Caribbean: TIA, tel: 418 1650; SVG Air; Mustique Airways, tel: 428 1638 (daily to Bequia and Grenada).
From Canada: Royal Airlines, tel: 228 2550; Air Trans At, tel: 428 1060.
From the UK: Britannia, tel: 428 1661; Caledonian, tel: 426 1959; Monarch, tel: 428 1661.
From Europe: Condor, tel: 428 1661; Caribbean Airways, tel: 428 5660.

BY SEA

More than 500,000 cruise ship passengers visit Barbados every year, part of a pattern of growth that seems likely to continue. Bridgetown's Deep Water Harbour is within easy reach of the centre (½ mile/1 km) and has a vast cruise ship passenger terminal, with duty-free shopping, banking and a variety of facilities for travellers. Unfortunately, most seafaring visitors remain only for a day or less. The following cruise lines include the island on their schedules; the "800" telephone numbers are toll free in the country of origin only.

Carnival Cruise Lines, tel: 800-327 9501
Celebrity Cruises, tel: 800-327 6700
Clipper Cruise Line, tel: 800-325 0010
Club Med, tel: 800 CLUBMED
Costa Cruises, tel: 800-462 6782
Crystal Cruises, tel: 800-446 6620
Cunard Line, tel: 800 5-CUNARD (including Cunard Sea Goddess)
Fred Olsen Cruise Line, tel: 44-01473 292200
Holland America Line, tel: 800-426 0327
P&O Cruises, tel: 800-551 1000
Premier Cruise Lines, tel: 800-327 7113
Princess Cruises, tel: 800-421 0522
Radisson Seven Seas Cruises, tel: 800-285 1835
Royal Caribbean Cruise Line, tel: 800-327 6700
Seabourn Cruise Line, tel: 800-5-CUNARD
Silversea Cruises, tel: 800-722 6655
Star Clippers, tel: 800-442 0551
Sun Cruises, tel: 0171-623 5974
Windstar Cruises, tel: 800-258-SAIL

On Departure from Barbados

If you are leaving by plane, be at the airport two hours before your scheduled flight. LIAT is the only airline requiring reconfirmation. It is a good idea to make sure the flight is on time before leaving for the airport.

On leaving Barbados, everyone, including children, will be required to pay a BDS$25 departure tax. If travelling on a package, check with the tour company – the tax may have been included in the price of the holiday. You will also be asked to surrender the remaining portion of the Immigration Card you filled out on arrival. Beyond the customs and immigration checkpoint, the airport departure area has duty-free shops and several refreshment stands. But once you have entered this area, you will not be permitted to leave until your flight is called.

'Green' website

Tourism Concern is a UK-based charity working for fairer tourism. It provides an extensive community tourism directory: www.gn.apc.org/tourismconcern

Practical Tips

Media

Barbadians are kept informed by two daily newspapers and various magazines. The state-owned TV station and seven radio stations also provide news on current events and entertainment.

CANA (the Caribbean News Agency) is based in Barbados, serving print and electronic media throughout the Caribbean region and the rest of the world. CANA also operates a radio service.

NEWSPAPERS

There are two daily papers: *The Advocate*, established in 1895, and *The Nation*, established in 1973. Weekly newspapers are *The Investigator*, a tabloid which comes out on Friday, the *Broad Street Journal*, a free paper which comes out on Wednesday, and *The Visitor*, a free paper for tourists produced by *The Nation*. *Caribbean Week is* a fortnightly regional paper. *The Barbados Sunseeker* is a bi-monthly tourist supplement in *The Advocate*.

MAGAZINES

Ins and Outs of Barbados and *Barbados in a Nutshell* are annual publications specifically for visitors, both free and kept in hotels, etc. Other free magazines published annually, and available on newsstands, are *Simply Barbados*, a lifestyle magazine, *Sporting Barbados*, which focuses on the island's sporting activities, and *Business Barbados*, an international business publication for those interested in investing on the island.

Ringbang (Green Man Publishing) is a specialist Caribbean music magazine. It is also on sale in the US, the UK and Canada. Tel: 421 6700 for stockists or e-mail: ringbang@caribsurf.com.

TELEVISION & RADIO

Television is broadcast on Channel 8 by the Caribbean Broadcasting Corporation (CBC). CBC-TV also broadcasts pay-television which includes USA-based Cable News Network (CNN) news from 6–10am daily. STV (Subscription TV) offers a selection of cable stations and Direct TV is a satellite service. Domestic and satellite dishes in many hotels and bars are also a popular route to US and other foreign channels and programmes.

There are seven radio stations: CBC broadcasts on AM 900KHz; on FM are Radio Liberty (98.1MHz), BBS – Barbados Broadcasting Service (90.7MHz), YESS (104.1MHz), VOB – Voice of Barbados (92.90KHz), Faith (102.1MHz), a religious station, and HOTT (95.3MHz). All feature music, talk shows, and local, regional and international news.

INTERNET

There are many information services for the Caribbean region and several specific Barbados sites:
Cyberweek Communications Inc.: http://www.funbarbados.com
Miller Publishing Co.: http://www.insandouts-barbados.com
Barbados Tourism Authority (with Systems Caribbean Ltd): http://www.barbados.org/bta

Postal Services

There are post offices in all 11 parishes, as well as the large, modern General Post Office in Cheapside, Bridgetown (tel: 436 4800), which houses the island's main post office, parcel post, philatelic and registration/money order departments, open Monday to Friday 7.30am–5pm. Most other branches are open Monday to Friday 8am–3.15pm (3pm closing on Monday).

Weights & Measures

Officially, Barbados uses the metric system, though spoken directions and descriptions of quantities are often phrased in miles and pounds. Given below are some standard equivalents of metric units:
1 inch = 2.54 centimetres
1 foot = 0.305 metre
1 mile = 1.609 kilometres
1 sq. mile = 2.69 sq. km
1 gallon = 3.785 litres
1 ounce = 28.35 grams
1 pound = 0.434 kilogram

Telecommunications

The country code is **246**.

Cable & Wireless Bartel Ltd (tel: 292 2273) operates a dependable island-wide service. Overseas calls may be made in conjunction with Cable & Wireless BET Ltd (tel: 292 6000). Check the telephone directory or dial 0 for current overseas rate information; for local directory enquiries dial 411.

Calls from hotel rooms can be considerably more expensive than from a domestic or public phone. Phone cards, with a value of between BDS$10 and BDS$60, are available from many of the larger shops in Bridgetown and from hotels and Super Centre and 9 other supermarkets. Coin-operated phone booths are located throughout the island but international calls can only be made from card telephones. Cellular phones are available for rent through Cellcom, tel: 434-CELL.

Faxes and e-mail can be sent through hotel operators and post offices. BET also offers telex, fax, e-mail, video conferencing and other high-tech facilities.

An Internet and Data Service is offered Monday to Friday, 9am–4pm, by Karibik B'dos Tours Inc., St Lawrence Gap, Christ Church; tel: 428 1035, fax: 428 3172, e-mail: karibik@sunbeach.net.

Embassies & Consulates

Australia: Bishop's Court Hill, Pine Road, St Michael, tel: 435 2834.
Canada: Canadian High Commission/High Commissariat du Canada, Bishops Court Hill, Pine Road, St Michael, tel: 429 3550.
France: French Consulate, Waverly House, Hastings, Christ Church, tel: 435 6847.
Haiti: Sugarlands Farm, Salters, St George, tel: 436 6144.
Netherlands: Chickmont Foods Barbados Ltd, Balls Plantation, Christ Church, tel: 418 8074.
United Kingdom: British High Commission Building, Lower Collymore Rock, St Michael, tel: 430 7800, fax: 430 7860.
United States: Bridgetown, tel: 436 4950.
Venezuela: Hastings, Christ Church, tel: 435 7619.

The Tourist Office

The main office of the **Barbados Tourism Authority (BTA)** is in Bridgetown at Harbour Road, tel: 427 2623, fax: 426 4080, with branches at the airport, cruise terminal and at Cave Shepherd, Broad Street, Bridgetown.

Tipping

From the time you step into the arrivals hall and the porters (Red Caps) begin hounding you for your luggage, tips will be expected. Red caps are entitled to BDS$1 per bag. People tend to tip higher, but if a Red Cap tries to insist on more you are not obliged to give it.

Most restaurants will include a 10 or 15 percent service charge on the bill, and anything beyond that is purely discretionary. Check the tab or ask if you are not sure. If service is not included, tip 15 percent.

If you have maid service in your accommodation, you should leave a tip when you depart.

Religious Services

Traditionally, the Anglican Church has claimed the most members in Barbados, but over 140 religious groups are represented on the island. Most welcome visitors (properly dressed). The Yellow Pages of the telephone book has a list. There are also religious radio broadcasts on Sunday, and throughout the week. Among the many religious services are the following:

AFRICAN METHODIST EPISCOPAL CHURCH

Sealy Memorial Church, Collymore Rock, St Michael, tel: 427 1046. Sunday, 10am and 6.30pm.

ANGLICAN

St James Parish Church, Holetown, St James, tel: 422 4117. Sunday, 7.30am and 9am.
St Lawrence Church, St Lawrence Gap, Christ Church, tel: 435 6596. Sunday, 8am and 9.30am; Tuesday, 7am; Wednesday, 7.30pm.
St Mathias Church, St Mathias Gap, Hastings, Christ Church, tel: 429 5733. Sunday, 7am and 9.30am; first Sunday in the month, 6pm. Wednesday, 6.30am, Holy Communion 8.30am.
St Michael's Cathedral, Bridgetown, tel: 427 0790. Sunday, 6.30am, 7.45am, 9am, 11am and 6pm; Wednesday, 9.45am.

BAPTIST

Emmanuel Baptist Church, President Kennedy Drive, Eagle Hall, St Michael, tel: 426 2697. Sunday 8am, 10.30am and 6pm. Third Sunday in the month, 10am and 6pm only; Wednesday, 7.30pm.

CHURCH OF THE NAZARENE

St Christopher, nr Silver Sands, tel: 428 6253. Sunday, 11am and 7pm.
Speightstown, St Peter, tel: 422 1991. Sunday school, 9am, services at 10.15am and 6.30pm. Youth service Friday, 7.30pm.

HINDU

Sanatan Dhuram Maha (Barbados Inc.), Synagogue Lane, Bridgetown. Study group meets Sundays, at 3pm, followed by SRF meditation at 4pm.

JEWISH

Nidhe Israel Synagogue, Synagogue Lane, Bridgetown, tel: 427 7611.
The Schaare Tzedeck Synagogue, Rockley New Road, Christ Church, tel: 428 8414. Friday 7.30pm.

METHODIST

Bethel Methodist Church, Bay Street, Bridgetown, tel: 426 2223. Sunday, 9am and 6pm.
Hawthorne, Worthing, Christ Church, tel: 436 6859. Sunday 9am and 5pm.
Holetown, St James, tel: 436 6859. Sunday, 9am.

MUSLIM

Juma Mosque, Kensington New Road, Bridgetown, tel: 425 7854. Service five times daily and special service 12.30pm on Friday.

PENTECOSTAL

Abundant Life Assembly, Bank Hall, St Michael, tel: 427 9166. Sunday, 9.15am, 6pm; Wednesday, 7pm.
The People's Cathedral, Bishop Court Hill, Collymore Rock, St Michael, tel: 429 2145. Sunday, 7.30am, 10am, 5pm and 7pm. Sunday school, 9am. Wednesday, 7pm; Thursday, 11am; Friday, 7pm.

ROMAN CATHOLIC

St Dominic's, Maxwell Main Road, Christ Church, tel: 428 7677.

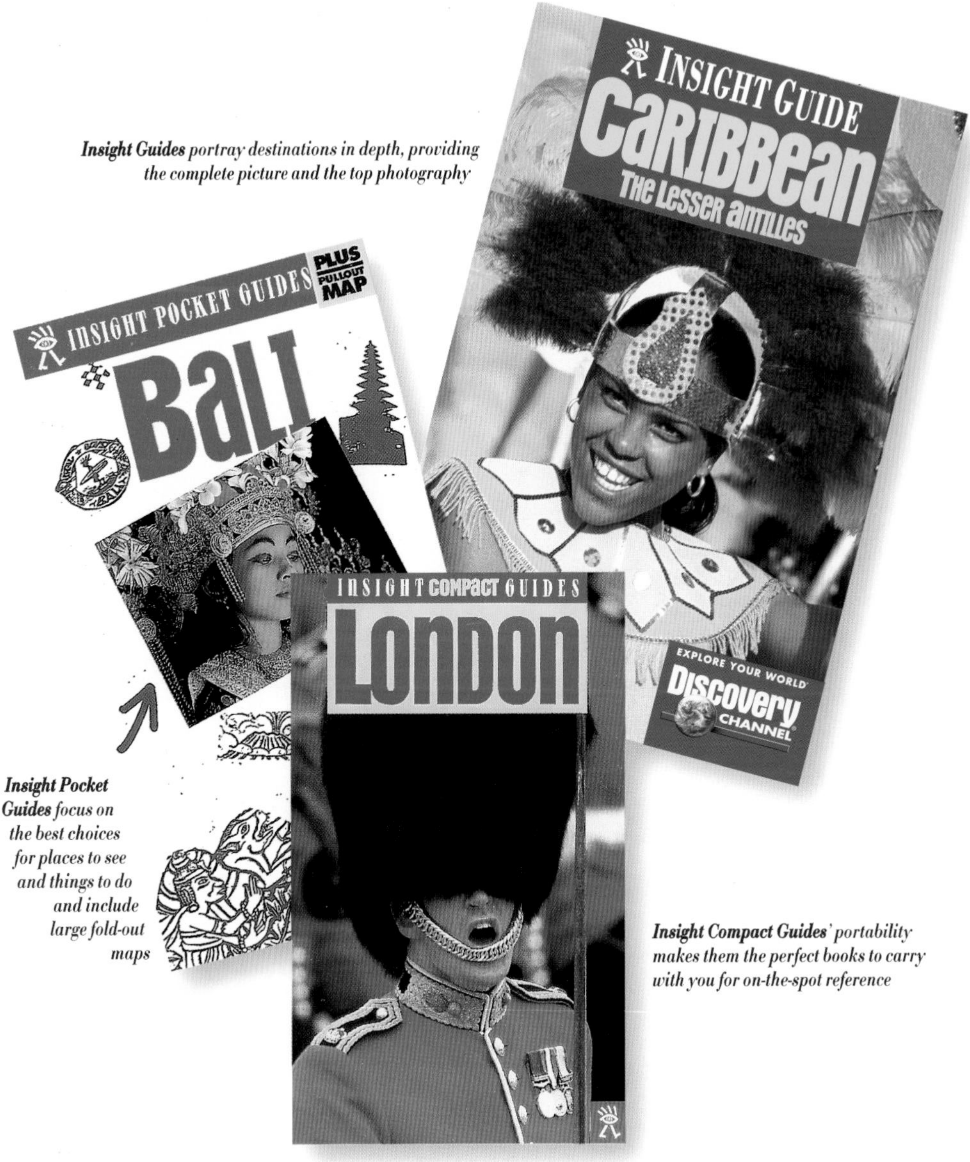

Sunday, 7.30am, 10am; Saturday, 6.30pm.
St Francis of Assisi, St James, tel: 422 2431. Sunday, 8am and 10.30am; Saturday, 5pm; Monday to Friday, 7am.
St Patrick's Cathedral, Jemmotts Lane, St Michael, tel: 426 2325. Sunday, 7am and 8.45am, and 6pm; Monday, Wednesday and Friday, noon; Saturday, 6pm.

- **Church of Jesus Christ of the Latter Day Saints**
Black Rock, St Michael; Rendezvous, Christ Church; Oistins, Christ Church, tel: 435 8595. Sunday, 10am.
- **Jehovah's Witness**
Kingdom Hall, Fontabelle, Bridgetown. Sunday, 9am.
- **Seventh Day Adventist**
Black Rock Church, Ellerslie Gap, Black Rock, St Michael, tel: 429 7234. Services in King Street, St Michael; Canevale, Christ Church; and Checker Hall, St Lucy.
- **Sons of God Apostolic Spiritual Baptists**
The Jerusalem Cathedral, Ealing Grove, Christ Church, tel: 436 0702. Service every Sunday at 3pm. The Zion Temple, Richmond Gap, St. Michael; service Wednesdays and Fridays at 7pm and the Beulah Temple, Bishops Tenantry, St. Lucy; service every Tuesday at 7pm.

Medical Treatment

There are a number of physicians and dentists in Barbados, particularly in and around Bridgetown, and medical provision is generally good. The general hospital, **Queen Elizabeth Hospital** (tel: 436 6450) is in St Michael; it operates a 24-hour accident and emergency department but waiting time can be between four and 24 hours. A modern, private facility, **Bay View Hospital** (tel: 436 5446), is also in St Michael. The Barbados Defence Force has a **decompression chamber** for divers. FMH is a private emergency medical clinic also in St Michael, tel: 228 6120, offering a quick, efficient service.
The **Get Help Service**, tel: 438 4357, is a private emergency service which provides a 24-hour Doctor on Call, ground and air ambulance services.

Medical insurance from recognised insurance plans may be accepted at private facilities, but you should verify this first. The Queen Elizabeth Hospital does not as a rule accept overseas medical plans, nor does it take credit cards.

Emergency Numbers

Police	Tel: 211
Fire	Tel: 311
Ambulance	Tel: 511
Coast Guard	Tel: 427 8819
Get Help Service	Tel: 438 4357
Samaritans	Tel: 429 9999

Helpline staffed 8–11pm Monday to Thursday; 5–11pm Friday; 1–11pm Saturday and Sunday.

Alcoholics Anonymous	Tel: 426 1600

Security & Crime

Use common sense in Barbados as you would in any other cosmopolitan area. Place valuables in the hotel safe; do not leave them unattended in your room or at the beach. Leave your key at the hotel reception desk before going out. Avoid walking alone after dark on deserted streets and beaches.

Etiquette

Good manners are extremely important in Barbados. Visitors are expected to act like guests: to say "please" and "thank you," and to ask permission before taking anyone's picture and offer a tip. It is considered impolite not greet someone with "good morning," "good afternoon," or "good evening," when you pass them on the road or enter a shop. Always use a greeting before asking a question – like asking for directions – or requesting service.

Getting Around

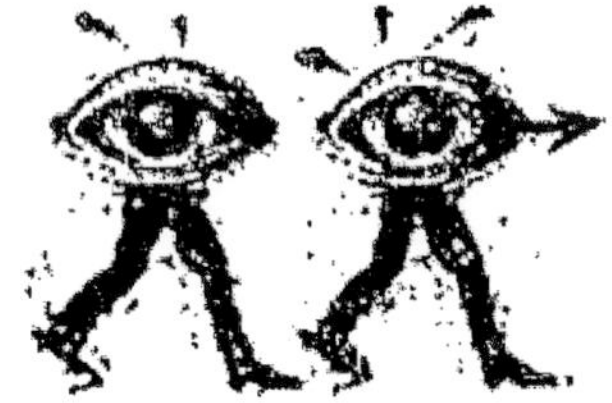

On Arrival

Just prior to arriving by land or sea, you will be asked to fill out an immigration form. Save the perforated stub. You will need it for departure. Also be prepared to show your return ticket and tell the Immigration Officer your address in Barbados. If you arrive at the airport without a hotel reservation, there are telephones and information on accommodation in the arrival area. You may make arrangements and report back to Immigration.

Airport baggage handlers assist arriving and departing passengers at a charge of BDS$1 per item.

Unless your package vacation includes airport transfers, or you have arranged to pick up a rental car, you will probably take a taxi to and from the airport.

Current fares from the airport (for government taxis – see next page) are:

North of Speightstown	BDS$55
Holetown	BDS$38
Garrison	BDS$24
Bridgetown Harbour	BDS$30
Sam Lord's Castle	BDS$22
St Lawrence Gap	BDS$20

Maps

Basic maps are available at most hotels and tourist information desks. The free *Barbados Island Guide* lists places of interest and suggests a sight-seeing tour route. A word of caution, though: depend only on the most current maps. Barbados has worked hard on its roads and older maps do not include all the improvements.

Barbados in a Nutshell is a free

publication available in hotels and tourist information offices, which provides good maps of the island, and the *Barbados Holiday Map* is another free map available everywhere.

Taxis

In Barbados, taxis do not have meters, but charge pre-determined fares, based on location and mileage. In general, the fare should not be greater than BDS$2.25 per mile or $1.50 per kilometre. Hourly rates should not be greater than $32. For an air-conditioned taxi add 25 percent to published rates. Be warned, however: these are government rates. Most taxis actually charge at least BDS$4 more.

Many taxi cab companies offer tour services as well. It is wise to establish the fare before embarking on your journey.

Public Transportation

You can travel to any part of Barbados by bus – either the larger Transport Board buses, smaller privately operated minibuses, or ZR vans. All cost BDS$1.50 for any journey. Board at numerous bus stops on most major thoroughfares. Bus stops will be marked "In to City" or "Out of City". In Bridgetown, the main Transport Board terminals are on Fairchild Street for south-bound commuters, or Lower Green and Princess Alice Highway for coastal routes. A few route numbers to watch out for are 12 to Sam Lord's Castle, 13a to St Christopher via the South Coast, 6 to Bathsheba and 4 to Harrison's Cave. Minibus and ZR van terminals are at Temple Yard, Probyn Street and River Road.

The Barbados Transport Board (tel: 436 6820) will provide additional information upon request.

Private Transportation

CAR RENTAL

Driving is the best way to appreciate the distinct character of Barbados' parishes, and the only way to reach a good share of attractions in a reasonable amount of time. In order to drive on the island, you must present a driver's licence from your home country along with a fee of BDS$10. Driving licences for visitors are available at police stations and from car rental companies. Most will deliver your licence along with your car. Alternatively, you can arrange car rental before you travel and have the car and licence waiting for you at the airport.

Car rental in Barbados is handled by local fleets and garages. Charges vary for an open-top Mini Moke, cross-country four-wheel-drive vehicles and saloon cars. Additional collision damage waivers cost about $10 per day. Some companies rent cars only for two days or more, and most require a substantial refundable deposit which can usually be paid by a recognised credit card.

Some of the larger car rental companies are:

Auto Rentals Ltd, Kendal Hill, Christ Church, tel: 228 1520, fax: 426 1583.
Coconut Car Rentals Ltd, Bayside, Bay Street, St Michael, tel: 437 0297, fax: 228 9820.
Corbin's Car Rentals Inc., Collymore Rock, St Michael, tel: 427 9531, fax: 427 7975, e-mail: corbin's@ndl.net.
Courtesy Rent-a-Car, Rendezvous, Christ Church, tel: 431 4133; 418 2500 (airport), fax: 429 6387.
Direct Car Rentals Ltd, Chelmead, Chelsea Gardens, St Michael, tel: 228 2491, fax: 228 2492.
Drive-a-matic, Lower Carlton, St James, tel: 422 4000; 435 7670 (Worthing), fax: 435 7537.
Stoutes Car Rentals Ltd, Kirtans, St Philip, tel: 435 4456, fax: 435 4435.

TWO-WHEEL RENTAL

Motor scooters can be rented for about US$50 per day, or US$210 per week. Usually there is an additional US$50 deposit to pay. Helmets are required by law and come with the rental. Also required is a motorcycle licence or driver's licence including a motorcycle endorsement. Motor scooters can be rented from **Caribbean Scooters**, Bridge House, Waterfront Marina, Bridgetown, tel: 436 8522. Hourly, daily and weekly rates. Pick up scooters from outlets at Bridgetown Port, Bridge House or the Material Things store (opposite Sandy Beach Hotel, Worthing).

Bicycles can be rented from **Rob's Mountain Bikes**, Hastings, Christ Church, tel: 437 3404 and **Jordan and Jorday**, Flamboyant Avenue, Sunset Crest, St. James, tel: 432-0178.

Driving Tips

- Most importantly, remember in Barbados you drive on the left-hand side of the road.
- At roundabouts, take the left lane if you intend turning first left; otherwise take the right lane. The vehicle on your right has the right of way (i.e. the vehicle approaching that is already on the roundabout).
- Barbadians honk their horns either as a warning of their presence, or as a greeting.
- If another driver flashes their lights at you, it means "after you".
- Avoid driving during the morning and evening rush hours, from 7.30–8.30am and 4.30–5.30pm.

Where to Stay

Accommodation Guide

Most of Barbados' expensive hotels are on the West Coast. The less expensive hotels are generally located on the South Coast. There are a few hotels dotted around the southeast and east coasts, each with their own ambience. Many places offer more than one type of accommodation, from basic rooms to luxury suites. The rates during the winter (15 December to 15 April) can be double the summer rates. Hotel tax is 7.5 percent; 10 percent service charge is usually added as well. Renting a villa or apartment is a good alternative to staying in a hotel, especially as many have maid service.

Hotel Price Guide

Winter (high season) rates for a double room (two people) per night:

$	less than BDS$300
$$	BDS$300–599
$$$	more than BDS$600

Hotels & Apartments

SOUTH COAST

Accra Beach Hotel, Rockley, Christ Church, tel: 435 8920, fax: 435 6794; e-mail: accrahotel@sunbeach.net. Completely refurbished, modern oceanfront complex. Comfortable rooms, lovely pool, restaurants and shops within the compound. Gym, squash, conference rooms. Standard rooms, penthouses, ocean or island view. Disabled access. **$$**

Asta Beach Hotel, Palm Beach, Hastings, tel: 427 2541, fax: 426-9566. Oceanfront studios and suites. Good choice for business people because it is close to town. Each room has a fully equipped kitchen. Pool. **$$**

Casuarina Beach Club, St Lawrence Gap, tel: 428 3600, fax: 4281970. Beachfront hotel and apartments with tennis courts, swimming pool and mini mart, set in tropical gardens. Rooms with garden or ocean view. Studio, one- and two-bedroom units, all with kitchen. Excellent service. Restaurant and bar. **$$**

Cleverdale Guesthouse Worthing, Christ Church, tel: 428 1035, fax: 428 3172. Colonial-style house with four bedrooms a stone's throw from Sandy Beach. Guests have use of whole house and verandah. **$**

Club Rockley, Golf Club Road, Rockley, Christ Church, tel: 435 7880, fax: 435 8015. All-inclusive resort with 9-hole golf course, pools and tennis. Not on the beach, but transportation provided. **$$$**

Coconut Court, Hastings, Christ Church, tel: 427 1655, fax: 429 8198. Beachfront apartments with pool, jacuzzi, restaurant and bar. **$**

Divi Southwinds Hotel and Beach Club, St Lawrence, Christ Church, tel: 428 7181, fax: 428 4674. Luxury spacious rooms. Pool, tennis, restaurant, mini mart, conference facilities. Central to the South Coast's nightlife. **$$**

Magic Isle Beach Apartments, Rockley, Christ Church, tel: 435 6760, fax: 435 8558. No frills self-catering beach apartments, one or two-bedroom, all with sea view. Oceanfront location, 20 minutes from airport, 10 minutes from town. Quiet, with shops and many restaurants within walking distance. Pool. Suitable for families and couples. **$$**

Sand Acres/Bougainvillea, Maxwell Coast Road, Christ Church, tel: 428 7141, fax: 428 2524 (Sand Acres); tel: 418 0900, fax: 418 0995 (Bougainvillea). Beachfront hotels set amidst lush tropical gardens. Suite accommodation, pools, tennis and a great restaurant. **$$$**

Sandy Beach, Worthing, Christ Church, tel: 435 8000, fax: 435 8053. Studios, one- and two-bedroom suites, apartments with kitchen. Relaxed, friendly, centrally located close to banks, shopping and restaurants. Lush gardens, pool and beach. **$$**

Sierra Guesthouse, St Lawrence Gap, Christ Church, tel: 428 1035, fax: 428 3172. Small three-bedroomed guesthouse on the edge of the Gap, 250 yds (230 metres) from beach. The whole house can be rented too. Garden. Room service. Close to good facilities. **$**

Silver Rock, Silver Sands, Christ Church, tel: 428 2866, fax: 420 6982. Home to the windsurfing fraternity. A little out of the way. **$**

Southern Palms, St Lawrence Gap, Christ Church, tel: 428 7171, fax: 428 7175. Two pools, tennis, watersports, beauty salon. Pleasant and centrally located. **$$**

Time Out at The Gap, St Lawrence Gap, Christ Church, tel: 420 5021, fax: 420 5034. Located across the road from Dover Beach, Caribbean-style architecture. All rooms with fridge, cable TV and comfy beds. Pub with three happy hours. Sporty atmosphere, ideal for young, active holiday-makers. **$**

Time Out at Rockley (formerly Blue Horizon), Rockley Main Road, Christ Church, tel: 435 8916, fax: 435 8153; e-mail: bhorizon@bluehorizon.com
Across the road from the popular Accra Beach. Rooms with garden or

Holiday Renting

Several local agents provide a range of villas, apartments and studio-apartments to rent:

Alleyne, Aguilar & Altman Ltd, St James, tel: 432 0340, fax: 432 2147.

Bajan Services Ltd, Gibbs, St Peter, tel: 422 2618, fax: 422 5366.

Karibik B'dos Tours Inc., St Lawrence Gap, Christ Church, tel: 428 1035, fax: 428 3172. Also provides rooms in guesthouses.

Realtas Ltd, St James, tel: 432-6930, fax: 432 6919.

Ronald Stoute & Sons Ltd, St Philip, 423 6800, fax: 423 9935.

Holiday rentals: http://www.holiday-rentals.co.uk./pages/barbados

ocean view, each with a fridge, cable TV and comfy beds. Sporty with two pools, small convenience store. **$**
Turtle Beach Resort, St Lawrence Gap, Christ Church, tel: 428 7131, fax: 428 6089. Luxurious all-inclusive resort with suites with ocean view. The only 5-star hotel on the South Coast. **$$$**
Woodville Beach Hotel, Hastings, Christ Church, tel: 435 6693, fax: 435 9211. Self-contained, no frills one- or two-bedroom units or studios, with air-conditioning or ceiling fan. Restaurant and bar. Quiet, relaxed and friendly, family-orientated. Pool. **$**

WEST COAST

Almond Beach Village, Heywoods, St Peter, tel: 422 4900, fax: 422 0617. All-inclusive resort. Rooms and suites with garden or ocean views. Pools, tennis, 9-hole golf course, watersports, conference room, fitness centre, squash, kids' facilities. Four restaurants, five bars. In the northwest. **$$$**
Cobblers Cove Hotel, Road View, St Peter, tel: 422 2291, fax: 422 1460. Elegant beachfront hotel built around a country house. Pool, beach, tennis, watersports. One- and two-bedroom suites, two with private pools. Excellent restaurant. Friendly and luxurious. **$$$**
Coconut Creek, Derricks, St James, tel: 432 0803, fax: 432 0272. All-inclusive resort set on a low bluff overlooking sandy coves. Pool, jacuzzi, watersports, bars and restaurants. Relaxed, informal atmosphere. Popular with couples. **$$**
Colony Club Hotel, Porters, St James, tel: 422 2335, fax: 422 0667. Elegant resort with pool, rooms and suites with garden and ocean view. Two restaurants, three bars, meeting facilities, beauty salon, tennis, fitness centre, luxury lagoon-style pool. Five-star accommodation, informal but very good service. **$$$**
Coral Reef Club, Holetown, St James, tel: 422 2372, fax: 422 1776. Family-owned 5-star beach resort with cottages set among 12 acres (5 hectres) of lush tropical gardens. Pools, restaurants, tennis and watersports. **$$$**
Crystal Cove Hotel, Appleby, St James, tel: 432 2683, fax: 432 8290. All-inclusive luxury hotel, with excellent facilities including two bars, two restaurants, pools, watersports, garden and ocean views. No meeting facilities. Vibrant tropical atmosphere. **$$$**
Discovery Bay Hotel, Holetown, St James, tel: 432 1301, fax: 432 2553. Plantation-house style, set in tropical gardens, with conference facilities. Close to fine dining and shops. Pool, garden and ocean view rooms, restaurant and bars. **$$$**
Glitter Bay Resort, Porters, St James, tel: 422 5555, fax: 422 3940. Great House with deluxe rooms, one- and two-bedroom suites and penthouses with garden or ocean views. Meeting facilities, three pools, tennis, fitness room, watersports. Royal Westmoreland golf course is nearby. **$$$**
Inn on the Beach, Holetown, St James, tel: 432 0385, fax: 432 2440. Ocean view studios. Restaurant and easy access to the shops, dining and watersports. **$**
Royal Pavillion, Porters, St James, tel: 422 5555, fax: 422 3940. Deluxe oceanfront suites set within 30 acres. Conference facilities, restaurants and bars. A sister property to Glitter Bay, it shares the same leisure facilities. **$$$**
Sandpiper, Holetown, St James, tel: 422 2251, fax: 422 1776. Beach-front, intimate resort, suites with garden and ocean views. Excellent restaurant, pool and watersports. **$$$**
Settlers Beach Villa Hotel, Holetown, St James, tel: 422 3052. Ocean-side villas set amongst lush tropical gardens. Pool, bar, Ile de France restaurant. Watersports, tennis and golf nearby. **$$$**
Tamarind Cove Hotel, Paynes Bay, St James, tel: 432 1332, fax: 432 6317. Large luxury hotel, rooms and suites with garden and ocean view. Pool, three great restaurants, three bars, meeting facilities. A stylish and popular hotel. **$$–$$$**
Treasure Beach Hotel, Paynes Bay, St James, tel: 432 1346, fax: 432 1094. Award-winning dining, fine rooms with pool, garden and ocean views. **$$$**

Hotel Price Guide

Winter (high season) rates for a double room (two people) per night:

$	less than BDS$300
$$	BDS$300–599
$$$	more than BDS$600

Children's Facilities

Most hotels give substantial discounts for children, and often children under 12 stay free in their parents' room. Many hotels have babysitters or can provide one on request. Some resorts also offer lessons in watersports that children will enjoy. Still, if you have young children, you may find that an apartment or villa with its own cooking facilities is more convenient than a hotel.

SOUTHEAST & EAST COASTS

Atlantis Hotel, Bathsheba, St Joseph, tel: 433 9445. Basic lodging. Wonderful Bajan cuisine. **$**
Crane Beach Hotel, St Philip, tel: 423 6220, fax: 433 9902. Dramatic oceanfront setting with a clifftop pool and tennis. Fantastic views and beach. Rooms with antique furnishings and four-poster beds. Excellent restaurant. **$$**
Edgewater Inn, Bathsheba, St Joseph, tel: 433 9900, fax: 433 9902. Secluded, ocean view rooms. Pool. Variable service. **$**
Sam Lord's Castle, Long Bay, St Philip, tel: 423 7350, fax: 423 6361. All-inclusive resort with suites and castle rooms, on a legendary pirate's estate. Three restaurants, four bars, secluded beach but rough sea. Live entertainment, tennis, pools, gym. Conference facilities. **$$**

Where to Eat

What to Eat

Barbados has restaurants featuring everything from traditional Bajan cuisine to Asian, Mediterranean and Italian. National dishes to try include the delicious (and ubiquitous) flying fish, "dolphin" fish (actually dorado), red snapper, hot saltfish cakes, pickled breadfruit, cake-like conkies, and pepperpot – a stew made in a pot so well-seasoned that it literally used to be passed down like an heirloom from generation to generation. As a rule Barbadian food is well seasoned and usually accompanied by rice and peas (pigeon peas), macaroni pie, plantain, yam or sweet potato. The Barbadian speciality of *cou-cou* (mashed cornmeal and okra) is also a popular side dish.

"Pudding" (black or white, made from pig's intestines) and "souse" (pickled pig's head or feet) are Barbadian poor man's foods, traditionally eaten on Saturday.

Barbados also has its share of fast food. A Bajan-style fast food is *roti* – a savoury pocket of curried chicken, beef, shrimp or potato that originated with Trinidad's East Indian population.

Where to Eat

Some of the grander hotels and restaurants offer international cuisine prepared under the direction of European chefs. However, there are also some international-class Barbadian chefs. Sample the home-grown talent by ordering fried fish on Thursday, Friday and Saturday evenings at Oistins – Friday night is the busiest.

Eating out in Barbados can be expensive; even some of the fast-food establishments charge more than you would pay at home. Best for less expensive eating is the South Coast.

Restaurants start serving around 6.30–7pm and take last orders around 10pm. It's advisable to make a reservation. In most cases VAT is included in the quoted price but 10 percent service charge is usually added to the restaurant bill.

SOUTH COAST

Café Sol, St Lawrence Gap, Christ Church, tel: 435 9531. Lively Mexican restaurant with indoor and outdoor dining. Two happy hour sessions. Open for dinner seven nights. Popular with locals. **$–$$**

Meal Price Guide

Cost of a three-course meal for one person, excluding drinks:

$	less than BDS$50
$$	BDS$51–90
$$$	BDS$91–149
$$$$	More than BDS$150 (top-class cuisine)

Captain's Carvery at **The Ship Inn**, St Lawrence Gap, Christ Church, tel: 435 6961. Lunch and dinner is Bajan buffet-style with salad bar. Casual with live entertainment every evening in a popular night spot. **$–$$**

Caribbean Bar, 2nd Ave., Worthing, Christ Church, tel: 435 8540. Casual beach bar on a sandy beach. Open daily for lunch and dinner. Live music on weekends. **$**

Champers, Hastings, Christ Church, tel: 435 6644. Extensive blackboard menu. Central South Coast seafront location. Lively bar. Excellent presentation and service. Open for lunch and dinner every day. **$$–$$$**

David's Place, St Lawrence Main Road, Worthing, Christ Church, tel: 435 9755. Authentic Barbadian cuisine. Excellent, friendly service. Open Tuesday to Sunday for dinner. **$$**

Jeremiah's Bistro, Maxwell Coast Road, Christ Church, tel: 420 3080. Casual, friendly atmosphere, good for families. Varied, affordable menu. Two happy hour sessions. Open Monday to Friday for lunch; dinner every night. **$$**

Josef's, St Lawrence Gap, Christ Church, tel: 435 8254. International cuisine using fresh ingredients at one of the top South Coast restaurants. Open for lunch and dinner. **$$$**

The Lunch Club, Hastings, Christ Church, tel: 228 3649. Tasty gourmet sandwiches, fresh chocolate chip cookies and freshly blended juices. Take away service available. Sandwiches BDS$9–18. Monday to Friday 9am–5pm, Saturday 10am–4.30pm. **$**

McBride's Pub and Cookhouse, St Lawrence Gap, Christ Church, tel: 435 6352. The only authentic Irish pub and restaurant in Barbados. Pool table, darts, satellite TV and nightly entertainment. **$–$$**

Shak Shak, Hastings, Christ Church, tel: 435 1234. Relaxed, sophisticated spot with a menu inspired by the sea. Pizzeria and bustling bar with live entertainment several nights a week. Excellent service. Open for lunch and dinner. **$–$$$**

39 Steps, Chattel Plaza, Hastings, Christ Church, tel: 427 0715. Wine bar and restaurant with delicious lunches and dinners at reasonable prices. Lively, informal atmosphere, live jazz every other Saturday. **$$**

WEST COAST

Bomba's, Paynes Bay, St James, tel: 432 0569. Beach bar popular with visitors and locals lunchtime and evening. Daily specials: pasta, vegetarian, chicken, fish, curries. Run by a Scottish chef and a Bajan Rasta. Open 11am–11pm. **$$**

Bourbon Street, Prospect, St James, tel: 424 4557. Authentic Louisiana/Cajan cuisine. Blues and jazz by the ocean. "Tasty Treats" menu for late night diners. Open for dinner daily except Monday. **$$$**

Carambola Restaurant, Derricks, St James, tel: 432 0832, fax: 432 6183. Romantic clifftop setting with delicious French and Caribbean and a touch of Asian cuisine. Ideal for special occasions. Occasional live music in the Copper Club Bar. Open for dinner only. **$$$**
The Cliff, Derricks, St James, tel: 432 1922. One of the island's top restaurants and among the most expensive. Excellent food, impeccable service and wonderful views. Open daily for dinner. **$$$$**
The Coach House, Paynes Bay, St James, tel: 432 1163. Recently revamped sports bar. Fish, steak and vegetarian cusine. Live entertainment nightly. Open for lunch. **$–$$**
Fathoms, Paynes Bay, St James, tel: 432 2568. Oceanfront restaurant with a varied menu. Seafood speciality. Quality dining at reasonable prices. Open for lunch and dinner. **$$**
Indigo Bar and Restaurant, Holetown, St James, tel: 432 2996. The menu changes daily, served in a friendly, casual but elegant setting. Open for lunch (around BDS$50) and dinner 11am–11pm, bar open late. **$$–$$$**
Kitchen Korner, 2nd Street, Holetown, St James, tel: 432 1684. Cosy, lovely spot and irresistible food to eat in or take away. Salads, pies, soups and quiches. **$–$$**
The Lone Star, The Garden, St James, tel: 419 0599. Beachfront place with Mediterranean, Caribbean and European dishes. Daily from 10am for lunch and dinner. **$–$$$**

Meal Price Guide

Cost of a three-course meal for one person, excluding drinks:

$	less than BDS$50
$$	BDS$51–90
$$$	BDS$91–149
$$$$	More than BDS$150 (top-class cuisine)

Mango's, Speightstown, St Peter, tel: 422 0704. Oceanfront elegance with friendly staff and fresh, simple food. **$**
The Mews, 2nd Street, Holetown, St James, tel: 432 1122, fax: 432 1136. Superb seafood dishes. Live jazz on Friday nights. Also a good after-dinner rendezvous spot. **$$$**
Mullins Beach Bar, Mullins Bay, St Peter, tel: 422 1878. Attractive beach-side property. The quality of the food varies but it is a popular place to stop after an island tour. Expensive and the service can be slow. **$$**
Nico's Champagne Wine Bar, Derricks, St James, tel: 432 6386. Wine bar with good food in an informal setting. The varied menu includes local lobster. Open daily for lunch and dinner. **$$–$$$**
Olives Bar & Bistro, 2nd Street, Holetown, St James, tel: 432 2112. Imaginative Caribbean/ Mediterranean cuisine served in a friendly, casually elegant atmosphere indoors or out in the courtyard. Upstairs bar serves pâté, salads, pasta and pizza. Open for dinner daily. **$$$**
Patisserie Flinat, 1st Street, Holetown, St James, tel: 432 2626. Fine pastries, savouries and desserts which can be enjoyed on the spot with coffee, or taken away. **$**
The Restaurant, Sandy Lane Golf Club, St James, tel: 432 2838. Flavours of the Caribbean and Asia. Open all day, closed on Monday. Elegant dining. **$$$$**

BRIDGETOWN & ST MICHAEL

Brown Sugar, Aquatic Gap, St Michael, tel: 436 7069. Authentic Creole cuisine, renowned Planter's buffet lunch served daily, except Saturday. Popular with the business set. Open for dinner too. **$–$$**
Rusty Pelican, upstairs at the Bridge House on the Careenage, Bridgetown, tel: 436 7778. Seafood and great atmosphere; live music. Popular for lunch and dinner. Closed for Sunday lunch and dinner on Monday, except January to April. **$$**
The South Deck, The Boatyard, Carlisle Bay, Bridgetown, tel: 436 2620. Five minutes walk from town. Mediterranean bistro-style menu, casual atmosphere. Lively party spot when the sun goes down. Views over Carlisle Bay. **$$–$$$**
Waterfront Café, The Careenage, Bridgetown, tel: 427 0093, fax: 431 0303. Traditional Bajan and Creole cuisine at reasonable prices with live music every night. Caribbean buffet on Tuesday nights. Open for lunch and dinner, closed Sunday. **$$**

Fast Food

- The **Chefette** chain has nine branches including six drive-thrus. Some have children's playgrounds and BBQ areas. The varied menu includes chicken, burgers, rotis, pizza, nuggets, fries, shakes and ice cream.
- The reasonably priced **BBQBarn Chefette** restaurants at Rockley, Holetown, Bridgetown and Warrens serve good barbequed steak, chicken, fish and burgers, with a great salad bar.
- There are seven **KFC** (Kentucky Fried Chicken) outlets: Bridgetown, Hastings, Collymore Rock, Black Roc and Speightstown.
- **Chicken Barn** in Worthing, Christ Church, serves delicious Bajan fast food, including rotisserie-cooked chicken.
- **Fat Andy's** in Hastings, Christ Church, tel: 435 8121, is a 1950s-style air-conditioned diner with take-away service too. Pizzas, burgers, chicken.
- **The Roti Hut,** Worthing Main Road, Christ Church, tel: 435 7362, has the largest selection of rotis on the island.
- **Pizzas** are made at Chefettes (pizza hotline, tel: 436 6000) and Fat Andy's, and also at:

Pizza Man Doc, St Lawrence Gap, Christ Church, tel: 435 8918.
Gigi's Pizzeria, Rockley, Christ Church, tel: 435 7768.
Pizzaz, Holetown, St James, tel: 432 0227.

Drinking Notes

Sugar may no longer be king on Barbados, but the island **rum** is certainly royalty among tropical drinks – and worth taking home. Mount Gay and Cockspur are two of the most popular brands, but don't forget Doorly's and Malibu. Caution: rum punches served in bars are stronger than they seem.

The local Banks **beer** is considered by those in the know to be among the best in the Caribbean and, some say, the world. Carib, a Trinidadian beer, is also increasingly popular.

Fresh **fruit juices**, a Caribbean staple, are available in any café or bar and from street vendors. Other drinks include mauby (from bark soaked in spices) – an acquired taste – fresh ginger beer, spicy sorrel, and coconut water (green coconuts are sold by roadside vendors, who supply you with a straw to drink direct from the fruit – and will open it up afterwards so you can eat the jelly-like flesh).

EAST COAST

Atlantis Hotel, Bathsheba, St Joseph, tel: 433 9445. Original West Indian dishes. Renowned Sunday buffet. Daily Bajan lunch has not changed in 20 years. **$**
Bonito Restaurant and Bar, Bathsheba, St Joseph, tel: 433 9034; 433 9451. Bajan home cooking with freshly caught fish, just across from the beach. Open 10am–6pm. **$$**
Edgewater Inn, Bathsheba, St Joseph, tel: 433 9900. Lunch with a view. Traditional Bajan food. A good place to stop for a swim in the pool and a drink. **$$**
Round House, Bathsheba, St Joseph, tel: 433 9678. Delicious, wholesome food cooked with fresh ingredients in a beautiful spot. Closed Monday. **$$**

Culture

Heritage

Established in 1961, the **Barbados National Trust** (BNT) owns many of the island's most significant heritage sites and historic properties; tel: 436 9033 for a programme.

The National Trust runs a **Heritage Passport** scheme, whereby passport holders are entitled to reductions in admission prices (or in a few cases, free admission) to BNT properties. The "passports" are now free and are available from hotels, restaurants, ticket offices, etc., or contact the Barbados National Trust, tel: 426 2421. The passport itself, a glossy colour booklet, makes a good souvenir to keep.

The Barbados National Trust also administers the **Open House Programme** – the annual opening of privately owned houses of historic or architectural interest (Wednesday afternoons, January to April).

For details of walks organised by the National Trust, often taking in heritage sites, see *Sport: Guided Hikes*.

Theatre & Dance

Venues for dance and theatrical performances throughout the year are the **Daphne Joseph-Hackett Theatre** and **The Steel Shed**, both run by the National Cultural Foundation at Queen's Park, Bridgetown, tel: 427 2345; **Combermere School Hall**, Waterford, St Michael, tel: 429 3431. **The Sherbourne Centre** on Two Mile Hill and the **National Stadium** in Bridgetown stage large events. Bridgetown's handsome **Frank Collymore Hall** in the Tom Adams Financial Centre (tel: 436 9083) hosts almost continuous events, from jazz concerts, to ballet, to theatre.

Other Performances

The **National Cultural Foundation (NCF)** organises various events, including a three-day Writers' Fest in April, with writing competitions, readings and workshops. Contact the NCF on 424 0907/9.

Interludes: innovative poetry and jazz performances by local poets and musicians of their own work, ranging from reggae-based rhythm poetry to poetry set to jazz or blues. Runs in multiple week seasons. Look in the local press for dates and venues or call 437 4136, fax: 437 4135.

VOICES (Barbados Writers Collective): meets monthly at The Barbados Museum & Historical Society. Performances are open to the public, and at the Open Mic Session members of the audience are invited to share their work too.

See the following *Festivals* section for information about annual cultural events.

Voice of Barbados

For a taste of Barbados' popular culture, and ideas about some offbeat things to do and see, tune in to the "Voice of Barbados" radio station (92.90KHz). You'll hear advertisements in Bajan dialect, short stories, the latest soca hits and announcements of up-coming events – festivals, concerts, picnic, dances – all of which welcome visitors.

Nightlife

After Dark

Barbados nights are for celebrating, whether you take a "round-the-island-with-rum-and-calypso" cruise aboard the *Jolly Roger* or *MV Harbour Master* catamarans (sailing Saturdays and Thursdays respectively; see *Excursions* for phone numbers), marvel at fire-eaters performing at the Plantation Restaurant, or just cruise the late-night eateries and wine bars. (Most bars have a Happy Hour around sundown.)

Bars and cafés that are particular hot spots with live music are: **39 Steps** (Chattel Plaza, Hastings), with live jazz on alternate Saturdays; the **Waterfront Café** (The Careenage, Bridgetown), offering either steel pan or jazz after dinner; **The Mews** (2nd Street, Holetown, St James), with jazz on Friday and Saturday. In St Lawrence Gap, **Café Sol** and **McBride's** are popular with British ex-pats, while **The Rum Shoppe** is a great place for cocktails and bar snacks.

During festival times (see the next section) the nightlife hots up even more, especially during Crop Over, the Jazz Festival and Holders Season.

Dinner Shows

Almost all the resort hotels offer live entertainment combined with dinner and dancing, including: **Sam Lord's Castle**, **Glitter Bay**, **The Colony Club** and the **Royal Pavilion**. Dinner shows in Barbados run the gamut from glitz to gala entertainment with superb dancers, as well as cultural and historical content. A couple of the most popular shows are:

Tropical Spectacular, The Plantation Restaurant and Garden Theatre, St Lawrence Road, Christ Church, tel: 428 5048. Wednesday and Friday from 6.30pm. Tropical Spectacular is the Caribbean's number one dinner show, as featured on CNN's travel guide and GMTV in the UK. An evening's entertainment with sensational costumes, dance and music, celebrating the mixed cultures of the Caribbean people. There is also a spectacle of limbo and fire-eating, followed by a party with some of the island's best musicians. Admission price includes dinner, drinks and transportation to and from the venue. Reservations are required, all major credit cards accepted. Inclusive cost: BDS$125.

1627 and All That, Barbados Museum, tel: 428 1627. Thursday 6.30–10pm. The inclusive deal includes a tour of the museum, transportation, open bar, buffet dinner and the historical and cultural folkloric show. Reservations recommended.

Nightclubs

Nightclubs start getting lively around 11pm, and stay open into the early hours. You can dance to the beat of local artists and bands at a wide variety of nightclubs, including: **Harbour Lights** and **The Boatyard**, Bay Street, Bridgetown; **Sunset Creek** in St James; **The Ship Inn**, **B4 Blues**, **The Reggae Lounge** and **After Dark** in St Lawrence Gap; and **The Casbah** at Baku Beach, Holetown, St James.

Sports Bars

Themed "sports" bars, with satellite television beaming a variety of sporting events, are currently very popular in Barbados. These include **Bubba's** and **Bert's Bar** in Worthing, and – with pool tables and darts board – **McBride's** in St Lawrence Gap, and **Crocodile's Den** and **The Coach House** at Paynes Bay, St James.

Festivals

Annual Events

January–February

Barbados Jazz Festival: weekend-long programme of events in January, featuring international artists. Tel: 429 2084.
Barbados Horticultural Society Open Gardens Programme: private gardens open to the public on Sunday during the winter. Tel: 428 5889.
National Trust Open House Programme: historic private homes open up to the public every Wednesday 2.30–5.30pm, January to April. Tel: 426 2421.
PWA Windsurfing Competition: February. Tel: 426 5837.
International Festival and Fair: first Saturday in February at Government House. Entertainment, art, crafts and food organised by the Multi-National Women's Group.
Holetown Festival: week-long festival commemorates the first settlers' landing on 17 February 1627. Street fair, concerts, parades and more. Tel: 430 7300.
Barbados Flower Show: late February at Balls Plantation. Tel: 428 5889.

March–April

National Trust Open House Programme: *see page 343.*
Holder's Season: major international opera, music and theatre festival held in the gardens of Holders House. Tel: 432 6385.
Test cricket series: carnival atmosphere at Kensington Oval when international teams compete against the West Indies.
Sandy Lane Gold Cup: prestigious horse race held at the Garrison Savannah.

Oistins Fish Festival: Easter weekend programme of events in Barbados' main fishing town – exhibitions, craft stalls, boat races. Tel: 428 6738.
De Congaline Carnival: nine-day village festival and street party featuring a huge human congaline. Tel: 424 0909.

May–June
Gospelfest: international festival of gospel music. Tel: 430 7300.
Celtic Festival: last two weeks in May. Celebration of Celtic culture in the Caribbean, with performers from many countries.
Barbados Rugby Sevens International Masters Festival: international teams compete at the Garrison Savannah.
Mount Gay Regatta: top-class yacht races based at the Boatyard.

July–August
Sir Garfield Sobers International Schools Tournament: school teams from all over the world come to Barbados to compete.
Crop Over Festival: Barbados' biggest and longest festival – see box. Tel: 424 0907/9.

September–December
International Surfing: at the Soup Bowl. Tel: 435 6377.
Sun, Sea and Slams International Bridge Festival: top bridge players pit their wits against each other in October.
National Independence Festival of Creative Arts (NIFCA): October/ November, culminating on Independence Day, 30 November when there is a military parade and street processions.
Run Barbados: 10 km and marathon races attracting international runners; early December.

Crop Over

This five-week festival, starting in early July and ending on Emancipation Day, is the highlight of the Barbados cultural calendar. It is a revival of the traditional celebration of the end of the sugar cane harvest. Community fairs, concerts and parades abound, including:

- Opening Ceremony at a plantation, with the "Delivery of the Last Canes"
- Decorated Cart Parade
- Calypso Competition and crowning of the Calypso Monarch
- Kadooment Day finale – a costumed carnival parade.

Excursions

Guided Tours

The following companies specialise in guided sightseeing and day trips in and around Barbados.

ON LAND

Island Safari, tel: 432 5337, fax: 422 1966.
L.E. Williams Tour Company Ltd, Hastings, Christ Church, tel: 427 1043, fax: 427 6007.
Bajan Tours, tel: 437 9389, fax: 437 7922.
Custom Tours, tel: 425 0099.
VIP Tour Services, tel: 429 4617.
Custom Tours and VIP Tour Services offer personalised or customised tours for a maximum of four people.

ON WATER

MV Harbour Master, tel: 430 0900, fax: 430 0901. Day and evening cruises on four decks. Great food and fun slide, a party atmosphere with loud music.
Jolly Roger Pirate Cruises, tel: 436 6424. Party cruises on a pirate ship.

The Ferry

The most economic way to visit other islands, or the South American mainland, is to take the ferry, ***M V Windward***, which accommodates up to 250 passengers. Options include a six-day round trip from Barbados, taking in St Vincent, Trinidad and Venezuela, or a weekend trip to St Lucia. Tel: 431 0449 or e-mail: windward@sjds.net

Small Cats, tel: 421 6419, fax: 421 7582. Small personalised catamaran cruises. Also available for private charter.
Tiami, tel: 430 0900. Lunch, sunset or moonlight catamaran cruises. Private charters.
Excellence, tel: 436 6424, fax: 429 8500. Catamaran sailing cruise. Private charter available.

BY AIR

Bajan Helicopters, The Wharf, Bridgetown, tel: 431 0069. Helicopter tours.

Island hopping

There are a number of islands near Barbados that you may want to visit for one or more days, such as St Vincent and the Grenadines – which include Mustique, Bequia and the Tobago Cays – St Lucia, Martinique, Dominica and Grenada. (*See the Island Hopping chapter, page 317*) They can all be reached by air charter, scheduled airline service or guided tours. **LIAT** (tel: 434 5428) offers special one-day fares to a host of island destinations on scheduled flights. The airline also offers a 30-day ticket deal which allows you to visit as many islands as you wish – but only once, except for connections.

Chartering a plane is a good solution if you are travelling with a small group, but it is not an inexpensive option. With a charter company such as **Trans Island Air (TIA)**, tel: 418 1654, fax: 428 0916, which has 8-16-seater planes, or **Mustique Airways**, tel: 428 1638, fax: 428 0140 (or call the head office in St Vincent: (1784) 458 4380), with 6-seaters, you decide where and when you want to go. The prices are set according the distance travelled.

TOUR COMPANIES

Safari Tours (tel: 429 5100, fax: 429 5446) and G & T Tours (tel: 435 8451, fax: 435 6444), specialise in excursions to one or more islands. Costs are approximately BDS$550 for some of the full day trips, with drinks and lunch included. Try also Chantours, tel: 432 5591, fax: 432 5540. Day and overnight trips available.

Entertaining Children

- **Playgrounds:** There is one at the Garrison Savannah and another at Three Houses in St Philip, both in quite good shape. The best playgrounds are located at some of the fast food restaurants, especially those run by Chefette. These are dotted around the island. The **Rum Factory and Heritage Park**, Four Square, St Philip, has the largest playground on the island and good facilities.
- The **Wildlife Reserve**, St Peter (tel: 422 8826), is a pleasant spot for the kids. It is cool, as almost the entire reserve is under tree cover, and the selection of animals is extensive by Barbados' standards.
- **Mini Golf** at the Academy of Golf, Christ Church (tel: 420 7405), can provide entertainment for the young at heart aged 2–92 years old. There's also a public driving range.
- The **Folkestone Marine Reserve and Visitors Centre** on the West Coast offers information on marine life, particularly turtles. It is an ideal place for snorkelling.
- **Highland Outdoor Tours** offers jitney rides and horseback rides in the countryside. Tel: 438 8069/70.
- **Ayshford Bird Park**, open daily 8am–5pm, tel: 438 6565 (entrance fee), may appeal to children between 2–6 years, although it is not worth a special trip – there are only a few exotic birds here, mostly different types of chicken and pigeon, plus emus and three ostriches.

Shopping

Shopping Areas

The main shopping destinations, especially for duty-free shopping, are: Broad Street, Bridgetown; Sunset Crest and Sunset Crest Chattel Village; Chattel House Village, St Lawrence Gap; Hastings Plaza; Quayside Center, Hastings; and, not least, the larger hotel boutiques and the cruise ship terminal.
Parking: the three main car parks are at Independence Square, Wharfside and City Centre and there are several smaller ones. Beware of friendly Bajans who offer to "find you a park" for a fee as they may park it illegally.
Dress code: people are expected to cover up in town and not go shopping in scanty dress.

What to Buy

First on the list must be **rum** – local production ensuring an excellent selection sold at good prices everywhere on the island. Both white and dark rums are available, as well as rum products such as Malibu and other liqueurs. Brands to look out for are Mount Gay (which operates the world's oldest distillery, established in 1663), Cockspur and Doorly's, each of which makes a range of rums.

There is a wide choice of locally made **arts and crafts**, and shops and galleries to buy them from, and in some cases you can buy directly from the artist or craftsperson. Handicrafts include objects made from wood – especially mahogany, of which the best selection is at Medford Mahogany Village just north of Bridgetown – batiks, pottery, and jewellery made with semi-precious stones.

You can select from a vast range of quality, locally-made **T-shirts**, from cheap souvenir T-shirts to silky designer T-shirts made from special sea island cotton.

Where to Buy

ART & CRAFTS

The shops and centres listed below specialise in fine arts and handicrafts made by Barbadians, sold exclusively or alongside work from other regions.

Best of Barbados: seven branches specialising in the work of Jill Walker, as well as gifts and souvenirs. Head office and information, tel: 421 6900.

Chattel House Village, Holetown. Various crafts, jewellery and swimwear.

Chattel House Village, St Lawrence Gap, tel: 428 2474. Variety of shops selling souvenirs and locally produced crafts.

Colours of de Caribbean, The Careenage, Bridgetown. Excellent designer jewellery, accessories, hand-painted cushions, placemats, napkins, rugs and furniture. Features the work of some of the region's leading designers and artists.

Daphne's Sea Shell Studio, Congo Road, St Philip, tel: 423 6180 or 432 7448 on the West Coast. Mirrors, picture frames, ornaments and a range of hand-painted clothing.

Earthworks Pottery, St Thomas, tel: 425 0223, fax: 425 3224. Pots, plates, lamp bases in blues and golds. Includes Potter's House Gallery, a showplace for Barbadian pottery, as well as batik and painted fabrics. Open Monday to Friday 9am–5pm, Saturday 9am–1pm.

Medford Mahogany Craft Village, Lower Barabees Hills, St Michael, tel: 427 3179. Carved wooden sculptures and functional objects. Watch the carpenters at work.

Pelican Craft Centre, Princess Alice Highway (by the port). Authentic Barbadian crafts. Sponsored by the Industrial Development Corporation (IDC), tel: 427 5350.

Portobello Exhibition, Batts Rock Road, Prospect, St James, tel: 424 1687. Colorful naïve paintings from Haiti. Buy or just admire. Monday through Saturday 10am–6pm.

Red Clay Pottery and **Fairfield Gallery**, Fairfield Cross Road, St Michael, tel: 424 3800, fax: 424 0072. Innovative, very Bajan, family pottery.

Temple Yard, Bridgetown, is where Rastafarians display their interesting leather work.

Wild Feathers Bird Art, St Philip, tel: 423 7758. Wood carvings of indigenous and migratory birds. Viewing by appointment.

JEWELLERY

Columbian Emeralds for jewellery and watches. Outlets at Cave Shepherd, on Broad Street, Bridgetown, and at the cruise ship terminal and airport.

One Stop Shopping in Bridgetown

DaCosta's Mall, Broad Street. Clinical air-conditioned shopping gallery behind a pink colonial facade. Jewellers' shops, boutiques, souvenirs.

Cave Shepherd, Broad Street. The island's main department store with a wide range of goods under one roof – perfumes, cosmetics, liquor, cigars, cameras, electronics, music, T-shirts and swimwear, designer clothing, souvenirs, etc. Also outlets at Sunset Crest, the cruise ship terminal and the airport.

Harrison's, Broad Street. A small department store selling cosmetics, skin care products, perfume, leather, china and crystal, sunglasses, T-shirts and liquor at the Liquor Den. All the top brand names including Gucci, Cartier, Fendi, Waterford, Lalique and Calvin Klein.

Duty-free Shopping

To purchase goods duty free, you need to present your immigration slip or passport and return ticket, so don't forget to take them with you when you go shopping. Purchases can be taken away immediately, except for alcohol and tobacco which will be sent to the airport for you to pick up on your departure. Duty-free prices are generally quite competitive.

Diamonds in Paradise, Nicholas House, Bridgetown, for diamonds and diamond jewellery.

International Diamonds, Lower Broad Street, Bridgetown, for diamonds.

Jewellers Warehouse, Norman Centre, Broad Street, Bridgetown, for jewellery and watches.

Little Switzerland, DaCosta's Mall, Bridgetown, for watches, fine jewellery, china and crystal.

Luna Jewellers, Bay Street, Bridgetown, tel: 430 0355. Handcrafted jewellery.

Royal Shop, Broad Street, Bridgetown, for watches and jewellery.

CLOTHING

Go to **Gabby boutiques** for exclusive evening and casual wear, shoes, hats, swimwear, jewellery and accessories; **Sandbox**, at the Rum Factory and Heritage Park, St Philip, for swim and beach wear, as well as household furnishings; or **UpBeat** for casual island wear. At **John C. Mayers Batik Gallery**, Cleaver Hill, Bathsheba, tel: 433 9668, you can buy hand-made batik fashions in a small chattel house.

BOOKS

Cloister Bookstore, Hincks Street, Bridgetown. Good selection and a wide variety of books on Barbados and related topics.

Sport

Sporting Choices

An abundance of sports draws visitors to Barbados: golf, tennis, horseback riding, and the whole array of watersports from windsurfing and scuba diving to parasailing and game fishing. Bajans themselves are sports mad. Cricket is a way of life; eager spectators (and gamblers) flock to the Barbados Turf Club races at the Garrison Savannah on the South Coast.

The local pastimes of a game of dominoes under the trees and road tennis played with wooden paddles can be enjoyed as spectator or participant. The Barbados Tourism Authority provides information on competitive events like Run Barbados at the beginning of December (from the airport to Almond Beach Village, north of Speightstown), the Barbados Open Independence Surfing Championship and the Barbados Open Golf Tournament.

Equipment Rental

Rob's Mountain Bikes, Hastings, Christ Church, tel: 437 3404. Bicycle hire; also rental of watersports equipment including water skis and jet skis, and fishing equipment.
Dread or Dead, Hastings, Christ Church, tel: 228 7349. Surfboard rental.

CRICKET

Barbados Cricket Association, Kensington Oval, Bridgetown, tel: 436 1397. For tickets to matches call the West Indies Ticketline: 1 800 744 GAME (toll free in Barbados only).

DEEP SEA FISHING

Barbados Game Fishing Association, tel: 422 2016.
Cannon II, tel: 424 6107. Big game fishing.
Barracuda Too, Christ Church, tel: 426 7252.
Blue Marlin, tel: 436 4322.

GOLF

Barbados Academy of Golf and Public Driving Range, Balls Complex, Christ Church, tel: 420 7405.
Almond Beach Village, St Peter, tel: 422 4900.
Club Rockley, Christ Church, tel: 435 7873.
Royal Westmoreland, St James, tel: 422 4653.
Sandy Lane, St James, tel: 432 1311. Although the course is being expanded, it is still open.

GYMS

World Gym, Haggat Hall, St Michael, tel: 228 3319.
West One Fitness Studios, DaCosta West Mall, Sunset Crest, St James, tel: 432 5760.

HORSEBACK RIDING

Highland Outdoor Tours, St Thomas, tel: 438 8069.
Wilcox Riding Stables, Christ Church, tel: 428 3610.

HORSE RACING

Barbados Turf Club, Garrison Savannah, Bush Hill, St Michael, tel: 426 3980; e-mail: barturf@sunbeach.net.

PARASAILING, SURFING & WINDSURFING

Barbados Windsurfing Association, Silver Rock Hotel, Christ Church, tel: 428 7277.
Barbados Surfing Association, tel: 429 2326.
Ultimate High Parasail Adventures, tel: 231 4386.

POLO

Barbados Polo Club, St James, tel: 427 6022.

SAILING

Barbados Yachting Association, tel: 428 7905.

SCUBA DIVING & SNORKELLING

There are plenty of dive operators with **Professional Association of Dive Operators** (**PADO**) qualified instructors (tel: 435 6542).
Hightide Watersports, Sandy Lane, St James, tel: 432 0931. Reef and wreck dives, night dives.
Coral Isle Divers, Bridgetown, tel: 434 8377.
Explore Sub Barbados, St Lawrence Gap, Christ Church, tel: 435 6542.
West Side Scuba Centre, Baku Beach, Holetown, tel: 432 2558.
Hazell's Water World Inc., Bay Street, Bridgetown, tel: 426 4043.
Atlantis Adventures, Shallow Draught, Bridgetown, tel: 436 8929, operate hourly dives, six days a week, in the *Atlantis Submarine* in which you are given a tour of the reef and a shipwreck, and see a dive show. Also tours on the *Seatrec* semi-submersible reef observation craft, and snorkelling tours.

West Coast Dive Sites

The calm waters of the Platinum Coast are ideal for scuba diving. A bar reef runs down the length of the coast about a mile offshore, marking where the coastline was at the end of the last ice age. Popular dive sites here include **Dottins**, **Tropicana**, **Fisherman's**, **Spawny** and the **Bright Ledge**.

There are three regularly dived wrecks along this coast. ***The Pamir***, a freighter, is located off Almond

Beach, north of Speightstown in St Peter, and the ***Lord Combermere***, a water barge, is off Prospect in St James. Both lie in about 60 ft (18 metres) of water. A little way north of the *Lord Combermere* is the ***Stavronikita***, sitting upright in 135 ft (60 metres) of water off Fitts village. This 356-ft (108-metre) Greek freighter ranks among the world's top 10 wreck dives.

SQUASH

Barbados Squash Club, Christ Church, tel: 427 7913.

TENNIS

Most large hotels and some smaller ones have courts which are open to guests and other visitors for a fee.

Guided Hikes

- **Sunday Hikes:** co-sponsored by the Barbados National Trust and the Future Centre Trust. Every Sunday at 6am sharp and 3.30pm. Free hikes at a leisurely pace, led by Dr Colin Hudson, who provides an informative commentary on the island's history, geology and wildlife. Something of an institution in Barbados. Each week's site is announced in the daily newspapers (calendars are also available at some hotels), or call the Future Centre Trust, tel: 425 2020 for details.
- **Arbib Nature and Heritage Trail:** two educational guided hikes around the attractions of the little-known northern part of the island, starting in Speightstown, St Peter. Choose between a 4½-mile/7.5-km route (approx. 3 hours) or a 3½-mile/5.5-km route (approx. 2 hours). Hikes are on Wednesday, Thursday and Saturday, at 9am and 2.30pm. There is a charge and you need to book by 3pm the day before with the Barbados National Trust, tel: 426 2421.

Further Reading

General

A–Z of Barbadian Heritage (multiple authors), Jamaica: Heinemann Publishers (Caribbean Ltd), 1990. Some fascinating inside stories.

Alleyne, Warren, ***Historic Houses of Barbados***. Bridgetown: Barbados National Trust.

Alleyne, Warren and Sheppard, Jill, ***The Barbados Garrison and its Buildings***. Macmillan, 1990. Well-researched background to the historic area of Barbados.

Allsopp, Dr Richard, ***A Dictionary of Caribbean Usage***. An excellent source for the comprehension and legitimization of the region's native languages.

Bell, G. ***Sir Garfield Sobers***. Nelson Caribbean.

Callender, Jean H., ***Barbadian Society: Past and Present***. Cave Hill: Main Library, University of the West Indies (Barbados), 1981.

Cozier, Tony (ed.), ***West Indies Cricket Annual***. Barbados: Caribbean Communications.

Fermor, Patrick Leigh, ***Traveller's Tree: A Journey Through the Caribbean Islands***. Penguin (out of print). A personal account of the islands and people the author met during travels in the late 1940s. Not always complimentary.

Hill, Barbara, ***Historic Churches of Barbados*** (ed. Henry Fraser). Bridgetown: Art Heritage Publishers, 1984.

Hughes, Griffith, ***Natural History of Barbados*** (1756). Ayer Co. Publishers, 1971.

Kent, David, ***Barbados and America*** by Arlington, Va: CM Kent, 1980.

LaBrucherie, Roger, ***Barbados – A World Apart***. Imágenes Press, 1995. Picture book with a personal approach. The photographs perceptively capture Barbados's rich heritage.

Marshall, Trevor, ***Folk Songs of Barbados***. Barbados: Cedar Press, 1981.

Watson Yates, Ann, ***Bygone Barbados***. Black Bird Studios, 1998. Picture book.

History

Beckles, Hilary, ***A History of Barbados: from Amerindian Settlement to Nation State***. Cambridge University Press, 1990. The first general history of Barbados by a professional historian, tracing the events and ideas that have shaped contemporary society.

Ferguson, James, ***A Traveller's History of the Caribbean***. Windrush Press, 1998. Comprehensive and easy to read. Highlights how Barbados' peaceful history contrasts with those of other islands.

Ligon, Richard, ***A True and Exact History of the Island of Barbadoes***. London: Frank Cass & Co. Ltd, 1970. The first history book of Barbados written by the Royalist author in an English debtors' prison in 1653, after staying in Barbados for three years. First published in 1657

Schomburgk, Sir Robert, ***History of Barbados*** (1848). Reprinted in 1998. For copies contact Tony Thomas, tel: 428 4015. History, geography and natural history.

Tree, Ronald, ***A History of Barbados***. New York: Beekman; London: Hart-Davis, MacGibbon, 1972. An entertaining account by one of the founders of the Barbados National Trust.

Barbadian Literature

Brathwaite, Kamau (Barbados' most eminent poet and the island's unofficial poet laureate):
Mother Poem. Oxford University Press, 1977.
Sun Poem. Oxford University Press, 1982.
Barabajan. An extensive work of literary criticism, poetry and history.

Callender, Timothy, ***It So Happen***. Collection of short stories describing the comic saga of life in the fictional St Elizabeth village.

Clarke, Austin, ***Growing Up Stupid Under the Union Jack***. Humorous tale of a black boy growing up in colonial Barbados.

Collymore, Sir Frank:

The Man who Loved Attending Funerals and Other Stories. Heinemann, 1993.

Collected Poems. A must for Bajan verse enthusiasts.

Drayton, Geoffrey, ***Christopher***. Heinemann, 1972. Poignant coming-of-age tale of a white boy in Barbados.

Ferguson, James, ***A Traveller's Literary Companion to the Caribbean***. A rich and diverse look at recent literature, with tantalising book extracts.

Jackman, Oliver, ***Saw The House in Half***. Washington, D.C.: Howard University Press, 1974.

Lamming, George:

The Emigrants. London: Allison & Busby, 1980.

In the Castle of My Skin. London: Longman, 1987. A difficult but worthwhile read, this novel – a Bajan classic – has been translated into 23 languages.

The Pleasure of Exile. London: Allison & Busby, Schocken, 1984.

Lovell, Glenville, ***Fire in the Canes***. A well-crafted contemporary novel.

Lynch, Louis, ***The Barbados Book***. An insight into the spirit of Bajan folk culture and its influence on literature.

Vaughn, H.A., ***Sandy Lane and Other Poems***. Collection published by the literary magazine *Bim*.

Voices I. An anthology of poems by Barbados' modern poets. Available from the National Cultural Foundation (NCF) or Queen's Park Gallery, Bridgetown.

Wickham, John, ***Casuarina Row***. A classic anthology of short stories.

Other Insight Guides

In Apa Publications' main series of more than 200 Insight Guides, destinations in this region include *Caribbean, Bahamas, Bermuda, Cuba, Jamaica, Puerto Rico*, and *Trinidad and Tobago*.

Discover the birthplace of calypso, steel drums and complex, cosmopolitan culture in *Insight Guide: Trinidad and Tobago*.

Insight Guide: Puerto Rico takes the adventurous visitor through the colourful streets of San Juan, into the richly populated waters of the Caribbean.

Insight Guide: Caribbean takes readers on a journey from the beauty of a tropical sunset to the charm of the Caribees.

POCKET GUIDES

Also available are companion volumes in the Pocket Guides series: *Bahamas*, Barbados, *Bermuda, Jamaica* and *Puerto Rico*. These books feature the author's personal recommendations and are especially suitable for visitors with limited time to spare. A practical and easy-to-use pullout map smooths the way through the islands and sights.

Insight Pocket Guide: Bahamas shows visitors the best of the beaches and the most fertile seas along this archipelago of 700 islands.

COMPACT GUIDES

Insight Compact Guides are handy mini encyclopedias which are both fact-packed and intensely practical, with text, pictures and maps all carefully cross-referenced. Titles in this series include *Bahamas*, Barbados, *Dominican Republic* and *Jamaica*.

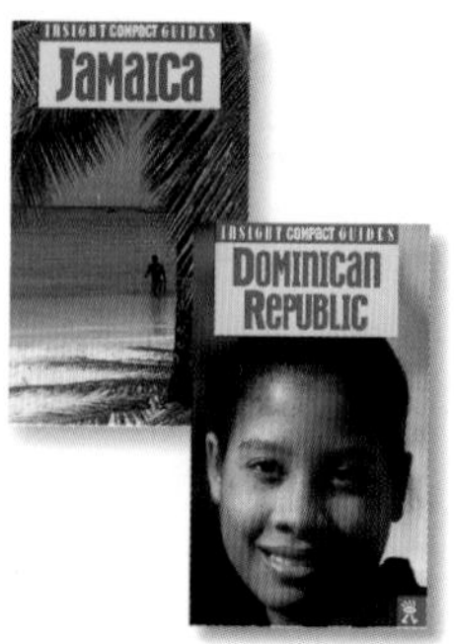

ART & PHOTO CREDITS

All Photography by Tony Arruza except for:

Herve Amiard 150
Ping Amranand 111
Allsport 88, 90, 93
The Art Foundry Barbados 98
Barbados Museum & Historical Society 24/25, 26, 28, 29, 35L, 36, 177, 267
Ronnie Carrington 213
Stephanie Calmenson 104
Ras Bongo Congo 99R
Courtesy of Jamaica National Library 32
Courtesy of the Government of Barbados 27, 48
Ian Cumming/Axiom 270, 306
Annalee Davis 97
Gang of 4 Art Studio 99L
Bill Grace 100, 220T
Robert Harding Picture Library 219
Edmond Van Hoorick 323
Dave G. Houser 126, 151
Hulton Getty Picture Collection 38/39
Volkmar E. Janicke 244, 264, 265T, 320, 324
Kirby Gallery 94/95, 196
Bob Krist 326, 327
David Lyons 325
Manning Selvage & Lee 248, 290
Media Crew Mitte 141, 145, 174
H. P. Merten 302T
Chantours, Barbados 317, 322
Lesley Player 2/3, 8/9, 22, 23, 37, 47L, 74, 84R, 108, 131, 132, 158, 204, 214, 262, 265, 294, 328
Martin Rosefeldt 1, 18, 19, 43, 44, 45, 47R, 49, 52/53, 58, 73, 89, 101, 128, 130, 152R, 161, 172/173, 178, 179, 180, 182, 183, 184T, 195, 196T, 198, 202, 205, 215, 217T, 218, 229T, 232T, 235, 235T, 245, 246T, 247T, 260T, 263T, 272, 274T, 276T, 279T, 288, 288T, 292, 292T, 306T, 310T
Wolfgang Rössig 80
Elizabeth Saft, Courtesy of New York Public Library 34
Geoffrey & Joanie Skecte 230T
Stephen Smith 35R, 40, 41, 106, 305
Terraqua 316
Mike Toy 4/5, 12/13, 14, 20, 42, 50/51, 54, 55, 72, 75, 76/77, 79, 82, 83, 86/87, 96, 102/103, 133, 143, 187, 190/191, 192, 193, 203, 208/209, 217, 231, 233T, 237, 252, 281, 290T, 299, 301, 319, 321
Marc Vorsatz/Media Crew Mitte 314/315
Bill Wassman 16, 17, 21, 30, 56L, 70/71, 112, 136, 152L, 153, 175, 179T, 181, 181T, 186, 186T, 194T, 200T, 201, 203T, 220, 222, 229, 230, 234T, 237T, 248T, 249, 259, 261, 261T, 280, 287, 289, 293, 300T, 309T, 321T, 323T
Willie Alleyne Associates 60, 140R

Cartographic Editor **Zoë Goodwin**
Production **Stuart A Everitt**
Design Consultants
Carlotta Junger, Graham Mitchener
Picture Research
Hilary Genin, Georgina Vacy-Ash

Picture Spreads

Pages 134-135
Top row, left to right: Martin Rosefeldt; Mike Toy; Willie Alleyne Associates; Martin Rosefeldt. *Centre row:* All pictures by Mike Toy; *Bottom row, left to right:* Willie Alleyne Associates; Mike Toy

Pages 206-207
Top row, left to right: courtesy Mount Gay Rum, Martin Rosefeldt, Mike Toy, Lesley Player; *Centre row, left to right:* Courtesy Mount Gay Rum, The Media Centre, Lesley Player; *Bottom row, left to right:* Tony Arruza, Martin Rosefeldt, Ian Cumming/Axiom, courtesy Malibu

Pages 240-241
Top row, left to right: Bill Wassman, Manning Selvage & Lee, Mike Toy, Blue Marlin Boat Co. *Centre row, left to right:* Sandy Lane Hotel, Mike Toy, Lesley Player; *Bottom row, left to right:* Lesley Player, Martin Rosefeldt, Lesley Player

Pages 282-283
Top row, left to right: Volkmar E. Janicke, Martin Rosefeldt, Robert Harding, Mike Toy *Centre row, left to right:* Lesley Player, Mike Toy, Mike Toy *Bottom row, left to right:* Bill Wassman, Mike Toy, Lesley Player, Bill Wassman

Pages 312-313
Top row, left to right: Cobblers Cove, Mike Toy, Martin Rosefeldt, Andrey Thomas; *Bottom row, left to right:* Martin Rosefeldt, Mike Toy, JGB Moulsdale, Martin Rosefeldt, Lesley Player, Martin Rosefeldt

Maps John Scott Graphics

Index

Numbers in italics refer to photographs

a

b

j

k

l

m

n

o

p